D1011374

# Introduction to Measurement Theory

**Mary J. Allen**
California State College
Bakersfield, California

**Wendy M. Yen**
CTB/McGraw-Hill
Monterey, California

Brooks/Cole Publishing Company
Monterey, California
A Division of Wadsworth, Inc.

Consulting Editor: Lawrence S. Wrightsman

Printed in the United States of America

10  9  8  7  6

**Library of Congress Cataloging in Publication Data**

Allen, Mary J
    Introduction to measurement theory.

    Bibliography:  p. 291
    Includes index.
    1.  Psychometrics.   I.  Yen, Wendy M., joint
author.   II.  Title.
BF39.A44        150'.28        78-25821
ISBN 0–8185–0283–5

Acquisition Editor: **Todd Lueders**
Production Editor: **Cece Munson**
Interior and Cover Design: **Katherine Minerva**
Illustrations: **Lori Gilbo**
Typesetting: **David R. Sullivan Company, Dallas, Texas**

# Preface

*Introduction to Measurement Theory* is intended to serve as a text and reference book for people who are using or constructing psychological tests and interpreting test scores and scales. The book is designed for people who understand college algebra and who have some familiarity with elementary statistics; for those lacking this familiarity or desiring a review, a chapter is included that covers the basic statistical terminology and concepts that are used in the remainder of the book. When more advanced mathematical topics are covered, they appear as optional sections or separate chapters that can be omitted without loss of continuity.

Measurement books currently available tend to be of three types: (1) extremely difficult, mathematically rigorous volumes, (2) books that discuss the statistical properties of measurements, but in a nonrigorous "cookbook" fashion, and (3) books that discuss different types of tests and the philosophy of measurement. The purpose of this book is to fill the gap between the first two categories, using some statistical sophistication in its presentation but at a level appropriate for upper-division undergraduates with minimal statistical competencies. We hope that this book will not dazzle or frighten the nonmathematical reader or bore or insult the more mathematically sophisticated reader.

Uniquely for a text at this level, classical true-score theory is examined critically, theoretical assumptions are stated and explained, and modern measurement models, controversies, and developments are discussed. We have presented most major concepts graphically and with formulas, as well as verbally, and provided simple examples whenever possible. Practical applications of theoretical topics are presented so that readers most interested in applying measurement theory, such as researchers, school personnel, and mental-health professionals, will find the book a useful reference source.

Almost every chapter includes an introduction, a summary, a vocabulary list, study questions, and computational problems. For classroom use, the study questions provide students with a set of comprehensive learning objectives, and the computational problems provide practice in applying mathematical concepts. Instructors may choose to base homework assignments and/or exams on these study questions and computational problems.

After mastering the material in this text, readers should be able to understand appropriate uses and limitations of common measures of test reliability and validity and to perform the basic item analyses necessary for test construction. They should also be able to judge published tests by American Psychological Association standards, understand the rationale and limitations of commonly used score scales, have a familiarity with controversies in testing, and have some knowledge of recent developments in test theory.

We would like to thank the following people, whose criticisms and comments at various stages of the project were extremely valuable: Rebecca Bryson, San Diego State University; Gerald Helmstadter, Arizona State University; Lawrence Jones, University of Illinois, Champaign-Urbana; Arthur Thomas, Central Michigan University; Steven Vandenberg, University of Colorado; James Wardrop, University of Illinois, Champaign-Urbana; and Sheldon Zedeck, University of California, Berkeley. The second author would like to thank George Burket and Ross Green, who have taught her so much about dealing with practical problems in measurement. The staff at Brooks/Cole has been very helpful in the editing and production of the manuscript. In particular, we would like to thank Cece Munson for her excellent editing. Jacki Kenneth typed and retyped the manuscript with great skill, and we thank her for her patience. Our husbands, Carey and Jin, helped search for errors and inconsistencies in the manuscript, and we are very grateful for their help and moral support.

Mary J. Allen
Wendy M. Yen

# Contents

**1**   **Introduction**   **1**

   1.1   The Use of Tests      1
   1.2   Definition of Measurement      2
   1.3   History of Testing and Measurement      2
   1.4   Organization of This Book      4
   1.5   Standards for Test Users      4
   1.6   Vocabulary      5
   1.7   Study Questions      5

**2**   **A Review of Basic Statistical Concepts**   **6**

   2.1   Introduction      6
   2.2   Levels of Measurement      6
   2.3   Common Statistical Notation and Definitions      9
   2.4   Distributions and Probabilities      12

vi    Contents

2.5    Descriptive Statistics    16
2.6    Inferential Statistics    18
2.7    The Normal Distribution    20
2.8    The Pearson Correlation Coefficient    23
2.9    Linear Regression    31
2.10   Influences on Correlation Coefficients    34
2.11   Alternative Measures of Association    36
2.12   Introduction to Advanced Topics    42
2.13   (Optional) Joint and Conditional Probabilities    42
2.14   (Optional) The Algebra of Expectations    44
2.15   Summary    48
2.16   Vocabulary    49
2.17   Study Questions    50
2.18   Computational Problems    52

# 3    Classical True-Score Theory    56

3.1    The Assumptions of Classical True-Score Theory    56
3.2    Summary of Classical True-Score Theory    60
3.3    Conclusions Derived from Classical True-Score Theory    60
3.4    (Optional) Proofs of Conclusions Derived from Classical True-Score Theory    65
3.5    Vocabulary    70
3.6    Study Questions    71
3.7    Computational Problems    71

# 4    Reliability    72

4.1    Introduction    72
4.2    Test/Retest Reliability Estimates    76
4.3    Parallel-Forms and Alternate-Forms Reliability Estimates    77
4.4    Internal-Consistency Estimates of Reliability: Split Halves    78
4.5    Internal-Consistency Reliability: The General Case    83
4.6    The Spearman-Brown Formula: The General Case    85

4.7    Comparison of Methods of Estimating
       Reliabilities    88
4.8    Standard Errors of Measurement and Confidence
       Intervals for True Scores    88
4.9    Summary    91
4.10   Vocabulary    92
4.11   Study Questions    92
4.12   Computational Problems    93

# 5    Validity    95

5.1    Introduction    95
5.2    Content Validity    95
5.3    Criterion-Related Validity    97
5.4    Correction for Attenuation    98
5.5    Estimating a Criterion from a Predictor    99
5.6    Screening into Dichotomous Categories    101
5.7    Taylor-Russell Tables    104
5.8    Multiple Predictors or Criteria    108
5.9    Construct Validity    108
5.10   Multitrait-Multimethod Validity    109
5.11   Factorial Validity    111
5.12   Summary    113
5.13   Vocabulary    114
5.14   Study Questions    115
5.15   Computational Problems    116

# 6    Principles of Test Construction    118

6.1    Introduction    118
6.2    Item Formats    119
6.3    Item Analysis Using Indices of Item Difficulty and
       Discrimination    120
6.4    Item Analysis Using Item Reliability and Validity
       Indices    124
6.5    Item Analysis Using Item-Characteristic
       Curves    127
6.6    Using Factor Analysis for Item Analysis and Test
       Development    130
6.7    Distributions of Test Scores    133
6.8    Some General Considerations in Item Analysis    138

6.9    Comparison of Item-Analysis Methods    140
6.10   Selecting a Published Test    140
6.11   Summary    142
6.12   Vocabulary    144
6.13   Study Questions    144
6.14   Computational Problems    145

# 7    Transforming and Equating Test Scores    148

7.1    Introduction    148
7.2    Percentiles    150
7.3    Age and Grade Scores    157
7.4    Expectancy Tables    160
7.5    Standard and Standardized Scores    161
7.6    Normalized Scores    163
7.7    Corrections for Guessing and Omissions    166
7.8    Equal-Interval Scales    168
7.9    Equating Test Scores    170
7.10   Summary    173
7.11   Vocabulary    174
7.12   Study Questions    175
7.13   Computational Problems    175

# 8    Scaling    178

8.1    Introduction    178
8.2    Determining the Level of Measurement    179
8.3    Levels of Measurement Produced by Selected Scales    182
8.4    Additional Methods for Obtaining Scales    184
8.5    Summary    190
8.6    Vocabulary    191
8.7    Study Questions    192
8.8    Computational Problems    192

# 9    Special Considerations in the Use of Measurements    193

9.1    Introduction    193
9.2    Group Heterogeneity    193
9.3    Combining Scores; Multiple Regression    200

9.4    Suppressor Variables, Moderator Variables, and Bias in Selection    204
9.5    Measuring Change    208
9.6    Profile Analysis    211
9.7    Implications of Measurement Theory for the Design and Interpretation of Research Studies    213
9.8    Summary    215
9.9    Vocabulary    216
9.10   Study Questions    217
9.11   Computational Problems    218

# 10  Controversies and Current Developments in Measurement    222

10.1    Introduction    222
10.2    Clinical and Statistical Prediction    222
10.3    Homogeneous and Nonhomogeneous Tests    224
10.4    Criticisms of Standardized Testing    225
10.5    Criterion-Referenced Tests    227
10.6    Strong True-Score Theories and Latent-Trait Models    229
10.7    Generalizability Theory    230
10.8    Bayesian Methods    232
10.9    Tailored Testing    232
10.10   Computer-Interpreted Testing    234
10.11   Summary    235
10.12   Vocabulary    236
10.13   Study Questions    237

# 11  Strong True-Score Theories and Latent-Trait Models    239

11.1    Introduction    239
11.2    Local Independence    241
11.3    Binomial-Error Models    242
11.4    Poisson Models    249
11.5    Normal-Ogive and Logistic Models    253
11.6    Rasch's Logistic Model    260
11.7    Test Information    262
11.8    Information Functions and the Logistic Models    267
11.9    Summary    269

11.10   Vocabulary    270
11.11   Study Questions    270
11.12   Computational Problems   272


Appendix: Areas under the Standard Normal Curve    275
Glossary of Symbols    278
Answers to Computational Problems    284
References    291
Name Index    296
Subject Index    298

# Introduction

## 1.1 The Use of Tests

A *test* is a device for obtaining a sample of an individual's behavior. The use of tests has become so widespread in American schools, clinics, industry, and government that it is difficult to imagine anyone who has not taken hundreds of tests. Unfortunately, many tests are written, administered, and interpreted by people who lack adequate training. This textbook will help you develop the technical skills necessary for responsible test use. We will describe and illustrate the basic principles of measurement theory so that you will gain the technical background necessary to interpret and compare test scores, to make maximum use of available testing instruments, and to develop tests to suit individual needs.

Tests have been designed that are useful for a number of different purposes. They can be used for selection, as when we select new employees from a group of job applicants or clients for psychological counseling from a pool of potential clients. Tests can be used for classification—for example, classifying a person as neurotic, brain-damaged, or weak in verbal skills and strong in mechanical skills. This classification can occur in placement settings, as when a student is placed in an

1

advanced French class or when a soldier is assigned to the motor pool. Tests can be used for evaluation, as when students are assigned grades in a class, individuals are certified to practice law or medicine, or the effectiveness of teaching programs is evaluated. Tests can be useful in counseling, as when we use an interest inventory to suggest potential careers or use a personality test to aid in marriage counseling. And test scores also are invaluable in research—for example, when classifying subjects in an experimental design or measuring different behaviors and examining their interrelationships.

A useful test measures accurately some property or behavior. To evaluate the usefulness of a test, we need to have a more precise statement of the meaning of the term *measurement*.

## 1.2 Definition of Measurement

*Measurement* is the assigning of numbers to individuals in a systematic way as a means of representing properties of the individuals. Numbers are assigned to the individuals according to a carefully prescribed, repeatable procedure. For example, a personality test generates scores by using the same instructions, questions, and scoring procedures for each examinee. Scores couldn't be compared meaningfully if examinees were each given different instructions or items or if different scoring procedures were used. In measurement, numbers are assigned systematically and can be of various forms. For example, labeling people with red hair ''1'' and people with brown hair ''2'' is measurement, since numbers are assigned to individuals in a systematic way and differences between scores represent differences in the property being measured (hair color). Similarly, giving an examinee a score of 98 on a mathematics exam or a score of 54 on a personality test would be measurement, if the numbers were systematically assigned to represent differences in mathematics performance or personality. *Measurement theory* is a branch of applied statistics that attempts to describe, categorize, and evaluate the quality of measurements, improve the usefulness, accuracy, and meaningfulness of measurements, and propose methods for developing new and better measurement instruments.

## 1.3 History of Testing and Measurement

Although this book deals basically with applied statistics, we will briefly discuss the history of testing and measurement to help put modern measurement theory into a broader perspective. If you are interested in exploring this topic in more detail, we recommend a book such as *A History of Psychological Testing* by Philip H. Du Bois (1970).

Du Bois attributes the increase in the use of testing to three major areas of development: civil-service exams, school exams, and the study of individual differences. Civil-service testing began in China about 3000 years ago when an emperor decided to assess the competency of his officials. Later, government positions were filled by persons who scored well on exams that covered topics such as music, horsemanship, civil law, writing, Confucian principles, and knowledge of public and private ceremonies. Such exams were eliminated in 1905 and were replaced by formal educational requirements. Paradoxically, as the Chinese were phasing out their exams, civil-service exams were being developed in Britain and the United States as a fair way of selecting among job applicants for government jobs. Early evidence of the effectiveness of the exams was anecdotal in nature, but the exams were popular because they removed decisions from the biases of political judgments.

Students in European schools were given oral exams until well after the 12th century, when paper began replacing parchment and papyrus. In the 16th century the Jesuits started using tests for the evaluation and placement of their students. Present-day students owe their exams to the later developments of printing presses and ditto machines.

The study of individual differences began in Great Britain when Sir Francis Galton (1822–1911) set up his famous Anthropometric Laboratory containing instruments to measure various sensory and motor skills. In 1884 visitors at the International Health Exhibition in London paid threepence each to be measured by Galton's tests, yielding a large data base for Galton's later studies. Another Englishman, Karl Pearson (1857–1936), the "founder of statistics," developed a number of statistical techniques that form the core of basic measurement theory. These include the well-known Pearson product-moment correlation coefficient and chi-square goodness-of-fit test. In France, Alfred Binet (1857–1911) developed the first individual tests of intelligence (1905) as part of his work on the study of individual differences. A German, William Stern (1871–1938), developed the intelligence quotient (IQ), which he defined as the ratio of mental (measured) age to chronological (actual) age. (The current definition of IQ differs markedly from Stern's definition.) Back in Great Britain, Charles Spearman (1863–1945) followed in the footsteps of Galton and Pearson, and his work led to our modern concepts of test reliability and factor analysis.

Most early tests were designed for administration to only one individual at a time. Although work had begun on tests that could be given to many examinees at once, group-administered tests did not become widely used or accepted until after their introduction by the United States Army in World War I. The success of military testing led to the widespread development and use of group tests in schools and industry.

According to Du Bois, measurement theory as a discipline began to blossom in the 1930s. In 1935 the journal *Psychometrika* was founded. *Educational and Psychological Measurement* followed in 1941, the *British Journal of Statistical Psychology* began in 1947, and *Multivariate Behavioral Research* began in 1966. The first textbook in measurement theory, E. L. Thorndike's *An Introduction to the Theory of Mental and Social Measurements,* appeared in 1904; many other measurement books have followed. Although most of the foundation for present-day measurement theory was completed by the 1950s, research into the methods of psychological measurement, or *psychometrics,* continues. Modern measurement theorists are currently developing alternative models and techniques to augment and in some cases to replace current measurement practices.

## 1.4  Organization of This Book

Chapter 2 reviews and summarizes some of the basic statistical methods that you will need to understand before continuing. A thorough mastery of Chapter 2 will greatly facilitate subsequent learning. Chapter 3 introduces classical true-score theory. Most of the early work in measurement theory was based on the assumptions of classical theory. Chapters 4 and 5 cover the two basic properties that all tests should have—reliability and validity. A test is reliable if it produces consistent measurements; it is valid if it measures those properties that it is designed to assess. Chapter 6 deals with test selection (where to find and how to choose a published test) and test construction (how to build a test and how to evaluate one). Chapter 7 covers common ways of reporting scores, such as percentiles and standardized scores. Chapter 8 discusses differences in types of score scales and surveys methods for the development of scales. Chapter 9 covers a number of special problems in measurement, such as the effects of group heterogeneity on test properties and the simultaneous use of several test scores. Chapter 10 discusses some of the current controversies in testing and describes some of the proposals intended to improve the usefulness of tests. The last chapter, Chapter 11, covers some of the more recently developed measurement models.

Parts of this book, particularly Chapter 11, are more difficult to read than others, because many recently developed measurement theories use advanced mathematical techniques. If you do not have a strong mathematical background, you may prefer to read that chapter for general understanding rather than rigorous mastery of the content. Even a casual awareness of recent developments is better than no awareness at all.

## 1.5  Standards for Test Users

As you read this book you might like to refer to the *Standards for Educational and Psychological Tests* (American Psychological Association, 1974) developed jointly by the American Psychological Association, the American Educational Research Association, and the National Council on Measurement in Education. The authors of the *Standards* state:

> The test user, in selecting, administering, scoring, or interpreting a test, should know his purposes, what he is doing to achieve those purposes, and their probable consequences. It is not enough to have benign purposes; the user must know the procedures necessary to maximize effectiveness and to minimize unfairness in test use. . . . Competence in test use is a combination of knowledge of psychometric principles, knowledge of the problem situation in which the testing is to be done, technical skill, and some wisdom [p. 6].

This book is designed to give you the required knowledge of psychometric principles and some technical skills in test construction and test use.

In *Standards for Educational and Psychological Tests,* standards for tests and test users are classified on three levels: essential, very desirable, and desirable. Included as essential for test users are the following:

1. a general knowledge of measurement theory,
2. explicit and well-formulated goals for test use,
3. a consideration of alternative and supplemental measurement procedures, especially for examinees coming from very different backgrounds,
4. a careful review of the development of the tests being considered for use,
5. the competence to administer each test used for decision-making purposes,
6. established conditions for test administration that enable all examinees to do their best,
7. a rationale for decisions based on test scores,
8. a consideration of alternative interpretations of scores,
9. the correct use of norms and the avoidance of scores that have technical problems—for example, age or grade scores (see Chapter 7), and
10. periodic reviews of the effectiveness of tests and decision-making procedures for institutional tests.

The section of the *Standards* on test use contains many more standards that are related to two general issues: technical competency and wise professional judgment (fairness).

Tests can be useful tools, but they can also be dangerous if misused. It is our professional obligation to ensure that we use tests as accurately and as fairly as possible.

## 1.6   Vocabulary

measurement
measurement theory
psychometrics
*Standards for Educational and Psychological Tests*
test

## 1.7   Study Questions

1. Describe five purposes for which tests are used.
2. Discuss the relationship between *measurement* and *measurement theory.*
3. Briefly describe the historical roots of modern tests.
4. Describe the essential requirements for test use according to the *Standards for Educational and Psychological Tests.*

# A Review of
# Basic Statistical
# Concepts

## 2.1 Introduction

In Chapter 1 we defined measurement as the assigning of numbers to individuals in a systematic way as a means of representing properties of the individuals. This definition is mathematical in nature, and much of measurement theory is expressed in mathematical terms. Measurement theory, as a branch of statistics, develops statistical models for test scores and other types of measurements. In order to fully understand measurement theory, it is necessary to have some knowledge of statistical concepts and to develop certain mathematical skills. This chapter reviews these necessary concepts and skills.

## 2.2 Levels of Measurement

Measurement can take place at four different levels—nominal, ordinal, interval, and ratio. Each *level of measurement* specifies how the numbers that are assigned to the individuals relate to the property being measured. The level of measurement is determined by noting the presence or absence of four characteristics—distinctiveness, ordering in magnitude, equal intervals, and an absolute zero. First we will discuss these four characteristics, and then we'll describe the four levels of measurement that can be obtained.

A measurement has the characteristic of *distinctiveness* if different numbers are assigned to individuals who have different values of the property being measured. For example, if we assign the number 1 to males and the number 2 to females, this measurement has the characteristic of distinctiveness. Assigned numbers can also indicate an *ordering in magnitude,* with larger numbers representing more of the property being measured than smaller numbers. For example, if a test score of 7 represents more knowledge of history than a test score of 5, then the scores have ordering in magnitude. *Equal intervals* are obtained if equivalent differences between measurements represent the same amount of difference in the property being measured. For example, if a two-point difference between the scores of 108 and 110 represents the same amount of difference in vocabulary level as a two-point difference between the scores of 92 and 94, the measurement has equal intervals. And a measurement has an *absolute zero* when a measurement of zero represents an absence of the property being measured. For example, if a score of 0 represents an absence of errors made while running a maze, the measurement has an absolute zero.

The four characteristics of measurement just described determine the four major levels of measurement: nominal, ordinal, interval, and ratio. Table 2.1 summarizes the relationship between the characteristics just described and the levels of measurement.

Table 2.1. Characteristics of the Levels of Measurement

| Characteristic | Level of Measurement | | | |
| --- | --- | --- | --- | --- |
| | Nominal | Ordinal | Interval | Ratio |
| Distinctiveness | yes | yes | yes | yes |
| Ordering in magnitude | no | yes | yes | yes |
| Equal intervals | no | no | yes | yes |
| Absolute zero | no | no | no | yes |

*Nominal* measurement has only the characteristic of distinctiveness; it does not reflect ordering in magnitude, equal intervals, or an absolute zero. If we arbitrarily label poodles ''0,'' German shepherds ''1,'' and chihuahuas ''2,'' we are measuring at the nominal level; the numbers serve only as names to distinguish among types of dogs. There is no ordering in magnitude, because a chihuahua, which is assigned the number 2, is not more of a dog than a German shepherd, which is assigned the number 1. There are no equal intervals; the fact that poodles, German shepherds, and chihuahuas are one unit apart doesn't mean that poodles and German shepherds are as similar as German shepherds and chihuahuas. And there is no absolute zero; the fact that poodles are assigned the number 0 does not mean that they aren't dogs. Further, arithmetic operations cannot meaningfully be performed on nominal data—a poodle plus two German shepherds doesn't equal a chihuahua, so $0 + (2 \times 1)$ does not equal 2.

*Ordinal* measurements assign higher numbers to individuals who possess more of the property being measured. You can see from Table 2.1 that the ordinal level of measurement possesses the characteristics of distinctiveness and ordering in magnitude. Perhaps the most common ordinal measurement is the rank order. For example, if we take a sample of people, line them up from shortest to tallest, and assign the shortest person the number 1, the next shortest the number 2, and so on, we have established a rank order. A larger number indicates a greater height (ordering in magnitude), but equal intervals between numbers cannot be assumed. For example, there may be a difference of two inches in height between person 5 and person 6, but a difference of one inch between person 3 and person 4. Also, there is no absolute zero; the score, or rank, of zero, indicating an absence of height, would be meaningless in this situation.

The *interval* level of measurement has the characteristics of distinctiveness, ordering in magnitude, and equal intervals. For example, temperature can be measured on an interval level using a Fahrenheit thermometer. A thermometer reading of 104°F represents more heat than a reading of 76°F (ordering in magnitude), and equivalent differences between scores represent equivalent differences in amounts of heat (equal intervals). Measuring heat on a Fahrenheit scale is an interval level of measurement, and lacks an absolute zero, because 0°F does not indicate an absence of heat.

The *ratio* level of measurement has all four characteristics. Length can be measured using a tape measure at a ratio level of measurement with distinctiveness (boards of different lengths are assigned different numbers), ordering in magnitude (longer boards are assigned higher measures), equal intervals (a difference of one inch at any length means the same thing), and an absolute zero (the measurement of zero means the absence of length). Meaningful ratios of measurements or scores can be calculated only when measurement is made on a ratio level. If height were measured at the ordinal level using the rank-order method described earlier, ratios of scores (ranks) would not make sense in terms of ratios of heights; a person with a rank of 2 would not necessarily be twice as tall as a person with a rank of 1. But when we measure at the ratio level, we can calculate meaningful ratios; for example, a 6-foot-tall person is twice as tall as a 3-foot-tall person.

The choice of statistical techniques to be used for analyzing a set of measurements depends, in part, on the level of measurement. For example, arithmetic manipulations of measurements made on a nominal level are not meaningful. Most common statistical techniques make sense only when used with an interval or ratio level of measurement, because most of these techniques involve taking differences among scores or sums of scores. The results of arithmetic manipulations of ordinal measurements must be interpreted with great care.

Section 8.2 discusses levels of measurement in more detail and includes a discussion of the procedures used to verify whether a set of measurements has reached a given level of measurement.

## 2.3 Common Statistical Notation and Definitions

Once measurements have been obtained, they are analyzed. In order to manipulate the data mathematically, you will need to be familiar with statistical notation. This section will discuss symbols used for constants, variables, and summations.

### Constants and Variables

A *constant* is a symbol for a specific unchanging number. Most constants are symbolized either with lower-case italic letters or with Greek letters. For example, the number of examinees who take a particular test is a constant that is usually symbolized by $n$. Once a constant is defined—as when $n = 25$ for a particular set of data—its value does not change. However, a *variable* is a symbol that can take on a variety of numerical values. In statistics, most variables are symbolized with capital italic letters, although sometimes lower-case italic or Greek letters are used. For example, the variable $X$ could represent vocabulary-test score, height, or any other measurement. Frequently, subscripted variables are used; the variables are subscripted with numbers or lower-case letters. These subscripts denote different variables, and they help simplify the expression. For example, suppose that we want to represent one person's score on five different tests. We could use a different letter to stand for each test score, but this is tedious and potentially confusing. It is simpler to let the score on test 1 be represented by $X_1$, the score on test 2 by $X_2$, and so on. Similarly, if we are dealing with the scores of $n$ different people on one test, $X_1$ is the first examinee's score, $X_2$ is the second examinee's score, and $X_i$ is the $i$th examinee's score. Sometimes variables have two or more subscripts; $X_{ij}$ can be the score of the $i$th examinee on the $j$th test.

When we want to express the fact that a variable has taken on a certain value, we usually use an equation such as $X = 10$. In some cases we use a lower-case $x$ to indicate in a general way that $X$ is taking on a specific value. For example, if $X$ can take on values from 0 to 10, we would write $0 \leqslant X \leqslant 10$. But the general statement would be $x_s \leqslant X \leqslant x_g$, where $x_s$ is the smallest value $X$ can have and $x_g$ is the greatest value $X$ can have. In another example of the use of the lower-case letter to indicate that a variable is taking on a specific value, suppose we want to express the average salaries of people with various amounts of education. We let $X$ equal average salary and $Y$ equal amount of education in years. In general terms we say that $X = x$ for $Y = y$. In specific terms we might say that $X = \$10,000$ for $Y = 11$, $X = \$11,000$ for $Y = 12$, and so on.

Another important distinction to make is between discrete and continuous variables. A *discrete variable* can take on only selected values. For example, if $X$ is a score indicating how many test items an examinee got correct, $X$ is discrete and can only take on the values 0, 1, 2, and so on. It is not possible for $X$ to take on a value such as 1.4. Variables that can take on any of an infinite number of values are called *continuous variables*. For example, if $X$ is the time required for a rat to run a maze, it is a continuous variable and can take on any value greater than 0.

## Summations

A basic tool in statistics is the *summation sign*, $\Sigma$ (Greek capital letter *sigma*). Values for variables following the sign are to be added together. For example,

$$\sum_{i=1}^{3} X_i$$

means that the values of variables $X_1$, $X_2$, and $X_3$ are to be added together, so that

$$\sum_{i=1}^{3} X_i = X_1 + X_2 + X_3.$$

If $X_1 = 20$, $X_2 = 0$, and $X_3 = 40$, then

$$\sum_{i=1}^{3} X_i = 20 + 0 + 40 = 60.$$

The "1" and "3" in the above summation are the *limits of summation*. To sum from $i = 1$ to $i = 3$, begin with $i = 1$ and increment $i$ by 1 until $i = 3$. If the limits of summation were 2 and 5, the summation would be $X_2 + X_3 + X_4 + X_5$.

The term that follows the summation sign may be simple, like $X_i$, or complex, like

$$\sum_{i=1}^{3} (X_i^2 - Y_i + 1) = (X_1^2 - Y_1 + 1) + (X_2^2 - Y_2 + 1) + (X_3^2 - Y_3 + 1).$$

Notice that the whole term following the summation sign is repeated for each value of $i$ within the stated limits. If $X_1 = 2$, $X_2 = 3$, $X_3 = -1$, $Y_1 = 0$, $Y_2 = 1$, and $Y_3 = -2$, then the above summation would equal $(4 - 0 + 1) + (9 - 1 + 1) + (1 + 2 + 1)$, or 18.

As stated earlier, sometimes variables have more than one subscript. For example, $X_{ij}$ may be the score of the $i$th examinee on the $j$th test. If it were necessary to symbolize the addition of all of the scores of $n$ examinees on $N$ tests, a double summation sign would be required:

$$\sum_{i=1}^{n} \sum_{j=1}^{N} X_{ij},$$

where the upper limit of $i$ is the last examinee (examinee $n$) and the upper limit of $j$ is the last test (test $N$).

There are three main rules for manipulating summation signs to simplify arithmetic and derive alternative formulas.

Rule 1.  $\displaystyle\sum_{i=1}^{n} b = nb$

Rule 2.  $\displaystyle\sum_{i=1}^{n} bX_i = b \sum_{i=1}^{n} X_i$

Rule 3.  $\displaystyle\sum_{i=1}^{n} (X_i + Y_i) = \sum_{i=1}^{n} X_i + \sum_{i=1}^{n} Y_i$

In these equations $b$ is a constant, and $X_i$ and $Y_i$ are variables.

Rule 1 states that summing a constant $n$ number of times is equivalent to calculating the product of $n$ and the constant. This rule is derived from

$$\sum_{i=1}^{n} b = b + b + \cdots + b,$$

where there are $n$ terms in this sum, which is equivalent to $n$ times $b$. From Rule 1 it is easy to see that $\sum_{i=1}^{4} 80 = 320$ and $\sum_{i=1}^{80} 25 = 2000$.

Rule 2 states that the summation of variables multiplied by a constant is equivalent to the constant times the sum of the variables. This is true because

$$\sum_{i=1}^{n} bX_i = bX_1 + bX_2 + \cdots + bX_n$$

$$= b(X_1 + X_2 + \cdots + X_n)$$

$$= b \sum_{i=1}^{n} X_i.$$

From Rule 2 we can see that, when $X_1 = 2, X_2 = 4$, and $X_3 = 12$, then

$$\sum_{i=1}^{2} 4X_i = 4(6) = 24$$

and

$$\sum_{i=1}^{3} 2080 X_i = 2080(18) = 37440.$$

Rule 3, the *distribution rule,* states that, if you are summing more than one term under the summation sign, the summation sign can be "distributed" to each term. Rule 3 holds because

$$\sum_{i=1}^{n} (X_i + Y_i) = (X_1 + Y_1) + (X_2 + Y_2) + \cdots + (X_n + Y_n)$$

$$= (X_1 + X_2 + \cdots + X_n) + (Y_1 + Y_2 + \cdots + Y_n)$$

$$= \sum_{i=1}^{n} X_i + \sum_{i=1}^{n} Y_i.$$

From Rule 3, when $X_1 = 1, X_2 = 2, X_3 = 0, Y_1 = 1, Y_2 = 1$, and $Y_3 = 4$,

$$\sum_{i=1}^{3} (X_i + Y_i) = \sum_{i=1}^{3} X_i + \sum_{i=1}^{3} Y_i = 3 + 6 = 9.$$

Taken together, the rules can be used sequentially to simplify complex expressions. For example,

$$\sum_{i=1}^{4} (104X_i - 2Y_i + 12) = \sum_{i=1}^{4} 104X_i - \sum_{i=1}^{4} 2Y_i + \sum_{i=1}^{4} 12$$

$$= 104 \sum_{i=1}^{4} X_i - 2 \sum_{i=1}^{4} Y_i + 4(12),$$

and    $$\sum_{i=1}^{3} (2X_i + 3Y_i)^2 = \sum_{i=1}^{3} (4X_i^2 + 12 X_iY_i + 9Y_i^2)$$

$$= \sum_{i=1}^{3} 4X_i^2 + \sum_{i=1}^{3} 12X_iY_i + \sum_{i=1}^{3} 9Y_i^2$$

$$= 4 \sum_{i=1}^{3} X_i^2 + 12 \sum_{i=1}^{3} X_iY_i + 9 \sum_{i=1}^{3} Y_i^2.$$

If $X_1 = 1$, $X_2 = -1$, $X_3 = 1$, $X_4 = 0$, $Y_1 = 2$, $Y_2 = 1$, $Y_3 = 0$, and $Y_4 = -1$, then

$$\sum_{i=1}^{4} (104X_i - 2Y_i + 12) = 148$$

and    $$\sum_{i=1}^{3} (2X_i + 3Y_i)^2 = 69.$$

Notice that $\sum_{i=1}^{3} X_iY_i = X_1Y_1 + X_2Y_2 + X_3Y_3$, which generally is not equal to $(\sum_{i=1}^{3} X_i)(\sum_{i=1}^{3} Y_i)$. Demonstrate this to yourself with an example of your own.

## 2.4  Distributions and Probabilities

### Frequency Distributions

There are a great variety of ways that values of a variable—for example, scores on a test—can be distributed among the examinees. A *frequency distribution* expresses the frequency of occurrence for each value of a discrete variable (for example, it expresses how many examinees obtained each score). Table 2.2 is a frequency distribution for a certain test score, $X$. The score values are labeled $x_i$, and the column showing the frequency of each $x_i$ is labeled $f(x_i)$.

Table 2.2. A Frequency Distribution

| $i$ | Score Value $x_i$ | Frequency $f(x_i)$ |
|---|---|---|
| 1 | 10 | 0 |
| 2 | 11 | 0 |
| 3 | 12 | 2 |
| 4 | 13 | 5 |
| 5 | 14 | 3 |
| 6 | 15 | 1 |
| 7 | 16 | 6 |
| 8 | 17 | 1 |
| 9 | 18 | 2 |
| 10 | 19 | 0 |

The test was taken by 20 people. No one received a score of 10 or 11, two examinees received a score of 12, five received a score of 13, and so on. Figure 2.1 is a graph of the frequency distribution from Table 2.2. Frequency distributions can be expressed in terms of *relative frequencies,* or the proportion of time a variable takes on each specific value (in our example, the proportion of examinees who received each score). Table 2.3 contains a relative frequency distribution based on the data from the frequency distribution in Table 2.2. There are 20 scores, so each frequency is divided by 20 to convert it to a relative frequency. Notice that the sum of the relative frequencies equals 1.0.

A graph of the relative frequencies appears in Figure 2.2. Notice that the shape of this graph is the same as that of the graph in Figure 2.1; only the numbers associated with the vertical axis have been changed.

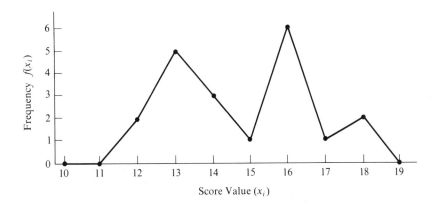

Figure 2.1. Example of a frequency distribution

Table 2.3. A Relative Frequency Distribution

| $i$ | Score Value $x_i$ | Relative Frequency |
|---|---|---|
| 1 | 10 | .00 |
| 2 | 11 | .00 |
| 3 | 12 | .10 |
| 4 | 13 | .25 |
| 5 | 14 | .15 |
| 6 | 15 | .05 |
| 7 | 16 | .30 |
| 8 | 17 | .05 |
| 9 | 18 | .10 |
| 10 | 19 | .00 |

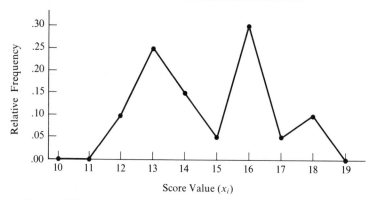

Figure 2.2. A frequency distribution expressed in terms of relative frequencies

## Probabilities

The *probability* that a discrete variable $X$ takes on a certain value $x_i$ in a population is defined to be the relative frequency of $x_i$ in that population. (A population is a specific and usually large group of individuals—for example, all ten-year-old children attending public schools in Illinois. Section 2.6 discusses populations further.) Such a probability is written

$$p(X = x_i) = p(x_i). \qquad (2.1)$$

If the data in Table 2.3 represent a population, $p(X = 10) = 0$, $p(X = 11) = 0$, $p(X = 12) = .10$, $p(X = 13) = .25$, and so on. The probability that $X$ takes on one of any two or more values is equal to the sum of the probabilities that $X$ takes on each of those values. For example, the probability that $X$ takes on the values 13 or 15 is $p(X = x_4$ or $X = x_6) = p(X = 13$ or $X = 15) = p(X = 13) + p(X = 15) = .25 + .05 = .30$.

The probability that $X$ has a value in a certain range can be expressed as

$$p(x_a \leqslant X \leqslant x_b) = \sum_{i=a}^{b} p(X = x_i). \tag{2.2}$$

For example, if $a = 3$ and $b = 5$, Equation 2.2 becomes

$$p(x_3 \leqslant X \leqslant x_5) = \sum_{i=3}^{5} p(X = x_i). \tag{2.3}$$

For the data in Table 2.3, Equation 2.3 is evaluated as $p(12 \leqslant X \leqslant 14) = .10$ + .25 + .15 = .50; the probability that $X$ has a value of 12, 13, or 14 is .50. Notice that evaluating Equation 2.3 is the same as adding the heights of the points at $X = 12, X = 13$, and $X = 14$ on the relative frequency curve (Figure 2.2).

The graphs for continuous variables look different from those for discrete variables. Figure 2.3 displays a distribution for a continuous variable, $X$. The vertical axis, labeled $f(x)$, is called the *density* of $x$. The density does not give the probability of observing the value $x$, but it can be used to determine the probability that the value observed for $X$ falls within a specified range of values. (Since $X$ is a continuous variable and can take on an infinite number of different values, the probability that $X$ has any one specific value, $x$, is zero.) The probability that $X$ has a value between $x_a$ and $x_b$ is

$$p(x_a \leqslant X \leqslant x_b) = \int_{x_a}^{x_b} f(x) \, dx, \tag{2.4}$$

where the right-hand side of this equation is the integral of $f(x)$ with respect to $x$ between the values of $x_a$ and $x_b$. The integral in the case of continuous variables is analogous to the summation in the case of discrete variables (Equation 2.2). Evaluating Equation 2.4 is the same as finding the area under the density curve between the values of $x_a$ and $x_b$.* To evaluate $p(x_a \leqslant X \leqslant x_b)$ for a continuous variable, $f(x)$

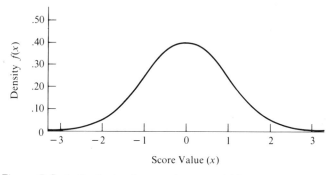

Figure 2.3. A distribution for a continuous variable

*If you are unfamiliar with calculus, you need understand integrals only at this level.

must be specified. In Section 2.7 the use of one type of continuous distribution, the normal distribution, is described in detail. The density function for a normal distribution is

$$f(x) = \frac{1}{\sigma\sqrt{2\pi}}\, e^{-(x-\mu)^2/2\sigma^2},\qquad\qquad(2.5)$$

where $e$ is the constant approximately equal to 2.72. Raising $e$ to a negative power is equivalent to taking the reciprocal of $e$ raised to the corresponding positive power. That is, $e^{-2} = 1/e^2 = .135$. The parameters $\mu$ and $\sigma$ are two constants that describe the normal distribution. For example, Figure 2.3 displays a normal distribution with $\mu = 0$ and $\sigma = 1$. Because the normal distribution is used so frequently, tables are available that give $p(x_a \leq X \leq x_b)$.

## 2.5  Descriptive Statistics

A number of statistics have been developed for describing properties of distributions. These *descriptive statistics* most commonly describe the two properties of central tendency and variability. The *central tendency* of a score distribution indicates where the center of the score distribution lies, and the *variability* indicates the degree to which the scores vary. A third descriptive statistic, *skewness*, indicates the degree to which the score distribution is asymmetrical.

### Central Tendency

The three most commonly used indexes of central tendency are the *mode* (the most frequently occurring score), the *median* (the score that half the examinees score at or below), and the *mean* (the arithmetic average of the scores). The mode is generally the easiest to locate and is useful for obtaining a rough estimate of central tendency. The mode of the frequency distribution in Figure 2.2 is 16. However, some distributions have more than one mode. Figure 2.4 is an example of a distribution with two modes, called a *bimodal distribution*.

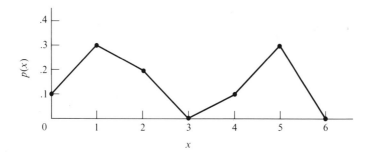

Figure 2.4. A bimodal distribution

The median is preferable as an index of central tendency for highly skewed (asymmetrical) distributions. The median of the frequency distribution in Figure 2.2 could have any value above 14 and less than 15. Conventionally, the median would be set at 14.5. (The median is the 50th percentile, and the calculation of percentiles is discussed in detail in Section 7.2.)

The mean is the most commonly used index of central tendency. The mean is a relatively stable statistic, although it is affected more than the mode or the median by the occurrence of a few scores that are extremely large or extremely small. The mean for a discrete variable $X$ is defined as

$$\bar{X} = \frac{1}{n} \sum_{i=1}^{n} X_i, \tag{2.6}$$

where $n$ is the number of scores in the frequency distribution and $X_i$ is the score of the $i$th examinee. The mean also can be expressed as

$$\bar{X} = \frac{1}{n} \sum_{i=1}^{I} x_i f(x_i), \tag{2.7}$$

where $x_i$ is one of $I$ possible values for $X$, $f(x_i)$ is the frequency of occurrence of $x_i$, and $n = \sum_{i=1}^{I} f(x_i)$ is the total number of observations.

Using Equation 2.7, the mean of the frequency distribution in Table 2.2 and Figure 2.1 can be calculated as

$$\frac{1}{(0 + 0 + 2 + 5 + 3 + 1 + 6 + 1 + 2 + 0)} \big[10(0) + 11(0) + 12(2) + 13(5)$$
$$+ 14(3) + 15(1) + 16(6) + 17(1) + 18(2) + 19(0)\big] = 14.75.$$

## Variability

There are three common measures of *variability*—the range, the variance, and the standard deviation. Each reflects the extent to which the scores in a set differ among themselves. Each of these three measures equals zero whenever all the scores in a set are identical, and each becomes larger as the spread of scores increases. The *range* is defined as the difference between the largest and smallest scores occurring in the distribution. For example, the range of scores for the frequency distribution in Figure 2.1 is $18 - 12 = 6$. Like the mode, the range is easy to calculate but is useful only for rough or preliminary work.

The *variance* of a discrete variable $X$ is defined as

$$s_X^2 = \frac{1}{n} \sum_{i=1}^{n} (X_i - \bar{X})^2 \tag{2.8}$$

$$= \frac{\left( \sum_{i=1}^{n} X_i^2 \right) - n\bar{X}^2}{n}. \tag{2.9}$$

The variance is the average squared deviation from the mean. (For some uses, the variance is defined with $(n - 1)$ instead of $n$ in the denominator; see Section 2.14.) Since the variance is defined in terms of squared units, it is often useful to use its positive square root, the *standard deviation*, as an index of variability.

The variance can also be expressed as

$$s_X^2 = \frac{\left[ \sum_{i=1}^{I} x_i^2 f(x_i) \right] - n\bar{X}^2}{n}. \tag{2.10}$$

For the data in Table 2.2,

$$\sum_{i=1}^{I} x_i^2 f(x_i) = 10^2(0) + 11^2(0) + 12^2(2) + 13^2(5)$$

$$+ 14^2(3) + 15^2(1) + 16^2(6) + 17^2(1) + 18^2(2) + 19^2(0)$$

$$= 4419.$$

From Equation 2.10 the variance is calculated as $\left[ 4419 - 20(14.75)^2 \right]/20 \doteq 3.39$. (The symbol "$\doteq$" is read "approximately equals.") The standard deviation is $\sqrt{3.39} \doteq 1.84$.

## Skewness

A distribution can also be described in terms of its symmetry or of its skewness. A distribution is *symmetrical* if the left half of the curve is the mirror image of the right half. Figures 2.3, 2.5a, and 2.5b are symmetrical distributions; Figures 2.2, 2.5c, and 2.5d are not symmetrical. Figure 2.5c displays a distribution that is *positively skewed* (skewed to the right). The distribution in Figure 2.5d is skewed to the left or *negatively skewed*.

## 2.6   Inferential Statistics

Whereas the purpose of descriptive statistics is to describe a distribution, *inferential statistics* are used to infer from a sample of scores properties of the entire population of scores from which the sample was drawn. Inherent in the development of inferential techniques is the concept of sampling from a population. A *population* is a specific (usually large) group of individuals, and a *sample* is a subset of individuals chosen from that population. Generally, researchers are not interested mainly in the sample but, instead, are interested in making generalizations about the population from which the sample was selected. For example, an experimental psychologist may conduct an experiment with five rats in order to make inferences about all the animals that this sample represents. Inferential techniques allow this researcher to generalize results to the entire population—which may be a specific

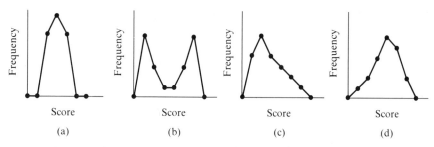

Figure 2.5. Examples of four frequency distributions

subspecies of hooded rats, all rats, or all mammals, depending upon the experimenter's assumptions.

Any statistical technique is based on some set of assumptions. Many techniques have very strict assumptions (for example, that the scores in the population have a normal distribution); others have weaker or less specific assumptions (for example, that people with higher scores possess more of the trait being measured). All common inferential methods share one assumption—that of random sampling. A *random sample* from a population is obtained if each object in the population is equally likely to be included in the sample. For example, suppose the population of interest is all U.S. citizens with Social Security cards. In order to obtain a random sample of *n* citizens, one could put all the known Social Security numbers in a giant bin, carefully mix them up, and blindly draw out *n* numbers. The citizens with these numbers would be a random sample from the population. A nonrandom sample can produce biased results. For example, if a sample of homeowners was used to represent the population of U.S. citizens, biased (nonrepresentative) results on an opinion poll concerning property taxes could result.

Inferential methods are divided into two major branches: hypothesis testing and estimation. *Hypothesis testing* involves several steps, including the construction of an appropriate hypothesis (for example, the test-score mean in the population is equal to 100), the selection of a sample, the collection of data in the sample, and the use of an appropriate statistical technique (for example, a *t* test) to test the hypothesis. The *estimation* approach uses a statistic based on the sample distribution to estimate a property of the population distribution. For example, the mean score in a sample can be used to estimate the mean score in a population. Estimates are usually stated in terms of confidence intervals. For example, one might state that, based on the sample results, a 95% confidence interval for the mean score in the population is from 85 to 115. This implies that, if 100 such intervals were constructed (based on 100 different samples drawn from the same population), the population mean would be expected to fall inside 95 of these intervals. Confidence intervals are discussed further in Section 2.9.

The symbols $\bar{X}$ and $s_{\bar{x}}^2$ are used for the mean and variance in a sample, respectively. Different symbols are needed to distinguish between sample statistics (the mean and variance of the sample) and population parameters (the population mean and variance). Unlike the sample statistics, which are random variables and fluctuate from sample to sample, the population *parameters* are fixed constants. Greek letters generally are used to represent population parameters. Two symbols are commonly used for the population mean: $\mu_X$ and $\mathcal{E}(X)$, the *expected value* of $X$. The symbol most commonly used for the population variance is $\sigma_X^2$, which is $\mathcal{E}(X - \mu_X)^2$, the expected or average squared deviation from the population mean. Expected values are discussed further in Section 2.14. The symbols $\mathcal{E}(X)$, $\mu_X$, and $\sigma_X^2$ are used frequently in following chapters. The symbol ``$\hat{\ }$'' is used to indicate an estimate. For example, $\hat{\mu}_X = \bar{X}$; an estimate of the population mean is the sample mean.

## 2.7  The Normal Distribution

Many standard statistical procedures rely on the assumption that the sample of scores being examined has been drawn from a population with a normal distribution. The *normal distribution* of scores is a bell-shaped curve, with many scores near the middle and fewer scores tapering off to the extremes, as can be seen in Figure 2.6. Many variables have an approximately normal distribution—for example, height and intelligence. Most people are in the middle (of average height, of average intelligence), and very few people are at the extremes (extremely short or tall, extremely low or high in intelligence). However, not all bell-shaped distributions are normal distributions; to have a normal distribution, a variable must be continuous and must have the density described in Equation 2.5.

Recall from Section 2.4 that the area under a density function between two values of a variable is the probability of observing values of the variable in that range. For the normal distribution, areas under the normal density curve have been

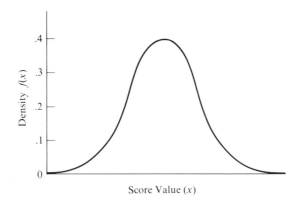

Figure 2.6. A normal distribution

tabled to make it easier to determine the probability that a normal variable will take on a specified range of values. The Appendix contains such a table, called a normal table, that gives the probabilities associated with what is called the *standard normal curve*, or *distribution*. The standard normal distribution has a mean of zero and a standard deviation of one. Since the normal curve is symmetrical, only the probabilities associated with the upper half of the curve (scores above 0) are given. The column labeled $z$ gives the value of the normal score from the standard normal distribution. The second column gives the probability of observing a score between 0 and $z$. The third column gives the probability of observing a score above $z$. Using the table, verify that the probability of observing a score above 1.5 is .0668 or $p(Z > 1.5) = .0668$, and the probability of observing a score between 0 and 2.67 is .4962 or $p(0 < Z < 2.67) = .4962$. Because the normal density curve is symmetrical, $p[Z < -1.5] = .0668$, and $p[-2.67 < Z < 0] = .4962$. This is easy to understand if you remember that the area under the normal curve above a score of 1.5 is identical to the area under the curve below $-1.5$ and that the area between the mean (zero) and 2.67 is identical to the area between the mean and $-2.67$.

The calculations of probabilities for a normal distribution are greatly simplified, especially for beginners, by drawing a picture to define the desired area. The following examples illustrate several such calculations. Notice that areas under the normal curve can be added or subtracted to find the exact area you want.

1. $p[-.80 < Z < .80]$
   $= p[-.80 < Z < 0] + p[0 < Z < .80]$
   $= .2881 + .2881 = .5762$
   (This is the area under the curve between $-.80$ and 0 plus the area between 0 and .80.)

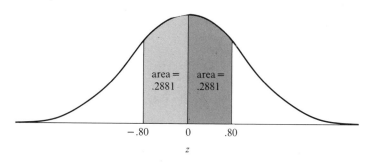

2. $p[.20 < Z < .90]$
   $= p[0 < Z < .90] - p[0 < Z < .20]$
   $= .3159 - .0793 = .2366$
   (This is obtained by subtracting the area between 0 and .20 from the area between 0 and .90.)

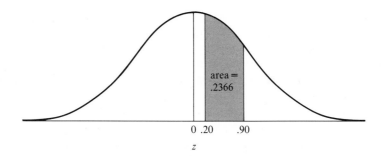

3. $p[-2.41 < Z < -1.03]$
   $= p[-2.41 < Z < 0] - p[-1.03 < Z < 0]$
   $= .4920 - .3485 = .1435$

(This is the area between $-1.03$ and 0 subtracted from the area between $-2.41$ and 0.)

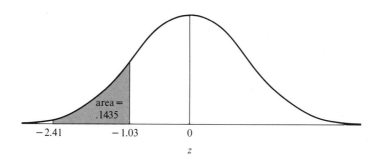

4. $p[-1.74 < Z < .46]$
   $= p[-1.74 < Z < 0] + p[0 < Z < .46]$
   $= .4591 + .1772 = .6363$

(This is the area between $-1.74$ and 0 plus the area between 0 and .46.)

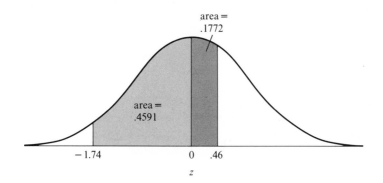

By reversing the process, you can determine the values associated with given probabilities. For example, determine what value, $z$, has 90% of the scores below it. If the probability of having a score less than $z$ is .90, the probability of having a score greater than $z$ is .10. By using the third column in the normal table and searching for .10, you find that $z \doteq 1.28$. Because the normal distribution is symmetrical, it is also clear that 10% of the scores fall below $-1.28$.

Not all normal distributions have a mean of 0 and a standard deviation of 1. However, the probabilities for any normal distribution can be ascertained by using the standard normal table and performing a simple transformation. If $X$ is a variable that has a nonstandard normal distribution with a known mean ($\mu_X$) and standard deviation ($\sigma_X$), then a new variable, $Z$, can be defined as

$$Z = \frac{X - \mu_X}{\sigma_X} \tag{2.11}$$

The variable $Z$ has the standard normal distribution—that is, $Z$ has a mean of 0 and a standard deviation of 1. $Z$ is called a $Z$ *score* or *standard score*.

The following example illustrates the use of this transformation. Imagine that an IQ test has a normal distribution of scores, with a mean of 100 and a standard deviation of 16. What is the probability of observing an IQ greater than 116? Here $x = 116$, $\mu_X = 100$, and $\sigma_X = 16$. Using Equation 2.11, $z = (116 - 100)/16 = 1.0$. From the normal table we determine that $p[Z > 1.0] = .1587$; therefore, about 16% of the scores are above 116. On this same test, what percentage of the population will score below 78? To use the table, we first calculate the standard normal score corresponding to 78: $z = (78 - 100)/16 \doteq -1.38$. Since $p[Z < -1.38] = .0838$, about 8% of the population will score below 78. What is the score on this test that 80% of the people will score below? From the table, we see that the $z$ corresponding to $(1.0 - .80) = .20$ in the third column is about .84. Since $.84 = (x - 100)/16$, the $x$ corresponding to a $z$ of .84 is $16(.84) + 100 = 113.44$. About 80% of the scores are below 113.44. Remember that these calculations were made under the assumption that the test scores are normally distributed. Since IQ scores are discrete and the normal distribution is continuous, these calculations can give only approximate values. The accuracy of these approximations depends upon how close the distribution of IQ scores is to the normal distribution.

## 2.8  The Pearson Correlation Coefficient

One of the basic concerns in the behavioral sciences is understanding the relationship between variables. For example, achievement-test scores and intelligence-test scores are related to each other in a positive way: those who have high intelligence-test scores tend to have high achievement-test scores. Sometimes variables are related negatively—for example, achievement-test scores and malnutrition. People rated higher in level of malnutrition tend to have lower achievement-test scores. Other variables are not related at all—for example, weight and intelligence. The most commonly used statistical index for the relationship between two variables is the *Pearson product-moment correlation coefficient*, which is sometimes called the *correlation coefficient, correlation*, or *intercorrelation*. The symbol for a sample correlation coefficient for variables $X$ and $Y$ is $r_{XY}$. (The symbol for the population correlation coefficient is $\rho_{XY}$, which is discussed in Section 2.14.)

Sample correlations are defined using the following formula.

$$r_{XY} = \frac{\frac{1}{n} \sum_{i=1}^{n} (X_i - \bar{X})(Y_i - \bar{Y})}{s_X s_Y} \tag{2.12}$$

$$= \frac{\frac{1}{n} \left[ \sum_{i=1}^{n} X_i Y_i \right] - \bar{X}\bar{Y}}{s_X s_Y} \tag{2.13}$$

$$= \frac{s_{XY}}{s_X s_Y} . \tag{2.14}$$

The numerator of a correlation, $s_{XY}$, called a *covariance*, is the average product of the deviations in $X$ and $Y$, where a *deviation* is a distance from the mean. For examinee $i$, $X_i - \bar{X}$ is the deviation from the group mean for variable $X$, and $Y_i - \bar{Y}$ is the deviation from the group mean for variable $Y$. The correlation is the covariance divided by the product of the standard deviations. Another way of writing the definition of $r_{XY}$ is

$$r_{XY} = \frac{1}{n} \sum_{i=1}^{n} Z_{X_i} Z_{Y_i}, \tag{2.15}$$

which is the average product of the standard ($Z$) scores for the two variables, where

$$Z_{X_i} = \frac{X_i - \bar{X}}{s_X}$$

and

$$Z_{Y_i} = \frac{Y_i - \bar{Y}}{s_Y} .$$

Notice that $r_{XY} = r_{YX}$.

When calculating a correlation from a set of scores, Equation 2.13 is an efficient formula to use. The standard deviations are calculated from

$$s_X = \sqrt{\left[ \sum_{i=1}^{n} X_i^2 \right] / n - \bar{X}^2} \tag{2.16}$$

and

$$s_Y = \sqrt{\left[ \sum_{i=1}^{n} Y_i^2 \right] / n - \bar{Y}^2}, \tag{2.17}$$

where

$$\bar{X} = \frac{1}{n} \sum_{i=1}^{n} X_i, \tag{2.18}$$

and
$$\bar{Y} = \frac{1}{n} \sum_{i=1}^{n} Y_i. \qquad (2.19)$$

Table 2.4 presents pairs of scores ($X_i$ and $Y_i$) for 13 examinees. The table also contains $X_i^2$, $Y_i^2$, and $X_i Y_i$ for each examinee, and the sums of all values appear at the bottom of the table. Using these values and the equations above, we obtain $\bar{X} = 53/13 \doteq 4.08$ and $\bar{Y} = 51/13 \doteq 3.92$. The standard deviations are $s_X \doteq \sqrt{(243/13) - (4.08)^2} \doteq 1.43$ and $s_Y \doteq \sqrt{(249/13) - (3.92)^2} \doteq 1.95$. The covariance is $s_{XY} \doteq (237/13) - (4.08)(3.92) \doteq 2.24$. The correlation between $X$ and $Y$ is $r_{XY} \doteq 2.24/(1.43)(1.95) \doteq .80$.

Table 2.4. Example of Data Used in the Calculation of a Correlation

| Examinee i | $X_i$ | $Y_i$ | $X_i^2$ | $Y_i^2$ | $X_i Y_i$ |
|---|---|---|---|---|---|
| 1 | 1 | 1 | 1 | 1 | 1 |
| 2 | 2 | 1 | 4 | 1 | 2 |
| 3 | 3 | 3 | 9 | 9 | 9 |
| 4 | 3 | 4 | 9 | 16 | 12 |
| 5 | 4 | 2 | 16 | 4 | 8 |
| 6 | 4 | 3 | 16 | 9 | 12 |
| 7 | 4 | 5 | 16 | 25 | 20 |
| 8 | 5 | 3 | 25 | 9 | 15 |
| 9 | 5 | 4 | 25 | 16 | 20 |
| 10 | 5 | 5 | 25 | 25 | 25 |
| 11 | 5 | 7 | 25 | 49 | 35 |
| 12 | ·6 | 6 | 36 | 36 | 36 |
| 13 | 6 | 7 | 36 | 49 | 42 |
| Sum | 53 | 51 | 243 | 249 | 237 |

The most common way to visually present the relationship between two variables is by using a *scatter plot*. Figure 2.7 is a scatter plot for the relationship between variables $X$ and $Y$ from Table 2.4. Each point represents a pair of scores for one examinee. The point labeled "5" represents the scores for examinee 5, who scored 4 on $X$ and 2 on $Y$. An examination of the scatter plot reveals that the two variables are positively related (positively correlated), since people who tend to score higher on $X$ also tend to score higher on $Y$.

Correlation coefficients are described in terms of their sign and their size. The sign of the correlation reflects the direction of the relationship; a correlation has a negative sign if the variables are negatively related and a positive sign if the variables are positively related. The size of the correlation, which can vary from zero to one, reflects the strength of the relationship—that is, how well one variable can be predicted from the other. Figure 2.8 displays four scatter plots representing correlations differing in sign and size. Figures 2.8a and 2.8b represent positive correlations; Figures 2.8c and 2.8d represent negative correlations. The relationships in Figures

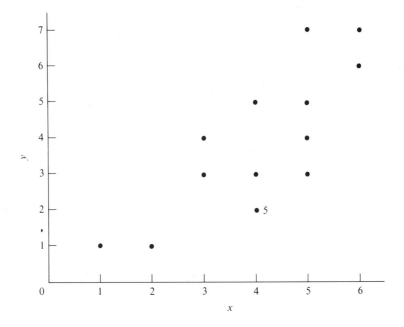

Figure 2.7. Scatter plot of the scores from Table 2.4

2.8a and 2.8c both have the same size for the correlation, .2, as do the relationships in Figures 2.8b and 2.8d, .8. Although the relationships in 2.8b and 2.8d are strong ($r \doteq \pm .8$), they are not perfect (a perfect relationship would be a straight line with $r = \pm 1.0$); therefore, precise predictions of X from Y or of Y from X are not possible. The larger correlation ($r \doteq \pm .8$) does mean, however, that the predictions in 2.8b and 2.8d would be more accurate than similar predictions made in 2.8a and 2.8c ($r \doteq \pm .2$).

The size of a correlation can be considered a measure of how well the points in the scatter plot "hug a line." If we draw a straight line through the bulk of the scatter plot, the points in Figures 2.8b and 2.8d would hug the line better than the points in Figures 2.8a and 2.8c. In fact, the correlation coefficient measures the

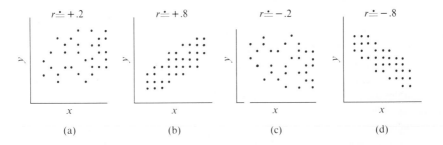

Figure 2.8. Scatter plots for positive and negative correlations

strength of the linear relationship between two variables. Although the relationship in Figure 2.9 is strong (there is good predictability of $Y$ from $X$), the correlation between the variables is low, because the relationship is curved or *curvilinear*. This leads us to a more precise description of the Pearson correlation coefficient: the Pearson correlation coefficient is a number between $-1$ and $+1$ that indicates the directionality and strength of the linear relationship between two variables. The sign indicates the direction of the relationship (whether it is positive or negative), and the size indicates the strength of the linear relationship. If X and Y have a *linear relationship*, $Y = c_1 X + c_2$, and $X = (Y - c_2)/c_1$, where $c_1$ and $c_2$ are constants and $c_1$ does not equal zero. When $r = +1$, the points in the scatter plot fall precisely on a straight line with a positive slope (direction); when $r = -1$, the points in the scatter plot fall precisely on a straight line with a negative slope. Correlations with magnitudes unequal to $\pm 1$ indicate scatter plots that deviate from a perfect line pattern. As these deviations become larger, predictability decreases, and the size of the correlation coefficient approaches zero.

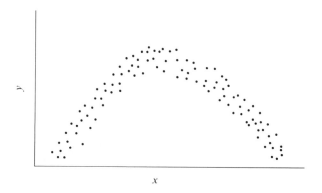

Figure 2.9. A curvilinear relationship

The *size* of a correlation is not affected by a linear transformation of either the X scores or the Y scores, but the *sign* of the correlation can be affected by such a linear transformation. A *linear transformation* of X means that the X score for each examinee is changed to a new score, $X^*$, by the following rule:

$$X_i^* = aX_i + b, \tag{2.20}$$

where $a$ is a constant not equal to zero, $b$ is another constant, and $i$ stands for an examinee. For example, if $a = -10$ and $b = +4$, then $X_i^* = -10X_i + 4$. If $X_i = 1$, then $X_i^* = -6$; if $X_i = 2$, then $X_i^* = -16$. The mean of $X^*$ scores, $\bar{X}^*$, is $a\bar{X} + b$. The standard deviation of the $X^*$ scores, $s_{X^*}$, is $|a|s_X$, where $|a|$ is the absolute value of $a$. Similarly, if $Y_i^* = cY_i + d$, then $\bar{Y}^* = c\bar{Y} + d$, and $s_{Y^*} = |c|s_Y$. The covariance between $X^*$ and $Y^*$ is $acs_{XY}$.

Using Equation 2.14, we find that

$$r_{X^*Y^*} = \frac{s_{X^*Y^*}}{s_{X^*} \, s_{Y^*}} \qquad (2.21)$$

$$= \frac{acs_{XY}}{|a| \, s_X \, |c| \, s_Y} \qquad (2.22)$$

$$= \frac{ac}{|a| \, |c|} r_{XY}. \qquad (2.23)$$

The term $ac/|a| \, |c|$ equals $\pm 1$. If $a$ is a negative number and $c$ is a positive number, or if $a$ is positive and $c$ is negative, then $r_{X^*Y^*} = -r_{XY}$. If $a$ and $c$ are both positive or both negative, then $r_{X^*Y^*} = r_{XY}$.

The most common interpretation of a correlation coefficient is in terms of its square. The squared correlation coefficient $(r_{XY}^2)$ is equal to the proportion of variance in $Y$ accounted for by a linear relationship with $X$. In order to fully explain what this means, we must develop a few concepts. Let $X$ and $Y$ be two variables that are being correlated. The scatter plot of the $X$ and $Y$ scores appears in Figure 2.10. (This is the same scatter plot as Figure 2.7 and is based on the data in Table 2.4.) Along the vertical edge, or margin, of the scatter plot, the frequency distribution of the $Y$ scores appears; the distribution of the $X$ scores appears (upside down) along the horizontal margin. The distributions of $X$ and $Y$ are called *marginal distributions* because they are drawn in the margins. Now consider the distribution of $Y$ scores for examinees with a fixed $X$ score. For example, for $X = 5$, one examinee has $Y_i = 7$, one has $Y_i = 5$, one has $Y_i = 4$, and one has $Y_i = 3$. The distribution of $Y$ scores for any fixed $X$ score is called the *conditional distribution* of $Y$ given $X$. There is a conditional distribution of $Y$ given $X$ for each value of $X$. Idealized (normal) marginal and conditional distributions are shown in Figure 2.11. The conditional distribution in Figure 2.11 is for $X = 10$.

Imagine that we are going to use the line $\hat{Y}_i = 1.1X_i - .57$ to predict $Y$ from $X$ in Figure 2.10. For example, at $X_i = 5$, $\hat{Y}_i$ is 4.93. For the conditional distribution of $Y$ for one value of $X$, $x$, we can calculate the average of the squared deviations of $Y_i$ from $\hat{Y}_i$ and call it $s_{Y \cdot x}^2$. (The "$\cdot$" in $s_{Y \cdot x}^2$ is read "given" and indicates that we are calculating the variance of $Y$ around $\hat{Y}$, which is based on $x$.) For example, for $x = 5$,

$$s_{Y \cdot x}^2 = \frac{1}{4} \left[ (7 - 4.93)^2 + (5 - 4.93)^2 + (4 - 4.93)^2 + (3 - 4.93)^2 \right]$$

$$\doteq 2.22.$$

Similarly, we can calculate an average squared deviation of $Y_i$ from $\hat{Y}_i$ averaged over all values of $X$ and call it $s_{Y \cdot X}^2$—the variance of $Y$ given $X$; then

$$s_{Y \cdot X}^2 = \frac{1}{n} \sum_{i=1}^{n} (Y_i - \hat{Y}_i)^2. \qquad (2.24)$$

For the data in Figure 2.10, $n = 13$, and $s_{Y \cdot X}^2 = (1/13) \left[ (1 - .53)^2 + (1 - 1.63)^2 + (3 - 2.73)^2 + (4 - 2.73)^2 + \cdots + (6 - 6.03)^2 + (7 - 6.03)^2 \right] \doteq 1.35$. The

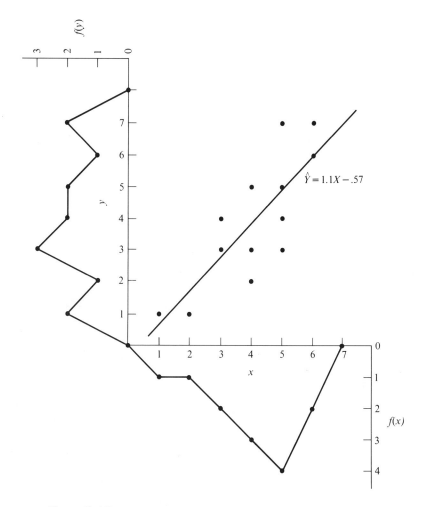

Figure 2.10. Illustration of linear prediction of $Y$ from $X$ and marginal distributions

square root of this variance, $s_{Y \cdot X}$, is called the sample *standard error of estimate*. If the conditional distribution of $Y$ given $X$ has the same variance for every value of $X$, the standard error of estimate, $s_{Y \cdot X}$, is the standard deviation of each of the conditional distributions; that is, $s_{Y \cdot X} = s_{Y \cdot x}$ for all $x$. For Figure 2.10, $s_{Y \cdot X} \doteq \sqrt{1.35} \doteq 1.16$.

If $Y$ could be predicted perfectly from $X$, $\hat{Y}_i$ would equal $Y_i$ for every examinee, and $s_{Y \cdot X}^2$ would equal zero. The conditional variance, $s_{Y \cdot X}^2$, reflects variance in $Y$ that is not explained by the prediction from $X$. Since $s_Y^2$ is the total variance in $Y$ and $s_{Y \cdot X}^2$ is the variance in $Y$ not explained by prediction from $X$,

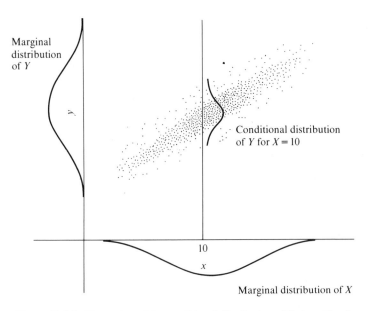

Figure 2.11. Illustration of the conditional distribution of $Y$ given $X$ and the marginal distributions of $X$ and $Y$

$s_Y^2 - s_{Y \cdot X}^2$ is the variance in $Y$ explained by or accounted for by prediction from $X$. The ratio

$$\frac{s_Y^2 - s_{Y \cdot X}^2}{s_Y^2}$$

is the proportion of variance in $Y$ that is explained by prediction from $X$.

  The prediction line $\hat{Y}_i = 1.1X_i - .57$ was found by linear regression, which is explained in detail in the next section. The formula for this prediction line is influenced by $r_{XY}$. In the case of perfect linear predictability ($r_{XY} = +1$ or $-1$), all the variance in $Y$ can be explained by linear prediction from $X$; therefore, $s_{Y \cdot X}^2 = 0$, and $s_Y^2 - s_{Y \cdot X}^2 = s_Y^2$. In the case of no linear predictability ($r_{XY} = 0$), none of the variance in $Y$ can be explained by linear prediction from $X$; if a linear prediction rule is used when $r_{XY} = 0$, $s_{Y \cdot X}^2 = s_Y^2$, and $s_Y^2 - s_{Y \cdot X}^2 = 0$. It can be shown that the maximum proportion of variance in $Y$ that can be explained by linear prediction from $X$ equals $r_{XY}^2$. This maximum is achieved when linear regression (Section 2.9) is used to construct the prediction line. When linear regression is used

$$r_{XY}^2 = \frac{s_Y^2 - s_{Y \cdot X}^2}{s_Y^2}, \tag{2.25}$$

and the squared correlation is the proportion of variance in $Y$ that is explained by the linear prediction from $X$.

  When $r_{XY}$ is relatively small, linear predictability is very weak. For example, when $r_{XY} = .2$, only 4% of the variance in $Y$ can be accounted for by linear prediction from $X$. When $r_{XY} = .7$, slightly less than half (49%) of the variance in $Y$ can be explained by linear prediction from $X$; that is, $s_{Y.X}^2$ is about half the size of $s_Y^2$. For the data in Figure 2.10, $r_{XY} \doteq .80$, $s_Y^2 \doteq (1.95)^2 = 3.80$, and $s_{Y.X}^2 \doteq 1.35$. The squared correlation between $X$ and $Y$ is $r_{XY}^2 \doteq .64$. The quantity $(s_Y^2 - s_{Y.X}^2)/s_Y^2$ $\doteq (3.80 - 1.35)/3.80 \doteq .64$. About 64% of the variance in $Y$ is explained by the linear prediction from $X$.

## 2.9  Linear Regression

In the previous section, correlation was defined, in part, by the word *predictability*. The size of the correlation reflects how well one variable can be linearly predicted from the other. Just as the correlation coefficient reflects the strength of the linear relationship between the two variables, it also reflects the accuracy of a linear prediction—a prediction based on a line. *Linear-regression* techniques allow us to determine the equation for the best prediction line, the *regression line*.

Examine the scatter plot in Figure 2.12. If we wish to linearly predict $Y$ from $X$, we need to determine the position for the best prediction line. Several lines are drawn through the scatter plot, some of which produce better predictions than others. In order to determine the best line, we need a definition of "best." One common statistical criterion for predictions is the *least-squares criterion*, in which we pick the procedure (line) that minimizes the sum of squared errors of prediction. If $Y_i$ is the

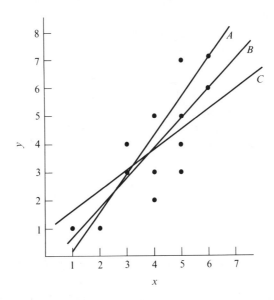

Figure 2.12. Possible prediction lines

observed score for examinee $i$ and $\hat{Y}_i$ is the predicted score for examinee $i$, then $(Y_i - \hat{Y}_i)$ is the amount of error involved in predicting $Y$ from $\hat{Y}$ for examinee $i$. The best prediction line that satisfies the least-squares criterion would minimize the function $\sum_{i=1}^{n} (Y_i - \hat{Y}_i)^2$, the sum of squared errors. Thus, this best prediction line minimizes $s_{Y \cdot X}^2$. It can be shown that the best least-squares prediction line in a sample is

$$\hat{Y}_i = r_{XY}\left(\frac{s_Y}{s_X}\right)(X_i - \bar{X}) + \bar{Y} \qquad (2.26)$$

$$= B_{Y \cdot X}(X_i - \bar{X}) + \bar{Y}. \qquad (2.27)$$

Equations 2.26 and 2.27 are called linear-regression equations. $B_{Y \cdot X} = r_{XY}s_Y/s_X$ and is called the sample *regression coefficient* for predicting $Y$ from $X$. The variables in Figure 2.12 have a correlation of .80, $\bar{X} \doteq 4.08$, $\bar{Y} \doteq 3.92$, $s_X \doteq 1.43$, and $s_Y \doteq 1.95$; and the equation for the regression line is $\hat{Y}_i \doteq (.80)(1.95/1.43)(X_i - 4.08) + 3.92 \doteq 1.1(X_i) - .57$. When $X_i = 2, \hat{Y}_i = 1.63$; when $X_i = 6, \hat{Y}_i = 6.03$. The $\hat{Y}$ represents the predicted $Y$ score for the given $X$ score. Line B in Figure 2.12 is the plot of the best least-squares regression line for these data.

Usually such regression lines are used when we want to use $X$ scores to predict unknown $Y$ scores. For example, a college admissions office may wish to predict future grade-point average $(Y)$ from scores on an entrance exam $(X)$, in order to decide which applicants should be admitted. The first step is to obtain a random sample from the current population of students, who have taken the entrance exam and whose later grade-point averages are available. The means, standard deviations, and correlations of $X$ and $Y$ from this sample are used to construct the regression equation (Equation 2.26). Then, when new applicants are considered, their exam scores can be entered into the regression equation to predict their future grade-point averages. Further discussion of the uses of linear regression can be found in Sections 5.5 and 9.3.

The $\hat{Y}_i$ is the best linear least-squares estimate of $Y_i$. Unless $r_{XY} = \pm 1$, it is unlikely that $Y_i$ exactly equals $\hat{Y}_i$. For this reason, we often want to estimate a range of values that is likely to include $Y_i$. This procedure is called *confidence-interval estimation*. The confidence interval makes it clear that the prediction is not exact and gives an idea of about how accurate the prediction is. The confidence interval for $Y_i$ is defined as

$$\hat{Y}_i - z_c s_{Y \cdot X} < Y_i < \hat{Y}_i + z_c s_{Y \cdot X}, \qquad (2.28)$$

usually written as $\hat{Y}_i \pm z_c s_{Y \cdot X}$, where

$$s_{Y \cdot X} = s_Y \sqrt{1 - r_{XY}^2}, \qquad (2.29)$$

and $z_c$ is the critical value for the given confidence level obtained from the normal table, and defined so that $p(-z_c < Z < +z_c) = c$.

The use of this confidence interval involves three major assumptions: (1) that the relationship between $X$ and $Y$ is linear, (2) that the conditional distribution of

$Y$ given $X$ is normal, and (3) that $s_{Y \cdot x}$ is the same for every $x$. The first assumption is required to justify the use of $\hat{Y}_i$, which is based on a linear equation. If the relationship were not linear, a linear regression line would not be reasonable. $z_c$ is the critical value for the given confidence probability from the normal table. For example, $z_c$ for a 95% confidence interval is 1.96, since $p(-1.96 < Z < 1.96) \doteq .95$; and $z_c$ for a 98% confidence interval is 2.33, since $p(-2.33 < Z < 2.33) \doteq .98$. In order to meet the second assumption and to justify the use of the normal table, we must assume that the distribution we are dealing with (the conditional distribution of $Y$ given $X$) is normal, as it is in Figure 2.11. The third assumption is called an assumption of *homoscedasticity,* which says that all $s_{Y \cdot x}$ are identical. (If the $s_{Y \cdot x}$ are different, the relationship between $X$ and $Y$ is said to exhibit *heteroscedasticity.*) Homoscedastic and heteroscedastic relationships are illustrated in Figure 2.13. Figure 2.13a displays a homoscedastic relationship. In Figure 2.13b the relationship is heteroscedastic, because $s_{Y \cdot x}$ increases for larger $x$. Homoscedasticity must be assumed when using Equation 2.29 to estimate $s_{Y \cdot x}$, since this estimate does not vary as a function of $x$. (If very large sample sizes are available, it would be possible to calculate $s_{Y \cdot x}$ separately for each $x$, so that the third assumption would not be necessary.)

If these three assumptions are met, the confidence intervals can be interpreted in the following manner. When a large number of confidence intervals at a certain level (let's say at a 95% level) are constructed for a large number of examinees, a specified percentage of these intervals (in this case 95%) are expected to contain the examinees' actual $Y$ values. When we are predicting unknown $Y$ scores, we cannot specify which examinees' confidence intervals would contain the examinees' actual $Y$ scores. But if we predict that every examinee's confidence interval contains his or her $Y$ score, we expect that our predictions would be correct for a certain percentage (95% in this case) of the examinees.

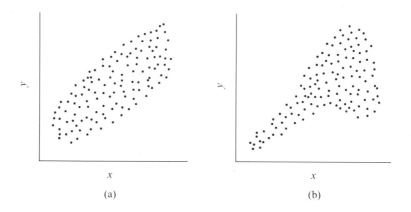

Figure 2.13. Examples of homoscedastic (a) and heteroscedastic (b) relationships

The relationship between $X$ and $Y$ in Figure 2.10 appears linear, satisfying Assumption 1, but the number of examinees is so small that it is difficult to judge the appropriateness of the two other assumptions. In any case, we will construct confidence intervals with these data for illustrative purposes. Referring to Figure 2.10, we see that when $X_i = 2$, the 90% confidence interval for $Y_i$ is approximately equal to

$$1.63 \pm (1.65)(1.95) \sqrt{1 - (.80)^2}$$

$$= 1.63 \pm (1.65)(1.17)$$

$$\doteq 1.63 \pm 1.93 \quad \text{or} \quad -.30 \text{ to } 3.56.$$

When $X_i = 6$, the 95% confidence interval for $Y_i$ is approximately

$$6.03 \pm (1.96)(1.17)$$

$$\doteq 6.03 \pm 2.29 \quad \text{or} \quad 3.74 \text{ to } 8.32.$$

Notice that the second interval is wider than the first interval. This occurs because a larger confidence probability was used to create the second interval. We are more confident (that is, there is a higher probability) that the wider interval contains the examinees' scores on variable $Y$.

The regression line and correlation coefficient are appropriately used in applied settings whenever the actual relationship between the two variables is linear in form. When the relationship is curvilinear, as in Figure 2.9, other methods, which are beyond the scope of this book, are more appropriate.

## 2.10   Influences on Correlation Coefficients

Correlation coefficients can be influenced by many factors. Two of these factors that are particularly important—restriction of range and combining groups—are discussed in this section.

If the range of one or both of the scores involved in a correlation is restricted or reduced, the correlation will tend to be smaller than a similar correlation based on an unrestricted range of scores. This effect is called *attenuation* (reduction) due to *restriction of range*. For example, a hypothetical relationship between IQ and high school achievement in a national sample of high school graduates is illustrated in Figure 2.14a, where the variables have a correlation of about .8. Suppose we then study this relationship among graduates entering very selective universities. In this university sample there will be restriction of range both in IQ and in achievement, as illustrated in Figure 2.14b. Since the size of the correlation indicates how well the points in the scatter plot hug a line, it is clear that the correlation will be higher in the unrestricted sample than in the restricted sample. Since the correlation coefficient indicates how well one variable can be linearly predicted from the other, the reduced correlation in a relatively homogeneous sample indicates that linear regression will not be as effective in the restricted group as in the unrestricted group. Therefore, it

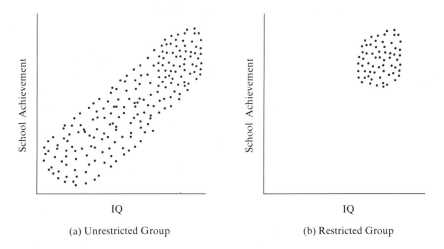

<table>
<tr><td>(a) Unrestricted Group</td><td>(b) Restricted Group</td></tr>
</table>

Figure 2.14. Scatter plots for the relationship between IQ and achievement

would not be as effective to use IQ as a predictor of school achievement in the example illustrated in Figure 2.14b as it would be in the example in Figure 2.14a.

Sometimes the relationship between two variables varies across groups. For example, the relationship between maternal protectiveness and achievement orientation among girls may be different from that among boys, as illustrated in Figure 2.15. In this example there is a positive relationship between protectiveness and achievement for boys and a negative relationship for girls. If a combined sample of boys and girls were studied, a very small or zero correlation would be observed, and

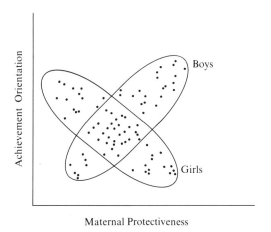

Figure 2.15. Example of scatter plots differing across groups

the conclusion might be made that there is no correlation between maternal protectiveness and achievement orientation among boys or girls. This conclusion would
not be true, and this example illustrates the problem of combining groups when the
groups differ with respect to the relationship between the variables studied. Combining groups can lead to conclusions that differ markedly from conclusions based
on the uncombined groups. Figure 2.16 illustrates several such situations. In Figure
2.16a the correlation between $X$ and $Y$ is zero within each group but is positive when
the groups are combined. In Figure 2.16b the correlation is negative in Group A,
positive in Group B, and negative in the combined group. In Figure 2.16c the
correlation is positive in Group A, zero in Group B, and positive in the combined
sample. And in Figure 2.16d the correlation is positive for each group but is reduced
in the combined sample. When correlations are reported for combined groups, it is
important to examine the possibility that the relationship between the variables
varies across groups. An examination of the scatter plots for the different groups
could aid considerably in interpreting the data.

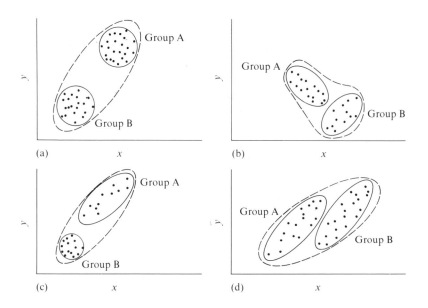

Figure 2.16. Examples of problems created by combining groups

## 2.11   Alternative Measures of Association

The Pearson correlation coefficient is the measure most commonly used for
indicating the strength of the relationship between two variables. Its use is appropriate when the variables are continuous or *multi-step* (having a large number of
possible values) and when the variables reach an interval or a ratio level of measure-

ment (see Section 2.2 and Chapter 8). The Pearson correlation frequently is used with ordinal variables, such as number-right test scores, and usually no problems arise. However, using the Pearson correlation with some ordinal variables can lead to misinterpretation of the relationship between the traits being measured. Care should be taken whenever the Pearson correlation is used with ordinal variables.

When the variables being correlated are not continuous or multi-step or when they are rank orders, the name and interpretation of the Pearson correlation coefficient can be altered or an alternative measure of association can be used. Six of these correlations or measures of association are reviewed briefly in this section: the phi coefficient, the tetrachoric correlation coefficient, the biserial correlation coefficient, the point-biserial correlation coefficient, the Spearman rank-order correlation coefficient, and Kendall's tau.

To simplify this discussion, a few distinctions should be drawn. A *dichotomous* variable is a variable that has only two values (for example, *zero* and *one*, *yes* and *no*, *on* and *off*). A dichotomous variable may be truly dichotomous (for example, *male* and *female*), or it may be *artificially dichotomized*. An example of an artificial dichotomy would be arbitrarily labeling people over 6 feet tall as "tall" and calling everyone else "short." If the underlying distribution of an artificially dichotomized variable (in this example, height) is normal, the variable is called an artificially dichotomized normal variable.

The *phi coefficient* ($\phi$) is used as an index of the strength of association between two dichotomous variables. If the dichotomous variables have the values "0" and "1" and a Pearson correlation coefficient is calculated on the set of scores, the resulting coefficient is the phi coefficient. Since each of the two variables takes on only two values, the computations can be simplified, so that

$$\phi_{XY} = \frac{p_c - p_X p_Y}{\sqrt{p_X(1 - p_X)p_Y(1 - p_Y)}} , \qquad (2.30)$$

where $X$ and $Y$ are the two variables, $p_c$ is the proportion of examinees scoring "1" on both $X$ and $Y$, and $p_X$ and $p_Y$ are the proportions of examinees scoring "1" on $X$ and $Y$, respectively. For the data in Table 2.5, $p_c = 16/40$, $p_X = 28/40$, $p_Y = 20/40$, $(1 - p_X) = 12/40$, and $(1 - p_Y) = 20/40$. The computed $\phi_{XY} \doteq .22$, which is a low positive correlation.

Because the phi coefficient is a special case of the Pearson correlation coefficient, one might expect that its range would be from $-1$ to $+1$. However, this is true only when $p_X$ and $p_Y$ are each equal to .5. When $p_X$ and $p_Y$ are not both equal to .5, the range of $\phi$ is restricted or reduced. For example, if $p_X = 5/20$ and $p_Y = 18/20$, the maximum positive $\phi$ is approximately .19 and the maximum negative $\phi$ is approximately $-.58$. (Verify this by calculating $\phi$ for the strongest relationships that are possible with the given values of $p_X$ and $p_Y$; namely, $p_c = 5/20$ and $p_c = 3/20$.)

The phi coefficient can be used in any situation in which a measure of the association between two dichotomous variables is desired. For example, the phi could be used to correlate the variable of gender with a variable indicating whether a

Table 2.5. Sample Data for Phi Coefficient Calculation

|   |   | x | | |
|---|---|---|---|---|
|   |   | 0 | 1 | Total |
| y | 0 | 8 | 12 | 20 |
|   | 1 | 4 | 16 | 20 |
|   | Total | 12 | 28 | 40 |

person has graduated from high school. In testing applications, $\phi$ can be used for the correlation between scores on two test items, where "1" means that the item was answered correctly. Such correlations are useful in test construction.

The *tetrachoric correlation coefficient* ($r_{tet}$) is used to correlate two artificially dichotomized variables, $X$ and $Y$, that have a bivariate normal distribution. A complete description of the bivariate normal distribution is beyond the scope of this book, but, in simplified terms, *bivariate normality* means that the distribution of $Y$ among examinees who have the same (fixed) value of $X$ is a normal distribution and that the distribution of $X$ among examinees who have the same value of $Y$ is a normal distribution. If $X$ and $Y$ have a bivariate normal distribution, then $X$ and $Y$ must each have a normal distribution. The calculation of the tetrachoric correlation involves corrections that approximate what the Pearson correlation coefficient would have been if the data had been continuous (nondichotomized) and the Pearson correlation coefficient could have been used. For example, one might assume that there is an underlying normal distribution for a trait and, if an examinee is above some value on that trait, that examinee will pass a given item. With this assumption, the appropriate index of association between such items would be the tetrachoric correlation coefficient. The actual calculation of the tetrachoric correlation cannot be reduced to a simple formula; tables and computer programs are available to compute it. (See Lord and Novick, 1968, for a further discussion of this statistic.)

Both the phi and tetrachoric correlations are used for relating two dichotomous variables, but the tetrachoric is used when the normality assumptions are reasonable. Both indexes are commonly used as measures of the association between scores on test items.

The *point-biserial correlation coefficient*, $r_{pbis}$, is used as an index of the association between a dichotomous variable and a continuous or multi-step variable. If the values that the dichotomous variable can have are 0 and 1 and if the Pearson correlation coefficient (Equation 2.13) is calculated between the 0/1 scores and the continuous or multi-step scores, the resulting number is the point-biserial correlation coefficient. In this case the calculation (Equation 2.13) can be reduced to a more simple computational formula,

$$r_{pbis} = \left[ \frac{\bar{Y}_1 - \bar{Y}}{s_Y} \right] \sqrt{\frac{p_X}{(1 - p_X)}} , \tag{2.31}$$

where $X$ is the dichotomous variable, $Y$ is the continuous or multi-step variable, $\overline{Y}_1$ is the mean of $Y$ scores for examinees with $X = 1$, $\overline{Y}$ is the overall mean of the $Y$ scores, $s_Y$ is the standard deviation of the $Y$ scores, and $p_X$ is the proportion of examinees with $X = 1$.

The point biserial is frequently used in test construction, where $X$ is the score on item $i$, $Y$ is the number-right score for the entire test, and the point biserial is written $r_{iY}$. For example, suppose we want to find the correlation between scores on the first item ($X = 1$ if the examinee passes item 1; $X = 0$ if the examinee fails item 1) and scores for the total number of right answers ($Y$) on a nine-item test. The observed data appear in Table 2.6. For these data, $p_X = 10/15 \doteq .667$. The overall mean of the $Y$ scores (using Equation 2.19) is $\overline{Y} = (1 + 4 + \cdots + 6 + 5)/15 \doteq 5.53$. The standard deviation of the scores (using Equation 2.17) is

$$s_Y = \sqrt{\left[ (1^2 + 4^2 + \cdots + 6^2 + 5^2)/15 \right] - (5.53)^2}$$
$$= \sqrt{(553/15) - 30.58} \doteq 2.51.$$

The mean of the $Y$ scores for those passing item 1 is $\overline{Y}_1 = (4 + 5 + \cdots + 6 + 5)/10 = 6.6$. Using Equation 2.31 the point-biserial correlation is

$$r_{1Y} = \left[ \frac{6.6 - 5.53}{2.51} \right] \sqrt{\frac{.667}{.333}} \doteq .60.$$

Table 2.6. Data Used in Calculating a Point-Biserial Correlation

| | Examinee | | | | | | | | | | | | | | |
|---|---|---|---|---|---|---|---|---|---|---|---|---|---|---|
| | 1 | 2 | 3 | 4 | 5 | 6 | 7 | 8 | 9 | 10 | 11 | 12 | 13 | 14 | 15 |
| $X$ | 0 | 0 | 0 | 0 | 0 | 1 | 1 | 1 | 1 | 1 | 1 | 1 | 1 | 1 | 1 |
| $Y$ | 1 | 4 | 0 | 5 | 7 | 4 | 5 | 7 | 9 | 8 | 6 | 9 | 7 | 6 | 5 |

The range of the point biserial, like the range of the phi coefficient, is reduced when $p_X$ is not approximately equal to one-half. For example, if the dichotomized variable has an underlying normal distribution and if $p_X$ or $(1 - p_X)$ is as extreme as .95 (on the item, almost everyone gets the right answer or almost everyone gets the wrong answer), the range of the point biserial is from about $-.5$ to $+.5$ (Lord & Novick, 1968, p. 340). Thus, the interpretation of the size of the point-biserial correlation coefficient depends on $p_X$.

The *biserial correlation coefficient*, $r_{bis}$, is related to the point-biserial correlation in the same way that the tetrachoric is related to the phi coefficient. The biserial correlation is used to correlate an artificially dichotomized, normally distributed variable with a continuous or multi-step variable. The calculations make corrections for the dichotomization, yielding an estimate of the Pearson correlation that would have been found had the data not been dichotomized. The formula for the biserial correlation is

$$r_{bis} = \left[ \frac{\overline{Y}_1 - \overline{Y}}{s_Y} \right] \left[ \frac{p_X}{f(z)} \right], \qquad (2.32)$$

where $X$, $Y$, $\bar{Y}$, $\bar{Y}_1$, $s_Y$, and $p_X$ are defined to be the same as for the point-biserial correlation, and $f(z)$ is the standard normal density evaluated at the value of a normal variate, $z$, above which $p_X$ of cases fall:

$$f(z) = \frac{1}{\sqrt{2\pi}} e^{-z^2/2}. \tag{2.33}$$

For example, if $p_X = .10$, then $z \doteq 1.28$ (found in the normal table in the Appendix) and $f(z) \doteq (.40)(2.72)^{-.82} \doteq .18$. (Tables of the normal density function are available in most collections of statistical tables.)

The calculation of a biserial correlation can be illustrated using the data from Table 2.6. From our calculations for the point-biserial correlation, we know that $\bar{Y} \doteq 5.53$, $\bar{Y}_1 = 6.6$, $s_Y \doteq 2.51$, and $p_X \doteq .667$. We look at the normal table in the Appendix to determine the $z$ above which $.667$ of the cases in the normal distribution fall, and we find $z \doteq -.43$. Evaluating Equation 2.33 at $z \doteq -.43$ gives $f(z)$ $\doteq (.40)(2.72)^{-.092} \doteq .36$. The biserial correlation (using Equation 2.32) is $r_{bis}$ $= \left[(6.6 - 5.53)/2.51\right] \left[.667/.36\right] \doteq .79$. This biserial correlation is the estimated correlation between $Y$ and a normally distributed trait that was dichotomized to produce $X$. Ghiselli (1964) presents a graph for finding $r_{bis}$ given $(\bar{Y}_1 - \bar{Y})/s_Y$ and $p_X$; this graph provides a way of estimating $r_{bis}$ without evaluating Equation 2.33. Lord and Novick (1968) present a further discussion of the biserial correlation.

The biserial and point-biserial correlations frequently are used as indices of the association between an item and a total test score. Such correlations are useful for item selection when tests are being created.

Another important type of correlation coefficient is the *Spearman rank-order correlation coefficient,* which is used to correlate two multi-step or continuous variables that are measured at the ordinal level of measurement. If the examinees are rank ordered on each of the two variables (from highest to lowest) and the ranks are correlated using the Pearson correlation coefficient, the resulting number is a Spearman rank-order correlation coefficient. This calculation is equivalent to the computational formula

$$r_S = 1 - \frac{6 \sum\limits_{i=1}^{n} D_i^2}{n^3 - n}, \tag{2.34}$$

where $n$ is the sample size and $D_i$ is the difference between the two rank orderings for the $i$th examinee. This calculation for the data in Table 2.7 yields a Spearman correlation of

$$1 - \frac{6\,(6)}{216 - 6} \doteq .83.$$

*Kendall's tau* ($\tau$) is an alternative to the Spearman rank-order correlation coefficient and is useful for ordinal-level data. The calculation for Kendall's tau is considerably more tedious than the calculation of the Spearman coefficient, particu-

Table 2.7. Data for Calculating the Spearman Rank-Order Correlation Coefficient

| Examinee (i) | $X_i$ | $Y_i$ | Rank $X_i$ | Rank $Y_i$ | $D_i$ | $D_i^2$ |
|---|---|---|---|---|---|---|
| 1 | 12 | 3 | 6 | 6 | 0 | 0 |
| 2 | 15 | 7 | 5 | 3 | 2 | 4 |
| 3 | 19 | 4 | 4 | 5 | $-1$ | 1 |
| 4 | 24 | 5 | 3 | 4 | $-1$ | 1 |
| 5 | 46 | 12 | 2 | 2 | 0 | 0 |
| 6 | 102 | 17 | 1 | 1 | 0 | 0 |
| Sum | | | | | | 6 |

larly when there is a large number of examinees. Consult a statistics book such as Hays (1973) for a discussion of Kendall's tau.

Table 2.8 summarizes the conditions under which each type of correlation coefficient is used.

Table 2.8. Types of Correlations Used under Various Conditions

| | Multi-step or continuous variable is measured at interval or ratio level | | Multi-step variable is a rank order |
|---|---|---|---|
| | Correlation of observed scores | Estimated correlation replacing dichotomous variable(s) with normal variable(s) | |
| Both variables dichotomous | phi $(\phi_{XY})$ | tetrachoric $(r_{tet})$ | |
| One variable dichotomous; other is multi-step or continuous | point biserial $(r_{pbis})$ | biserial $(r_{bis})$ | |
| Both variables multi-step or continuous | Pearson coefficient $(r_{XY})$ | | Spearman coefficient $(r_S)$ or Kendall's tau $(\tau)$ |

## 2.12   Introduction to Advanced Topics

Although most of basic measurement theory can be understood using the information surveyed to this point, a number of topics require a somewhat more advanced understanding of mathematical statistics. Section 2.13 covers joint and conditional probabilities; Section 2.14 covers the algebra of expectations, presenting techniques that must be mastered to follow the optional proofs at the end of Chapter 3 and the derivations in later chapters. Although mastery of these two sections is necessary for a complete understanding of some of the developments in later chapters, these sections are not essential for a mastery of their basic conclusions.

## 2.13 (Optional)   Joint and Conditional Probabilities

Conditional distributions were introduced in Section 2.8 in the discussion of correlation. This section describes how conditional distributions are calculated for discrete variables.

Table 2.9 presents hypothetical data relating the probability of a successful outcome of therapy to the educational level of the clients. The main entries in the table (.30, .15, .12, and .43) are *joint probabilities*: that is, they show the probabilities of the two events occurring simultaneously (jointly). For example, the joint probability of a client having a college degree and being successful in therapy is .30. This can be expressed by the formula

$$p(X = x_1, Y = y_1) = .30.$$

Table 2.9. Probabilities of Therapeutic Outcome and Educational Level

|  |  | *Therapeutic outcome (X)* | | |
| --- | --- | --- | --- | --- |
|  |  | *Success (x₁)* | *Failure (x₂)* | *Total* |
| *College degree (Y)* | *Yes (y₁)* | .30 | .15 | .45 |
|  | *No (y₂)* | .12 | .43 | .55 |
|  | *Total* | .42 | .58 | 1.00 |

The row and the column labeled "Total" contain the sums of the joint probabilities and indicate the probabilities of the outcomes for one of the variables. These are called the *marginal probabilities* of the variables, and these marginal probabilities form marginal distributions. For example, the marginal probability of therapeutic success is .30 + .12 = .42. These probabilities can be summed because there are only two ways to have successful therapy: either be successful and be a college graduate or be successful and not be a college graduate. The formula for this relationship is

$$p(X = x_1) = p(X = x_1, Y = y_1) + p(X = x_1, Y = y_2).$$

This formula is a specific example of the general statistical rule

$$p(X = x) = \sum_{j=1}^{J} p(X = x, Y = y_j),$$

where the summation occurs over all possible values of $y_j$.

The data in Table 2.9 can be used to calculate conditional probabilities. A *conditional probability* is the probability of a specific outcome for one variable given (conditional on) a specific outcome for another variable. The conditional probability that $X$ takes on the value $x$ given that $Y$ takes on the value $y$ can be found from the rule

$$p(X = x \mid Y = y) = \frac{p(X = x, Y = y)}{p(Y = y)}, \tag{2.35}$$

which states that the conditional probability that $X$ equals $x$ given that $Y$ equals $y$ is the joint probability that $X$ equals $x$ and $Y$ equals $y$, divided by the probability that $Y = y$. The vertical bar, $\mid$, in Equation 2.35 is read "given," and sometimes $p(X = x \mid Y = y)$ is written $p(X = x \mid y)$. Similarly,

$$p(Y = y \mid X = x) = \frac{p(X = x, Y = y)}{p(X = x)}. \tag{2.36}$$

For example, the probability of success in therapy, given that the client has a college degree, is

$$p(X = x_1 \mid Y = y_1) = \frac{p(X = x_1, Y = y_1)}{p(Y = y_1)}$$

$$= \frac{.30}{.45} \doteq .67.$$

The probability of success among those without college degrees is

$$p(X = x_1 \mid Y = y_2) = .12/.55 \doteq .22.$$

In this example, information about a person's educational level aids considerably in predicting the success or failure of the therapy. Using Equation 2.36, the probability of those people who are successful in therapy having a college degree is

$$p(Y = y_1 \mid X = x_1) = .30/.42 \doteq .71,$$

and the probability of their having a college degree, given that their therapy is unsuccessful, is

$$p(Y = y_1 \mid X = x_2) = .15/.58 \doteq .26.$$

Therefore, knowledge of therapeutic outcome aids in predicting a client's educational level.

Conditional probabilities are used in a number of ways. For example, the probability of a student's graduation from medical school given a score of 152 on an admissions exam is a conditional probability. If we know that $p$(graduation with a score of 152) $= .2$ and $p$(score of 152) $= .4$, then we can determine that $p$(graduation $\mid$ score of 152) $= .2/.4 = .5$.

Two variables are said to be *independent* if

$$p(X = x, Y = y) = p(X = x)p(Y = y). \tag{2.37}$$

For example, suppose that a person's sex and the probability of his or her being successful in therapy are independent of each other. The probabilities of each outcome appear in Table 2.10. Notice that each joint outcome equals the product of its associated marginal probabilities. For example, the probability of someone in this group being a man and being successful in therapy equals the probability of someone in this group being a man times the probability of being successful or $p(Y = y_1, X = x_1) = p(Y = y_1)p(X = x_1)$, which is $.12 = (.30)(.40)$.

Table 2.10. Example of Probabilities of Outcomes When Variables Are Independent

|  | Success ($x_1$) | Failure ($x_2$) | Total |
|---|---|---|---|
| Men ($y_1$) | .12 | .18 | .30 |
| Women ($y_2$) | .28 | .42 | .70 |
| Total | .40 | .60 | 1.00 |

If two variables are independent,

$$p(X = x \mid Y = y) = p(X = x) \tag{2.38}$$

and

$$p(Y = y \mid X = x) = p(Y = y). \tag{2.39}$$

These statements clearly follow from the definition of conditional probabilities (Equations 2.35 and 2.36) and the definition of independence (Equation 2.37). For example, the probability of having successful therapy among women ($.28/.70 = .40$) equals the marginal probability of having successful therapy.

If two variables are independent, their correlation must be zero. However, if two variables have a zero correlation, they are not necessarily independent. A zero correlation means that the variables are not linearly related, but the variables could have a zero correlation and have a curvilinear relationship, as in Figure 2.9. However, if each of the two variables has a normal distribution, the only type of relationship they can have is a linear relationship; normally distributed variables cannot have a curvilinear relationship. Thus, if two normally distributed variables have a zero correlation, the variables are independent.

## 2.14 (Optional)   The Algebra of Expectations

The *expected value* of the discrete variable $X$ is defined as

$$\mathcal{E}(X) = \sum_{i=1}^{I} x_i p(X = x_i), \tag{2.40}$$

where $x_i$ is the $i$th possible value of $X$, $p(X = x_i)$ is the probability that $X$ takes on the value $x_i$, and the summation is taken over all $I$ possible values of $x_i$. The expected value is a type of average. Table 2.11 displays the calculation of an expectation; for these data the expected value is 105.45.

Table 2.11. Calculation of an Expectation

| $i$ | $x_i$ | $p(X = x_i)$ | $x_i p(X = x_i)$ |
|-----|-------|--------------|-------------------|
| 1 | 103 | .10 | 10.30 |
| 2 | 104 | .15 | 15.60 |
| 3 | 105 | .20 | 21.00 |
| 4 | 106 | .30 | 31.80 |
| 5 | 107 | .25 | 26.75 |
| Sum | | 1.00 | 105.45 |

The expected value of a product of discrete variables is

$$\mathcal{E}(XY) = \sum_{i=1}^{I} \sum_{j=1}^{J} x_i y_j p(X = x_i, Y = y_j), \tag{2.41}$$

where the summations are taken over all values of $X$ and $Y$.

In Section 2.3 the algebra of summation signs was reviewed, and three rules were developed and demonstrated. Expected-value signs can be manipulated in similar ways using the following rules.

Rule 1. $\mathcal{E}(b) = b$

Rule 2. $\mathcal{E}(bX) = b\mathcal{E}(X)$

Rule 3. $\mathcal{E}(X + Y) = \mathcal{E}(X) + \mathcal{E}(Y)$

And, if $X$ and $Y$ are independent, the following rule can be used:

Rule 4. $\mathcal{E}(XY) = \mathcal{E}(X)\mathcal{E}(Y)$

Rule 1 states that the expected value of a constant is that constant. This rule may be easier to understand if you remember that an expected value of a variable is its mean, and the mean of a constant is the constant.

Rule 2 states that the expected value of a constant times a variable is the constant times the expected value of the variable. Imagine a set of scores with a given mean. It should be apparent that, if each score is multiplied by a constant, the mean of these new scores will equal the mean of the original scores multiplied by the constant.

Rule 3, the distribution rule, states that one can distribute an expectation across terms. Again, this rule is intuitively reasonable.

Rule 4 states that, when variables are independent, the expected value of their product is the product of their expected values. The proof of Rule 4 is straight-forward.

There are other useful definitions and relationships among expectations.

$$\mu_X = \mathcal{E}(X); \tag{2.42}$$

$\mu_X$ is the population mean of $X$ or expectation of $X$.

$$\sigma_X^2 = \mathcal{E}(X - \mu_X)^2 \tag{2.43}$$

$$= \mathcal{E}(X^2) - \mu_X^2; \tag{2.44}$$

$\sigma_X^2$ is the population variance of $X$; $\sigma_X$ is the population standard deviation of $X$.

$$\sigma_{XY} = \mathcal{E}(X - \mu_X)(Y - \mu_Y) \tag{2.45}$$

$$= \mathcal{E}(XY) - \mu_X\mu_Y \tag{2.46}$$

$$= 0, \text{ if } X \text{ and } Y \text{ are independent}; \tag{2.47}$$

$\sigma_{XY}$ is the population covariance between $X$ and $Y$. If $X = Y$, $\sigma_{XY} = \sigma_{XX} = \sigma_X^2$; the covariance of a variable with itself is the variance of the variable. Notice from Rules 1 and 3 and from Equation 2.43 that $\sigma_{X+b}^2 = \sigma_X^2$ when $b$ is a constant.

$$\rho_{XY} = \frac{\sigma_{XY}}{\sigma_X\sigma_Y} ; \tag{2.48}$$

$\rho_{XY}$ is the population correlation between $X$ and $Y$, and it equals their covariance divided by the product of their standard deviations. The fact that independent variables are uncorrelated follows directly from Rule 4 and Equations 2.46 and 2.48.

$$\beta_{Y \cdot X} = \frac{\sigma_{XY}}{\sigma_X^2} ; \tag{2.49}$$

$\beta_{Y \cdot X}$ is the population regression coefficient for predicting $Y$ from $X$, and it equals the covariance of $X$ and $Y$ divided by the variance of $X$.

$$\sigma_{(W + X, Y + Z)} = \sigma_{WY} + \sigma_{WZ} + \sigma_{XY} + \sigma_{XZ}; \tag{2.50}$$

the covariance between two sums equals the sum of all cross covariances.

$$\sigma_{(X + Y)}^2 = \sigma_X^2 + \sigma_Y^2 + 2\sigma_{XY}; \tag{2.51}$$

the variance of a sum of two variables equals the sum of their variances plus twice their covariance. This equation can be generalized to form the following:

$$\sigma_{(X_1 + X_2 + \cdots + X_n)}^2 = \sum_{i=1}^{n} \sigma_{X_i}^2 + \left[ \sigma_{X_1X_2} + \sigma_{X_1X_3} + \cdots + \sigma_{X_1X_n} \right.$$

$$\left. + \sigma_{X_2X_1} + \sigma_{X_2X_3} + \cdots + \sigma_{X_2X_n} + \cdots + \sigma_{X_{n-1}X_n} \right]$$

$$= \sum_{i=1}^{n} \sigma_{X_i}^2 + \sum_{\substack{i=1 \\ i \neq j}}^{n} \sum_{j=1}^{n} \sigma_{X_iX_j}. \tag{2.52}$$

The variance of the sum of $n$ variables equals the sum of the variances of the $n$ variables plus the sum of all the different covariances.

If the expected value of an estimator of a population value equals that population value, the estimator is said to be *unbiased*. For example, the sample mean,

$$\bar{X} = \frac{1}{n} \sum_{i=1}^{n} X_i,$$

is an unbiased estimator of the population mean, $\mu_X$, since $\varepsilon(\bar{X}) = \mu_X$. The sample variance defined as

$$s_X^2 = \sum_{i=1}^{n} (X_i - \bar{X})^2/n$$

is a biased estimator of the population variance $\sigma_X^2$. The sample variance defined as

$$s_X^2 = \sum_{i=1}^{n} (X_i - \bar{X})^2/(n - 1)$$

is an unbiased estimator of $\sigma_X^2$. When the variance of scores in a sample is being used as a descriptive statistic, $n$ usually is used in the denominator; when the variance of scores in a sample is being used as an inferential statistic, $(n - 1)$ is used in the denominator. When $n$ is large, the alternative use of $n$ and $(n - 1)$ will make little difference in the calculated variance.

*Conditional expectation* is the expectation of one variable given a fixed value of another variable. The conditional expectation of $Y$ given $X = x$ is

$$\varepsilon(Y \mid x) = \sum_{i=1}^{l} y_i p(Y = y_i \mid X = x), \tag{2.53}$$

where $p(Y = y_i \mid X = x)$ is defined as the conditional probability of $Y$ given $X$. $\varepsilon(Y \mid x)$ is read "expectation of $Y$ given $x$." $\varepsilon(Y \mid x)$ also is defined to be the *regression* of $Y$ on $X$. The regression of $Y$ on $X$ may be, but does not have to be, linear (that is, of the form $\varepsilon(Y \mid x) = ax + b$, where $a$ and $b$ are constants).

The probabilities in Table 2.12 can be used to calculate $\varepsilon(Y \mid x)$, which appears at the bottom of the table. Using Equation 2.53 we find that $\varepsilon(Y \mid x = 1) = 0(1.00) + 1(.00) + 2(.00) + 3(.00) = 0$; $\varepsilon(Y \mid x = 2) = 0(.10) + 1(.80) + 2(.10)$

Table 2.12. Conditional Probabilities $p(Y = y_i \mid X = x)$ and Expectations $\varepsilon(Y \mid x)$

|  |  | $x$ | | | |
|---|---|---|---|---|---|
|  |  | *1* | *2* | *3* | *4* |
| | 0 | 1.00 | .10 | .00 | .00 |
| | 1 | .00 | .80 | .25 | .00 |
| $y_i$ | 2 | .00 | .10 | .50 | .00 |
| | 3 | .00 | .00 | .25 | 1.00 |
| | $\varepsilon(Y \mid x)$ | .00 | 1.00 | 2.00 | 3.00 |

+ 3(.00) = 1.00; and so on. We could express this regression as $\varepsilon(Y \mid x) = x - 1$, which is a linear regression. However, not all regressions are necessarily linear.

## 2.15  Summary

Because much of measurement theory is expressed in mathematical terms, Chapter 2 presented some basic mathematical and statistical concepts. A variable can be measured on a nominal, ordinal, interval, or ratio level. Each level of measurement produces different conclusions about differences between values of the variables and is consistent with a different type of mathematical manipulation.

A constant is a symbol for a specific, unchanging number, and a variable is a symbol that can take on different numerical values. Most variables are symbolized with capital letters, and the values that the variables can take on usually are symbolized with lower-case letters. Variables and values can be subscripted to indicate different variables or different values of variables. Although a discrete variable can take on only selected values, a continuous variable can take on an infinite number of values within a specified range. Summation signs are useful for defining and calculating various statistics.

A frequency distribution expresses the frequency of occurrence of each value of a discrete variable. The proportion of time that a variable takes on a specific value is called its relative frequency, and probabilities can be defined as relative frequencies obtained in populations. The density conveys the distribution for a continuous variable; the area under a density curve in a selected range of values equals the probability that a continuous variable takes on a value in that range.

Statistical methods can be classified as being either descriptive or inferential. Descriptive methods describe and summarize distributions. For example, common descriptors of central tendency are the mean ($\overline{X}$, $\mu_X$), the mode, and the median. The standard deviation ($s_X$, $\sigma_X$), variance ($s_X^2$, $\sigma_X^2$), and range are used as descriptors of variability. Inferential techniques allow us to generalize from a sample to the population it represents through hypothesis testing or estimation.

Many standard statistical procedures rely on the assumption that the set of scores being examined has a normal distribution or is drawn from a population with a normal distribution. Tables are available for the standard normal distribution ($\mu_Z = 0$, $\sigma_Z = 1$). Any other normal distribution with a different mean ($\mu_X$) and standard deviation ($\sigma_X$) can be examined by transforming the original scores ($X$) to standard normal scores ($Z$) by using the formula

$$Z = \frac{X - \mu_X}{\sigma_X}.$$

The direction and strength of the relationship between two multi-step or continuous variables ($X$ and $Y$) can be described by using a Pearson correlation coefficient ($r_{XY}$, $\rho_{XY}$). A Pearson correlation expresses the strength of the linear relationship between the two variables, how well a scatter plot of the two variables hugs a line, and whether the relationship is positive or negative. The most common interpretation of a correlation $(r_{XY})$ is that $r_{XY}^2$ is the proportion of variance in $Y$ that can be accounted for by linear prediction from $X$.

Correlation and linear regression are intimately related, because a correlation influences the accuracy of a linear prediction. The equation for the best least-squares regression line in a sample is

$$\hat{Y}_i = r_{XY} \frac{s_Y}{s_X} (X_i - \bar{X}) + \bar{Y}.$$

Using this equation to predict $Y_i$ from $X_i$ minimizes the sum, over examinees, of squared errors of prediction, where $(Y_i - \hat{Y}_i)$ is the error of prediction for the $i$th examinee. Confidence-interval estimates for $Y_i$ can also be calculated if we assume that $X$ and $Y$ are linearly related, that the conditional distribution of $Y$ given $X$ is normal, and that the relationship between $X$ and $Y$ is homoscedastic.

Restriction of range and combining disparate groups can lead to complications in the interpretation of correlations. A correlation coefficient will tend to be attenuated or reduced in samples with restricted variability. Combining groups with very different scatter plots can lead to conclusions that are not true for the groups considered separately.

Correlations and alternative measures of association are available for use with dichotomous and rank-order variables. These include the phi coefficient and tetrachoric correlation (for two dichotomous variables), the biserial and point-biserial correlations (for one dichotomous and one continuous or multi-step variable), and the Spearman rank-order correlation and Kendall's tau (for rank orders).

Two additional topics have been covered as optional readings: joint and conditional probabilities and the algebra of expectations. These topics are necessary for a complete understanding of some of the developments in later chapters but are not required for a mastery of the basic conclusions of these later chapters.

## 2.16  Vocabulary

absolute zero
artificially dichotomized variable
attenuation
bimodal distribution
biserial correlation coefficient
bivariate normality
central tendency
conditional distribution
confidence interval
constant
continuous variable
correlation
correlation coefficient
covariance

curvilinear relationship
density
descriptive statistics
deviation
dichotomous variable
discrete variable
distinctiveness
distribution rule
equal intervals
estimation
expected value
frequency distribution
heteroscedasticity
homoscedasticity

hypothesis testing
inferential statistics
intercorrelation
interval measurement
Kendall's tau ($\tau$)
least-squares criterion
level of measurement
limits of summation
linear regression
linear relationship
linear transformation
marginal distribution
mean
median
mode
mu ($\mu$)
multi-step variable
negatively skewed
nominal measurement
normal distribution
ordering in magnitude
ordinal measurement
parameter
Pearson product-moment
    correlation coefficient
phi coefficient ($\phi$)
point-biserial correlation
    coefficient
population
positively skewed

probability
random sample
range
ratio measurement
regression coefficient
regression line
relative frequency
restriction of range
rho ($\rho$)
sample
scatter plot
sigma ($\Sigma$—summation sign;
    $\sigma$—population standard
    deviation)
skewed distribution
Spearman rank-order correlation
    coefficient
standard deviation
standard error of estimate
standard normal distribution
standard score
subscripted variable
summation sign
symmetrical distribution
tau ($\tau$)
tetrachoric correlation coefficient
variability
variable
variance
Z score

## Optional Vocabulary

conditional expectation
conditional probability
expected value
independent variables

joint probability
marginal probability
regression
unbiased estimator

## 2.17  Study Questions

1. Describe the characteristics of the four major levels of measurement.
2. Define a *constant,* a *variable,* and a *value of a variable.* Give an example of each.
3. What are subscripted variables? Why are they useful?
4. Define *discrete variable* and *continuous variable.* Give an example of each.

5. What does a summation sign mean? Explain how to calculate summations.
6. What are the limits of summation? How are they used?
7. What are the three rules for manipulating summation signs? Explain their use.
8. Define *frequency distribution*, *relative frequency distribution*, *probability*, and *density*.
9. Explain how to calculate the probability that a discrete or continuous variable will take on a value in a specified range.
10. Describe the uses of descriptive and inferential statistics.
11. Define and compare the three major indicators of central tendency.
12. Define and compare the three major indicators of variability.
13. What is a bimodal distribution?
14. What is a symmetric distribution? Give an example of a negatively skewed distribution and of a positively skewed distribution.
15. How are a random sample and a population related?
16. How are sample statistics (such as $\bar{X}$ and $s^2$) related to population parameters (such as $\mu$ and $\sigma^2$)?
17. Explain how to use the normal tables for problems similar to those illustrated in Section 2.7.
18. What is the standard normal distribution? How is it related to other normal distributions?
19. Can discrete test scores have a normal distribution? Explain.
20. What is a scatter plot? Draw scatter plots representing curvilinear relationships and positive, negative, and zero correlations.
21. How is a correlation calculated?
22. Explain how to interpret the sign and size of a Pearson correlation coefficient.
23. How are the sign and the size of a correlation influenced by the linear transformation of one or both of the variables entering into the correlation?
24. How is the concept of linearity related to the Pearson correlation coefficient?
25. Explain the following phrases: *conditional distribution of Y given X, marginal distribution of Y,* and *the proportion of variance in Y explained by linear relationship with X.*
26. What is the standard error of estimate? How is it related to the correlation?
27. How is the Pearson correlation coefficient related to linear regression?
28. What criterion is minimized to determine the regression line?
29. What assumptions are necessary to compute confidence intervals for $Y$ based on predictions from $X$? Why is each assumption necessary?
30. Explain how to calculate and interpret a confidence interval.
31. How does restriction of range affect correlations?
32. How can combining groups create problems in the interpretation of correlation coefficients?
33. When is each of the following correlations used: Pearson, biserial, point-biserial, phi, tetrachoric, Spearman, and tau?
34. How is the Pearson correlation related to each of the following correlations: biserial, point-biserial, phi, tetrachoric, and Spearman?
35. How are biserial, point-biserial, phi, and Spearman correlations calculated?

36. How might each of the correlations listed in Question 33 be used in a measurement application?

### Optional Questions

37. Define *joint probability*, *marginal probability*, and *conditional probability*.
38. How is each of the probabilities in Question 37 calculated?
39. Define *independence*.
40. How are independence and a zero correlation related?
41. Define *expected value*.
42. What are the four rules for manipulating expected-value signs?
43. What is an unbiased estimator of a population value? Give examples of an unbiased and a biased estimator.
44. Define *conditional expectation* and *regression*.

## 2.18   Computational Problems

1. If $X_1 = 2, X_2 = -1, X_3 = 0, Y_1 = 4, Y_2 = 0$, and $Y_3 = 1$, what are the values of the following?

    a. $\sum\limits_{i=1}^{3} (X_i - 4)$

    b. $\sum\limits_{i=1}^{3} (5X_i - 3X_iY_i + Y_i^2)$

    c. $\sum\limits_{i=1}^{3} (15X_i - 3Y_i^2 + 2)$

2. a.  Calculate the frequency distribution and the relative frequency distribution of the data in the following table:

| Examinee (i) | $X_i$ |
|:---:|:---:|
| 1 | 5 |
| 2 | 3 |
| 3 | 1 |
| 4 | 2 |
| 5 | 5 |
| 6 | 7 |
| 7 | 3 |
| 8 | 6 |
| 9 | 5 |
| 10 | 4 |
| 11 | 0 |
| 12 | 1 |
| 13 | 2 |
| 14 | 5 |
| 15 | 6 |

| Examinee (i) | $X_i$ |
|:---:|:---:|
| 16 | 3 |
| 17 | 1 |
| 18 | 4 |
| 19 | 2 |
| 20 | 6 |

  b. What is $p(3 \leqslant X \leqslant 5)$?
3. What are the mean, median, and mode of the distribution in Question 2?
4. What are the range, variance, and standard deviation of the distribution in Question 2?
5. If $X$ has a normal distribution, with $\mu = 50$ and $\sigma = 4$, what are the values of the following?
  a. $p(X > 52)$
  b. $p(X > 46)$
  c. $p(48 < X < 54)$
  d. $p(42 < X < 46)$
  e. the proportion of people obtaining a score below 50
  f. the score that 40% of the population scores below
  g. the score that 80% of the population scores above
6. Draw the scatter plot and calculate the Pearson correlation coefficient for the relationship between *Introversion* and *Social dominance* for the following data.

| | | Examinee | | | | | | |
|---|---|---|---|---|---|---|---|---|
| | *1* | *2* | *3* | *4* | *5* | *6* | *7* | *8* |
| Introversion score | 0 | 0 | 1 | 1 | 2 | 2 | 4 | 5 |
| Social-dominance score | 4 | 5 | 4 | 2 | 1 | 3 | 2 | 1 |

7. a. What is the equation for the regression line for predicting *Social dominance* from *Introversion* for the data given in Question 6?
  b. What is the predicted *Social-dominance* score for an examinee with an *Introversion* score of 2?
  c. What is the standard error of estimate for predicting *Social dominance* from *Introversion*?
  d. What is the 90% confidence interval for the *Social-dominance* score for an examinee with an *Introversion* score of 3?
8. If $r_{XY} = -.8$, what proportion of the variance in $Y$ is explained by a linear relationship with $X$?
9. What is the phi coefficient for the following data? Interpret this coefficient.

| | | Length of hair | |
|---|---|:---:|:---:|
| | | Short | Long |
| Sex | Male | 16 | 4 |
| | Female | 8 | 12 |

10. Teachers were asked whether they liked or disliked the pupils in their classes. A score of 0 was recorded for "dislike" responses and a score of 1 was assigned to "like" responses. Use a point-biserial correlation to summarize the relationship between this variable and grades on a midterm exam from the data in the following table.

| | | | | | Pupil | | | | | |
|---|---|---|---|---|---|---|---|---|---|---|
| | *1* | *2* | *3* | *4* | *5* | *6* | *7* | *8* | *9* | *10* |
| Teacher attitude | 0 | 0 | 0 | 0 | 1 | 1 | 1 | 1 | 1 | 1 |
| Midterm score | 5 | 7 | 4 | 7 | 9 | 5 | 9 | 11 | 13 | 15 |

11. Calculate the biserial correlation for the data presented in Question 10. ($z = -.25$, and $f(z) = .387$.)

12. Two personality tests measure empathy and nurturance on an ordinal level. Calculate and interpret the Spearman rank-order correlation for the data below.

| | | | Examinee | | | | |
|---|---|---|---|---|---|---|---|
| | *1* | *2* | *3* | *4* | *5* | *6* | *7* |
| Empathy | 3 | 5 | 8 | 10 | 9 | 17 | 12 |
| Nurturance | 2 | 4 | 7 | 5 | 6 | 10 | 14 |

13. (Optional) An experimenter gave either a drug or a placebo (sugar pill) to a group of 100 volunteers, who were then asked to report the occurrence of hallucinations. The data from this experiment appear in the following table.

| | Report Hallucinations | | |
|---|---|---|---|
| | *Yes* | *No* | *Total* |
| Drug | 18 | 22 | 40 |
| Placebo | 2 | 58 | 60 |
| Total | 20 | 80 | 100 |

a. What is the marginal probability that a volunteer reports hallucinations?

b. What is the joint probability of reporting hallucinations and being given a placebo?

c. What is the conditional probability of reporting hallucinations, given that the volunteer received the drug?

d. What is the probability of reporting hallucinations among those given the placebo?

14. (Optional) Below are a set of conditional probabilities, $p(Y = y_i \mid X = x)$.

a. Calculate $\mathcal{E}(Y \mid x)$ for each $x$, and plot $\mathcal{E}(Y \mid x)$ as a function of $x$.

b. Is the regression of $Y$ on $X$ linear?

| | | | | $x$ | | |
|---|---|---|---|---|---|---|
| | | 0 | 1 | 2 | 3 | 4 |
| | 0 | 1.00 | 0.25 | 0.00 | 0.25 | 1.00 |
| $y_i$ | 1 | 0.00 | 0.50 | 0.20 | 0.50 | 0.00 |
| | 2 | 0.00 | 0.25 | 0.60 | 0.25 | 0.00 |
| | 3 | 0.00 | 0.00 | 0.20 | 0.00 | 0.00 |

15. (Optional) If you roll a fair die, each of its six sides has an equal chance of occurring (1/6). Imagine that you will be rolling the die a large number of times, and recording the number shown each time. Call the number shown variable $X$. What is the expected value of $X$?

16. (Optional) If $\sigma_X^2 = 16$, $\sigma_Y^2 = 25$, and $\rho_{XY} = .8$, what is the variance of $(X + Y)$?

17. (Optional) Determine whether the variables $X$ and $W$ and the variables $Y$ and $Z$, whose joint probabilities appear in the following tables, are independent.

a.

|        | $w_1$ | $w_2$ | Total |
|--------|-------|-------|-------|
| $x_1$  | .09   | .11   | .20   |
| $x_2$  | .36   | .44   | .80   |
| Total  | .45   | .55   | 1.00  |

b.

|        | $y_1$ | $y_2$ | Total |
|--------|-------|-------|-------|
| $z_1$  | .10   | .15   | .25   |
| $z_2$  | .55   | .20   | .75   |
| Total  | .65   | .35   | 1.00  |

# Classical
# True-Score Theory

## 3.1 The Assumptions of Classical True-Score Theory

Most of the standard procedures for creating and evaluating tests are based on a set of assumptions, commonly called *classical* (or *weak*) *true-score theory*. This chapter examines these assumptions in detail. Chapters 4, 5, and 6 describe how the few simple assumptions of classical true-score theory expand into principles for test construction and for evaluation of a test's reliability and validity. Chapter 11 presents alternative test theories, called strong true-score theories and latent-trait models.

A *test theory*, or *test model*, is a symbolic representation of the factors influencing observed test scores and is described by its assumptions. Classical true-score theory is a simple, quite useful model that describes how errors of measurement can influence observed scores. The model assumes certain conditions to be true; if these assumptions are reasonable, then the conclusions derived from the model are reasonable. However, if the assumptions are not reasonable. then use of the model leads to faulty conclusions. First we will list the assumptions of classical true-score theory, and then we'll explain each one in detail.

## Assumptions of Classical True-Score Theory

1. $X = T + E$.
2. $\mathcal{E}(X) = T$.
3. $\rho_{ET} = 0$.
4. $\rho_{E_1 E_2} = 0$.
5. $\rho_{E_1 T_2} = 0$.
6. If two tests have observed scores $X$ and $X'$ that satisfy Assumptions 1 through 5, and if, for every population of examinees, $T = T'$ and $\sigma_E^2 = \sigma_{E'}^2$, then the tests are called *parallel tests*.
7. If two tests have observed scores $X_1$ and $X_2$ that satisfy Assumptions 1 through 5, and if, for every population of examinees, $T_1 = T_2 + c_{12}$, where $c_{12}$ is a constant, then the tests are called *essentially $\tau$-equivalent tests*.

In the assumptions for this model, $X$ is an *observed score* for an examinee. Assumption 1, $X = T + E$, states that this observed score is the sum of two parts: $T$, the *true score*, and $E$, the *error score*, or *error of measurement*. For example, if on an IQ test Joe's true score is 108 but his observed score is 112, then $X$ is 112, $T$ is 108, and $E$ is $+ 4$. If Joe is tested again and his observed score is 100, then $X$ becomes 100, $T$ is still 108, and $E$ is $- 8$. For any given examinee and test, $T$ is assumed to be a fixed value, although $E$ and $X$ vary for that examinee on different testing occasions.

In classical true-score theory, the true scores and error scores are assumed to add (rather than to have some other relationship, such as a multiplicative one). The assumption of additivity is commonly made in statistical work, because it is mathematically simple and appears reasonable. Other well-known additive models underlie analysis of variance (see Hays, 1973) and factor analysis (Sections 5.11 and 6.6).

Assumption 2, $\mathcal{E}(X) = T$, states that the expected value (population mean) of $X$ is $T$. This assumption is the definition of $T$: $T$ is the mean of the theoretical distribution of $X$ scores that would be found in repeated independent testings of the same person with the same test. For example, if we test Joe an infinite number of times, the mean of his observed scores would be 108. For this definition of $T$, we assume that the testings are independent—that is, that each testing has no influence on any subsequent testing. Because this lack of contamination among testings is impossible in practice and an infinite number of testings are not available, $T$ must remain a theoretical construct. However, as we shall see, this theoretical construct leads to some useful results.

From Assumption 2 we also can see that $T$ is defined in terms of an expected test score rather than in terms of any "real" trait of the examinee. Some examples of the implications of this assumption can be given. Suppose that a test measures spatial reasoning and has a maximum possible score of 10 points. Mike and Tony take the test, and each receives a score of 10. We look into a crystal ball and discover that Mike actually is better at spatial reasoning than Tony. But the test was too easy, and therefore both people earned the top score. This result is called a *ceiling effect,* and a test with too low a ceiling fails to discriminate among people with high ability. Here, although Mike's ability is higher, his true score on the test may be the same as Tony's. Or suppose that an intelligence test is administered in English to Maria, who does not speak English well. She takes the test and receives a fairly low score. If Maria took the test a large number of times, the resulting observed scores would be consistently low and would produce a low true score. Maria may be above average in intelligence, but unfamiliarity with English interferes with her test performance. In the classical model, the true score is the theoretical mean of the results of repeated independent testings. Whether this true score accurately reflects some theoretical ability or characteristic is a question of test validity, which is discussed in Chapter 5.

Assumption 2 deals with a theoretical distribution of observed scores over different testing occasions for one examinee on one test. Assumptions 3 through 5 deal with true and error scores for one or two tests for many examinees on one test-ing occasion.

Assumption 3, $\rho_{ET} = 0$, is extremely important for further derivations. It states that the error scores and the true scores obtained by a population of examinees on one test are uncorrelated. This assumption implies that examinees with high true scores do not have systematically more positive or negative errors of measurement than examinees with low true scores. This assumption would be violated if, for example, on one administration of a college entrance exam, students with low true scores copied answers from those students with high true scores; this situation would create a negative correlation between true scores and error scores. Or suppose a teacher places the worst students in the class in the front of the room to ensure that they understand the instructions for an achievement test. Because of acoustical problems, the better students in the back of the room have a great deal of difficulty hearing and understanding the instructions, and they do worse than they normally would have on the test. Such a situation would produce a negative correlation between true scores and error scores. If the situation were reversed and the better students were in the front of the room, a positive correlation between true scores and error scores could be produced.

In Assumption 4, $\rho_{E_1E_2} = 0$, $E_1$ is the error score for Test 1, and $E_2$ is the error score for Test 2. This assumption states that the error scores on two different tests are uncorrelated—that is, if a person has a positive error score on Test 1, he or she is not more likely to have a positive or a negative error score on Test 2. This assumption is not reasonable if the test scores are greatly affected by factors such as fatigue, practice effects, the examinee's mood, or effects of the environment. For example, suppose that two tests are usually administered alone, but on one occasion they are given as the last tests in a long battery of tests. Some of the examinees may have become fatigued during the testing and consequently perform unusually poorly on the last two tests, resulting in negative errors of measurement on those two tests.

Other examinees may have benefited from the practice provided by the earlier tests and therefore perform unusually well on the last two tests, resulting in positive errors of measurement on both those tests. A situation such as this would produce a positive correlation between errors of measurement on the two tests; if we knew what a person's error of measurement was for one of the tests, we could predict his or her error of measurement for the other test. Other factors also influence the correlation between errors of measurement. A person who is momentarily depressed while taking two ability tests may have high negative error scores on both tests. Or if two tests are taken in a room with many interruptions or distractions, some examinees will tend to have negative errors of measurement on both tests.

If we want to apply classical true-score theory to tests that are greatly influenced by practice effects, fatigue, or environmental conditions, then we should make an attempt to ensure that the testing conditions are as homogeneous as possible for all examinees on all tests over all testing occasions. This control will reduce the sizes of the errors of measurement on each test as well as the correlations of errors of measurement between tests.

Assumption 5, $\rho_{E_1 T_2} = 0$, states that the error scores on one test $(E_1)$ are uncorrelated with the true scores on another test $(T_2)$. This assumption would be violated if Test 2 measures a personality trait or ability dimension that influences errors on Test 1. It would also be violated under the same conditions that lead to violation of Assumption 3.

Assumptions 1 through 5 present classical true-score theory's definition of error of measurement. Error of measurement is an *unsystematic,* or random, deviation of an examinee's observed score from a theoretically expected observed score. *Systematic* errors are not called errors of measurement in classical theory. For example, in Maria's case, if her actual intelligence (obtained via the crystal ball) is consistently underestimated by 20 points in each testing, then the 20-point difference is a systematic error and is not considered to be error under classical theory.

Assumption 6 presents the definition of parallel tests. $X$ is an observed score for one test, $T$ is its true score, and $\sigma_E^2$ is its error variance. The error variance is the variance of error scores for that test among the examinees in a particular population. $X'$, $T'$, and $\sigma_{E'}^2$ are the observed score, the true score, and the error variance, respectively, for a second test. Assumption 6 states that the tests are parallel if $T = T'$ and $\sigma_E^2 = \sigma_{E'}^2$ for every population of examinees taking both tests. Parallel tests are sometimes called *parallel test forms* or *parallel forms*. For $\sigma_E^2$ to equal $\sigma_{E'}^2$, the conditions leading to errors of measurement, such as mood and environmental effects, must vary in the same way for the two tests. The definition of parallel tests also implies that parallel tests will have equal observed-score means, variances, and correlations with other observed test scores (see Section 3.3). You should note, however, that scores on two parallel tests are not necessarily perfectly correlated with each other. For example, parallel tests of aggression will yield the same true scores, error variances, observed-score variances, and relationships with other scores, but the observed aggression-test scores will not be perfectly correlated with each other unless there is no error variance. Error variance is not predictable, so if the error variance is not 0, the parallel aggression-test scores cannot be perfectly correlated. The concept of parallel tests becomes important later in this book, because such tests are involved in one method of estimating reliability as well as being involved in some important derivations.

Assumption 7 states the definition of essentially $\tau$-equivalent tests. The Greek letter $\tau$ (tau) represents the true score, $T$. Tests that are essentially $\tau$-equivalent have true scores that are the same except for an additive constant, $c_{12}$. For example, on one test four examinees have true scores of 10, 11, 13, and 18. If this test and a second test are essentially $\tau$-equivalent with $c_{12} = 3$, the examinees have true scores of 13, 14, 16, and 21 on the second test. Unlike parallel tests, essentially $\tau$-equivalent tests can have unequal error variances; true scores may be measured more accurately by one of the $\tau$-equivalent tests than by the other. Notice that parallel tests meet stronger restrictions than essentially $\tau$-equivalent tests; if two tests are parallel, they more than satisfy the definition of essentially $\tau$-equivalent tests. However, two tests that are essentially $\tau$-equivalent are not necessarily parallel. The concept of essential $\tau$-equivalence is important in describing one method of estimating test reliability, which is discussed in Sections 4.4 and 4.5.

## 3.2   Summary of Classical True-Score Theory

Classical true-score theory involves an additive model. An observed test score $X$ is the sum of two components: a stable true score $T$ and a random error score $E$. Error scores on a test are assumed to be uncorrelated with true scores on that test and with true and error scores on all other tests. Parallel tests have the same true scores and error variances. Essentially $\tau$-equivalent tests have true scores that differ by an additive constant. The assumptions for classical true-score theory can be violated by a number of conditions that affect test scores. However, because we usually cannot determine $T$ and $E$, we cannot directly verify the appropriateness of the assumptions, and we can only surmise when they would be appropriate.

True scores and error scores are unobservable theoretical constructs. Only $X$'s can be observed. When we speak of true scores, it is necessary to remember that a true score—an average score taken over repeated independent testings with the same test—is a theoretical idea. This score will not completely reflect the "true" characteristic of interest unless the test has perfect validity—that is, unless the test measures exactly what it purports to measure. (See Chapter 5 for a discussion of the concept of test validity.)

## 3.3   Conclusions Derived from Classical True-Score Theory

The assumptions of classical true-score theory can lead to a large number of conclusions. If the assumptions are reasonable, the conclusions must be true; if they are not reasonable, the conclusions and their corresponding applications may not

•

adequately reflect reality. Some of these conclusions will be listed and then briefly described. Then in Section 3.4 a proof, based on classical assumptions, is given for each conclusion. These proofs are optional, and you will suffer no loss of continuity if you choose to skip them. More practical applications of these conclusions are discussed in detail in later chapters.

### Conclusions Drawn from Classical True-Score Theory

1. $\mathcal{E}(E) = 0$;

   the expected value (population mean) of the error scores for any examinee is 0. If a person were tested repeatedly with the same test, the average error score for these testings would be 0 (assuming that the repeated testings were independent and did not influence one another). Positive and negative errors would cancel out in the long run, and there would be no tendency to underestimate or overestimate an examinee's true score.

   Conclusions 2 through 18 deal with the behavior of observed, true, and error scores for one or more tests for a population of examinees. These conclusions assume that an observed score, a true score, and an error score could be obtained for every examinee and that expectations (as well as variances, correlations, and so on) of these scores would be taken over all examinees.

2. $\mathcal{E}(ET) = \sigma_{ET} = 0$;

   the expected value of the product of error and true scores is 0. The covariance between error and true scores, $\sigma_{ET}$, which equals $\mathcal{E}(ET) - \mathcal{E}(E)\mathcal{E}(T)$, also equals 0. The terms $\mathcal{E}(ET)$ and $\sigma_{ET}$ would be computed based on error and true scores for many examinees on one test. In other words, if an error score and a true score could be obtained for every examinee in a given population for one test, and if $\mathcal{E}(ET)$ and $\sigma_{ET}$ were computed, they would be equal to 0. These relationships simplify a number of the proofs in Section 3.4.

3. $\sigma_X^2 = \sigma_T^2 + \sigma_E^2$;

   observed-score variance is the sum of true-score variance and error-score variance. If an observed score, a true score, and an error score could be obtained for every examinee in a given population for a particular test, the variance of the observed scores would equal the sum of the variance of the true scores and the variance of the error scores. If measurement is made without error, all error scores will equal 0, and there will be no variance in error scores. If $\sigma_E^2 = 0$, then $\sigma_X^2 = \sigma_T^2$; all observed-score differences among examinees represent true-score differences. If measurement is made with some error, $\sigma_E^2$ will be greater than 0, and observed-score differences among examinees will reflect both true-score differences and error. The larger $\sigma_E^2$ becomes, relative to $\sigma_X^2$ or $\sigma_T^2$, the more likely it is that small observed-score differences between examinees represent differences due to errors of measurement rather than true-score differences.

4. $\rho_{XT}^2 = \dfrac{\sigma_T^2}{\sigma_X^2}$;

the squared correlation between observed and true scores is the ratio of true-score variance to observed-score variance. This statement implies that the proportion of variance in true scores explained by a linear relationship with observed scores is $\sigma_T^2/\sigma_X^2$ (see Section 2.8). Observed scores best account for, predict, or explain true scores when this ratio is 1.0—that is, when all observed-score variance is true-score variance.

5. $\rho_{XT}^2 = 1 - \dfrac{\sigma_E^2}{\sigma_X^2}$;

the squared correlation between observed and true scores is 1 minus the ratio of error-score variance to observed-score variance. This conclusion gives us an alternative way of understanding or interpreting $\rho_{XT}^2$. When error-score variance is small, relative to observed-score variance, the proportion of variance in true scores explained by observed scores is large. When error variance is large, relative to observed-score variance, observed scores account for, predict, or explain true scores less well.

6. $\sigma_X^2 = \sigma_{X'}^2$;

if $X$ and $X'$ are scores on parallel tests (as defined by Assumption 6), their observed-score variances are identical. If a researcher develops "parallel" tests that do not have identical observed-score variances, they are not truly parallel.

7. $\rho_{XY} = \rho_{X'Y}$;

if $X$ and $X'$ are scores on parallel tests, and $Y$ is any other score or variable, the correlations between the parallel tests and $Y$ are equal. Parallel-test scores correlate equally with all other test scores. This fact provides another check for true parallelism between two tests.

8. $\rho_{XX'} = \dfrac{\sigma_T^2}{\sigma_X^2} = \dfrac{\sigma_{T'}^2}{\sigma_{X'}^2}$ ;

the correlation between scores on two parallel forms of a test ($X$ and $X'$) is equal to the ratio of true-score variance to observed-score variance determined on the basis of either test. Parallel forms correlate perfectly with each other (that is, $\rho_{XX'} = 1.0$) only when this ratio is 1.0. This situation occurs when measurements are made without error—that is, when $\sigma_E^2 = 0$, so that $\sigma_T^2 = \sigma_X^2$, and when $\sigma_{E'}^2 = 0$, so that $\sigma_{T'}^2 = \sigma_{X'}^2$.

9. $\rho_{XX'} = 1 - \dfrac{\sigma_E^2}{\sigma_X^2}$ ;

the correlation between scores on two parallel tests equals 1 minus the ratio of error variance to observed-score variance. The correlation between parallel forms will equal 1.0 when error variance equals 0; this correlation will equal 0 when error variance equals observed-score variance.

10. $\rho_{XX'} = 1 - \rho_{XE}^2$;

the correlation between scores on two parallel tests equals 1 minus the squared correlation between observed scores and error scores. The correlation between parallel tests will equal 1.0 when observed scores and error scores are uncorrelated. The correlation between parallel tests will equal 0 when observed scores and error scores are perfectly correlated.

11. $\rho_{XT}^2 = \rho_{XX'}$;

the squared correlation between observed and true scores is equal to the correlation between parallel-test scores. If parallel tests are available, $r_{XX'}$ (the observed correlation between scores on the parallel tests) can be used to estimate $\rho_{XT}^2$. This fact is important, because true scores are never known, and the correlation between $X$ and $T$ can never be calculated directly.

12. $\sigma_T^2 = \sigma_{XX'}$;

true-score variance is equal to the covariance between observed scores on parallel tests. Thus, the observed covariance between scores on parallel tests ($s_{XX'}$) can provide an observable estimate of true-score variance.

13. $\sigma_E^2 = \sigma_X^2 (1 - \rho_{XX'})$;

error variance is equal to observed-score variance times 1 minus the correlation between observed scores for parallel tests. The square root of the error variance, $\sigma_E$, is called the *standard error of measurement*. This formula can be used in obtaining an estimate for $\sigma_E^2$; $\hat{\sigma}_E^2 = s_E^2 = s_X^2 (1 - r_{XX'})$.

14. $\rho_{T_X T_Z} = \dfrac{\rho_{XZ}}{\sqrt{\rho_{XX'} \rho_{ZZ'}}}$ ;

the correlation between true scores for two tests equals the correlation between observed scores for the two tests divided by the square root of the product of the correlations of each observed test score with a parallel-test score. The scores $X$ and $X'$ are observed scores on parallel tests, where $X = T_X + E_X$, and $X' = T_X + E_{X'}$. The scores $Z$ and $Z'$ are observed scores on two other tests that are parallel to each other, and $Z = T_Z + E_Z$, and $Z' = T_Z + E_{Z'}$. Since

$\sqrt{\rho_{XX'} \, \rho_{ZZ'}}$ must always be less than or equal to 1, $\rho_{T_X T_Z}$ must always be greater than or equal to $\rho_{XZ}$. The correlation between observed scores is said to be attenuated (reduced) relative to the correlation between true scores. Conclusion 14 is called the *correction for attenuation*, and it is discussed further in Section 5.4. By using correlations between observed test scores ($r_{XZ}$, $r_{XX'}$, and $r_{ZZ'}$) in the correction for attenuation, it is possible to estimate the correlation between true scores for any two tests.

15. $\sigma_{T_X}^2 = N^2 \sigma_{T_Y}^2$;

if $X$ is the sum of $N$ parallel-test scores,

$$X = \sum_{i=1}^{N} Y_i,$$

and if $Y_i$ is one of these parallel tests, then the true-score variance of $X(\sigma_{T_X}^2)$ is $N^2$ times the true-score variance of one of the $Y_i$'s ($\sigma_{T_Y}^2$). If a test is made $N$ times longer by combining parallel versions of it, the true-score variance of the lengthened test will be $N^2$ times the true-score variance of the original test. This result and the one to follow are essential for the development of the Spearman-Brown formula (Conclusion 17).

16. $\sigma_{E_X}^2 = N \sigma_{E_Y}^2$;

if $X$ and $Y$ are defined as in the discussion of Conclusion 15, error variance in $X(\sigma_{E_X}^2)$ is $N$ times the error variance in any $Y_i(\sigma_{E_Y}^2)$. If a test is made $N$ times longer by combining parallel versions of it, the error variance of the longer test will be $N$ times the error variance of one of its component tests. Combining the implications of Conclusions 15 and 16, we can see that true-score variance will increase more than error-score variance when a test is lengthened by adding parallel components. Thus, lengthening a test with parallel forms will improve the accuracy of measurement.

17. $\rho_{XX'} = \dfrac{N \rho_{YY'}}{1 + (N - 1)\rho_{YY'}}$ ;

this is the Spearman-Brown formula, where $X$, $Y$, and $N$ are defined as in Conclusion 15, $\rho_{YY'}$ is the correlation between any two of the $N$ parallel-test scores contained in $X$, and $\rho_{XX'}$ is the correlation between $X$ and a test score, $X'$, that is parallel to $X$. This formula allows us to estimate the effects that changes in test length will have on the correlation of the test with a parallel test. This concept is developed in more detail in Chapter 4.

18. If $\rho_{YY'} \neq 0$, $\lim\limits_{N \to \infty} \rho_{XX'} = 1$;

this statement is read "If $\rho_{YY'}$ does not equal 0, the limit, as $N$ goes to infinity, of

$\rho_{XX'}$ is 1.'' $X$, $X'$, and $N$ are defined as in Conclusion 15. This statement implies that, as tests are made infinitely long by adding parallel components to them, the correlation between the longer parallel-test scores draws closer and closer to unity (1.0). Since $\rho_{XX'} = 1 - (\sigma_E^2/\sigma_X^2)$ (Conclusion 9), a test composed of an infinite number of parallel components would measure without error ($\sigma_E^2 = 0$).

Each of these 18 conclusions is derivable from the classical true-score-model assumptions using the techniques described in Sections 2.3 and 2.14. There will be no loss of continuity if you choose to skip the next section, which contains the derivations of these conclusions.

## 3.4 (Optional)  Proofs of Conclusions Derived from Classical True-Score Theory

1. To prove $\varepsilon(E) = 0$:

   $\varepsilon(X) = \varepsilon(T) + \varepsilon(E)$        (by Assumption 1 and Rule 3, Section 2.14)

   $\quad = T + \varepsilon(E).$        (by Rule 1, Section 2.14)

   $\varepsilon(X) = T.$        (by Assumption 2)

   Therefore,

   $\varepsilon(E) = 0.$

2. To prove $\varepsilon(ET) = \sigma_{ET} = 0$:

   $\varepsilon(ET) = \varepsilon(ET) - 0$

   $\quad = \varepsilon(ET) - \varepsilon(E)\varepsilon(T)$        (by Proof 1)

   $\quad = \sigma_{ET}.$        (by Equation 2.46)

   $\rho_{ET} = \sigma_{ET}/\sigma_E\sigma_T$        (by Equation 2.48)

   $\quad = 0.$        (by Assumption 3)

   Therefore,

   $\varepsilon(ET) = \sigma_{ET} = 0.$

3. To prove $\sigma_X^2 = \sigma_T^2 + \sigma_E^2$:

   $\sigma_X^2 = \sigma_{T+E}^2$        (by Assumption 1)

   $\quad = \sigma_T^2 + \sigma_E^2 + 2\sigma_{ET}$        (by Equation 2.51)

   $\quad = \sigma_T^2 + \sigma_E^2.$        (by Proof 2)

4. To prove $\rho_{XT}^2 = \sigma_T^2/\sigma_X^2$:

$$\rho_{XT}^2 = \left[\frac{\sigma_{XT}}{\sigma_X\sigma_T}\right]^2 \qquad \text{(by Equation 2.48)}$$

$$= \frac{[\mathcal{E}(XT) - \mathcal{E}(X)\mathcal{E}(T)]^2}{\sigma_X^2\sigma_T^2} \qquad \text{(by Equation 2.46)}$$

$$= \frac{[\mathcal{E}[(T+E)T] - \mathcal{E}(X)\mathcal{E}(T)]^2}{\sigma_X^2\sigma_T^2} \qquad \text{(by Assumption 1)}$$

$$= \frac{[\mathcal{E}(T^2) + \mathcal{E}(ET) - (\mathcal{E}(T))^2]^2}{\sigma_X^2\sigma_T^2} \qquad \begin{array}{l}\text{(by Assumption 2 and}\\ \text{Rules 1 and 3, Section 2.14)}\end{array}$$

$$= \frac{[\mathcal{E}(T^2) - (\mathcal{E}(T))^2]^2}{\sigma_X^2\sigma_T^2} \qquad \text{(by Proof 2)}$$

$$= [\sigma_T^2]^2/\sigma_X^2\sigma_T^2 \qquad \text{(by Equation 2.44)}$$

$$= \sigma_T^2/\sigma_X^2.$$

5. To prove $\rho_{XT}^2 = 1 - (\sigma_E^2/\sigma_X^2)$:

$$\rho_{XT}^2 = \sigma_T^2/\sigma_X^2 \qquad \text{(by Proof 4)}$$

$$= \frac{\sigma_X^2 - \sigma_E^2}{\sigma_X^2} \qquad \text{(by Proof 3)}$$

$$= 1 - (\sigma_E^2/\sigma_X^2).$$

6. To prove $\sigma_X^2 = \sigma_{X'}^2$, where $X$ and $X'$ are observed scores on parallel tests:

$$\sigma_X^2 = \sigma_T^2 + \sigma_E^2 \qquad \text{(by Proof 3)}$$

$$\sigma_{X'}^2 = \sigma_{T'}^2 + \sigma_{E'}^2 \qquad \text{(by Proof 3)}$$

$$= \sigma_T^2 + \sigma_E^2 \qquad \text{(by Assumption 6)}$$

$$= \sigma_X^2.$$

7. To prove $\rho_{XY} = \rho_{X'Y}$, where $X$ and $X'$ are scores on parallel tests:

$$\rho_{XY} = \frac{\sigma_{XY}}{\sigma_X\sigma_Y} \qquad \text{(by Equation 2.48)}$$

$$= \frac{\sigma_{(T+E)Y}}{\sigma_X\sigma_Y} \qquad \text{(by Assumption 1)}$$

$$= \frac{\sigma_{TY} + \sigma_{EY}}{\sigma_X\sigma_Y} \qquad \text{(by Equation 2.50)}$$

$$= \frac{\sigma_{TY}}{\sigma_X\sigma_Y} \qquad \text{(by Assumptions 4 and 5)}$$

$$= \frac{\sigma_{T'Y}}{\sigma_{X'}\sigma_Y} \qquad \text{(by Assumption 6 and Proof 6)}$$

$$= \rho_{X'Y}. \qquad \text{(by Equation 2.48)}$$

8. To prove $\rho_{XX'} = \sigma_T^2/\sigma_X^2 = \sigma_{T'}^2/\sigma_{X'}^2$, where $X$ and $X'$ are scores on parallel tests:

$$\rho_{XX'} = \frac{\sigma_{XX'}}{\sigma_X\sigma_{X'}} \qquad \text{(by Equation 2.48)}$$

$$= \frac{\sigma_{(T+E)(T'+E')}}{\sigma_X^2} \qquad \text{(by Assumptions 1 and 6 and Proof 6)}$$

$$= \frac{\sigma_{TT'} + \sigma_{ET'} + \sigma_{TE'} + \sigma_{EE'}}{\sigma_X^2} \qquad \text{(by Equation 2.50)}$$

$$= \frac{\sigma_T^2}{\sigma_X^2} \qquad \text{(by Assumptions 4, 5, and 6)}$$

$$= \frac{\sigma_{T'}^2}{\sigma_{X'}^2}. \qquad \text{(by Assumption 6 and Proof 6)}$$

9. To prove $\rho_{XX'} = 1 - \dfrac{\sigma_E^2}{\sigma_X^2}$ :

$$\rho_{XX'} = \sigma_T^2/\sigma_X^2 \qquad \text{(by Proof 8)}$$

$$= (\sigma_X^2 - \sigma_E^2)/\sigma_X^2 \qquad \text{(by Proof 3)}$$

$$= 1 - \frac{\sigma_E^2}{\sigma_X^2}$$

10. To prove $\rho_{XX'} = 1 - \rho_{XE}^2$:

$$\rho_{XE}^2 = \left[\frac{\sigma_{XE}}{\sigma_X\sigma_E}\right]^2 \qquad \text{(by Equation 2.48)}$$

$$= \frac{(\sigma_{TE} + \sigma_E^2)^2}{\sigma_X^2\sigma_E^2} \qquad \text{(by Assumption 1 and Equation 2.50)}$$

$$= \frac{(\sigma_E^2)^2}{\sigma_X^2\sigma_E^2} \qquad \text{(by Proof 2)}$$

$$= \frac{\sigma_E^2}{\sigma_X^2}$$

$$\rho_{XX'} = 1 - \frac{\sigma_E^2}{\sigma_X^2} \qquad \text{(by Proof 9)}$$

$$= 1 - \rho_{XE}^2.$$

11. To prove $\rho_{XT}^2 = \rho_{XX'}$, where $X$ and $X'$ are scores on parallel tests:

$\rho_{XT}^2 = \sigma_T^2/\sigma_X^2$                (by Proof 4)

$\quad = \rho_{XX'}.$              (by Proof 8)

12. To prove $\sigma_T^2 = \sigma_{XX'}$, where $X$ and $X'$ are scores on parallel tests:

$\rho_{XX'} = \sigma_T^2/\sigma_X^2.$         (by Proof 8)

$\rho_{XX'} = \sigma_{XX'}/\sigma_X^2.$       (by Equation 2.48 and Proof 6)

Therefore,

$\sigma_T^2 = \sigma_{XX'}.$

13. To prove $\sigma_E^2 = \sigma_X^2 (1 - \rho_{XX'})$, where $X$ and $X'$ are scores on parallel tests:

$\sigma_E^2 = \sigma_X^2 - \sigma_T^2$            (by Proof 3)

$\quad = \sigma_X^2 - \sigma_X^2 \rho_{XX'}$       (by Proof 8)

$\quad = \sigma_X^2 (1 - \rho_{XX'}).$

14. To prove $\rho_{T_X T_Z} = \rho_{XZ}/\sqrt{\rho_{XX'}\rho_{ZZ'}}$, where $X = T_X + E_X$, $Z = T_Z + E_Z$, $X$ and $X'$ are scores on parallel tests, and $Z$ and $Z'$ are scores on parallel tests:

$\rho_{XZ} \;=\; \dfrac{\sigma_{XZ}}{\sigma_X \sigma_Z}$          (by Equation 2.48)

$\quad = \dfrac{\sigma_{T_X T_Z} + \sigma_{T_X E_Z} + \sigma_{E_X T_Z} + \sigma_{E_X E_Z}}{\sigma_X \sigma_Z}$      (by Assumption 1 and Equation 2.50)

$\quad = \dfrac{\sigma_{T_X T_Z}}{\sigma_X \sigma_Z}$          (by Assumptions 4 and 5)

$\rho_{T_X T_Z} = \dfrac{\sigma_{T_X T_Z}}{\sigma_{T_X} \sigma_{T_Z}}$          (by Equation 2.48)

$\quad = \dfrac{\rho_{XZ}\, \sigma_X \sigma_Z}{\sigma_{T_X} \sigma_{T_Z}}$

$\quad = \dfrac{\rho_{XZ}}{\dfrac{\sigma_{T_X}}{\sigma_X}\dfrac{\sigma_{T_Z}}{\sigma_Z}}$

$\quad = \dfrac{\rho_{XZ}}{\sqrt{\rho_{XX'}\rho_{ZZ'}}}$          (by Proof 8)

15.  To prove $\sigma_{T_X}^2 = N^2 \sigma_{T_Y}^2$, where $X = \sum_{i=1}^{N} Y_i$, and the $Y_i$'s are parallel test scores with $\mathcal{E}(Y_i) = T_Y$ and $\sigma_{E_{Y_i}}^2 = \sigma_{E_Y}^2$:

$$T_X = \mathcal{E}(X) \qquad \text{(by Assumption 2)}$$

$$= \mathcal{E}\left[\sum_{i=1}^{N} Y_i\right]$$

$$= \sum_{i=1}^{N} \mathcal{E}(Y_i) \qquad \text{(by Rule 3, Section 2.14)}$$

$$= NT_Y. \qquad \text{(by Rule 1, Section 2.3)}$$

$$T_X - \mathcal{E}(T_X) = NT_Y - \mathcal{E}(NT_Y)$$

$$= NT_Y - N\mathcal{E}(T_Y) \qquad \text{(by Rule 2, Section 2.14)}$$

$$= N\left[T_Y - \mathcal{E}(T_Y)\right].$$

$$\sigma_{T_X}^2 = \mathcal{E}\left[T_X - \mathcal{E}(T_X)\right]^2 \qquad \text{(by Equation 2.43)}$$

$$= \mathcal{E}\left[N(T_Y - \mathcal{E}(T_Y))\right]^2$$

$$= N^2 \mathcal{E}\left[T_Y - \mathcal{E}(T_Y)\right]^2 \qquad \text{(by Rule 2, Section 2.14)}$$

$$= N^2 \sigma_{T_Y}^2. \qquad \text{(by Equation 2.43)}$$

16.  To prove $\sigma_{E_X}^2 = N\sigma_{E_Y}^2$, where $X$ and $Y$ are defined as in Proof 15:

$$E_X = X - T_X \qquad \text{(by Assumption 1)}$$

$$= \sum_{i=1}^{N} Y_i - NT_Y \qquad \text{(by Proof 15)}$$

$$= NT_Y + \sum_{i=1}^{N} E_{Y_i} - NT_Y \qquad \text{(by Assumption 1 and Rules 1 and 3, Section 2.3)}$$

$$= \sum_{i=1}^{N} E_{Y_i}.$$

$$\sigma_{E_X}^2 = \sum_{i=1}^{N} \sigma_{E_Y}^2 + \sum_{i=1}^{N} \sum_{\substack{j=1 \\ i \neq j}}^{N} \sigma_{E_{Y_i} E_{Y_j}} \qquad \text{(by Equation 2.52)}$$

$$= N\sigma_{E_Y}^2. \qquad \text{(by Assumption 4 and Rule 1, Section 2.3)}$$

17.  To prove $\rho_{XX'} = N\rho_{YY'} / \left[1 + (N - 1)\rho_{YY'}\right]$, where $X$ and $Y_i$ are defined as in

Proof 15, $\rho_{YY'}$ is the correlation between any two of the $Y_i$'s, and $X'$ is a test score parallel to $X$:

$$\rho_{XX'} = \frac{\sigma_{T_X}^2}{\sigma_X^2} \qquad \text{(by Proof 8)}$$

$$= \frac{N^2 \sigma_{T_Y}^2}{\displaystyle\sum_{i=1}^{N} \sigma_{Y_i}^2 + \sum_{i=1}^{N} \sum_{\substack{j=1 \\ i \neq j}}^{N} \sigma_{Y_i Y_j}} \qquad \begin{array}{l} \text{(by Proof 15 and} \\ \text{Equation 2.52)} \end{array}$$

$$= \frac{N^2 \sigma_{T_Y}^2}{N \sigma_Y^2 + (N^2 - N) \sigma_{T_Y}^2} \qquad \begin{array}{l} \text{(by Proofs 6 and 12 and} \\ \text{Rule 1, Section 2.3)} \end{array}$$

$$= \frac{N^2 \rho_{YY'} \sigma_Y^2}{N \sigma_Y^2 + N(N-1) \rho_{YY'} \sigma_Y^2} \qquad \text{(by Proof 8)}$$

$$= \frac{N \rho_{YY'}}{1 + (N-1) \rho_{YY'}} .$$

18. To prove that the limit of $\rho_{XX'}$ as $N \to \infty$ is 1, where $X$ and $Y$ are defined as in Proof 15, and $\rho_{YY'} \neq 0$:

$$\rho_{XX'} = \frac{N \rho_{YY'}}{1 + (N-1) \rho_{YY'}} \qquad \text{(by Proof 17)}$$

$$= \frac{\rho_{YY'}}{\dfrac{1}{N} + \dfrac{N-1}{N} \rho_{YY'}} .$$

As $N \to \infty$, $1/N \to 0$, $(N-1)/N \to 1$, and $\rho_{XX'} \to \rho_{YY'}/\rho_{YY'} = 1$, if $\rho_{YY'} \neq 0$.

## 3.5  Vocabulary

| | |
|---|---|
| ceiling effect | parallel tests |
| classical true-score theory | standard error of measurement |
| correction for attenuation | systematic error |
| error of measurement | test model |
| error score | test theory |
| essentially $\tau$-equivalent tests | true score |
| observed score | unsystematic error |
| parallel forms | weak true-score theory |

## 3.6  Study Questions

1. What is a test theory or test model?
2. Explain each assumption of classical true-score theory.
3. Why is classical theory considered to be an additive model?
4. What are $X$, $T$, and $E$ in classical true-score theory? How are they related?
5. Why is $T$ defined by the test rather than by the trait being measured?
6. Why is it impossible to actually observe a true score?
7. How can practice effects, fatigue, examinee's mood, or environmental effects lead to violations of classical theory?
8. What conditions can lead to nonzero correlations between true scores and error scores?
9. Under what situations would error scores on two tests be correlated?
10. Compare parallel tests and essentially $\tau$-equivalent tests.
11. Describe the 18 conclusions reached by classical true-score theory.
12. (Optional) Prove the 18 conclusions reached by classical true-score theory.

## 3.7  Computational Problems

1. If $X = 10$ and $E = 2$, what does $T$ equal?
2. If $\sigma_T^2 = 5$ and $\sigma_X^2 = 10$, what does $\sigma_E^2$ equal?
3. If $\sigma_T^2 = 3$ and $\sigma_X^2 = 9$, what does $\rho_{XT}^2$ equal?
4. If $\sigma_E^2 = 1$ and $\sigma_X^2 = 4$, what does $\rho_{XT}^2$ equal?
5. $X$ and $X'$ are scores on two parallel tests. If $\sigma_X^2 = 10$ and $\rho_{XY} = 0.3$, what are $\sigma_{X'}^2$ and $\rho_{X'Y}$?
6. $\rho_{XX'} = 0.8$, and the observed test-score variance is 25.
   a. What are $\sigma_T^2/\sigma_X^2$, $\sigma_E^2/\sigma_X^2$, $\rho_{XE}^2$, and $\rho_{XT}^2$?
   b. What are the true-score variance and the error variance?
7. If $\rho_{XX'} = 0.6$ and $\sigma_X^2 = 25$, what are the true-score variance, the error variance, and the standard error of measurement?
8. If $\rho_{XY} = 0.5$, $\rho_{XX'} = 0.7$, and $\rho_{YY'} = 0.8$, what is $\rho_{T_X T_Y}$?
9. Scores on two parallel tests ($Y_1$ and $Y_2$) have a correlation of 0.6. The two tests are combined to make one long test ($X = Y_1 + Y_2$).
   a. What is the size of the true-score variance of the longer test ($\sigma_{T_X}^2$) relative to the size of the true-score variance of one of the shorter tests ($\sigma_{T_Y}^2$)?
   b. What is the size of the error variance of the longer test ($\sigma_{E_X}^2$) relative to the error variance of one of the shorter tests ($\sigma_{E_Y}^2$)?
   c. What is $\rho_{XX'}$?

# Reliability

## 4.1 Introduction

There are several ways of defining and interpreting test *reliability*. For example, a test is reliable if its observed scores are highly correlated with its true scores. That is, if observed and true scores could be obtained for every examinee for a test, the squared correlation between observed and true scores ($\rho_{XT}^2$) is called the reliability coefficient for that test. Or reliability can be expressed as a correlation coefficient between observed scores on two parallel tests. If two parallel tests are given to a population of examinees and the resulting observed scores are correlated, this correlation (symbolized $\rho_{XX'}$, where $X$ and $X'$ are observed scores for the two parallel tests) is the reliability coefficient. In most cases true scores cannot be obtained, and it is not possible to verify that tests are parallel. Therefore, reliability must be estimated by other methods. But before we investigate the common methods for estimating reliability, we will consider six ways of defining or interpreting reliability coefficients. We will retain $\rho_{XX'}$ as the symbol for the reliability coefficient even when parallel tests are not used to define reliability.

### Alternative Interpretations of the Reliability Coefficient

The following list presents six alternative ways of looking at reliability coefficients.

1. $\rho_{XX'}$ = the correlation between observed scores on parallel tests.

2. $\rho_{XX'}^2$ = the proportion of variance in $X$ explained by a linear relationship with $X'$.

3. $\rho_{XX'} = \sigma_T^2/\sigma_X^2$.

4. $\rho_{XX'} = \rho_{XT}^2$.

5. $\rho_{XX'} = 1 - \rho_{XE}^2$.

6. $\rho_{XX'} = 1 - \sigma_E^2/\sigma_X^2$.

Interpretation 1 states that the reliability of a test equals the correlation of its observed scores with observed scores on a parallel test. If each examinee obtains the same observed score when tested with a parallel form and there is some variance in observed scores within each testing, the tests have perfect reliability ($\rho_{XX'} = 1$). If examinees have observed scores on one test that are uncorrelated with their observed scores on a parallel test ($\rho_{XX'} = 0$), the tests are totally unreliable.

Interpretation 2 is the standard interpretation for the Pearson correlation coefficient, which we discussed at length in Section 2.8. A squared correlation can always be interpreted as the proportion of variance in one of the variables that is explained by a linear relationship with the other variable. Thus, $\rho_{XX'}^2$ can be viewed as the proportion of variance in one test score explained by its linear relationship with scores on a parallel test.

Interpretation 3, $\rho_{XX'} = \sigma_T^2/\sigma_X^2$, is that the reliability coefficient is the ratio of true-score variance to observed-score variance or the proportion of observed variance that is true-score variance. For a perfectly reliable test, $\rho_{XX'} = 1$, so $\sigma_T^2/\sigma_X^2 = 1$, and all of the observed variance reflects true-score variance rather than error variance. If $\rho_{XX'} = 1$, any differences between examinees' observed scores reflect differences between their true scores. If $\sigma_X^2 = \sigma_T^2$, then $\sigma_E^2$ must be 0. Since $\varepsilon(E) = 0$, all errors must equal 0 when $\sigma_E^2 = 0$. Thus, when $\rho_{XX'} = 1$, measurement is made without error. When $\rho_{XX'} < 1$, error is present in the measurement. When $\rho_{XX'} = 0$, then $\sigma_X^2 = \sigma_E^2$, which means that all scores reflect only error and, therefore, that differences between examinees' observed scores reflect random error rather than true-score differences.

As the reliability of a test increases, the error-score variance becomes relatively smaller. When error variance is relatively slight, an examinee's observed score is very close to his or her true score. However, when error variance is relatively large, observed scores give poor estimates of true scores. Figure 4.1 illustrates these relationships. The curves represent the theoretical distributions of observed scores

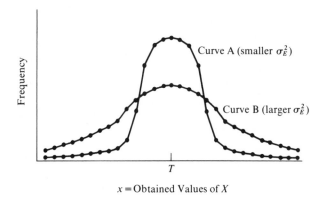

Figure 4.1. The effect of the size of $\sigma_E^2$ on the similarity of $T$ to an obtained value of $X$

for one fixed true score—that is, the distribution of observed scores for one examinee. The examinee's true score is indicated by $T$ in the figure. Remember that, when the true score is fixed or constant, $\sigma_T^2 = 0$, and the observed-score variance equals the error variance. Under curve A, which has a smaller error variance, most observed scores are very close to $T$; under curve B, which has a larger error variance, many observed scores are very far from $T$.

Interpretation 4, $\rho_{XX'} = \rho_{XT}^2$, presents the reliability coefficient as the square of the correlation between observed and true scores. For example, if $\rho_{XX'} = .81$, then $\rho_{XT} = .9$; if $\rho_{XX'} = .25$, then $\rho_{XT} = .5$. This relationship is illustrated in Figure 4.2. Whenever $0 < \rho_{XX'} < 1$, we can see that $\rho_{XT} > \rho_{XX'}$; an observed test score will correlate higher with its own true score than with an observed score on a

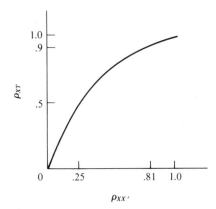

Figure 4.2. The relationship between $\rho_{XX'}$ and $\rho_{XT}$

parallel test. In fact, since a test score cannot correlate more highly with any other variable than it can with its own true score, the maximum correlation between an observed test score and any other variable is $\sqrt{\rho_{XX'}} = \rho_{XT}$. If a test, $X$, is used to predict a criterion, $Y$, then $\rho_{XY}$ is called the validity coefficient. Because $\rho_{XY}$ cannot be larger than $\rho_{XT}$, $\rho_{XY}$ cannot be larger than $\sqrt{\rho_{XX'}}$; therefore, unreliability affects validity. Although a validity coefficient cannot be higher than the square root of the reliability coefficient, the validity coefficient can be greater than the reliability coefficient itself. For example, if $\rho_{XX'} = .49$, then $\rho_{XT} = .7$. In this situation $\rho_{XY}$ (the validity coefficient) can be as large as .7 and, therefore, can be higher than the reliability coefficient. Chapter 5 contains a further discussion of validity coefficients.

Interpretation 5, $\rho_{XX'} = 1 - \rho_{XE}^2$, states that the reliability coefficient is 1 minus the squared correlation between observed and error scores. Ideally, $\rho_{XE}$ should be 0, but $\rho_{XE} = 0$ only when $\rho_{XX'} = 1.0$. The relationship between $\rho_{XE}$ and $\rho_{XX'}$ is illustrated in Figure 4.3.

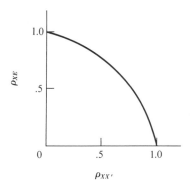

Figure 4.3. The relationship between $\rho_{XX'}$ and $\rho_{XE}$

Interpretation 6, $\rho_{XX'} = 1 - \sigma_E^2/\sigma_X^2$, relates reliability to error-score variance and observed-score variance. As described earlier, when $\rho_{XX'} = 1$, $\sigma_E^2 = 0$; and when $\rho_{XX'} = 0$, $\sigma_E^2 = \sigma_X^2$. The degree of heterogeneity (variance) of the observed scores obtained for a group of examinees can have an important impact on reliability. If a test is given to a population with a restricted range of observed scores (for example, if we give an IQ test to a group of mentally retarded people), $\sigma_X^2$ will be reduced. If the error variance is the same in the restricted group as it is in the more heterogeneous group, then the reliability will be smaller for the restricted group. In other words, reliability estimates based on the heterogeneous group will tend to be higher than estimates based on the more homogeneous group. This point is discussed further in Section 9.2.

In summary, when $\rho_{XX'} = 1$, we can see that:

1. the measurement has been made without error (all $E = 0$),
2. $X = T$ for all examinees,
3. all observed-score variance reflects true-score variance ($\sigma_X^2 = \sigma_T^2$),
4. all differences between observed scores reflect true-score differences,
5. the correlation between observed scores and true scores is 1 ($\rho_{XT} = 1$), and
6. the correlation between observed scores and error scores is 0 ($\rho_{XE} = 0$).

When $\rho_{XX'} = 0$, we can see that:

1. only random error is included in the measurement,
2. $X = E$ for all examinees,
3. all observed variance reflects error variance ($\sigma_X^2 = \sigma_E^2$),
4. all differences between scores reflect errors of measurement,
5. the correlation between observed scores and true scores is 0 ($\rho_{XT} = 0$), and
6. the correlation between observed scores and error scores is 1 ($\rho_{XE} = 1$).

When $0 \leqslant \rho_{XX'} \leqslant 1$, we can see that:

1. the measurement can include some error,
2. $X = T + E$,
3. observed-score variance includes some true-score variance and some error variance ($\sigma_X^2 = \sigma_T^2 + \sigma_E^2$),
4. differences between scores can reflect errors of measurement as well as true-score differences,
5. the correlation between observed scores and true scores, $\rho_{XT}$, equals $\sqrt{\rho_{XX'}}$,
6. the correlation between observed scores and error scores, $\rho_{XE}$, is $\sqrt{1 - \rho_{XX'}}$,
7. reliability is the proportion of observed-score variance that is true-score variance ($\rho_{XX'} = \sigma_T^2/\sigma_X^2$), and
8. the larger $\rho_{XX'}$ is, the more confidently we can estimate $T$ from $X$, because error variance will be relatively smaller.

The three common methods for estimating the reliability coefficient are: test/retest, parallel forms, and internal consistency. In general, each of these three methods will yield different estimates of $\rho_{XX'}$. To avoid confusion, remember that the methods to be described yield *estimates* for $\rho_{XX'}$; the real value of this coefficient is unobservable.

## 4.2  Test/Retest Reliability Estimates

*Test/retest reliability,* as the name suggests, yields a reliability estimate, $r_{XX'} = \hat{\rho}_{XX'}$, that is based on testing the same examinees twice with the same test and then correlating the results. If each examinee receives exactly the same observed score on the second testing as he or she did on the first, and if there is some variance in the observed scores among examinees, then the correlation is 1.0, indicating perfect reliability. Or, more generally, if the observed scores for all examinees obtained from one testing are perfectly linearly related to the observed scores from the second testing, then the estimated reliability is 1.0 (see Section 2.8). But, if the set of scores from the first testing is not related to the set of scores from the second, the estimate of $\rho_{XX'}$ is 0. The test/retest method seems to yield the most reasonable estimate of test reliability, but some complications are inherent with this method.

The most serious problem with the test/retest reliability estimate is the potential for a *carry-over effect* between testings: the first testing may influence the second testing. This contamination of scores can occur in a number of ways. The examinees might remember the answers they gave the first time and simply repeat them. If most examinees did this, $r_{XX'}$ would overestimate $\rho_{XX'}$. Or, on some tests, there may be a carry-over due to practice effects. For example, most people tend to improve with repeated testing on dexterity tests and on some ability tests. If some people improved more than others, the correlation of the observed scores for the two testings would probably underestimate $\rho_{XX'}$, unless the degree of improvement was highly correlated with scores on either the first or second testing.

A change in examinees' attitudes or degree of information could also cause other carry-over effects. Uncooperative examinees might object to the second testing and deliberately mismark the second test, resulting in a low reliability coefficient between the testings. Or, after the first testing, some examinees might seek advice or information about how to improve their scores. If some of the examinees did this, the test/retest correlation coefficient would tend to underestimate $\rho_{XX'}$. Carry-over effects can yield different results, sometimes overestimating and sometimes underestimating the real test reliability.

A second problem with test/retest reliability involves the length of time between the two test administrations. A very short time interval would make carry-over effects due to memory, practice, or mood more likely; a long interval would make effects due to changes in information or moods more likely. If the trait that the test is measuring varies over time, such as cognitive ability in children, long intervals would tend to lead to underestimates of the reliability of the test for one occasion. Different lengths of time can affect the reliability estimate in different ways, sometimes overestimating and sometimes underestimating the real reliability.

Test/retest reliability estimates are based on a straightforward design of simply correlating the results of two administrations of the same test. Carry-over effects and the length of the time interval between the two testings can influence the size of the test/retest reliability estimate. Test/retest reliability estimates are most appropriate for tests measuring traits that are not susceptible to carry-over effects and that are stable across the time interval used. For example, test/retest procedures are appropriate for estimating the reliability of sensory discrimination tasks (like visual or auditory acuity tests)

## 4.3  Parallel-Forms and Alternate-Forms Reliability Estimates

A *parallel-forms reliability* estimate is the correlation, $r_{XX'}$, between observed scores on two parallel tests. In practice, it usually is not possible to verify that two tests are parallel, and alternate test forms are often used in place of parallel test forms. *Alternate test forms* are any two test forms that have been constructed in an effort to make them parallel, and they may have equal (or very similar) observed-score means, variances, and correlations with other measures. However, beyond having these features, there is no proof available that the alternate forms are parallel. The correlation between observed scores on the alternate test forms, $r_{XZ}$, is an estimate of the reliability of either one of the alternate forms. This correlation will reflect how reliable the tests are, as well as how parallel they are. Thus alternate-forms reliability estimates will tend to be different from corresponding test/retest or parallel-forms reliability estimates taken over a similar time period. However, using alternate or parallel forms doesn't always eliminate the possibility of carry-over effects, especially those related to response styles, moods, or attitudes. As with test/retest reliability estimates, these carry-over effects may yield over- or under-estimates of $\rho_{XX'}$ or $\rho_{ZZ'}$. Timing also is a problem. Short intervals between the two testings allow for contamination due to memory, practice, or mood; long intervals are inappropriate for traits that change with time.

When alternate test forms, $X$ and $Z$, are not parallel, $r_{XZ}$ generally will be an inaccurate estimate of $\rho_{XX'}$ or $\rho_{ZZ'}$. For example, let $X = T_X + E_X$ and $Z = T_Z + E_Z$. If $T_X = T_Z$ but $\sigma^2_{E_X} > \sigma^2_{E_Z}$, then $X$ is less reliable than $Z$. The correlation $r_{XZ}$ will tend to overestimate $\rho_{XX'}$ and underestimate $\rho_{ZZ'}$. If $T_X \neq T_Z$, it is possible that the tests are measuring different traits, and $r_{XZ}$ will tend to underestimate both $\rho_{XX'}$ and $\rho_{ZZ'}$. For example, if $X$ is a score on a math computation test and $Z$ is a score on a math reasoning test, $r_{XZ}$ is the correlation between the math computation and math reasoning scores and is not necessarily a good estimate of the reliability of either test.

It is possible for alternate forms to have unequal true scores and error variances, even though the correlation between their observed scores is equivalent to a parallel-forms correlation. For example, let $X = T_X + E_X$ and $X' = T_{X'} + E_{X'}$, where $X$ and $X'$ are scores on parallel tests. Let $Z = aX' + b$, where $a$ and $b$ are constants and $a > 0$; that is, $Z$ is a linear function of $X'$ (see Section 2.8). Although $Z$ and $X$ are not parallel test scores ($T_Z \neq T_X$ and $\sigma^2_{E_Z} \neq \sigma^2_{E_X}$), $\rho_{XZ} = \rho_{XX'}$. Since $Z$ is a linear function of $X'$, the correlation of $X$ with $Z$ will equal the correlation of $X$ with $X'$. This result occurs because correlations are not affected by linear transformations of either of the variables entering into the correlation (see Section 2.8).

In summary, a correlation between observed scores on alternate forms will produce a good estimate of test reliability if the alternate forms are parallel or if they are linear functions of parallel test scores and if carry-over effects and changes in scores over time do not influence the correlation.

## 4.4 Internal-Consistency Estimates of Reliability: Split Halves

*Internal-consistency reliability* is estimated using only one test administration and thus avoids the problems associated with repeated testings. The most widely known method using this approach yields a *split-half* reliability estimate. The test is divided into two parts, which are alternate forms of each other, and an attempt is made to choose these parts so that they are parallel or essentially $\tau$-equivalent (see Section 3.1). If the halves of the test are parallel, the reliability of the whole test is estimated using the *Spearman-Brown formula*. If the halves are essentially $\tau$-equivalent, *coefficient* $\alpha$ (Greek letter alpha) can be used to calculate the reliability of the entire test.

To use the Spearman-Brown formula, scores from the parallel test halves (call them $Y$ and $Y'$) are correlated, producing $\rho_{YY'}$. This correlation would be a reasonable measure of the reliability of one half of the test. The reliability of the entire test, $X = Y + Y'$, would be greater than the reliability of either half taken alone. The Spearman-Brown formula, which gives the reliability of the whole test, is

$$\rho_{XX'} = \frac{2\,\rho_{YY'}}{1 + \rho_{YY'}} . \tag{4.1}$$

As shown in Table 4.1, $\rho_{XX'}$ is usually larger than $\rho_{YY'}$, because $\rho_{XX'}$ is the reliability of the whole test and $\rho_{YY'}$ is the reliability of only half the test.

Table 4.1. Correlation between Parallel Halves of a Test ($\rho_{YY'}$) and the Reliability of the Entire Test ($\rho_{XX'}$)

| $\rho_{XX'}$ | $\rho_{YY'}$ |
|---|---|
| .00 | .00 |
| .33 | .20 |
| .57 | .40 |
| .75 | .60 |
| .89 | .80 |
| 1.00 | 1.00 |

The Spearman-Brown formula can be used to obtain the reliability of the whole test if the halves of the test are parallel. But, if the scores for the halves have unequal variances or there is some other indication that the halves are not parallel, coefficient $\alpha$ (Cronbach, 1951) can be used to estimate the reliability of the whole test. If the halves (call them $Y_1$ and $Y_2$) are essentially $\tau$-equivalent, coefficient $\alpha$ gives the reliability of the whole test. If the test halves are not essentially $\tau$-equivalent, coefficient $\alpha$ will give a lower bound for the test's reliability. (That is, the test's reliability must be greater than or equal to the number produced by the coefficient-$\alpha$ formula.) If coefficient $\alpha$ produces a high value, you know that the test reliability must be high; if coefficient $\alpha$ is low, you may not know whether the test actually has low reliability or whether the halves of the test are not essentially $\tau$-equivalent. The formula for coefficient $\alpha$ for split halves is

$$\rho_{XX'} \geq \alpha = \frac{2\left[\sigma_X^2 - (\sigma_{Y_1}^2 + \sigma_{Y_2}^2)\right]}{\sigma_X^2} , \tag{4.2}$$

where $\sigma_{Y_1}^2$ and $\sigma_{Y_2}^2$ are the variances of scores on the two halves of the test, and $\sigma_X^2$ is the variance of scores on the whole test, with $X = Y_1 + Y_2$.

An examination of this formula can yield an intuitive feeling for its use. The variance of $X$ equals the sum of the variances of $Y_1$ and $Y_2$ plus two times the covariance of $Y_1$ and $Y_2$ (Equation 2.51). Thus, the numerator of coefficient $\alpha$ is a function of the covariance between the two halves of the test, and coefficient $\alpha$ can be expressed as

$$\frac{2\left[2 \times \text{covariance between halves}\right]}{\text{total test score variance}}.$$

As the covariance (and correlation) between the halves increases in size, coefficient $\alpha$ increases.

The quantities produced by coefficient $\alpha$ and the Spearman-Brown formula will be large if the test halves are highly correlated and small if they are not. The halves will correlate highly only if they measure traits that are the same or that are highly correlated; thus, the Spearman-Brown and coefficient-$\alpha$ reliabilities are indices of the test's internal consistency or homogeneity.

If the variances of the observed scores for the test halves are equal, the Spearman-Brown formula and coefficient $\alpha$ are equal. If the variances of the observed scores for the test halves are equal but the halves are not essentially $\tau$-equivalent, both the Spearman-Brown formula and coefficient $\alpha$ will underestimate the test's reliability. If the observed-score variances of the test halves are equal and the halves are essentially $\tau$-equivalent, the Spearman-Brown formula and coefficient $\alpha$ will both equal the test reliability.

The use of the split-half reliability estimates can be illustrated with an example. (In practice, estimates of reliabilities and variances replace the population values in Equations 4.1 and 4.2.) Suppose the correlation between the scores on two halves of a test is .5. The variances of scores on the test halves are 7 and 5, and the variance of the total test scores is 17.9. Using the Spearman-Brown formula (Equation 4.1), the reliability of the total test score is estimated to be

$$r_{XX'} = \frac{2(.5)}{1 + .5} \doteq .67.$$

The reliability of the total test score is estimated by coefficient $\alpha$ (Equation 4.2) to be

$$r_{XX'} \geqslant \frac{2\left[17.9 - (7 + 5)\right]}{17.9} \doteq .66.$$

In this example coefficient $\alpha$ produces a reliability estimate that is only slightly smaller than the Spearman-Brown estimate.

The major advantage of internal-consistency reliability estimates is that the test need be given only once to allow calculation of the reliability estimate. However, the internal-consistency methods are not appropriate when the test cannot be divided into parts that are parallel or essentially $\tau$-equivalent or when the test does not have independent items that can be separated. For example, some apparatus tests in which examinees must manipulate objects in a fixed time period cannot be broken down into parts, because the manipulation of each object depends on the timing and errors made while working with other objects. In situations such as this, test/retest, parallel-forms, or alternate-forms reliability estimates must be used.

Three methods for forming test halves are commonly used. The first method, called the *odd/even* method, classifies items by whether they are odd- or even-numbered on the test. Each examinee obtains a score for the odd-numbered items and a score for the even-numbered items. A second method is to form the halves in *order*; each examinee obtains a score on the first half of the test and a score on the second half of the test. In general, halves formed by order are less satisfactory than odd/even halves, because some examinees may improve with practice (inflating their second-half scores) and some examinees may not be able to finish the test (deflating their second-half scores). However, the problem of some examinees not finishing the second half of the test can be solved by separately timing the two halves. That is, examinees are given so many minutes to finish the first half of the test, and, when the time is up, all examinees proceed to the second half of the test. The examinees are given the same amount of time to complete the second half of the test as they were for the first half. This type of split-half test is equivalent to administering two short alternate forms, with only a short time lapse between them.

The third method for forming equivalent test halves is more sophisticated than the two methods just described. This method, called the method of *matched random subsets* (Gulliksen, 1950), involves several steps. First, two statistics are computed for each item: (1) the proportion of examinees passing the item (the item difficulty) and (2) the biserial or point-biserial correlation between the item score and the total test score (see Section 2.11). Then each item is plotted on a graph using these two statistics. Items that are close together on the graph are paired, and one item from each pair is randomly chosen for one half of the test. The remaining items form the other half of the test. For example, Figure 4.4 shows six items that have been plotted and then grouped into pairs. If item *A* is chosen for one half of the test, item *B* will appear on the other test half, and so on. Possible test groupings include items *ACE* and *BDF, ADE* and *BCF, ACF* and *BDE,* and so on. This method helps ensure that the two halves are of approximately the same difficulty and are measuring approximately the same thing (thus yielding about the same true scores).

Tests are often considered along a dimension with speed at one end and power at the other. A pure *speed test* consists of items that all examinees could answer correctly given enough time, but the test is given with a short time limit to see how quickly examinees can work. For example, as a test of clerical speed and accuracy, 100 items involving name matching, like the ones below, could be given with a 60-second time limit.

Are the two names identical or different?

| | | |
|---|---|---|
| 1. | John McIntyre | John McIntire |
| 2. | Fred Perez | Fred Perez |
| 3. | Mary Johnasen | Mary Johansen |

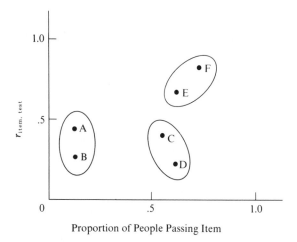

Figure 4.4. Selection of matched random subsets by graphing

At the other extreme is the *power test,* in which items are so difficult that even without time limits each examinee, depending on his or her ability, could correctly answer only a certain number of items. Time limits are generous to ensure that each examinee can attempt each item. Most ability and achievement tests fall somewhere between these two extremes, testing both speed and power.

A split-half reliability estimate should not be calculated for speed tests, because it would yield an unreasonable estimate of the test's reliability. On a pure speed test most people would get most attempted items correct, so that if a person completed 30 items, the odd and even scores would probably each be 15. In general the odd and even scores for each examinee would be nearly identical, forcing the split-half reliability estimate to be close to 1. And, if the split-half reliability estimate were based on correlating scores on the first half to scores on the second half of a speed test, the reliability estimate would be close to 0, since most examinees would earn nearly perfect scores on the first half and small scores on the second half. In this case, the correlation between scores on the test halves would reflect the relationship between errors on the first half and speed on the second half. The method of matched random subsets is not well suited for speed tests either, because the item difficulty and item/test correlation would be functions of the position of the item in the test, rather than functions of properties of the item itself.

The split-half method is based on examining halves of a test. Imagine breaking the test into thirds, fourths, and so on and then examining the relationships among these test components. If this process were carried to the limit, each item could be viewed as a test component, and relationships among items could be used as an indication of the internal consistency of the test. If all the components of a test intercorrelate highly, the test will have a high reliability estimate, indicating internal agreement or consistency among the components of the test. The next section describes a method of using the relationships among many components of a test to estimate the test's reliability.

## 4.5 Internal-Consistency Reliability: The General Case

The techniques for dividing a test in halves (odd/even, by order, or matched random subsets) can be generalized for dividing a test into more than two components. For example, the odd/even method can be modified to create thirds for a nine-item test by including the first, fourth, and seventh items in one third of the test, the second, fifth, and eighth items in another third, and the third, sixth, and ninth items in the last third. The method of matched random subsets would involve forming triplets of items by the graphical method illustrated in Figure 4.4 and then randomly choosing one item from each triplet to contribute to each third of the test.

This section assumes that a test has been divided into $N$ components. The variances of scores on these components and the variance of the total test score are used to estimate the reliability of the test. If the components (for example, items or sets of items) are all essentially $\tau$-equivalent (see Section 3.1), the formulas presented in this section will produce the test's reliability; if the components are not essentially $\tau$-equivalent, these formulas will underestimate the test's reliability. In addition, these formulas produce good estimates of reliability only when the test measures one trait—that is, when the test is homogeneous in content. For example, a test measuring algebraic reasoning may be homogeneous, but a typical intelligence test, which measures a collection of verbal, spatial, and quantitative skills, would be heterogeneous. Internal-consistency measures of reliability are not suited for use on heterogeneous tests. Nor are these measures suited for use on speed tests, since the internal consistency of the components of a speed test is not a good indication of the reliability of such a test.

The formula for internal-consistency reliability in the general case is coefficient $\alpha$:

$$\rho_{XX'} \geq \alpha = \left[\frac{N}{N-1}\right]\left[\frac{\sigma_X^2 - \sum_{i=1}^{N} \sigma_{Y_i}^2}{\sigma_X^2}\right], \tag{4.3}$$

where  $X$ = the observed score for a test formed from combining $N$ components, $X = \sum_{i=1}^{N} Y_i$,

$\sigma_X^2$ = the population variance of $X$,

$\sigma_{Y_i}^2$ = the population variance of the $i$th component, $Y_i$, and

$N$ = the number of components that are combined to form $X$; for example, if $N = 3$, the test score, $X$, is based on three components.

If each component test, $Y_i$, is a dichotomous item, Equation 4.3 takes on the following special form:

$$\rho_{XX'} \geqslant KR20 = \left[\frac{N}{N-1}\right] \left[\frac{\sigma_X^2 - \displaystyle\sum_{i=1}^{N} p_i (1 - p_i)}{\sigma_X^2}\right], \tag{4.4}$$

where $p_i$ is the proportion of examinees getting item $i$ correct, which is a measure of item difficulty. Equation 4.4 reflects the fact that the variance of scores on item $i$, when the scores on these items can take on only the values 1 or 0, equals $p_i(1 - p_i)$, where $p_i$ is the proportion of examinees in a population who get a score of 1 on the item (that is, who pass the item). Equation 4.4 is often referred to as *Kuder-Richardson formula 20,* abbreviated KR20, because it was the 20th formula presented by Kuder and Richardson (1937). Another name for this formula is *coefficient $\alpha$-20,* abbreviated $\alpha(20)$, after Cronbach (1951).

Another Kuder-Richardson formula that can be useful when every $Y_i$ is a dichotomous item is

$$\rho_{XX'} \geqslant KR21 = \left[\frac{N}{N-1}\right] \left[\frac{\sigma_X^2 - N\bar{p}(1 - \bar{p})}{\sigma_X^2}\right], \tag{4.5}$$

where $\bar{p}$ is the average of the item difficulties. Because $\bar{p}$ is straightforward to calculate using $\bar{p} = \varepsilon(X)/N$, Equation 4.5 can be calculated from the mean and variance of an $N$-item test. Equation 4.5 is a special case of KR20 and is usually referred to as KR21 or $\alpha(21)$. Further,

$$KR20 \geqslant KR21. \tag{4.6}$$

The two formulas will be equal only if the item difficulties are all equal. If the item difficulties are not equal, KR21 will be less than KR20 and will underestimate the test's reliability.

The quantities produced by Equations 4.3 and 4.4 will be less than or equal to the reliability of the test and will equal the test reliability only if the $Y_i$'s are essentially $\tau$-equivalent (that is, have essentially the same true scores). KR21 will equal the test reliability only if the items are of equal difficulty and are essentially $\tau$-equivalent. The quantities produced by Equations 4.3, 4.4, and 4.5 will be large if the components that make up the total test score intercorrelate highly, and they will be small if the components do not intercorrelate highly. The components will intercorrelate highly only if they measure the same or highly correlated traits. Thus the formulas presented in this section are indices of a test's internal consistency or homogeneity.

The following examples illustrate the use of these formulas for estimating internal-consistency reliability. (In practice, estimates of the variances of the components, $s_{Y_i}^2$, item difficulties, $\hat{p}_i$, and test variance, $s_X^2$, are used in place of the population values, $\sigma_{Y_i}^2$, $p_i$, and $\sigma_X^2$ in Equations 4.3, 4.4, and 4.5.)

1. A creativity test is split into thirds. If the variance of the scores on the first third, $s_{Y_1}^2$, is 5.2, the variance of scores on the second third, $s_{Y_2}^2$, is 4.8, and the variance of scores on the last third, $s_{Y_3}^2$, is 5.0, then the sum of these variances is

15. The variance of total test scores, $s_X^2$, is 25. The estimated lower bound of the reliability of the test (from Equation 4.3) is $[3/2][(25-15)/25] = .6$. If the thirds of the test are essentially $\tau$-equivalent, .6 is the estimate of the test's reliability.

2. A five-item test of autonomy is given to a group of elementary school teachers. The variance of observed test scores, $s_X^2$, is 3, and the mean of the observed scores, $\overline{X}$, is 2. The proportions of teachers passing the items $(\hat{p}_i)$ are .3, .4, .7, .5, and .1. The sum of the item score variances, $\Sigma_{i=1}^5 \hat{p}_i(1-\hat{p}_i)$, is $.21 + .24 + .21 + .25 + .09 = 1.00$. Using Equation 4.4, the estimated lower bound of the test's reliability is $[5/4][(3-1)/3] \doteq .833$. If the items are essentially $\tau$-equivalent, the test reliability is estimated to equal .833. A lower bound also could be obtained using KR21. The average estimated item difficulty, $\overline{p}$, is $2/5 = .4$, and $N\overline{p}(1-\overline{p}) = 1.2$. The estimated lower bound of the test reliability using Equation 4.5 is $[5/4][(3-1.2)/3] = .75$. KR21 produces a smaller lower-bound estimate than KR20 because the items are of unequal difficulty.

## 4.6  The Spearman-Brown Formula: The General Case

Another method for calculating a test's reliability is the Spearman-Brown formula, which utilizes information about the reliability of parallel components of the test. The Spearman-Brown formula is also used in predicting the effects that changes in test length will have on reliability. This formula was discussed with reference to split-half reliability estimates in Section 4.4 and was also presented as Conclusion 17 in Chapter 3. In its general form, the Spearman-Brown formula is

$$\rho_{XX'} = \frac{N\rho_{YY'}}{1 + (N-1)\rho_{YY'}}, \qquad (4.7)$$

where $X$ = the observed total test score for a test formed from combining $N$ parallel component test scores, $X = \Sigma_{i=1}^N Y_i$,

$Y_i$ = a component test score that is a part of $X$,

$\rho_{XX'}$ = the population reliability of $X$,

$\rho_{YY'}$ = the population reliability of any $Y_i$, and

$N$ = the number of parallel test scores that are combined to form $X$.

The Spearman-Brown formula expresses the reliability of a test, $\rho_{XX'}$, in terms of the reliability of parallel components of the test. Notice that in this formula $\rho_{XX'}$ is always greater than or equal to $\rho_{YY'}$; the reliability of a test that is composed of parallel components must be greater than or equal to the reliability of any one of the components. $\rho_{XX'}$ is sometimes called a *stepped-up reliability*, because it is an upward adjustment of the reliability of a shorter, component test.

Figure 4.5 illustrates the general effects that changes in test length will have on $\rho_{XX'}$ for tests with component reliabilities, $\rho_{YY'}$, of .2, .4, .6, and .8. Using Figure 4.5, any two of the three numbers ($N$, $\rho_{XX'}$, and $\rho_{YY'}$) can be used to find the third. For example, if $\rho_{YY'} = .4$, and a test with $\rho_{XX'}$ equal to .8 is desired, the test developer will need a test that is six times as long as the original test. Figure 4.5 also

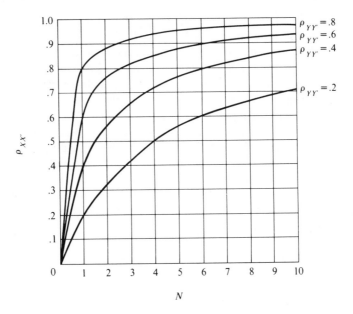

Figure 4.5. The relationship between test length and reliability. (From *Theory of Mental Tests*, by H. Gulliksen. Copyright 1950 by John Wiley & Sons, Inc. Reprinted by permission.)

demonstrates that increasing the length of a relatively unreliable test, even by a factor of ten, does not guarantee perfect reliability. However, as $N \rightarrow \infty$, the reliability of a test composed of $N$ parallel components will go to 1.0, as long as $\rho_{YY'} \neq 0$ (see Conclusion 18, Chapter 3).

Equation 4.7 is useful when we know $N$ and $\rho_{YY'}$ and want to solve for $\rho_{XX'}$. When we know the reliability of a test, $\rho_{XX'}$, and want to determine the reliability, $\rho_{YY'}$, of a shorter version of the test that is $1/N$ as long, the Spearman-Brown formula can be used to obtain

$$\rho_{YY'} = \frac{\dfrac{1}{N}\,\rho_{XX'}}{1 + \left(\dfrac{1}{N} - 1\right)\rho_{XX'}}. \qquad (4.8)$$

In a situation in which we know $\rho_{YY'}$ and we want $\rho_{XX'}$ to be some desired value, we can use a rearrangement of the Spearman-Brown formula,

$$N = \frac{\rho_{XX'}\,(1 - \rho_{YY'})}{\rho_{YY'}\,(1 - \rho_{XX'})}, \qquad (4.9)$$

to determine the $N$ necessary to reach the desired $\rho_{XX'}$.

The following examples illustrate some practical applications of Equations 4.7, 4.8, and 4.9. In using these Spearman-Brown formulas, estimates of reliabilities ($r_{XX'}$ and $r_{YY'}$) replace the population values of the reliabilities ($\rho_{XX'}$ and $\rho_{YY'}$). The reliability estimates used in these formulas can be test/retest, parallel-forms, alternate-forms, or internal-consistency reliabilities.

1. You have a five-minute test with an estimated reliability of .6. If you make the test three times as long by adding parallel components, what is the estimated reliability of the longer test? Here $N = 3$, and $r_{YY'} = .6$. Using Equation 4.7, we obtain

$$r_{XX'} = \frac{3(.6)}{1 + (2)(.6)} \doteq .82.$$

This reliability could also be obtained from Figure 4.5.

2. You have a 50-item test with an estimated reliability of .9. If you remove a ten-item component of the test, what is the estimated reliability of the ten-item test? Here $N = 5$, $r_{XX'} = .9$, and we are solving for $r_{YY'}$. Using Equation 4.8, we obtain

$$r_{YY'} = \frac{\frac{1}{5}(.9)}{1 + \left(\frac{1}{5} - 1\right).9} \doteq .64.$$

3. You have a ten-item test with an estimated reliability of .8. How long would the test have to be to have a reliability of .9? Here $r_{YY'} = .8$, $r_{XX'} = .9$, and we are solving for $N$. Using Equation 4.9, we obtain

$$N = \frac{(.9)(1-.8)}{(.8)(1-.9)} = 2.25.$$

The new test would have to be 2.25 times as long, or about 23 items long.

Remember that the Spearman-Brown formula is based on the assumption that parallel components are being added together to form a longer test. We cannot casually add items to a carefully devised test and expect the reliability to increase. If a test is lengthened carelessly, the reliability could actually decrease. However, longer tests are generally more reliable, because, under the assumptions of classical true-score theory, as $N$ increases, true-score variance increases faster than error variance (see Chapter 3, Conclusions 15 and 16).

If component tests are not parallel, the Spearman-Brown formula can under- or overestimate the reliability of a longer test. For example, suppose that we have a ten-item test with a reliability of .6. The Spearman-Brown formula states that doubling the test by adding a parallel ten-item test will result in a test with a reliability of $[2(.6)]/[1 + .6] = .75$. However, suppose that the test is lengthened, not by adding a parallel test, but by adding a ten-item test whose scores have no variance. Lengthening the test in this manner would have the effect of adding a constant to every examinee's score, which would not add to the test's reliability. In this case, the reliability of the 20-item test would equal .6 (that is, it would equal the reliability of the original ten-item test), and an inappropriate application of the Spearman-Brown formula would overestimate the reliability of the 20-item test.

In other situations, the Spearman-Brown formula can underestimate the test reliability. For example, suppose that a ten-item test has a reliability of 0. The Spearman-Brown formula would estimate that doubling the length of the test with a parallel component would produce a 20-item test with a reliability of $\left[2(0)\right]\big/\left[1 + 0\right] = 0$. However, if the original test is lengthened by adding a non-parallel ten-item test with a reliability of .7, the reliability of the resulting 20-item test would be greater than 0. In this case, inappropriate use of the Spearman-Brown formula would underestimate the reliability of the 20-item test. The reliability produced by the Spearman-Brown formula is accurate only when parallel test components are involved in the calculations.

There are two additional practical implications of the Spearman-Brown formula. First, when comparing the reliabilities of two tests of different lengths, the longer test may look better only because it is longer. An application of the Spearman-Brown formula will allow you to estimate the reliabilities the tests would have if they were of equal length. Second, because very short subtests tend to have substantially lower reliabilities than the longer test from which they are drawn, you should be careful when shortening tests or when comparing scores on short tests.

## 4.7    Comparison of Methods of Estimating Reliabilities

The previous discussion explained that there are different ways to estimate the reliability of a test and that the different methods yield different estimates. In determining reliability estimates for speed tests, test/retest, alternate-forms, or parallel-forms estimates should be used, because most internal-consistency measures would be inaccurate. Use of coefficient $\alpha$ and the Kuder-Richardson methods produces a lower bound for a test's reliability. This lower bound equals the test reliability if the components in the test are essentially $\tau$-equivalent. Coefficient $\alpha$ and the Kuder-Richardson formulas should be used only for homogeneous tests, since these formulas basically reflect item homogeneity. If the test measures a variety of traits, coefficient $\alpha$ and the Kuder-Richardson reliability will be inappropriately low. The Spearman-Brown formula can over- or underestimate a test's reliability if the components of the test are not parallel; when the components of a test are parallel, the Spearman-Brown formula is very useful for judging the effects that changes in test length have on reliability.

The same test can produce different reliability estimates when it is administered to different samples of examinees under different conditions. A test model called generalizability theory, which can be used to examine such systematic effects on reliability, is described in Section 10.7.

## 4.8    Standard Errors of Measurement and Confidence Intervals for True Scores

Consider again the assumptions of classical true-score theory and the distribution of observed scores for a specific examinee over repeated independent testings with the same test or parallel tests (Figure 4.6). This distribution is centered

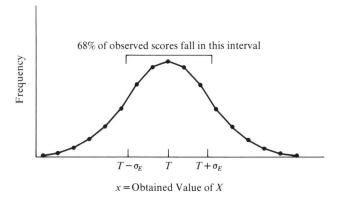

Figure 4.6. Approximately normal distribution of observed scores for repeated testings of one examinee

at $T$ and has a standard deviation, $\sigma_E$, where $\sigma_E$ is the standard error of measurement. Unless $\sigma_E = 0$, it is unlikely that an examinee's observed score will exactly equal his or her true score. It is more likely that a particular observed score falls within a range of values near the true score. Figure 4.6 represents an approximately normal distribution of observed scores for one examinee, resulting from repeated independent testings with the same test or parallel tests. From the normal-distribution table in the Appendix we can determine that 68% of the examinee's observed scores would be expected to fall in the interval from $T - \sigma_E$ to $T + \sigma_E$, or $T \pm \sigma_E$. When an observed score, $x$, falls in the interval $T \pm \sigma_E$, the observed score can be no farther from $T$ than $\sigma_E$, and $T$ can be no farther than $\sigma_E$ from $x$. For example, let $T = 10$ and $\sigma_E = 2; T \pm \sigma_E$ covers the interval from 8 to 12. If $x$ is contained in $T \pm \sigma_E$, $x$ could be as small as 8 or as large as 12. If $x = 8$, $x \pm \sigma_E$ covers the interval from 6 to 10, which includes $T$; if $x = 12$, $x \pm \sigma_E$ covers the interval 10 to 14, which also includes $T$. Thus, if intervals of the form $x \pm \sigma_E$ are constructed for every observed score, 68% of these intervals would be expected to include $T$. In a practical situation where $T$ is not known, we would know that 68% of the intervals $x \pm \sigma_E$ include $T$, but we could not identify which particular intervals are the ones that actually contain $T$.

Constructing an interval $x \pm \sigma_E$ requires an estimate of $\sigma_E$. Typically, the test user does not have the results of many independent testings of one examinee, so an estimate of $\sigma_E$ based on many scores for that examinee is not available. However, if we assume that $\sigma_E$ is the same for all the examinees in a sample, then the estimate $\hat{\sigma}_E = s_E = s_X\sqrt{1 - r_{XX'}}$ (Chapter 3, Conclusion 13) can be used in constructing the intervals.

These considerations lead to a method for the construction of *confidence intervals for true scores*. A confidence interval for the true score of an examinee can be constructed if the following assumptions are met: (1) the assumptions of classical true-score theory (Section 3.1), (2) the assumption that, for the given examinee, errors of measurement are normally distributed, and (3) the assumption that $\sigma_E$ is the same for all examinees (an assumption of *homoscedasticity*). When these assumptions are met, a confidence interval for an examinee's true score can be constructed as

$$x - z_c s_E \leq T \leq x + z_c s_E,$$    (4.10)

which is usually written,

$$x \pm z_c s_E,$$    (4.11)

where $x$ is the observed score for the examinee, $s_E$ is the estimated standard error of measurement ($s_E = s_X \sqrt{1 - r_{XX'}}$), and $z_c$ is the critical value of the standard normal deviate at the desired probability level (Section 2.9). For example, if an examinee has an observed score of 25, and $s_E = 4$, a 90% confidence interval for the examinee's true score is constructed as $25 \pm (1.65)(4)$, or from 18.4 to 31.6. If for the same examinee a 68% confidence interval were constructed instead, it would be $25 \pm (1)(4)$, or from 21 to 29. Notice that a lower confidence level is associated with a narrower confidence interval.

The confidence intervals for true scores can be interpreted in either of two ways. The intervals can be expected to contain a given examinee's true score a specified percentage of the time when the intervals are constructed using observed scores that are the result of repeated independent testings of the examinee with the same test or parallel tests. Or the intervals can be expected to cover a specified percentage of examinees' true scores when many examinees are tested once with the same test or parallel tests and a confidence interval is calculated for each examinee.

The main advantage of the use of confidence intervals is that they make it clear that an observed score contains a certain amount of measurement error. If a test score is unreliable, confidence intervals for true scores will be very wide, indicating that observed scores are not very good indicators of true scores. On the other hand, if a test has good reliability, confidence intervals for true scores will be narrow, indicating that observed scores can be expected to be close to true scores.

The main disadvantage of the use of confidence intervals is the difficulty in interpreting them correctly. When we say that we are 90% confident that a certain examinee's true score falls between 18.4 and 31.6, what we mean is that 90% of the confidence intervals constructed in a similar manner will contain true scores; we cannot say whether a specific confidence interval does or does not contain a given examinee's true score. In fact, an examinee's true score can be far outside a confidence interval. We might be tempted to make a statement such as "90% of the examinees with observed scores of 25 have true scores between 18.4 and 31.6," but such a statement would not necessarily be accurate. For example, suppose our sample contains only examinees with true scores of 33, and some of these examinees have obtained observed scores of 25. In this sample none of the examinees with observed scores of 25 had true scores between 18.4 and 31.6.

Another disadvantage of the use of confidence intervals of the form $x \pm z_c s_E$ is that the assumptions of normality and homoscedasticity may not be true. For example, it is easy to imagine that some examinees who are erratic or moody will have larger standard errors of measurement than the more stable examinees. It is also easy to imagine that the distribution (over repeated independent testings) of observed scores for an examinee with a very high true score will tend to be negatively skewed (Section 2.5); that is, because of a ceiling effect, most of this examinee's observed scores would be the maximum possible test score, and few observed scores would fall below the maximum score. Similarly, a floor effect would be expected to produce a positively skewed distribution. If standard errors of measurement are not homoscedastic and errors are not normally distributed, confidence intervals of the form $x \pm z_c s_E$ will be misleading.

The binomial-error model, presented in Section 11.3, describes a method of estimating standard errors of measurement that does not depend on the assumption of homoscedasticity. The model also assumes that a distribution of observed scores (over repeated independent testings) for one examinee is a binomial distribution. The binomial distribution can be positively or negatively skewed, and in many cases (for example, when there are floor or ceiling effects) the binomial-distribution assumption makes more sense than a normal-distribution assumption. Use of the binomial error model involves more complex mathematics than that used so far in this book. When a test developer or test user is unable to use a more complex model, the easily obtained $s_E = s_X \sqrt{1 - r_{XX'}}$ can be used as a rough estimate of $\sigma_E$, and the normal-distribution assumption can be used to obtain rough estimates of confidence intervals. However, the test user should be aware that standard errors and confidence intervals based on the assumptions of homoscedasticity and normality can be inaccurate and misleading, particularly for true scores that are far away from the average true score for a sample.

## 4.9  Summary

Reliability (symbolized by $\rho_{XX'}$) can be defined in several ways—such as the proportion of observed-score variance that is true-score variance, the squared correlation between true scores and observed scores, or the correlation between observed scores on two parallel tests. Several estimates of $\rho_{XX'}$ are widely used, including test/retest, parallel-forms, alternate-forms, and internal-consistency estimates. These estimates have different properties and generally are not identical.

Coefficient $\alpha$ and the Kuder-Richardson method (Equations 4.2 through 4.5) provide a lower-bound estimate for a test's reliability, using scores based on one administration of the test. Coefficient $\alpha$ (Equations 4.2 and 4.3) and the Kuder-Richardson formulas give the test reliability if the components of the test are essentially $\tau$-equivalent. Kuder-Richardson formula 20 (KR20, Equation 4.4) gives the reliability of a test where components are dichotomous items. Kuder-Richardson formula 21 (KR21, Equation 4.5) is less than or equal to KR20; KR21 equals the test reliability if the dichotomous items in the test have equal difficulties.

The Spearman-Brown formula (Equations 4.1 and 4.7) is useful for estimating the reliability of a test with altered length. It offers reasonable estimates if the test length is changed by adding or omitting parallel versions of the original test items.

Since reliability tends to be lower for shorter tests, test users should be careful when shortening tests and when comparing scores based on short tests.

The standard error of measurement, $\sigma_E$, is the standard deviation of error scores for a specific examinee under repeated independent testings with the same test or parallel tests. The standard error of measurement can be estimated from the standard deviation of the observed scores and the estimated reliability for a group of examinees, using the formula $\hat{\sigma}_E = s_E = s_X \sqrt{1 - r_{XX'}}$, if it is assumed that $\sigma_E$ is equal for all examinees. By making several assumptions, the standard error of measurement can be used to make confidence-interval estimates for true scores. However, great care must be taken in interpreting these confidence intervals.

## 4.10   Vocabulary

$\alpha(20)$

$\alpha(21)$

alternate-forms reliability

carry-over effect

coefficient $\alpha$

confidence intervals for true scores

homoscedasticity

internal-consistency reliability

KR20

KR21

Kuder-Richardson formulas

matched random subsets

odd/even reliability

parallel-forms reliability

power test

reliability

Spearman-Brown formula

speed test

split-half reliability

stepped-up reliability

test/retest reliability

## 4.11   Study Questions

1. Explain the implications of each of the alternative interpretations of the reliability coefficient.
2. Describe how each of the following reliability estimates is calculated:
   a. test/retest
   b. parallel forms
   c. alternate forms
   d. internal consistency by split halves
   e. internal consistency in general
   f. Spearman-Brown
3. What are the differences between parallel forms and alternate forms? When does an alternate-forms reliability, $\rho_{XZ}$, equal a parallel-forms reliability, $\rho_{XX'}$?
4. How can carry-over effects affect test/retest, parallel-forms, and alternate-forms reliability estimates?

5. How can the length of the time interval between testings affect test/retest, parallel-forms, and alternate-forms reliability estimates?

6. Explain why the Spearman-Brown formula or coefficient $\alpha$ is used when split-half reliabilities are calculated.

7. Show that the Spearman-Brown formula (Equation 4.1) produces the same result as coefficient $\alpha$ (Equation 4.2) when $\sigma_{Y_1}^2 = \sigma_{Y_2}^2$. (Hint: use Equations 2.48 and 2.51.)

8. Describe three methods for choosing split halves of a test. How can each of these methods be used to form thirds of a test?

9. Explain why internal-consistency estimates of reliability are inappropriate for speed tests.

10. Explain why coefficient $\alpha$ and Kuder-Richardson reliability estimates should be used only for homogeneous tests
   a. by examining the coefficient $\alpha$ and Kuder-Richardson formulas.
   b. by examining the definition of essential $\tau$-equivalence.

11. What assumptions are necessary for appropriate use of the Spearman-Brown formula?

12. Explain how to use the Spearman-Brown formula
   a. to calculate the reliability of a test of a different length.
   b. to calculate the length of test required to achieve a given reliability.
   c. to compare the reliabilities of two tests that are of different lengths.

13. Explain how to calculate confidence intervals for true scores.

14. What assumptions underlie the calculation of confidence intervals for true scores, and how might these assumptions be violated?

15. How are confidence intervals for true scores interpreted?

## 4.12  Computational Problems

1. If $\rho_{XX'} = .8$ and $\sigma_X^2 = 25$, what are $\rho_{XT}, \rho_{XE}, \sigma_T^2,$ and $\sigma_E^2$?

2. If $\sigma_E^2 = 0$, what are $\rho_{XT}$ and $\rho_{XX'}$?

3. You calculate a split-half reliability estimate and observe a correlation of .8 between the two halves. What is the estimated reliability of your test?

4. What is the estimated reliability of a test if the variance of scores on the first half of the test is 20, the variance of scores on the second half of the test is 25, and the variance of total test scores is 60?

5. A test is split in half. The scores on the first half of the test have a variance of 10, and scores on the second half of the test have a variance of 15. The correlation between the scores on the two halves is .50. The variance of the total test score is 37.2.
   a. Calculate the reliability of the entire test using coefficient $\alpha$.
   b. Calculate the reliability using the Spearman-Brown formula.

6. Form two matched random subsets using the items below.

| | | | | Item | | | | |
|---|---|---|---|---|---|---|---|---|
| | 1 | 2 | 3 | 4 | 5 | 6 | 7 | 8 |
| $r_{\text{item, test}}$ | .7 | .4 | .1 | .5 | .7 | .8 | .8 | .2 |
| % passing item | .1 | .3 | .9 | .3 | .2 | .6 | .7 | .9 |

7. For the items below, calculate (a) the Kuder-Richardson formula 20 and (b) the Kuder-Richardson formula 21 reliability estimates. The total test score variance for this test is 5.

| | | | | Item | | | | |
|---|---|---|---|---|---|---|---|---|
| | 1 | 2 | 3 | 4 | 5 | 6 | 7 | 8 |
| $p_i$ | .3 | .4 | .1 | .2 | .8 | .3 | .4 | .5 |

8. A 20-item test has an observed-score variance of 10 and a mean of 12. What is the KR 21 reliability for this test?

9. You have an 80-item test with an estimated reliability of .9. Estimate the reliability of a 40-item version of this test.

10. You have a 25-item test with an estimated reliability of .7. If you expanded it to a 100-item test by adding parallel items, what reliability would you expect to have?

11. You have a 50-item test with an estimated reliability of .75. How long would the test have to be in order to expect a reliability of .90?

12. An examinee receives a score of 107 on a test with a standard deviation of 10 and a reliability of .85. What is the 90% confidence interval for the examinee's true score?

# Validity

## 5.1 Introduction

A test has *validity* if it measures what it purports to measure. For example, a test that is used to screen job applicants is valid if its scores are highly related to examinees' future performance on the job. A valid intelligence test discriminates among people who vary in intelligence. A valid personality test generates scores that reflect meaningful differences in personality. Both the test developer and the test user have a responsibility to ensure that the tests they provide and use are valid tests.

Validity can be assessed in several ways, depending on the test and its intended use. The three major types of validity are content validity, criterion-related validity, and construct validity. Determinations of criterion-related validity and construct validity involve the calculation and examination of correlations or other statistics. Content validity, however, does not involve any statistical calculations.

## 5.2 Content Validity

*Content validity* is established through a rational analysis of the content of a test, and its determination is based on individual, subjective judgment. There are two main types of content validity: face validity and logical validity.

*Face validity*, sometimes called "armchair" validity, is established when a person examines the test and concludes that it measures the relevant trait. The person making this examination can be anyone from an expert to an examinee. If people disagree, face validity is in question. Face validity may be sufficient to justify the use of some tests. The classroom exam, when carefully prepared, has face validity. For example, an arithmetic test, on the "face" of it, measures arithmetic performance. Face validity may be essential for some tests because of their intended use. For example, it would be bad for a firm's public relations if the test used to screen job applicants had no apparent relationship to the job, even if the test was effective in identifying those people most likely to be good workers. Face validity can be crucial for effective test use, although in some cases face validity is not essential if the test is valid in other ways.

*Logical* or *sampling validity* is a more sophisticated version of face validity. It involves the careful definition of the domain of behaviors to be measured by a test and the logical design of items to cover all the important areas of this domain. Logical validity is especially useful in the development of achievement tests. The grid in Figure 5.1 represents a possible plan for an achievement test in history. The top left element in the grid represents all the items that measure knowledge of dates in African history. Other test items would sample the content areas of the other cells in the grid. The test could be developed with either equal or unequal proportions of items representing each cell, depending on the test developer's evaluation of each cell's relative importance.

Because content validity is based on subjective judgments, the determination of this type of validity is more subject to error than are other types of validity. But, generally, establishing content validity is the first concern in the development of all tests, and items are written to meet content-validity requirements. Through statistical item-analysis techniques, the test can be revised and improved to guarantee that other aspects of good measurement are achieved. Usually, the mere fact that a test has content validity is not a sufficient justification for its use. Before it is used, the test should have proven effectiveness, such as criterion-related validity.

|  | African History | Asian History | European History | Latin-American History | North-American History |
|---|---|---|---|---|---|
| Dates |  |  |  |  |  |
| Economic Changes |  |  |  |  |  |
| Social Changes |  |  |  |  |  |
| Political Movements |  |  |  |  |  |

Figure 5.1. Plan for a history-achievement test

## 5.3   Criterion-Related Validity

*Criterion-related validity* is used when test scores can be related to a criterion. The *criterion* is some behavior that the test scores are used to predict. For example, in order to have criterion-related validity, scores on a test designed to screen job applicants must be related to the criterion of work effectiveness. Similarly, in order to have criterion-related validity, scores on a school-admissions test must be related to some relevant criterion, such as later grade-point averages of the accepted students or percentage of students who complete their programs and receive degrees.

Criterion-related validity typically is expressed as a correlation coefficient —the correlation between the test (*predictor*) score and the criterion score. This correlation is symbolized $\rho_{XY}$, where $X$ is the test score and $Y$ is the criterion score. The *validity coefficient*, $\rho_{XY}$, is estimated in one of two ways, resulting in either a predictive- or a concurrent-validity estimate.

Predictive validity involves using test scores to predict future behavior. A *predictive-validity coefficient* is obtained by giving the test to all relevant people, waiting a reasonable amount of time, collecting criterion scores, and calculating the validity coefficient. For example, the predictive validity for an employment test would be established by testing every job applicant, hiring every applicant, waiting a few weeks or months until the criterion can be assessed reasonably and reliably (for example, by supervisors' ratings or by some other measure of job performance), and correlating the scores on the predictor (the test) and the criterion (job performance). This procedure would give a good indication of how well the test scores predict future behavior, but it can be expensive and time consuming. If the employer is not willing to hire all applicants, there probably will be restriction of range on both the predictor and criterion. As shown in Section 2.10, restriction of range generally attenuates (reduces) an observed correlation coefficient, leading to an underestimate of the predictive-validity coefficient.

When a test is used to predict future behavior, predictive validity should be established. A less desirable alternative in this situation is to use a concurrent-validity coefficient. A *concurrent-validity coefficient* is a correlation between test and criterion scores when both measurements are obtained at the same time. For the employment-test examples just given, the concurrent-validity coefficient would be the correlation between the predictor and the criterion scores when both measurements are made on present employees at the same time, rather than being separated by a time interval. This often involves a large restriction of range, especially on the criterion, since most people who could not or do not perform satisfactorily on the job would not be hired or would be fired by the time the validity study took place. Thus, the concurrent-validity coefficient would tend to underestimate a predictive-validity coefficient.

Concurrent-validity coefficients are appropriate when the test scores are used to estimate a concurrent criterion rather than to predict a future criterion. For example, the *Minnesota Multiphasic Personality Inventory* (MMPI) is an extremely long (almost 600-item) personality test. A counselor might give a brief personality test to all clients and reserve the MMPI for clients whose scores on the brief test suggest that they might have particularly interesting MMPI scores. This two-step process would be reasonable only if the scores on the brief test were related to the MMPI scores. The counselor needs to demonstrate concurrent validity for the brief test as the predictor and the MMPI scores as the criteria.

## 5.4   Correction for Attenuation

We pointed out in Section 4.1 that the reliability of a test affects the validity of the test, since, theoretically, a test cannot correlate more highly with any other score than it correlates with its own true score; that is, $\rho_{XY} \leqslant \rho_{XT}$ or $\rho_{XY} \leqslant \sqrt{\rho_{XX'}}$. If both a test score, $X$, and a criterion score, $Y$, are unreliable, the validity coefficient, $\rho_{XY}$, may be reduced in value (attenuated) relative to the value of the validity coefficient that would be obtained if $X$ and $Y$ did not contain measurement error. An estimate of the correlation that would be found if $X$ and $Y$ were perfectly reliable can be obtained with the *correction for attenuation,* which was first developed by Spearman (1904). The correction for attenuation gives the correlation between $T_X$ and $T_Y$ under the classical model,

$$\rho_{T_X T_Y} = \frac{\rho_{XY}}{\sqrt{\rho_{XX'} \rho_{YY'}}} .$$  (5.1)

In this equation, $\rho_{T_X T_Y}$ is the correlation between the true score for $X$ and the true score for $Y$ or the correlation between $X$ and $Y$ if there is no error of measurement in either observed score; $\rho_{XY}$ is the correlation of observed scores $X$ and $Y$, which includes error of measurement; and $\rho_{XX'}$ and $\rho_{YY'}$ are the reliabilities of $X$ and $Y$. The correction for attenuation appears as Conclusion 14 in Chapter 3.

We can also correct for attenuation due to unreliability only in the predictor or only in the criterion. For example,

$$\rho_{XT_Y} = \frac{\rho_{XY}}{\sqrt{\rho_{YY'}}}$$  (5.2)

would be the correlation between $X$ and $Y$ if the measurement of $Y$ were perfectly reliable. This would be a reasonable correction when a validity coefficient is attenuated due to unreliability in the criterion measurement.

The correction for attenuation has one application that is particularly useful. Suppose that a single test is needed to predict an important criterion. There are several brief tests (of approximately the same length) under consideration, each with a different reliability and validity. The test developer wants to choose the most promising test and lengthen it to improve its reliability. Given the data in Table 5.1, which test is best? Tests A and B have the same validity coefficients but different reliabilities. Test C has a lower validity coefficient but is also the least reliable.

Table 5.1. Hypothetical Reliabilities and
Validities for Three Tests

| Test | Reliability | Validity |
|------|-------------|----------|
| A | .3 | .5 |
| B | .4 | .5 |
| C | .2 | .4 |

Assuming that the reliability of each of the tests can be improved by adding more items, the test with the largest corrected validity coefficient is the one with the highest potential validity. If the reliability of the criterion is .95, the corrected validities are $.5/\sqrt{(.3)(.95)} \doteq .937$ for A, $.5/\sqrt{(.4)(.95)} \doteq .811$ for B, and $.4/\sqrt{(.2)(.95)} \doteq .918$ for C. Therefore, the greatest validities can be expected by lengthening test A or test C.

The calculations in the preceding paragraph do not guarantee a validity greater than .9. The corrected values are the maximum coefficients that are obtainable if measurement errors could be totally eliminated. Since total elimination of measurement error generally is not possible, we cannot expect to observe the values of correlations corrected for attenuation. Also, it is important that accurate reliability estimates be used in the correction for attenuation. If a reliability is underestimated, a misleading overestimate of $\rho_{T_X T_Y}$ will be obtained from Equation 5.1. Furthermore, the error of measurement that affects $\rho_{XY}$ should be the same error of measurement that affects $\rho_{XX'}$ and $\rho_{YY'}$. For example, an estimate of $\rho_{XY}$ that is obtained from the results of one testing session will not be attenuated by changes in $X$ or $Y$ due to changes in mood or testing conditions over a long time lapse. If $\rho_{XX'}$ or $\rho_{YY'}$ were estimated using an alternate-forms design with a three-week time lapse between testings, error of measurement would be included in $\rho_{XX'}$ or $\rho_{YY'}$ (that is, error of measurement due to the time lapse and change in test form) that would not be included in $\rho_{XY}$. The result would be an underestimate of $\rho_{XX'}$ and $\rho_{YY'}$ and an overestimate of $\rho_{T_X T_Y}$. When $\rho_{XY}$ is estimated by administering $X$ and $Y$ during one testing session, $\rho_{XX'}$ and $\rho_{YY'}$ can be estimated by appropriate internal-consistency methods (Sections 4.4 and 4.5) using scores for $X$ and $Y$ from that testing session.

## 5.5  Estimating a Criterion from a Predictor

This section describes how scores on a test can be used to estimate or predict criterion scores. The discussion uses an example from a predictive-validity study, but all the developments in this section are equally applicable to a concurrent-validity study.

The first step in predicting a criterion is to secure a representative sample of examinees and obtain a predictor score, $X$, and a criterion score, $Y$, for each examinee. From these data, a predictive equation is obtained that can be used for subsequent predictions for examinees with known predictor scores and unknown criterion scores. For example, the sample might consist of all the freshmen at a certain college who have taken a particular entrance examination. Exam scores, $X$, and grade-point averages, $Y$, are obtained for everyone in the sample. As described in Section 2.9, the best linear least-squares prediction of $Y$ for the $i$th person is

$$\hat{Y}_i = r_{XY} \left(\frac{s_Y}{s_X}\right) (X_i - \bar{X}) + \bar{Y}. \tag{5.3}$$

$\hat{Y}_i$ is the best *point estimate* (single-number estimate) for $Y_i$ in terms of least squared error. The statistics necessary to use this equation ($r_{XY}$, $s_X$, $s_Y$, $\bar{X}$, and $\bar{Y}$) are calculated from the representative sample. Entrance-exam scores, $X_i$, can then be used to predict future grade-point averages, $\hat{Y}_i$, for all applicants to the college in later years.

Unless there is perfect prediction, $r_{XY} = \pm 1$, a person's $\hat{Y}_i$ is not expected to exactly equal his or her (unknown) $Y_i$; that is, the point estimate of a criterion score rarely is identical to the person's actual criterion score. Although $\hat{Y}_i$ is not expected to equal $Y_i$ exactly, a confidence interval for $Y_i$ can be constructed. Section 2.9 describes the three assumptions required to derive a confidence-interval estimate: (1) the relationship between $X$ and $Y$ is linear, (2) $s_{Y \cdot x}$ is the same for all $x$ (this is an assumption of homoscedasticity), and (3) the conditional distribution of $Y$ given $X$ is normal. When these assumptions are met, the confidence interval for $Y_i$ is

$$\hat{Y}_i \pm z_c \, s_{Y \cdot X}, \tag{5.4}$$

where $z_c$ is the critical value from the normal table and

$$s_{Y \cdot X} = s_Y \sqrt{1 - r_{XY}^2}. \tag{5.5}$$

A 90% confidence interval, $\hat{Y}_i \pm (1.65)s_{Y \cdot X}$, is illustrated in Figure 5.2. The approximate normal curve is the conditional distribution of $Y$ for a fixed value of $X$, $X_i$. This conditional distribution has mean $\hat{Y}_i$ (the point on the regression line

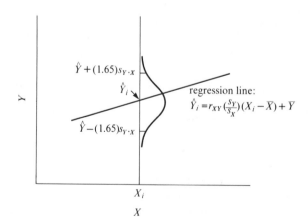

Figure 5.2. Illustration of a confidence interval for linear regression

corresponding to the fixed $X_i$) and standard deviation $s_{Y \cdot X}$. If such confidence intervals are created for every examinee and the assumptions of linearity, homoscedasticity, and normality are true, 90% of the confidence intervals will contain examinees' $Y_i$ scores.

Reporting predicted scores in terms of confidence intervals makes it clear that the prediction can contain error. For example, let us calculate the point estimate, $\hat{Y}_i$, and interval estimate, $\hat{Y}_i \pm z_c s_{Y \cdot X}$, for the example of the college-admissions exam. Assume that $X$ is the admissions-test score and $Y$ is the grade-point average. Further assume that $r_{XY} = .6, \bar{X} = 10, \bar{Y} = 2, s_X = 3$, and $s_Y = 1$. The $i$th person's test score, $X_i$, equals 8. The estimate of $Y_i$ is

$$\hat{Y}_i = .6 \left(\frac{1}{3}\right) (8 - 10) + 2 = 1.6.$$

The 90% confidence-interval estimate for $Y_i$ is
$$1.6 \pm (1.65)(1) \sqrt{1 - (.6)^2}$$

$$= 1.6 \pm 1.32, \text{ or } .28 \text{ to } 2.92.$$

The point estimate, $\hat{Y}_i = 1.6$, suggests that the person's predicted grade-point average is almost half a standard deviation below average. The confidence-interval estimate indicates that the point estimate may be far from accurate. The width of this confidence interval demonstrates the general need to consider carefully the implied accuracy of point estimates. This is especially true when $r_{XY}$ is low.

Keep in mind that if any of the three required assumptions are not true, confidence intervals of the form $\hat{Y}_i \pm z_c s_{Y \cdot X}$ can be misleading. These assumptions are likely to be violated if there is a floor or ceiling effect for $X$ or $Y$. Also, the confidence intervals developed in this way do not take errors due to unreliability of measurement into account in any direct way, although unreliability will tend to attenuate $r_{XY}$, producing wider intervals. If measurement is made with some error due to unreliability, a person's $X$ will vary with repeated measurements of $X$, yielding different confidence intervals for $Y$ for the different observed values of $X$.

## 5.6    Screening into Dichotomous Categories

A criterion-related test is often used for screening people into dichotomous categories (for example, "hire" and "do not hire" or "accept" and "do not accept"). This procedure involves setting a *cutting score* and placing people who obtain a score equal to or higher than the cutting score in one category and all other people in the other category. Table 5.2 shows the two types of errors that are possible in this process: predicting that a "successful" person will be "unsuccessful" and predicting that an "unsuccessful" person will be "successful."

If we make a number of predictions, a reasonable index of predictive accuracy is the *hit rate*—the percentage of predictions that are correct. For the data in Table 5.3, 100 predictions are made. Of the 40 people who are predicted to be successful, 30 actually are successful. Of the 60 people who are predicted to be

Table 5.2. Possible Outcomes in a Dichotomous Screening Situation

|  |  | Predicted Outcome | |
|  |  | Successful | Unsuccessful |
| --- | --- | --- | --- |
| Actual Outcome | Successful | correct | error |
|  | Unsuccessful | error | correct |

Table 5.3. Illustration of a 70% Hit Rate

|  |  | Predicted Outcome | | |
|  |  | Successful | Unsuccessful | Total |
| --- | --- | --- | --- | --- |
| Actual Outcome | Successful | 30 | 20 | 50 |
|  | Unsuccessful | 10 | 40 | 50 |
|  | Total | 40 | 60 | 100 |

Hit rate = (30 + 40)/100 = .70.

unsuccessful, 40 actually are unsuccessful. For this data the hit rate is 70%, and the error rate is 30%.

What represents a good hit rate? At first glance 90% would appear to be a good hit rate and 25% would appear to be poor. However, 90% is not good if an alternative test yields a 100% hit rate, and 25% may be excellent if the best alternative procedure has a 5% hit rate. In these examples the 100% and the 5% are base rates. A *base rate* is the best hit rate among all procedures that are possible alternatives to the procedure (test) being examined. To be valuable, a test should improve upon the base rate. For example, for the data in Table 5.4, the hit rate is 83%. If there is no alternative test for psychopathology, to what base rate can we compare the 83%? Notice that 90% of the people in the sample do not have any psychopathology. Therefore, if "no psychopathology" is predicted for each of the 100 people in the sample, the prediction would be correct 90% of the time. By making the same prediction each time (without using any test), a hit rate of 90% could be obtained. Thus, 90% could be used as the base rate. Since 83% is less than 90%, our test is worse than no test at all! For situations in which base rates for alternative tests or procedures are not available, the proportion of people with the more frequently occurring actual outcome is the base rate for comparisons. In the dichotomous case illustrated in Table 5.3, the base rate calculated in this way is 50%. Even poor tests often have hit rates greater than 50%. As the base rate becomes larger, it becomes harder for a test to improve on the base rate. Therefore, predictions of rare events (such as severe psychopathology) are extremely difficult to make with a hit rate greater than the base rate.

Table 5.4. Illustration of a 90% Base Rate

|  |  | Predicted Outcome | | Total |
|  |  | Psychopathology | No Psychopathology | |
|---|---|---|---|---|
| Actual Outcome | Psychopathology | 7 | 3 | 10 |
| | No Psychopathology | 14 | 76 | 90 |
| | Total | 21 | 79 | 100 |

Hit rate = (7 + 76)/100 = .83.

In determining the hit rate in the preceding discussion, we assumed that both types of errors were equal in importance. However, there are cases in which making one type of error is much more severe than making the other type of error. Suppose, in the preceding example, that the psychopathology in question leads the person to commit violent crimes and that preventive therapy (with or without psychopathology present) is, at the worst, merely inconvenient. In such a situation, predicting psychopathology when none is actually present would not be so severe an error as predicting no psychopathology when it is actually present. Consider the data in Table 5.4, and imagine that facilities are available for treating no more than 21 people (that is, 21% of the sample). If the test were used for selecting people for therapy, Table 5.4 indicates that 14 people would have unnecessary therapy, seven people would be deterred from violence, and three would commit violent crimes. If no one is treated, ten people would commit violent crimes. If 21 randomly selected people are treated, then about two people (21% of the ten people with psychopathology) will be deterred from violence and about eight will commit violent crimes. In this situation the use of the test would lead to fewer violent crimes. If no better test were available and if the therapist could not treat every person, the test would be recommended over the only alternatives, which are to treat no one or to treat as many randomly selected people as possible. (The recommendation to use this test does not imply that a better test should not be sought.)

To find the best cutting score for a test, test-score frequency distributions for successful and unsuccessful people are computed as illustrated in Table 5.5. In this example a score of 17 is earned by eight successful people and one unsuccessful person. What cutting score will yield the best hit rate? If the cutting score is 16 (that is, those with scores of 16 or higher are predicted to be successful), the hit rate would be 84.5%, as shown in Table 5.6. Since no other cutting score could improve this hit rate (try a few yourself to verify this), the best cutting score is 16. Therefore, we would predict that anyone scoring 16 or higher would be successful. However, if the two kinds of classification errors differ in importance, this cutting score would not be ideal. If predicting that an unsuccessful person is successful is the more severe error, the best cutting score might be 19. On the other hand, if predicting that a potentially successful person would be unsuccessful is the worse error, the cutting score should

Table 5.5. Test Score Frequency Distributions for Successful
and Unsuccessful People

| Score | Successful | Unsuccessful |
|-------|-----------|--------------|
| 20 | 3 | 0 |
| 19 | 5 | 0 |
| 18 | 12 | 2 |
| 17 | 8 | 1 |
| 16 | 10 | 2 |
| 15 | 4 | 5 |
| 14 | 1 | 8 |
| 13 | 1 | 10 |
| 12 | 2 | 7 |
| 11 | 1 | 5 |
| 10 | 1 | 4 |
| 9 | 0 | 3 |
| 8 | 0 | 2 |
| *Total* | 48 | 49 |

Table 5.6. Classification of People Using a Cutting Score of 16

|  |  | Predicted Outcome | | Total |
|--|--|-------------------|--|-------|
|  |  | Successful | Unsuccessful | |
| Actual Outcome | Successful | 38 | 10 | 48 |
|  | Unsuccessful | 5 | 44 | 49 |
|  | Total | 43 | 54 | 97 |

Hit rate = (38 + 44)/97 $\doteq$ 84.5.

be lower—perhaps as low as 10. The concept of expected utility, which is described in Section 9.4, can be used when choosing cutting scores in order to take into consideration the differential importance of different types of classification errors.

Because the cutting score influences decisions that affect individuals, the person who sets the cutting score should consider carefully the relative importance of the errors, as well as classification errors due to unreliability of test measurement. In addition, the position of the cutting score should be evaluated periodically and altered, if necessary.

## 5.7   Taylor-Russell Tables

In the previous section the effectiveness of a test is evaluated by comparing its hit rate to the base rate. Predictive- or concurrent-validity coefficients can be compared in a similar fashion. However, demonstrating that one validity coefficient is significantly better than another or significantly different from zero does not help in understanding how much the test can improve predictive accuracy in applied settings. For example, if a test's validity coefficient is .50, should the test be used in selecting job applicants? The answer depends on many things, including the *base rate* (the proportion of applicants who would be successful) and the *selection ratio* (the proportion of applicants who are chosen or admitted).

Taylor and Russell (1939) developed a technique that is helpful in evaluating the effectiveness of a test used for selection decisions, such as hiring job applicants or admitting students to a school. This technique assumes that the test scores, $X$, are used to predict criterion scores, $Y$ (such as job-performance ratings or grade-point averages), and that the criterion can be dichotomized into "successful" and "unsuccessful" categories. For example, workers who produce more than 18 units per hour on an assembly line could be classified as successful, and all other workers would be classified as unsuccessful. Or, students who obtain a "C" average or better could be classified as successful, and all other students would be classified as unsuccessful. If a test with a known validity coefficient, $\rho_{XY}$, is available and the base rate and selection ratio are known, we can estimate what proportion of applicants who are selected on the basis of their test scores will be classified as successful. Taylor and Russell calculated these proportions by assuming that the distribution of the predictor scores, $X$, and the criterion scores, $Y$, is bivariate normal (see Section 2.11). The assumption of bivariate normality would be violated if either $X$ or $Y$ exhibits a floor or ceiling effect (Sections 3.1 and 6.7).

Using the assumption of bivariate normality, Taylor and Russell developed a series of tables like the one reproduced in Table 5.7. The numbers in the body of a *Taylor-Russell table* give the probability that an applicant selected on the basis of a test score will be successful, given the specific base rate, validity coefficient, and selection ratio. Table 5.7 gives this information for a base rate of .60; that is, if every applicant were selected, 60% of them would be successful. (Tables for other base rates are available from Taylor and Russell [1939].) If a test has a validity coefficient of .50 and the top 10% of job applicants are selected (a selection ratio of .10), we can see from the table that 90% of those selected would be successful. The test improves upon the base rate by .30.

An examination of the Taylor-Russell table reveals a number of interesting points. Glance down a few columns and notice that, as the validity of the test increases, predictive accuracy also increases, as you would expect. Glance across a few rows and notice that, as the selection ratio increases, predictive accuracy decreases. If we apply these observations to our preceding example, we will see that, when it is necessary to hire a larger proportion of job applicants, the chances of hiring some poor workers increase. This effect would occur even with perfect validity; since the base rate is 60%, if more than 60% of the applicants are hired, some poor workers must be hired. Scanning the table reveals that even a test with a low validity can substantially improve on the base rate if the selection ratio is very low, because only those applicants who have unusually high test scores are hired. As before, the base rate is important. The highest possible improvement over the base rate is 1

Table 5.7. Taylor-Russell Table for a Base Rate of .60*

| Validity $(\rho_{XY})$ | Selection Ratio | | | | | | | | | | |
|---|---|---|---|---|---|---|---|---|---|---|---|
| | .05 | .10 | .20 | .30 | .40 | .50 | .60 | .70 | .80 | .90 | .95 |
| .00 | .60 | .60 | .60 | .60 | .60 | .60 | .60 | .60 | .60 | .60 | .60 |
| .05 | .64 | .63 | .63 | .62 | .62 | .62 | .61 | .61 | .61 | .60 | .60 |
| .10 | .68 | .67 | .65 | .64 | .64 | .63 | .63 | .62 | .61 | .61 | .60 |
| .15 | .71 | .70 | .68 | .67 | .66 | .65 | .64 | .63 | .62 | .61 | .61 |
| .20 | .75 | .73 | .71 | .69 | .67 | .66 | .65 | .64 | .63 | .62 | .61 |
| .25 | .78 | .76 | .73 | .71 | .69 | .68 | .66 | .65 | .63 | .62 | .61 |
| .30 | .82 | .79 | .76 | .73 | .71 | .69 | .68 | .66 | .64 | .62 | .61 |
| .35 | .85 | .82 | .78 | .75 | .73 | .71 | .69 | .67 | .65 | .63 | .62 |
| .40 | .88 | .85 | .81 | .78 | .75 | .73 | .70 | .68 | .66 | .63 | .62 |
| .45 | .90 | .87 | .83 | .80 | .77 | .74 | .72 | .69 | .66 | .64 | .62 |
| .50 | .93 | .90 | .86 | .82 | .79 | .76 | .73 | .70 | .67 | .64 | .62 |
| .55 | .95 | .92 | .88 | .84 | .81 | .78 | .75 | .71 | .68 | .64 | .62 |
| .60 | .96 | .94 | .90 | .87 | .83 | .80 | .76 | .73 | .69 | .65 | .63 |
| .65 | .98 | .96 | .92 | .89 | .85 | .82 | .78 | .74 | .70 | .65 | .63 |
| .70 | .99 | .97 | .94 | .91 | .87 | .84 | .80 | .75 | .71 | .66 | .63 |
| .75 | .99 | .99 | .96 | .93 | .90 | .86 | .81 | .77 | .71 | .66 | .63 |
| .80 | 1.00 | .99 | .98 | .95 | .92 | .88 | .83 | .78 | .72 | .66 | .63 |
| .85 | 1.00 | 1.00 | .99 | .97 | .95 | .91 | .86 | .80 | .73 | .66 | .63 |
| .90 | 1.00 | 1.00 | 1.00 | .99 | .97 | .94 | .88 | .82 | .74 | .67 | .63 |
| .95 | 1.00 | 1.00 | 1.00 | 1.00 | .99 | .97 | .92 | .84 | .75 | .67 | .63 |
| 1.00 | 1.00 | 1.00 | 1.00 | 1.00 | 1.00 | 1.00 | 1.00 | .86 | .75 | .67 | .63 |

The numbers in the body of the table show the proportions of people who will be judged successful when selection is made on the basis of a test of given validity when the base rate is .60.

*From "The Relationship of Validity Coefficients to the Practical Effectiveness of Tests in Selection: Discussion and Tables" by H. C. Taylor and J. T. Russell, *Journal of Applied Psychology,* 1939, *23,* 565–578. Copyright (1939) by the American Psychological Association. Reprinted by permission.

minus the base rate, or .40 for a base rate of .60. For a lower base rate, a greater improvement over the base rate can be obtained.

The Taylor-Russell tables can be used in several ways, as illustrated by the following problems.

1. Suppose we have a base rate of 60% and a validity coefficient of .40. If there are 400 job applicants and 80 workers are hired, how many of those hired probably will be good workers?

Since the base rate is .60, we can use Table 5.7. With validity = .40 and a selection ratio of 80/400 = .20, we obtain a probability of .81. Of the 80 hired workers, 81% (or about 65 workers) should be good employees.

2. Suppose the base rate is 60%, 30% of the job applicants will be hired, and we want at least 95% of those hired to be successful. What is the minimum validity a test must have to satisfy these requirements?

Searching in Table 5.7 for a selection ratio of .30 and a table entry of .95, we find that the required minimum validity coefficient is .80.

3. Suppose the base rate is .60 and the test has a validity of .40. If there are 100 applicants and 42 good workers are needed, how many people should be hired?

In Table 5.7 we must find a selection ratio such that, when validity equals .40, 42 good workers are hired. If the selection ratio is .60, 70% of 60 hired workers would be good. To obtain 42 good workers, at least 60 applicants should be hired.

The preceding examples illustrate how the Taylor-Russell tables can aid the industrial psychologist or personnel manager. However, the use of the tables is not restricted to management problems. The Taylor-Russell tables can be applied to any situation with a dichotomous criterion and a fixed selection ratio. For example, a therapist might classify clients into two categories: ''substantially improved'' and ''not substantially improved.'' A personality test could be used as the predictor, and the selection ratio would be the proportion of potential clients who are accepted into therapy. Suppose the base rate (proportion of clients who are substantially improved) is .60 and the therapist can accept 70% of the potential clients. If the test has a validity of .65, the therapist could increase his or her proportion of substantially improved clients to .74—an increase of .14 over the base rate.

There is one major problem associated with the use of the Taylor-Russell tables: only one type of error is taken into account. The proportions in the body of the table are the probabilities that selected people are successful. However, the unselected people who could have been successful are ignored. From the economic perspective of the employer, the worse error is to hire a poor worker; therefore, the Taylor-Russell tables are sufficient for cost-efficient recruiting. However, from the perspective of the applicant who is not selected, the untabled error is much more important. This untabled error can be calculated. For example, if there are 200 applicants, the selection ratio is .20, the validity coefficient is .60, and the base rate is .60, then 90% of the selected applicants will be successful. Using this information, a table can be constructed, such as the one given in Table 5.8. As an exercise, verify the numbers in this table. (The numbers 4, 84, and 76 are obtained by subtraction.) For this example 84/160, or 52.5%, of those not selected would have been successful.

Recall that the Taylor-Russell tables are based on an assumption of bivariate normality of predictor and criterion scores. In many cases this assumption will not be appropriate. However, unless this assumption is violated badly, the Taylor-Russell tables can be used to obtain approximate information.

Table 5.8. Example of Computing All Outcomes When Using Taylor-Russell Tables

|              | Selected | Not Selected | Total |
|--------------|----------|--------------|-------|
| Successful   | 36       | 84           | 120   |
| Unsuccessful | 4        | 76           | 80    |
| Total        | 40       | 160          | 200   |

## 5.8  Multiple Predictors or Criteria

In some situations several tests are used to predict a single criterion or multiple criteria. For example, an employer may use one battery of tests for all job applicants. The test scores could then be treated differently for different jobs. That is, verbal tests might be more important for predicting secretarial performance than assembly-line performance, and manual-dexterity tests might be more important for predicting assembly-line performance than secretarial performance. The test scores would be combined in such a way that predictive errors for both jobs are minimized. Methods for dealing with the case of multiple predictors or criteria are examined in Chapter 9.

## 5.9  Construct Validity

Construct validity is the most recently developed form of validity (Cronbach & Meehl, 1955). A test's *construct validity* is the degree to which it measures the theoretical construct or trait that it was designed to measure. Establishing construct validity is an ongoing process. Based on current theory regarding the trait being measured, the test developer makes predictions about how the test scores should behave in various situations. These predictions are then tested. If the predictions are supported by the data, construct validity is enhanced. If the predictions are not supported by the data, there are at least three alternative conclusions that can be drawn: (1) the experiment was flawed, (2) the theory was wrong and should be revised, or (3) the test does not measure the trait. Although establishing construct validity is an unending process, the test developer can demonstrate the construct validity for a test in specific situations.

Any testable prediction can be made to support construct validity, including predictions of content- and criterion-related validity. Other possible predictions include:

1. Group differences. If the theory implies group differences (or no group differences) in test scores, this prediction could be studied by collecting data and conducting a reasonable statistical test of the hypothesis. For example, one might predict differences between children and adults on a test of social maturity, or one might predict no differences among cultural groups on a "culture-fair" ability test.

2. Changes. The theory may imply that test scores change with time or after experimental intervention. For example, a test measuring oral-communication skills should yield higher scores as children grow older or as children attend relevant classes in school. The theory also may predict changes in some scores but not others. For example, an assertion-training experience should increase assertiveness scores but not affect vocabulary scores.

3. Correlations. The theory might lead the test developer to predict that one or more correlations are positive, negative, or zero. For example, we might expect scores

on a test of short-term memory to be positively correlated with age and uncorrelated with sex. The predictions may involve large sets of correlations (such as in multitrait-multimethod validity, Section 5.10, and factorial validity, Section 5.11).

4. Processes. Suppose a mathematical-reasoning test contains word problems that use extremely difficult words. Based on one theory we might predict that all examinees are processing or thinking about the test items in the same way. However, another theory may lead us to expect that some examinees may be able to do the mathematics but cannot begin the problems because their vocabulary is weak. In this example the test measures mathematical reasoning for some examinees and vocabulary level for other examinees. An examination of item content and correlations among item scores or an analysis of interviews with examinees as they solve the test items may help us choose between theories about the cognitive processes underlying solutions to the test items. It may also be reasonable to predict that different processing is occurring among different individuals or groups. For example, there are sex differences on most tests of spatial reasoning. A researcher may predict that the two sexes will process spatial-test items in different ways and then test these predictions.

## 5.10  Multitrait-Multimethod Validity

*Multitrait-multimethod validity* is an aspect of construct validity that was developed by Campbell and Fiske (1959). This method is used when two or more traits are being measured by two or more methods. Suppose the two traits of introversion and neuroticism are being measured by two methods, a true-false (T-F) test and a multiple-choice (M-C) test. All four tests are given to a sample of people, and the resulting multitrait-multimethod validity matrix appears in Table 5.9. The validity matrix is similar to a *correlation matrix,* which is a rectangular display of correlations. The correlation appearing at the intersection of each row and column is the correlation between the scores labeling that row and column. For example, the correlation between neuroticism T-F scores and introversion T-F scores is .20. Usually a correlation matrix has 1.0s on its main diagonal (which runs from the upper left corner to the lower right corner of the matrix); that is, the correlation of each variable with itself is, by definition, equal to 1.0. The *multitrait-multimethod validity matrix* is a correlation matrix with 1.0s replaced by estimated reliabilities. For example, the estimated reliability of the introversion T-F scores is .80.

Consider the properties that entries in this multitrait-multimethod matrix should have. The reliabilities in the main diagonal should be large. Correlations between two different measures of one trait also should be high. Correlations between measures of unrelated traits should be low. Correlations between test scores measuring different traits should be smaller than correlations between test scores measuring the same trait. Table 5.10 summarizes the results for good multitrait-multimethod validity for traits A and B measured by methods 1 and 2.

Table 5.9. A Multitrait-Multimethod Validity Matrix

|  | Introversion T-F | Neuroticism T-F | Introversion M-C | Neuroticism M-C |
|---|---|---|---|---|
| Introversion T-F | .80 | .20 | .75 | .17 |
| Neuroticism T-F | .20 | .85 | .15 | .71 |
| Introversion M-C | .75 | .15 | .83 | .21 |
| Neuroticism M-C | .17 | .71 | .21 | .91 |

Table 5.10. Ideal Multitrait-Multimethod Validity Matrix for the 2 × 2 Case

|  | $A_1$ | $B_1$ | $A_2$ | $B_2$ |
|---|---|---|---|---|
| $A_1$ | high | low | high | low |
| $B_1$ | low | high | low | high |
| $A_2$ | high | low | high | low |
| $B_2$ | low | high | low | high |

Two main types of multitrait-multimethod validity are illustrated in Table 5.10: convergent validity and discriminant validity. *Convergent validity* is demonstrated by high correlations between scores on tests measuring the same trait by different methods (for example, $r_{A_1A_2}$, $r_{B_1B_2}$). These high correlations show that the tests converge on the trait. *Discriminant validity* is demonstrated by low correlations between scores on tests measuring different traits (for example, $r_{A_1B_1}$, $r_{A_1B_2}$, $r_{A_2B_1}$, $r_{A_2B_2}$), especially when using the same methods ($r_{A_1B_1}$, $r_{A_2B_2}$). These low correlations show that the tests discriminate between different traits. The correlations in Table 5.9 display both discriminant and convergent multitrait-multimethod validity.

When there are more than two traits or methods, the multitrait-multimethod validity matrix is larger and slightly more complicated. However, the same types of patterns should occur to demonstrate convergent and discriminant validity. The correlational pattern should have high values for reliabilities and within-trait correlations, low values for across-trait correlations, and correlations that demonstrate that there is no bias due to method. *Method bias* is present if the correlations between scores for different traits are higher when the same method is used to measure both traits than when different methods are used to measure the traits. For example, if $r_{A_1B_1}$ and $r_{A_2B_2}$ are much larger than $r_{A_1B_2}$ and $r_{A_2B_1}$, method bias is suggested because larger correlations were found when the traits were measured by the same method. However, if $r_{A_1B_1}$ is about the same as $r_{A_1B_2}$, $r_{A_2B_1}$, and $r_{A_2B_2}$, there is evidence that the traits are being measured without method bias.

## 5.11 Factorial Validity

*Factorial validity* is a form of construct validity that is established through factor analysis. *Factor analysis* is a term that represents a large number of different mathematical procedures for analyzing the interrelationships among a set of variables and for explaining these interrelationships in terms of a reduced number of variables, called factors. A *factor* is a hypothetical variable that influences scores on one or more observed variables. For example, look at the correlation matrix in Table 5.11. Although there are three test scores being correlated, it is obvious that only one factor is being measured, because of the high correlations among the test scores. Instead of requiring three scores for each person, one score alone is sufficient.

Consider the correlations in Table 5.12. Two factors are being measured by the four tests; tests 1 and 2 measure one factor, and tests 3 and 4 measure the other factor. The two factors are uncorrelated, because the two pairs of tests are uncorrelated, as indicated by the zeros in the matrix.

Now consider the correlations in Table 5.13. Again, two factors are being measured; tests 1 and 2 measure one factor, and tests 3 and 4 measure the other factor. However, this time the two factors appear to be slightly correlated, as indicated by the low correlations (.10, .20, and .30) in the matrix.

The preceding examples involve an "eyeball" method of factor analysis. From a mere visual examination of the matrix, it is obvious how many factors are present. However, when there are many variables in the correlation matrix and the interrelationships among them are complex, it is not quite so simple to determine how many factors there are, and even experts may disagree on the number of factors and their interrelationships. However, the logic underlying our simple examples remains the same for the complex cases. For a further discussion of the mathematical techniques underlying factor analysis, consult Mulaik (1972) or Gorsuch (1974).

When a factor analysis is conducted on a correlation matrix, tests that are influenced by certain factors are said to have high factor loadings or to load highly on those factors. A *factor loading* is a number that is very much like a correlation coefficient in size and meaning. When the factors are uncorrelated with one another, the loadings usually are presented as correlations between the tests and the factors. When the factors are correlated with one another, the loadings are not correlations but are generally interpretable as if they were correlations, unless the factors are highly intercorrelated.

Table 5.11. Hypothetical Correlation Matrix for Three Tests
Displaying One Factor

|  |  | Test | | |
|---|---|---|---|---|
|  |  | *1* | *2* | *3* |
|  | *1* | 1.00 | .98 | .95 |
| *Test* | *2* | .98 | 1.00 | .97 |
|  | *3* | .95 | .97 | 1.00 |

Table 5.12. Hypothetical Correlation Matrix for Four Tests
Displaying Two Uncorrelated Factors

|  |  | Test | | | |
|---|---|---|---|---|---|
|  |  | 1 | 2 | 3 | 4 |
| Test | 1 | 1.00 | .90 | 0 | 0 |
|  | 2 | .90 | 1.00 | 0 | 0 |
|  | 3 | 0 | 0 | 1.00 | .90 |
|  | 4 | 0 | 0 | .90 | 1.00 |

Table 5.13. Hypothetical Correlation Matrix for Four Tests Displaying
Two Correlated Factors

|  |  | Test | | | |
|---|---|---|---|---|---|
|  |  | 1 | 2 | 3 | 4 |
| Test | 1 | 1.00 | .90 | .20 | .20 |
|  | 2 | .90 | 1.00 | .30 | .10 |
|  | 3 | .20 | .30 | 1.00 | .90 |
|  | 4 | .20 | .10 | .90 | 1.00 |

Table 5.14 contains the correlations of six tests of spatial ability. Three of the tests involve mental rotation (orientation) of objects (ORIENT); the other three tests involve mental alteration (visualization) of objects (VISUAL). Table 5.15 contains the loadings of the same six tests on two uncorrelated factors. The ORIENT tests all have relatively high loadings on the first factor and relatively low loadings on the second factor; therefore, the first factor could be called a spatial-orientation factor. The last two VISUAL tests have high loadings on the second factor and low loadings on the first factor; therefore, the second factor could be called a spatial-visualization factor. Performance on test VISUAL-1 appears to be influenced to a small degree by both factors. Through the use of factor analysis, the relationship among six test scores has been reduced to a consideration of two factors.

Factor analysis, as mentioned earlier, can be used to examine the construct validity of a test. Factor analysis can also be used in test development, which will be discussed in Chapter 6. Factorial validity is established by conducting a factor analysis on the test in question as well as on a set of tests that produce known factors (*marker tests*). For example, a new test for verbal fluency would be administered with a battery of marker tests measuring verbal fluency and other verbal skills. The matrix of correlations of all the test scores would be obtained and factor analyzed. Presumably a verbal-fluency factor, as well as the other verbal factors, would be produced. The factorial validity for the new test would be indicated by its loading on the verbal-fluency factor. The new test's loadings on the other verbal factors should be low. In terms of the discussion in the previous section, convergent validity would be demonstrated if all the verbal-fluency tests (including the new one) converge on the verbal-fluency factor. Discriminant validity would be demonstrated if the verbal-fluency tests (including the new one) do not load highly on the other verbal

Table 5.14. Correlation Matrix of Spatial Test Scores

|            | 0-1  | 0-2  | 0-3  | V-1  | V-2  | V-3  |
|------------|------|------|------|------|------|------|
| ORIENT-1   | 1.00 | .51  | .57  | .52  | .29  | .49  |
| ORIENT-2   | .51  | 1.00 | .91  | .40  | .43  | .49  |
| ORIENT-3   | .57  | .91  | 1.00 | .50  | .33  | .53  |
| VISUAL-1   | .52  | .40  | .50  | 1.00 | .32  | .59  |
| VISUAL-2   | .29  | .43  | .33  | .32  | 1.00 | .79  |
| VISUAL-3   | .49  | .49  | .53  | .59  | .79  | 1.00 |

Table 5.15. Factor Loadings of the Tests in Table 5.14

|          | Factor |       |
|----------|--------|-------|
| Test     | 1      | 2     |
| ORIENT-1 | .46    | .04   |
| ORIENT-2 | .56    | .02   |
| ORIENT-3 | .62    | − .03 |
| VISUAL-1 | .29    | .24   |
| VISUAL-2 | − .14  | .74   |
| VISUAL-3 | .05    | .63   |

factors. Each marker test used to establish factorial validity should be as pure a measure of the factor in question as possible (that is, it should load highly on one, and only one, factor).

Factor analyses of sets of test scores help investigators identify the important variables that influence performance on heterogeneous achievement- or ability-test batteries. For example, factor analyses of the subtest scores of standard intelligence tests have described important dimensions of performance on the tests, and these dimensions have been examined to see if they have value for diagnosing and explaining learning disabilities.

## 5.12  Summary

A test is valid if it measures what it purports to measure. The major types of validity are content validity, criterion-related validity, and construct validity.

Content validity is based on a subjective examination of the test items. There are two types of content validity: face validity and logical validity. A test has face validity if an examination of the items leads to the conclusion that the items are measuring what they are supposed to be measuring. Logical or sampling validity is based on a careful comparison of the items to the definition of the domain being measured.

When a test score, $X$, can be related to a criterion score, $Y$, criterion-related validity can be determined. The validity coefficient, $\rho_{XY}$, can be based on a predictive or a concurrent study. Reliability limits validity, because $\rho_{XY} \leq \sqrt{\rho_{XX'}}$. The correction for attenuation,

$$\rho_{T_X T_Y} = \frac{\rho_{XY}}{\sqrt{\rho_{XX'} \rho_{YY'}}} ,$$

allows us to estimate the maximum validity coefficient, $\rho_{T_X T_Y}$, that is possible if measurement errors due to unreliability are eliminated. A predictor score, $X$, can be used to predict a criterion score, $Y$, using linear regression. Predictions of a criterion score for the $i$th examinee, $Y_i$, can be expressed as a confidence interval, $\hat{Y}_i \pm z_c s_{Y \cdot X}$, if linearity, homoscedasticity, and normality are all assumed. Confidence intervals make it explicit that point estimates, $\hat{Y}_i$, may not be accurate.

When the criterion is dichotomous, a hit rate (the proportion of decisions that are correct) can be compared to base rates calculated from other classification procedures or to a base rate determined by the more frequently occurring outcome. Taylor-Russell tables allow the test user to estimate the number of correct decisions that use of a test score will produce, based on the test-validity coefficient, selection ratio (the proportion of applicants who are chosen), and the base rate (the proportion of applicants who would be successful). Use of the Taylor-Russell tables assumes that the predictor (test) scores and criterion scores have a bivariate normal distribution.

The most recently developed conceptual framework for validity is construct validity. Establishing construct validity is an ongoing process that involves the verification of predictions made about the test scores. Multitrait-multimethod validity is a type of construct validity that is based on examining the pattern of correlations among tests measuring a set of traits in different ways. Tests measuring the same trait should correlate highly, converging on the trait. Tests measuring different traits should correlate less highly, discriminating among the traits. There should be no method bias revealed in the correlations. Factorial validity is assessed by the process of factor analyzing the correlations of scores from selected tests and obtaining a predicted factor-loading pattern.

## 5.13  Vocabulary

base rate
concurrent-validity
  coefficient
construct validity
content validity
convergent validity
correction for attenuation
correlation matrix
criterion
criterion-related validity
cutting score
discriminant validity
face validity

factor
factor analysis
factorial validity
factor loading
hit rate
logical validity
marker test
method bias
multitrait-multimethod
  validity
multitrait-multimethod
  validity matrix
point estimate

predictive-validity coefficient          Taylor-Russell tables
predictor                                validity
sampling validity                        validity coefficient
selection ratio

## 5.14  Study Questions

1. What is a valid test? Briefly define the three major types of validity.
2. Give your own examples of situations in which
   a. content validity is crucial.
   b. content validity is not crucial.
   c. content validity is detrimental.
3. How are face validity and logical validity established?
4. How are predictive validity and concurrent validity different? When would each be used?
5. a. When is the correction for attenuation used?
   b. How do we interpret a correlation coefficient that has been corrected for attenuation?
   c. Describe how to apply the correction-for-attenuation formula.
   d. What cautions should be taken when using the correction for attenuation?
6. a. Explain how to construct confidence intervals for a prediction.
   b. How are these confidence intervals interpreted?
7. Why is it informative to determine confidence-interval estimates in addition to point estimates?
8. What errors are possible when screening people into dichotomous categories (see Table 5.2)?
9. What is a good hit rate?
10. Describe how to establish the cutting score that
    a. maximizes the hit rate.
    b. minimizes the misclassification of people who would be ''successful.''
    c. minimizes the misclassification of people who would be ''unsuccessful.''
11. When can Taylor-Russell tables be used? Describe how to use Taylor-Russell tables for problems similar to those in Section 5.7 and how to calculate the proportion of ''not hired, successful workers,'' as illustrated at the end of Section 5.7.
12. Compare the hit rate in the dichotomous-screening situation (Section 5.6) to the entries in the body of the Taylor-Russell tables (Section 5.7).
13. Which is more difficult to obtain, an improvement of .10 over a base rate of .50 or an improvement of .10 over a base rate of .80? Why?
14. a. How is construct validity established?
    b. If a construct-validity prediction is not upheld, what conclusions are possible?
    c. What types of predictions can be made for a construct-validity study?

15. Explain the ideal correlational pattern for multitrait-multimethod validity.
16. a. Explain how factor analysis is used to reduce the number of variables.
    b. How can factor analysis be used for construct validity?
17. Describe how to do ''eyeball'' factor analyses.

## 5.15   Computational Problems

1. Test score $X$ has a reliability of .75, and criterion $Y$ has a reliability of .80. The observed validity coefficient is .60. If you could increase the reliability of your measurements, how big could your validity coefficient be?
2. A predictor and a criterion have a correlation of .62. If the reliabilities of the predictor and the criterion are .73 and .82, respectively, what is the estimated correlation between the predictor observed score and the criterion true score?
3. Determine the 90% confidence interval for $Y_i$ when $X_i = 112, \bar{X} = 100, s_X = 10,$ $\bar{Y} = 50, s_Y = 5,$ and $r_{XY} = .6.$
4. For the data in the following table:
    a. What is the base rate?
    b. What cutting score yields the best hit rate? What is the best hit rate?
    c. If predicting a successful therapy outcome when in fact therapy would fail were the more severe error, what would be a reasonable cutting score?
    d. If predicting a failure outcome for a potentially successful client were the more severe error, what would be a reasonable cutting score?

| Score | Successful Therapy | Unsuccessful Therapy |
|-------|--------------------|----------------------|
| 10    | 8                  | 0                    |
| 9     | 7                  | 1                    |
| 8     | 12                 | 2                    |
| 7     | 9                  | 3                    |
| 6     | 4                  | 2                    |
| 5     | 8                  | 4                    |
| 4     | 2                  | 3                    |
| 3     | 1                  | 6                    |
| 2     | 0                  | 8                    |
| 1     | 0                  | 19                   |

5. Use the Taylor-Russell table (Table 5.7) to solve the following problems. Assume that 60% of randomly selected students graduate.
    a. Your admissions test has a validity of .70, and you accept the top 40% of the 200 applicants to your school. How many of the accepted students are expected to graduate?
    b. Your school admits 50% of the students who apply. You want at least 80% of these students to graduate. What minimum validity must your admissions test have?
    c. You have 200 applicants, and your admissions test has a validity of .40. How many students should be admitted to have a graduating class of at least 60 students?

6. There are 500 applicants for a job, the base rate is .60, the validity of your test is .50, and you hire 100 workers. How many potentially good workers were *not* hired?

7. You are measuring two traits (A and B) with three methods (1, 2, and 3). Does the following multitrait-multimethod matrix demonstrate good validity? Explain your answer.

|    | *A1* | *B1* | *A2* | *B2* | *A3* | *B3* |
|----|------|------|------|------|------|------|
| *A1* | .93 | .65 | .34 | .46 | .87 | .34 |
| *B1* | .65 | .90 | .35 | .78 | .22 | .21 |
| *A2* | .34 | .35 | .95 | .47 | .43 | .75 |
| *B2* | .46 | .78 | .47 | .87 | .24 | .43 |
| *A3* | .87 | .22 | .43 | .24 | .92 | .19 |
| *B3* | .34 | .21 | .75 | .43 | .19 | .85 |

8. Perform "eyeball" factor analyses of the following correlation matrices. State how many factors are present, and determine which tests load on each factor.

a.

|  | | *Test* | | |
|---|---|---|---|---|
| | *1* | *2* | *3* | *4* |
| *1* | 1.0 | .0 | .9 | .0 |
| *2* | .0 | 1.0 | .0 | .8 |
| *3* | .9 | .0 | 1.0 | .0 |
| *4* | .0 | .8 | .0 | 1.0 |

(*Test* labels the rows 1–4)

b.

|  | | *Test* | | |
|---|---|---|---|---|
| | *1* | *2* | *3* | *4* |
| *1* | 1.0 | .8 | .1 | .9 |
| *2* | .8 | 1.0 | .2 | .9 |
| *3* | .1 | .2 | 1.0 | .1 |
| *4* | .9 | .9 | .1 | 1.0 |

(*Test* labels the rows 1–4)

c.

|  | | | *Test* | | |
|---|---|---|---|---|---|
| | *1* | *2* | *3* | *4* | *5* |
| *1* | 1.0 | .8 | .1 | .2 | .9 |
| *2* | .8 | 1.0 | .2 | .2 | .9 |
| *3* | .1 | .2 | 1.0 | .9 | .1 |
| *4* | .2 | .2 | .9 | 1.0 | .1 |
| *5* | .9 | .9 | .1 | .1 | 1.0 |

(*Test* labels the rows 1–5)

# Principles of Test Construction

## 6.1 Introduction

Anyone who develops or uses tests—including teachers who write classroom exams and clinicians who interpret test scores, as well as professional measurement specialists—should be familiar with the procedures of test development and evaluation. The following list outlines the basic steps in test development.

1. Plan the test. Systematically lay out the exact areas to be covered by the items. This planning is crucial for logical or sampling validity (Section 5.2).
2. Write items for each of the areas in the plan. (Types of item formats are discussed in Section 6.2.) Write one and a half to three times as many items as the final version of the test will contain. Then item-analysis procedures can be used to identify poor items, which can be discarded or altered.
3. Administer all the items to a reasonably large sample of at least 50 (and preferably several hundred) examinees. This sample should be representative of the population with which the final version of the test will be used. For example, if the test is designed for use with fourth- and fifth-grade students, at least 50 fourth- and 50

118

fifth-grade students should be tested. Set ample time limits for test administration (unless the test is a speed test), so that the examinees can attempt all items. The conditions of test administration should be uniform or standard for all examinees; that is, all examinees should receive the same directions, practice items, time to complete the test, and so on.

4. Conduct an item analysis (Section 6.3 to 6.9). Select the best items, and refine them if necessary. (Steps 3 and 4 are called the *item tryout*.)

5. Administer the revised test to another representative sample of examinees. The test is administered under the same standardized conditions that will be used for the final version of the test. If the test is satisfactory, this sample can produce test norms (see Section 7.2). This step is called *test norming* or *test standardization*. If the test is not satisfactory, return to Step 2 or Step 4.

The remainder of this chapter briefly describes different item formats (Section 6.2) and then turns to a detailed discussion of item-analysis techniques (Sections 6.3 to 6.9). Each *item-analysis* technique provides a way of using data from the item tryout to evaluate the quality and usefulness of test items and to choose the best items for inclusion in the final edition of the test. Item analysis can also offer information about ways in which poor items might be improved. Although many methods have been proposed for conducting item analyses, four methods that are in common use are discussed here. These four methods involve examination of (1) item difficulties and item-discrimination indices or item/total-test-score point-biserial correlations, (2) item-reliability and item-validity indices, (3) item-characteristic curves, and (4) factor analysis.

Often a test user is interested not in developing a new test but in selecting a published test. Section 6.10 discusses the characteristics that a good test should have and describes reference books that provide useful information about published tests.

## 6.2  Item Formats

A large number of *item formats,* or different ways of asking questions on a test, are possible. Items can be free-response or *essay* questions, in which examinees are asked to write their answers in a word or two or in an essay form. For example, "List all the possible uses you can think of for a brick" or "Explain the major causes and effects of sunspots." The use of such items allows the examiner to obtain an accurate idea of what an examinee knows or feels. However, it is frequently difficult to standardize the scoring of free-response and essay items, and any scoring method that is developed will be relatively expensive to implement.

*Multiple-choice* items give the examinee a choice among two or more answers. Examples of multiple-choice items are: "Most employees steal from their employers: __true or __false" and "If Jane bought three pencils and each pencil cost 5¢, how much did Jane spend? a. 5¢ b. 10¢ c. 15¢ d. 20¢." The standardization of the scoring of multiple-choice items is straightforward, and frequently such items can be scored by machines, saving a great deal of money and human labor. Some critics feel that multiple-choice items are necessarily superficial or that they penalize the more creative examinees. However, carefully constructed multiple-choice items can measure complex thought processes, comprehension of nuances of meaning, and creativity.

Several books summarize suggestions for writing good items. Stanley and Hopkins (1972) and Ebel (1972) include suggestions for essay, true/false, and multiple-choice items. Wesman (1971) reviews the literature on item writing and makes a number of valuable suggestions. He concludes that none of the studies in the literature is definitive and that "item writing continues to be an art" (p. 86). According to Wesman the most important qualities for the item writer are "soundness of values, precision of language, imagination, knowledge of subject matter, and familiarity with examinees" (p. 86). Bearing this in mind, you should realize that the "art" of item writing involves careful planning and analysis to ensure unambiguous, efficient, nontrivial questions.

## 6.3    Item Analysis Using Indices of Item Difficulty and Discrimination

Using item difficulties and item-discrimination indices or item/total-test-score point-biserial correlations, an item analysis is fairly easy to conduct and is suitable for classroom teachers or test developers who do not have access to a computer. The measure of item difficulty is useful in evaluating whether the difficulty of an item is suited to the level of examinees taking the test. The item-discrimination index and the item/total-test-score point-biserial correlation indicate the degree to which responses to one item are related to responses to the other items in the test. These two statistics indicate whether a person who does well on the test as a whole (that is, a person who presumably is high on the trait being measured) is more likely to get the particular item correct than a person who does poorly on the test as a whole. In other words, the item-discrimination index and the item/test point-biserial correlation indicate whether an item discriminates between those examinees who do well and those who do poorly on the test as a whole. Taking the item difficulty and the item-discrimination index or item/test point-biserial correlation into consideration, the test developer hopes to construct a test that conveys the most information possible about differences in the examinees' levels on the trait being measured. In other words, the test developer desires to construct a test that discriminates well among examinees with varying levels of the trait.

The *item difficulty* for item $i$, $p_i$, is defined as the proportion of examinees who get that item correct. An item with a difficulty of .3 is more difficult than an item with a difficulty of .8, because fewer examinees responded correctly to the former item. Although the proportion of examinees passing an item traditionally has been called the item difficulty, this proportion logically should be called the item *easiness*, because the proportion increases as the item becomes easier.

The words *difficulty* and *correct* are best suited for discussions of ability or achievement tests. If a personality test is being developed, a "correct" response is a response that counts toward the trait and the "difficulty" of an item reflects the popularity of the "correct" response—that is, the proportion of examinees who choose this response. To simplify the discussion, the remainder of this chapter will use phrases suitable for ability or achievement tests; if you are more interested in personality-test development, you should translate the phrases when necessary.

The item difficulty, $p_i$, is very useful for item analysis. If $p_i$ is close to 0 or 1, the item generally should be altered or discarded, because it is not giving any information about differences among examinees' trait levels or abilities. If $p_i = 0$, no one got the item right; this item is too difficult and not at all useful. If $p_i = 1$, everyone got the item right, and again no differential information is provided. In both of these cases, the item does not discriminate among examinees with different trait levels. An item offers the maximum amount of information about differences among examinees when $p_i = .5$. When $p_i = .5$, the variance in item scores, which equals $p_i(1 - p_i)$, is maximized. This leads to the suggestion that all items should have $p_i = .5$, but the usefulness of this suggestion is influenced by intercorrelations among items. In the extreme, if the items all intercorrelated perfectly and had difficulties of .5, half of the examinees would receive a total test score of 0, and the other half would receive a perfect total test score; there would be no fine discrimination among examinees' trait levels. Therefore, it is best to choose items with a range of difficulties that average about .5. The range should be rather narrow for heterogeneous tests and wider for homogeneous tests. For example, Henryssen (1971, p. 153) suggests a range from $p_i = .4$ to $p_i = .6$ if the average (biserial) correlation between the item scores and the total test score is .3 to .4. If the average item/test biserial is higher than .4 (that is, if the test is more homogeneous), a wider range of item difficulties is suggested; if the average item/test biserial is less than .3 (that is, if the test is more heterogeneous), a narrower range of item difficulties can be used. The test developer might also choose to include some easy items early in the test for motivational reasons.

The choice of appropriate item difficulties also depends on the types of items used. A difficulty level of .5 for a true/false item can occur when all examinees randomly guess at the answer. Lord (1953) suggests that for multiple-choice tests the optimum difficulty level is slightly less than halfway between 1.0 and the *chance success level*—that is, the proportion of correct answers produced by guessing. Thus, for a four-option multiple-choice item, the chance success level is about .25, and the optimal difficulty level is about .60.

Generally, item difficulties of about .3 to .7 maximize the information the test provides about differences among examinees. One major exception occurs when the test is to be used for selection of an extreme group and a cutting score has been chosen (Section 5.6). In this case, the best test contains items that are passed by about 50% of the examinees whose total scores equal the cutting score (Lord, 1953; Richardson, 1936). A test used to select graduate students for a university that admits about 10% of the applicants should contain extremely difficult items. A test used to select children for a remedial-education program should contain very easy items. In both of these cases, there will be maximum discrimination among examinees near the crucial cutting score and very little discrimination among examinees not near the cutting score.

In summary, if maximum discrimination among examinees over all levels of performance is desired, a range of difficulty levels from about .3 to .7 is best. If maximum discrimination at some specific cutting score is desired, difficulty levels should relate to this cutting score.

The *item-discrimination index* for item $i$, $d_i$, is calculated by the formula

$$d_i = \frac{U_i}{n_{iU}} - \frac{L_i}{n_{iL}} , \qquad (6.1)$$

where

$U_i =$ the number of examinees who have total test scores in the upper range of total test scores and who also have item $i$ correct,

$L_i =$ the number of examinees who have total test scores in the lower range of total test scores and who also have item $i$ correct,

$n_{iU} =$ the number of examinees who have total test scores in the upper range of total test scores, and

$n_{iL} =$ the number of examinees who have total test scores in the lower range of total test scores.

If $n_{iU} = n_{iL} = n_i$, this formula reduces to

$$d_i = \frac{U_i - L_i}{n_i} . \qquad (6.2)$$

We can see from the definition that $d_i$ is the difference between the proportion of high-scoring examinees who get the item correct and the proportion of low-scoring examinees who get the item correct. Upper and lower ranges generally are defined as the upper and lower 10% to 33% of the sample, with examinees ordered on the basis of their total test scores. If the total test scores are normally distributed, it is optimal to use the 27% of the examinees with the highest total test scores as the upper range and the 27% of the examinees with the lowest total test scores as the lower range. When total test scores are normally distributed, using the upper and lower 27% produces the best estimate of $d_i$ (Kelley, 1939). If the distribution of total test scores is flatter than the normal curve, the optimum percentage is larger and approaches 33% (Cureton, 1957). For most applications, any percentage between 25 and 33 will yield similar estimates of $d_i$.

A measure of item discrimination that is an alternative to $d_i$ is the *item/ total-test-score point-biserial* correlation, $r_{iX}$, between scores on item $i$ and total test scores, $X$:

$$r_{iX} = \frac{\bar{X}_i - \bar{X}}{s_X} \sqrt{\frac{p_i}{1 - p_i}} , \qquad (6.3)$$

where $\bar{X}_i$, is the mean of the $X$ scores among examinees passing item $i$, $\bar{X}$ and $s_X$ are the mean and standard deviation of the $X$ scores among all examinees, and $p_i$ is the item difficulty. Sometimes $r_{ix}$ is converted to a biserial correlation (see Section 2.11). The correlation between item scores and total test scores, whether it be a point-biserial or a biserial correlation, behaves similarly to $d_i$: as responses on an item become more highly related to total test scores, $d_i$ and $r_{ix}$ will both increase in value.

When performance on an item is uncorrelated with performance on all the other items in a test, the item/total-test-score point biserial still will be positive, because the item score is included in the total test score. To control for this effect, an item point biserial can be calculated using test scores, $X'$, in which the item score is not included. For example, if we are dealing with the point biserial for the first item in a 25-item test, the examinees' scores on the 24 items excluding Item 1 would be used in place of $X$ in evaluating Equation 6.3. The point biserial for the second item would be based on the examinees' scores on the 24 items excluding Item 2, and so on. Obviously, the calculation of point biserials using $X'$ scores is more laborious than the calculation of point biserials using total test scores. The correlation $r_{ix'}$ will be lower than $r_{ix}$, and, if there are few items in a test, it is valuable to obtain $r_{ix'}$ in place of $r_{ix}$. However, if there are a large number of items in the test, $r_{ix'}$ and $r_{ix}$ will be very similar in value, and little will be gained by the use of $X'$ in place of $X$.

The item-discrimination index, $d_i$, and the item/test correlation, $r_{ix}$, are valuable pieces of information. On any reasonable item, $d_i$ and $r_{ix}$ should be positive; more high-scoring examinees than low-scoring examinees should answer the item correctly. An item with a negative value for $d_i$ or $r_{ix}$ apparently measures the opposite of what the bulk of the test measures. A negative $d_i$ or $r_{ix}$ might suggest that an error was made in the scoring of the item or that the item is poorly worded. Items with low or negative $d_i$'s or $r_{ix}$'s generally should be improved or eliminated.

When conducting an item analysis for a multiple-choice test, the examination of item difficulties and item discriminations or item/test correlations is usually valuable. It is also valuable to consider the proportion of examinees in different ability groups who mark each answer choice. (The answer choices that are incorrect are called *distractors*.) In Table 6.1 examinees are classified into the upper ($U$), middle ($M$), or lower ($L$) third of the sample, based on their total test scores. Within each third, the proportion of examinees marking each answer choice is noted for three hypothetical items. The answer marked with an asterisk is the correct answer; the three other answers for each item are distractors. Item 1, with a $p_i$ of .37, a $d_i$ of .5, and an $r_{ix}$ of .45, is a fairly good item. The three distractors ("a," "c," and "d") function well, although distractor "a" attracts twice as many examinees as each of the other distractors. Item 2 is very poor; it has a negative discrimination index and point-biserial correlation. Distractors "c" and "d" serve no function. Distractor "b" is too appealing, especially for high-scoring individuals. This item should be changed substantially or eliminated. Item 3 is too easy. As mentioned earlier, items with either very low or very high difficulty levels do not allow for discrimination among examinees, as this example illustrates. This item should be eliminated, unless the test will be used in selection to separate the bottom 10% of the examinees from the top 90%.

Table 6.1. Data for Item Analysis Using $p_i$, $d_i$, $r_{ix}$, and Proportions Choosing Each Answer

|        | Item 1 |     |     |        | Item 2 |     |     |        | Item 3 |     |      |
|        | L   | M   | U   |        | L   | M   | U   |        | L   | M   | U    |
|--------|-----|-----|-----|--------|-----|-----|-----|--------|-----|-----|------|
| a.     | .50 | .30 | .20 | *a.    | .70 | .30 | .10 | a.     | .07 | .03 | .00  |
| *b.    | .10 | .40 | .60 | b.     | .30 | .70 | .90 | b.     | .04 | .04 | .00  |
| c.     | .20 | .15 | .10 | c.     | .00 | .00 | .00 | *c.    | .80 | .90 | 1.00 |
| d.     | .20 | .15 | .10 | d.     | .00 | .00 | .00 | d.     | .09 | .03 | .00  |

$$p_i \doteq .37 \qquad\qquad p_i \doteq .37 \qquad\qquad p_i = .90$$
$$d_i = .50 \qquad\qquad d_i = -.60 \qquad\qquad d_i = .20$$
$$r_{ix} \doteq .45 \qquad\qquad r_{ix} \doteq -.53 \qquad\qquad r_{ix} \doteq .23$$

*Correct answer

## 6.4    Item Analysis Using Item Reliability and Validity Indices

Suppose that, as the result of an item-tryout study, a test developer has data for $N$ items and, of these, wants to choose the $k$ best items. This section discusses how the $k$ items can be chosen to maximize the internal-consistency reliability, $r_{XX'}$, or criterion-related validity, $r_{XY}$, of the $k$-item test.

In this discussion we will let $X^*$ be a total test score for a test composed of all $N$ items, $X$ be a score for a test composed of $k$ selected items, and $Y$ be a score on a criterion of interest.

To choose the best items, four statistics are needed for each item, $i$: (1) the item difficulty ($p_i$), (2) the item-score standard deviation ($s_i = \sqrt{p_i(1 - p_i)}$), (3) the *item-reliability index* ($s_i r_{ix}^*$, where $r_{ix}^*$ is the point-biserial correlation between the item score and the $N$-item test score), and (4) the *item-validity index* ($s_i r_{iY}$, where $r_{iY}$ is the point-biserial correlation between the item score and the criterion score). Once we know these four statistics, we can use the following formulas to estimate the mean, standard deviation, reliability, and validity of a test score, $X$, based on $k$ selected items:

$$\bar{X} = \sum_{i=1}^{k} p_i, \tag{6.4}$$

$$\hat{s}_X = \sum_{i=1}^{k} s_i r_{ix}^*, \tag{6.5}$$

$$\hat{r}_{XX'} = \frac{k}{k-1} \left[ 1 - \frac{\sum_{i=1}^{k} s_i^2}{\left( \sum_{i=1}^{k} s_i r_{ix}^* \right)^2} \right], \tag{6.6}$$

$$\text{and} \qquad \hat{r}_{XY} = \frac{\displaystyle\sum_{i=1}^{k} s_i r_{iY}}{\displaystyle\sum_{i=1}^{k} s_i r_{iX^*}} \qquad\qquad (6.7)$$

In each of these formulas, the sums are made over the $k$ selected items, and

$p_i$ = difficulty for item $i$,

$X$ = the score for a test composed of $k$ items,

$X^*$ = the test score composed of all $N$ items, $N \geqslant k$,

$\bar{X}$ = the mean of test score $X$,

$\hat{s}_X$ = the estimated standard deviation of test score $X$,

$\hat{r}_{XX'}$ = the estimated (Kuder-Richardson) reliability of test score $X$,

$\hat{r}_{XY}$ = the estimated validity of test score $X$,

$s_i^2 = p_i(1 - p_i)$ = variance of scores on item $i$,

$s_i r_{iX^*}$ = item-reliability index, and

$s_i r_{iY}$ = item-validity index.

Derivations of these formulas are available in Gulliksen (1950). If all $N$ of the original items are retained, then $k = N$, and the preceding formulas give exact values rather than estimates. From the formula for estimated reliability (Equation 6.6), we see that internal-consistency reliability, $\hat{r}_{XX'}$, is maximized when item/test correlations, $r_{iX^*}$, are maximized. From Equation 6.7 we can see that, since the validity, $\hat{r}_{XY}$, must lie between $-1$ and $+1$ (that is, in Equation 6.7 the numerator must be smaller in absolute value than the denominator), the sum of the item-reliability indices must be greater than or equal to the sum of the item-validity indices. Maximum validity is achieved when item-validity indices are as large as the item-reliability indices, which occurs when $Y$ is a parallel form of $X$.

To choose items for a test with maximum internal-consistency reliability, we can plot item-score standard deviations, $s_i$, and reliability indices, $s_i r_{iX^*}$, as in Figure 6.1. The best items have high item/test correlations; these items appear along the right-hand edge of the plot.

To choose items for a test with maximum validity, we can plot the item-validity indices, $s_i r_{iY}$, and item-reliability indices, $s_i r_{iX^*}$, as in Figure 6.2. The best items would have validity indices close to their reliability indices; these items appear in the upper edge of the plot.

When attempting to maximize both internal-consistency reliability and validity, we can create a dilemma, since different items might be chosen to reach each of the two goals. The test developer should decide which goal is more important in order to determine which method to use for item selection. Keep in mind that, if items are chosen to maximize validity, the resulting test may not have good internal-consistency reliability. However, it may have good test/retest or parallel-forms reliability, particularly when the selected items measure heterogeneous traits.

The formulas in this section provide estimates rather than exact values, because the reliability indices, $s_i r_{iX^*}$, are calculated using all $N$ items in the item

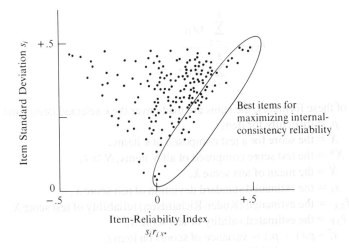

Figure 6.1. Item selection to produce a test with maximum internal-consistency reliability

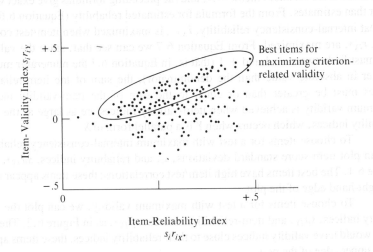

Figure 6.2. Item selection to produce a test with maximum criterion-related validity

pool, not just the $k$ items that are selected. If a few items are to be selected from a large number of items (that is, if $k$ is much smaller than $N$), the estimated reliability and validity for a $k$-item test (Equations 6.6 and 6.7) may be quite inaccurate. If few items are to be selected, it would be wise to recalculate the reliability indices after the least-desirable items have been eliminated from the item pool.

## 6.5   Item Analysis Using Item-Characteristic Curves

An *item-characteristic curve* (ICC) is a graphical display of the relationship between the probability of passing a particular item and the examinee's position on the underlying trait that is measured by the test. Since scores on the underlying trait generally are not available, observed test scores are used as estimators of trait values. For each item, then, the ICC is estimated by a plot with total test scores on the horizontal axis and the proportion of examinees passing the item on the vertical axis, as shown in Figure 6.3. The item in Figure 6.3 appears to be a reasonable item because the estimated ICC has a positive slope: high-scoring examinees are more likely to pass the item than are low-scoring examinees. It should be emphasized that using total test scores as estimates of the trait may produce ICCs that are very different from those obtained if trait scores are used.

The rationale underlying item analysis using ICCs is similar to the rationale for item analysis using item difficulty and discrimination indices (Section 6.3). Estimated ICCs for five items are given in Figure 6.4. Item A is a poor item, because it does not discriminate among examinees with different total test scores. Item B is also poor; it is negatively related to total test score. (The estimated ICC for Item B is what one would expect for the proportion of people choosing one particular distractor.) Items C and D are reasonable items. Item E has an estimated ICC that is flatter than those for C and D; it would not be as effective a discriminator among examinees who do not differ greatly in their total test scores.

The steepness of the ICC can be used as an index of item discrimination. For example, the estimated ICC in Figure 6.5 is very steep between the scores of 7 and 8.

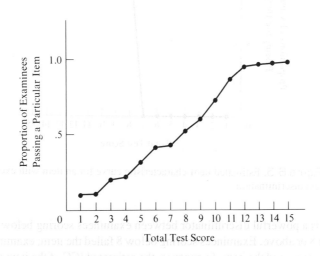

Figure 6.3. An estimated item-characteristic curve

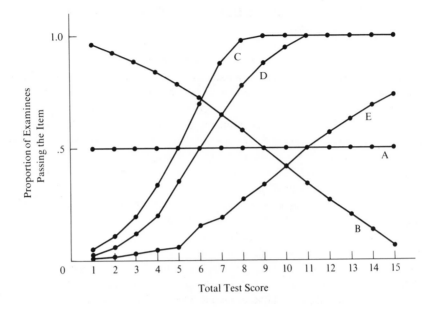

Figure 6.4. Examples of estimated item-characteristic curves

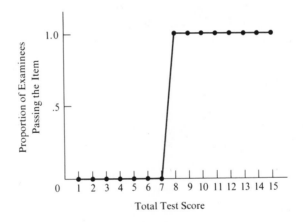

Figure 6.5. Estimated item-characteristic curve for an item with excellent discrimination

The item is a powerful discriminator between examinees scoring below 8 and those scoring at 8 or above. Examinees scoring below 8 failed the item; examinees scoring at 8 or above passed the item. In contrast, the estimated ICC of the item appearing in Figure 6.6 is not steep, and the item is a poor discriminator. Examinees with low

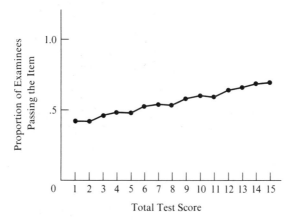

Figure 6.6. Estimated item-characteristic curve for an item with poor discrimination

total test scores have about the same chance of passing the item as examinees with high total test scores; knowing whether an examinee passes the item will not help much in determining whether the examinee has a high or low total test score.

An index of item difficulty also can be obtained from an ICC. For an ICC, an item's difficulty is defined to be the total test score corresponding to a proportion of .50 on the vertical axis—that is, the total test score needed to have a 50% chance of passing the item. This item-difficulty index, unlike the $p_i$ defined in Section 6.3, is larger for more difficult items. Using this item-difficulty index, we can see that in Figure 6.4 Item C has a difficulty of 5, Item D has a difficulty of 6, and Item E has a difficulty of 11; therefore, Item D is more difficult than Item C, and Item E is more difficult than Items D and C.

An ICC for a good item should display a positive slope and a moderate difficulty level. If a test is going to be used to select applicants above (or below) a specific cutting score, the difficulty level of the items should equal the cutting score, and the ICC should display high discrimination (maximum positive slope) at the cutting score. For example, if we wanted to select among examinees with high scores, Item E in Figure 6.4 would be most useful; Items C and D would be more useful in making decisions about lower-scoring examinees.

ICCs can be useful in identifying items that perform differently for different groups of examinees. For example, a test developer may be concerned that some reading-comprehension items dealing with farms may measure different processes for rural children and urban children. To examine this question, the test developer would administer the test to both groups of children and determine the ICC for each item in each group. If an item is measuring the same thing in both groups, the ICCs for that item should look the same in both groups. If the item is measuring different things in the two groups, the ICCs can appear different. Items whose ICCs are substantially affected by the group membership of the examinees can be revised or deleted from the test. Item-characteristic curves are discussed further in Section 11.5.

## 6.6    Using Factor Analysis for Item Analysis and Test Development

The technique of factor analysis was introduced in Section 5.11 as a way of determining factorial validity. Factor-analytic methods also can be used in test development.

Factor analysis can be used in test construction to help determine whether a set of items is homogeneous—that is, has one major factor influencing it—and to select items that are homogeneous. For example, the items whose correlations appear in Table 6.2 are homogeneous, with the exception of Item 7. A factor analysis of these correlations probably would produce two factors, but the factor defined by Item 7 would not be very important. It would be possible to report two scores for each examinee, one based on Items 1 through 6 and another based on Item 7. However, rarely is one item sufficiently reliable and valid to make it worthwhile to report its score alone. Thus, in this case it would be appropriate to delete Item 7 from the test and to use one score for each examinee—a total test score based on Items 1 through 6.

The item correlations in Table 6.3 would produce two important factors. In this case it would be appropriate to report two scores for each examinee, one based on Items 1 through 4 and the other based on Items 5 through 8. (Usually we factor analyze many more than seven or eight items and report scores based on more than just three or four items. The reliability and validity of any scores that are reported should be carefully examined.)

Factor analysis can be used to assess construct validity, as discussed in Section 5.11. By carefully choosing items with particular factor-loading patterns, a sophisticated form of content validity can be achieved. In this way the test developer can ensure that each item contributes to the test score or scores in a meaningful way.

When factors are correlated with one another, the factor-intercorrelation matrix can be factored (that is, the factors can be factored) to obtain *second-order*

Table 6.2. Hypothetical Item Correlations Producing One Important Factor

|  | | *Item* | | | | | |
|  | *1* | *2* | *3* | *4* | *5* | *6* | *7* |
|---|---|---|---|---|---|---|---|
| *1* | 1.00 | .72 | .75 | .86 | .91 | .84 | −.10 |
| *2* | .72 | 1.00 | .81 | .77 | .70 | .73 | .21 |
| *3* | .75 | .81 | 1.00 | .85 | .68 | .69 | .17 |
| *Item*    *4* | .86 | .77 | .85 | 1.00 | .91 | .76 | .03 |
| *5* | .91 | .70 | .68 | .91 | 1.00 | .77 | −.05 |
| *6* | .84 | .73 | .69 | .76 | .77 | 1.00 | .14 |
| *7* | −.10 | .21 | .17 | .03 | −.05 | .14 | 1.00 |

Table 6.3. Hypothetical Item Correlations Producing Two Important Factors

|  |  | 1 | 2 | 3 | Item 4 | 5 | 6 | 7 | 8 |
|---|---|---|---|---|---|---|---|---|---|
|  | 1 | 1.00 | .74 | .65 | .77 | .02 | −.03 | .06 | .14 |
|  | 2 | .74 | 1.00 | .83 | .81 | .21 | .11 | .22 | −.19 |
|  | 3 | .65 | .83 | 1.00 | .68 | .03 | −.09 | .08 | .01 |
| Item | 4 | .77 | .81 | .68 | 1.00 | −.12 | .07 | .11 | .02 |
|  | 5 | .02 | .21 | .03 | −.12 | 1.00 | .73 | .75 | .79 |
|  | 6 | −.03 | .11 | −.09 | .07 | .73 | 1.00 | .81 | .82 |
|  | 7 | .06 | .22 | .08 | .11 | .75 | .81 | 1.00 | .87 |
|  | 8 | .14 | −.19 | .01 | .02 | .79 | .82 | .87 | 1.00 |

*factors*. For example, the *Sixteen Personality Factor Questionnaire* (the 16PF, developed by R. B. Cattell) has 16 factors that resolve into four second-order factors. These second-order factors are slightly different for males and females. Table 6.4 summarizes the pattern of factor loadings for males. The second-order factors can be interpreted in terms of the *first-order factors* that load on them. For example, males tend to score high on the anxiety second-order factor if they are affected by feelings and are conscientious, shy, suspicious, practical, apprehensive, undisciplined in self-conflict, and tense. Test users can choose to use scores on the 16 first-order factors, scores on the four second-order factors, or both sets of scores to describe personality.

The results of factor analysis can lead to the development of new types of tests. Factor analyses of large numbers of ability-test scores led Thurstone to identify tests measuring a few "primary mental abilities" (Thurstone, 1938). Interpretation of the results of factor analyses made by many different investigators led researchers at the Educational Testing Service to describe and provide tests intended to measure more than 20 cognitive factors (French, Ekstrom, & Price, 1963). Guilford (1967) has based a model of the "structure of the intellect" on a long series of factor analyses. Guilford's model has led to many hypotheses about intellectual processes that had not been examined before Guilford suggested them.

Because the number of significant factors produced is influenced by the type of correlation coefficient used, we must use caution in factoring items.* Also, the factors produced for a set of items or scores can be altered by adding additional items or scores to the set. Factors can also be influenced by examinees' age, education, socioeconomic status, sex, ethnic group, degree of special training, and so on (Anastasi, 1970). Two or more groups of examinees can be given the same set of items, and factor-analytic solutions for the groups can be compared. This process might aid in the investigation of possible differences in item or score interpretations across groups. The test developer may choose to delete items that appear to measure different factors in different groups.

---

*If tetrachoric correlations are used and generate one factor, the use of phi coefficients for the same set of items would in general generate more than one factor (Lord & Novick, 1968, p. 382).

Table 6.4. Pattern of Factor Loadings for the 16PF Second-Order Factors for Males

|  | First-Order Factor | Extro-version | Anxiety | Tough Poise | Inde-pendence |
|---|---|---|---|---|---|
|  |  | *Second-Order Factor** | | | |
| A | Reserved—Outgoing | + |  | − |  |
| B | Dull—Bright |  |  | + | + |
| C | Affected by feelings—<br>Emotionally stable |  | − | + |  |
| E | Humble—Assertive | + |  | + | + |
| F | Sober—Happy-go-lucky | + |  | + |  |
| G | Expedient—Conscientious | + | + | − | − |
| H | Shy—Venturesome | + | − | + | + |
| I | Tough-minded—Tender-minded | − |  | − |  |
| L | Trusting—Suspicious |  | + | − | + |
| M | Practical—Imaginative |  | − | + | + |
| N | Forthright—Astute | − |  | − | − |
| O | Self-assured—Apprehensive | − | + | − | − |
| Q₁ | Conservative—Experimenting |  |  | − | + |
| Q₂ | Group dependent—Self-sufficient | − |  | + | + |
| Q₃ | Undisciplined self-conflict—<br>Controlled |  | − | − | + |
| Q₄ | Relaxed—Tense | + | + | + | − |

*Pluses indicate that high scores on the first-order factor (that is, scores in the direction of the second descriptor of the first-order factor) contribute to the second-order factor. Minuses indicate that low scores on the first-order factor (that is, scores in the direction of the first descriptor of the first-order factor) contribute to the second-order factor.

Another complication introduced by using factor analysis for test development is that different factor-analytic techniques can produce different results from the same data. Since any researcher using factor analytic techniques to develop a test or analyze data can arbitrarily select the type of factor analysis to be conducted, different researchers may reach different conclusions about the factors influencing the same set of items and the relationships among the factors. A test developer should have sound theoretical reasons for selecting a type of factor analysis and should be aware that other techniques could produce different results.

The theory and techniques underlying the use of factor analysis in test development and item selection are still being developed. There are a number of complications in choosing a factor-analytic technique, and there are some technical problems in estimating usable *factor scores*—that is, in estimating what an examinee's score would be on a factor rather than on a set of items. Keep in mind that factor analysis does not reveal the existence of "real" traits or "factors of the mind." Factor analysis is a method of describing statistical relationships among observed scores and cannot be applied haphazardly, despite ready access to computer programs for factor analysis. The quality and usefulness of any factor analysis depend on the thought and care that have gone into choosing the variables, the examinees and the analysis techniques. Factor analysis will not make sense out of a jumble of ill-conceived data (as factor analysts say, ''garbage in—garbage out''). However, when used appropriately, factor analysis is a powerful tool for item selection and test development. More detailed information about factor analysis can be obtained from Mulaik (1972) and Gorsuch (1974).

## 6.7  Distributions of Test Scores

For many psychological and educational tests, the observed-score distribution is approximately normal, with the bulk of examinees having scores near the average score and few examinees having scores near the extremes. For example, most people are of average intelligence, and very few people are either extremely high or extremely low in intelligence. Most people are of average temperament, neither extremely manic nor extremely depressive. Although it is not necessary for a test to produce a normal curve, and although many score distributions are not normal, deviations from normality sometimes indicate that there is a problem with the test. Skewed or bimodal distributions can occur for reasons that should be corrected.

Consider a personality test with questions that most people answer in the same way but that a few schizophrenic people answer in a very different way. On such a test, the scores would pile up at one tail (that is, at one end of the range of scores), resulting in a skewed distribution, as illustrated in Figure 6.7a and 6.7b. In this example, the test need not produce a normal curve for the trait to be accurately measured.

However, suppose we administer an ability test that is too easy, so that most people get a very high score (Figure 6.7a), or too hard, so that most people get a very low score (Figure 6.7b). In the case of the too-easy test, the trait being measured might have a normal distribution, but all the people who would be in the upper tail if the test were harder are crowded into the upper range of possible scores. This situation results in a *ceiling effect* and is represented in Figure 6.8. The distribution of the trait is represented by the normal curve, and the distribution of the test scores is represented by the negatively skewed curve. The total areas under the two curves are the same, but the people in the upper tail of the trait distribution are crowded into the upper range of the distribution of test scores.

A test that is too hard has the opposite effect and results in a distribution of observed scores that is skewed to the right (positively skewed), as in Figure 6.9. On the too-hard test, all the people who would be in the lower tail of the trait distribution are crowded into the lower range of the test-score distribution, resulting in a *floor effect*.

If an observed-score distribution is skewed due to a floor or ceiling effect, the test developer may choose to include more items that would discriminate among examinees at the appropriate tail of the trait distribution. If there is a ceiling effect, more difficult items should be added; if there is a floor effect, more easy items are needed. In effect, these additional items would pull the examinees into the appropriate tail and allow the test-score distribution to more accurately reflect the distribu-

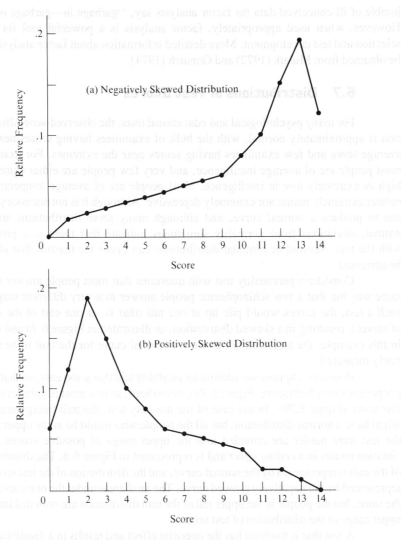

Figure 6.7. Skewed distributions of test scores

tion of the trait being measured. However, if the test developer believes that the trait being measured is positively (or negatively) skewed (as in our example of schizophrenics on the personality test) or that it is impossible or unnecessary to discriminate among examinees at the floor (or ceiling) of the test, then the test would not require change. For example, an aptitude test used to screen graduate-school applicants needs to discriminate only among people in the upper tail; in such a case a positively skewed raw-score distribution would not necessarily require change.

A *leptokurtic* test-score distribution, such as the one in Figure 6.10, results

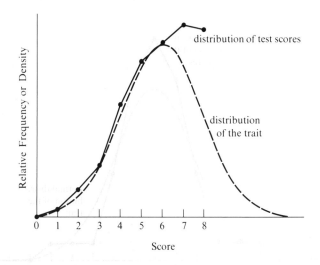

Figure 6.8. A ceiling effect

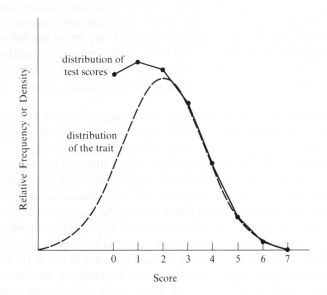

Figure 6.9. A floor effect

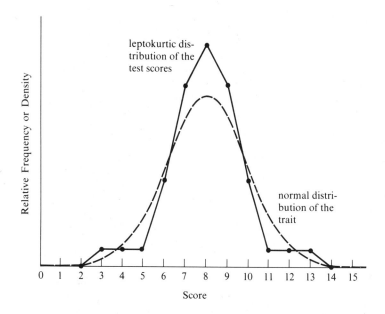

Figure 6.10. A leptokurtic distribution of test scores

when the test items fail to discriminate among examinees near the center of the curve. (A leptokurtic distribution is taller and thinner than a normal distribution.) If half of the test items were extremely easy and the other half were extremely hard, the examinees would get almost all of the easy items and very few of the difficult items correct. The result would be a piling up of scores in the center of the distribution and a leptokurtic score distribution. To correct this situation, the test developer could include more items of intermediate difficulty to discriminate among "average" examinees.

A *platykurtic* test-score distribution, as shown in Figure 6.11, is flatter and broader than a normal distribution. Such a score distribution can be produced by a test with items of moderate difficulty and good discriminating power.

If the test-score distribution is bimodal, as illustrated in Figure 6.12, it may suggest that the sample of examinees contains two disparate groups. If the sample of examinees does contain two groups with very different score distributions, the two distributions when combined produce a bimodal distribution with one mode for each group. For example, suppose a test reveals a large difference between males and females on some attitude. If the test is given to a sample containing equal numbers of both sexes, the resulting curve might resemble Figure 6.12. But, if the sample contains a larger proportion of one sex, the resulting distribution might resemble Figure 6.13. In these cases, the nonnormality of the score distributions accurately represents the trait distributions and does not mean that there is anything wrong with the test.

In an extreme case, a distribution can be *U-shaped,* as in Figure 6.14. Such

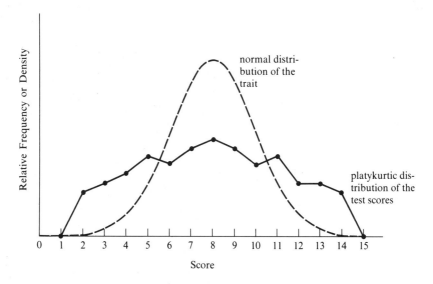

Figure 6.11. A platykurtic distribution of test scores

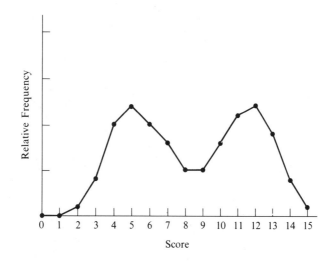

Figure 6.12. A bimodal distribution resulting from the combination of two dissimilar samples with equal numbers of examinees

a distribution can be produced by a test with items of moderate difficulty and extremely high discriminating power. A raw-score distribution such as this is ideal if we want to discriminate between examinees who are above or below a particular cutting score. However, such a test will not offer information about differences among examinees within either tail of the distribution. To gain this information, both easier and more difficult items must be added to the test.

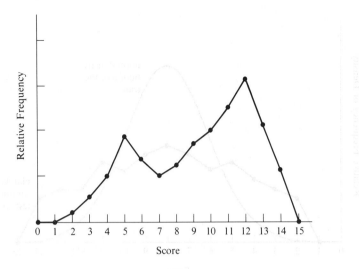

Figure 6.13. A distribution resulting from the combination of two dissimilar samples with unequal numbers of examinees

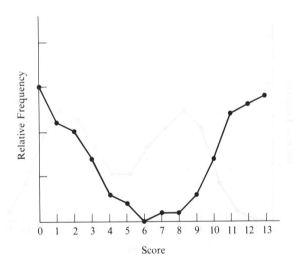

Figure 6.14. A U-shaped distribution

## 6.8  Some General Considerations in Item Analysis

Item analysis using any of the procedures described in the preceding sections appears to be largely a statistical matter. Appropriate numbers are calculated, and items with optimal statistical properties are selected. However, a test cannot be formed through consideration of these statistical criteria alone; other issues must be considered as well.

One issue that cannot be ignored is logical or sampling validity. It is crucial for the test developer to carefully examine the items for content coverage. A statistically ideal test that omits a crucial area of a trait cannot validly measure that trait.

Another requirement for an effective item analysis is that the test developer obtain appropriate samples and sample sizes for the item tryout. It is clear that an item difficulty, $p_i$, can be easily altered by changes in the sample. The statistics in Equations 6.1 to 6.7 and the results of factor analysis also can be altered by sample changes. The ICC is less easily affected by changes in the sample, and the item-difficulty and the discrimination (slope) obtained from an ICC also will tend to be stable over samples of examinees.

The test developer should be aware that the values of item statistics can fluctuate when different samples of examinees are tested. Any test that is the result of item selection based on an item tryout should be subjected to *cross validation*—a rechecking of the statistical properties of the test based on a new sample of examinees. For example, items that are chosen on the basis of high criterion-related validities in a tryout sample will tend to have smaller item validities in a cross-validation sample. The extent of this *shrinkage* must be examined.

It is not uncommon for some examinees to omit or fail to attempt some items, and handling these nonattempting examinees complicates the item analysis. Should nonattempting examinees be scored as if they got the items wrong, or should they be eliminated from the calculations? If the test is a power test and nonattempters are eliminated, the item statistics may be inaccurate. For example, if examinees who are lower in the trait fail to attempt difficult items, and if these examinees are eliminated from the item analysis, the result would be estimated item difficulties, $p_i$, that are too high and correlations between the items and other measures that are generally too low (because of attenuation due to restriction of range). On the other hand, if unattempted items are scored as errors, the item statistics will be inaccurate if some of the nonattempting examinees could have passed the items if given more time.

None of the item statistics discussed in this chapter considers the effect of guessing. If people can guess the correct answers to items, relationships between items and other measures (for example, the total test score or a criterion) can be affected. Some possible corrections for guessing and omissions are discussed in Section 7.7.

The intended use for the test affects item selection. As discussed earlier in this chapter, tests can be designed (1) to have maximum internal consistency or homogeneity, (2) to have maximum discrimination at one or more crucial cutting scores or to have discrimination throughout the range of scores, or (3) to have maximum validity. Tests designed for one purpose generally will not optimally meet other possible requirements. Similarly, a published test developed for multiple uses may not be as effective for a specific use as a test designed especially for that particular application.

Item selection also is confounded if there are linguistic or cognitive differences among members of the population to be tested. For example, an item on a test for children that assumes knowledge of tractor parts would be biased in favor of rural children. Similarly, an item that assumes familiarity with orchestral instruments would be biased against children raised in environments that exclude this information. Unless the function of the test is to assess familiarity with tractor parts, orchestral instruments, or other restricted areas of knowledge, items that involve biases of this type should be eliminated. More subtle biases may be introduced through the format of the test instructions or through the grammar of the instructions or items. Test instructions and items should be tried out on different subgroups of the population for which the test will be used. If different item statistics are obtained for the subgroups, the test may need revision, it may need to be written in multiple versions, or it may need to have separate norms and predictive equations for the subgroups.

## 6.9    Comparison of Item-Analysis Methods

There are a number of similarities among the item-analysis techniques discussed in this chapter. The discrimination index, $d_i$, the item/total-test-score point-biserial correlation, $r_{ix}$, the method illustrated in Table 6.1, the item-reliability index, and the slope of the ICC can all be used to assess the relationship of item responses to the total test score. The difficulty level of an item can be assessed by $p_i$ or by the total test score needed to obtain a .5 probability of passing the item.

The choice of method for item analysis depends on the availability of a computer and the item-tryout sample size. Factor analysis requires a computer and large samples. The use of ICCs also requires large samples, so that a reasonable number of examinees obtain rare scores. Item-difficulty levels, $p_i$, discrimination indices, $d_i$, and item/test point biserials, $r_{ix}$, provide useful information and, for moderate sample sizes, can be calculated without a computer. The tabular method illustrated in Table 6.1 does not require large samples and carries much the same information as an ICC; it also allows examination of the effectiveness of each distractor. Item-reliability and item-validity indices can be calculated fairly easily for moderately sized samples with a desk calculator or small computer. The test developer has an array of alternatives available and may choose to use several techniques for item selection.

## 6.10    Selecting a Published Test

Most test users do not develop their own tests. Instead, they select a published test and use the scoring system described in the test manual. Before examining alternative tests, the test user should know the answers to the following questions.

1. What minimum reliability is required? (How fine a discrimination among examinees must be made?)
2. What types of validity are important?
3. What population or populations should the reference (norm) group or groups represent?
4. What is the appropriate reading level of the test?
5. How much time is available for testing and for scoring the tests?
6. How much money is available to purchase the tests and to pay for computer scoring and professional administration, if required?

After these decisions are made, the test user generally can narrow the choice to several tests. The search for these tests could involve consultations with local measurement specialists, the screening of publishers' catalogs, professional journals, or textbooks (such as Anastasi, 1976; Cronbach, 1970; Thorndike & Hagen, 1977), and reference to three test guides: *Tests in Print II*, the *Mental Measurements Yearbook*, and *Measures for Psychological Assessment*.

*Tests in Print II* (Buros, 1974) is an index of all tests published for use with English-speaking examinees. Included for each test, when applicable, are (1) the test title, (2) the population of examinees for which it is suitable, (3) the range of copyright dates, (4) the acronym for the test title, (5) a description of subtest scores, (6) an indication of the absence of a manual, (7) any questionable updating of test materials, (8) authors, (9) publisher, (10) country of publication, if not the United States, and (11) cross references to *Mental Measurements Yearbook, Personality Tests and Reviews* (1970), and relevant journal articles. Tests are tabled by content areas; for example, all achievement tests are grouped together.

The *Mental Measurements Yearbook* (now in the seventh edition, Buros, 1972) is a collection of critical reviews and information on published tests for English-speaking examinees. Test users generally consider the *Mental Measurements Yearbook* (MMY) the best source for an objective, critical test assessment. The editor (Buros) and the reviewers have a somewhat missionary zeal in their reviews, hoping that their high standards will ''rub off'' on test publishers. However, according to Buros (p. xxvii, Volume I), their accomplishments in this area have been ''disappointingly modest. Test publishers continue to market tests which do not begin to meet the standards of the rank and file of MMY and journal reviewers. At least half the tests currently on the market should never have been published. Exaggerated, false, or unsubstantiated claims are the rule rather than the exception.'' Although the responsibility for the marketing of poor tests must be borne mainly by the test developer, the test users who uncritically accept and use such tests must share the blame.

*Measures for Psychological Assessment* (Chun, Cobb, & French, 1975) was created to supplement *Tests in Print II* and the *Mental Measurements Yearbook*. It provides a comprehensive bibliography for measures of mental health and related concepts mentioned in the literature between 1960 and 1970. It includes all tests, even those that were not published for public use or that did not prove valuable.

Cross-references allow the reader to trace the use of tests in various applications and avoid redundancy in test development. *Measures for Psychological Assessment* should prove to be a valuable reference book, especially for researchers and people who are developing their own tests.

Once several possible tests are selected, the test user should obtain *specimen sets*, which generally include a copy of the test, scoring instructions, and a test manual. Then, keeping in mind the requirements for the test, the user must choose the most appropriate test or, as an alternative, develop a new test or test battery. The test user should examine critically and carefully the published claims for a test and the evidence used to substantiate the claims.

The American Psychological Association (APA) has summarized the requirements for adequate test use in *Standards for Educational and Psychological Tests* (1974). Listed as "essential" for inclusion in the test manual or supplementary material are:

1. clear discussions of intended purposes and applications, with supporting evidence for each claim,
2. summaries of the test-development procedures, rationale, and item analyses, with a clear distinction between preliminary results and results obtained with the test in final or revised form,
3. clearly defined norm groups and information about how they were obtained,
4. a discussion of the reliability and validity of the test and subpart scores, together with information about how these statistics were obtained,
5. clear instructions for test administration and scoring, including required qualifications for the test administrator and interpreter,
6. information necessary for correct interpretation of test scores and warnings about foreseeable misuses, and
7. a discussion of the variables known to affect test scores or their reliability or validity (for example, regional, race, creed, or sex differences and differences due to different answer sheets or alternate forms of the test).

Every test user has the obligation to demonstrate that the tests he or she uses are the best instruments and methods available for rational, objective decision making.

## 6.11 Summary

Anyone who develops or uses tests should be familiar with the procedures for test development and evaluation. Tests are planned and items are developed, tested, and analyzed by means of various methods that allow the developer to select the best items for inclusion in the final edition of the test. Four major techniques for item analysis are reviewed.

Item difficulties, $p_i$, item-discrimination indices, $d_i$, and item/total-test-score point-biserial correlations, $r_{ix}$, can be used in item analysis. For general use, item $p_i$'s should be between about .3 and .7, and $d_i$'s and $r_{ix}$'s should be positive, indicating that the items discriminate well among examinees and that examinees with higher scores on the test are more likely to get the item correct than are examinees with lower scores on the test. If the test is to be used for selection and a cutting score is chosen, the best items are those that examinees at the cutting score have a 50% chance of passing and that have maximum discrimination at that cutting score. If multiple-choice items are used, the proportions of examinees marking each answer choice who score in the lower, middle, or upper ranges in terms of total test score can be examined. This information is then used for item selection or improvement.

If internal-consistency reliability or criterion-related validity are important, item analyses using item-reliability and item-validity indices are appropriate. Using these indices, the mean, variance, Kuder-Richardson reliability, and validity of a test based on selected items can be estimated (Equations 6.4 to 6.7). Maximizing internal-consistency reliability and validity simultaneously may not be possible, because different items may be selected for each goal.

An item-characteristic curve, ICC, displays the relationship between the probability of passing an item and values of the underlying trait influencing performance. If total test scores are used to estimate trait levels, ICCs may be approximated, although differences between the trait and test score can distort the ICC. Good items for a test for general use should have moderate difficulty levels and good discrimination (steep, positive slopes). If a test is to be used for selecting examinees and a cutting score has been chosen, a good item has an ICC with about 50% of the examinees who have the cutting score passing the item and with maximum slope at the cutting score.

Factor analysis can be used in several ways for test development. Items can be selected and grouped to measure important factors. Both content and construct validity can be aided by factor analysis. Group differences in factor results can lead to differences in item selection or test interpretation. Factor analysis can influence the type of scores that are reported. Batteries of tests can be factor analyzed to lead to a better understanding of what each test assesses and to the development of new tests. Factor analysis is a sophisticated mathematical technique, requiring careful thought on the part of the user, and provides a powerful method for analyzing items or tests.

The test developer should carefully examine the score distribution resulting from a new test. Examination of the score distribution may suggest problems with the test that should be corrected. Problems exist in all test-development methods. Sufficiently large samples of examinees must be tested to ensure that item statistics are reasonably stable. Cross validation of the final test is essential. Examinees who omit or guess on items introduce complications into the analyses. The intended purpose of the test influences the types of items that should be included. Finally, the possibility of biases in the test or item content or formats should be considered.

Most test users select a published test that best serves their needs. Several reference books can aid in this selection, including *Tests in Print II,* the *Mental Measurements Yearbook,* and *Measures for Psychological Assessment.* Manuals for specific tests should provide the user with all the information required to select and use the tests and to interpret the test scores in meaningful ways.

## 6.12  Vocabulary

ceiling effect
chance success level
cross validation
distractor
essay item
factor score
first-order factor
floor effect
item analysis
item-characteristic curve
item difficulty
item-discrimination index
item format
item-reliability index
item/total-test-score point
  biserial

item tryout
item-validity index
leptokurtic distribution
*Measures for Psychological
  Assessment*
*Mental Measurements
  Yearbook*
multiple-choice item
platykurtic distribution
second-order factor
shrinkage
specimen set
test norming
*Tests in Print II*
test standardization
U-shaped distribution

## 6.13  Study Questions

1. What are the basic steps in test development?
2. What properties are desirable for item-difficulty indices, item-discrimination indices, and item/total-test-score point-biserial correlations?
3. In general, why is an item difficulty of .01 or .99 undesirable?
4. Why is a negative or zero discrimination index or item/test-score point biserial undesirable?
5. Why is an item difficulty of .5 undesirable for a true/false item?
6. When is it desirable to select items with a range of difficulty levels?
7. How can the distractors in multiple-choice items be evaluated?
8. How can item reliability and validity indices be used to form a test with high internal-consistency reliability or with high criterion-related validity?
9. Describe how to calculate estimates of the mean, standard deviation, reliability, and validity of a $k$-item test if the item difficulties, reliability indices, and validity indices are known for an $N$-item test that includes the $k$ items.
10. Explain the dilemma created when we try to choose items to maximize both internal-consistency reliability and validity.
11. What properties are desirable for an ICC?
12. How is item difficulty assessed when ICCs are used? How is this measure of item difficulty related to $p_i$?

13. How is item discrimination assessed with ICCs?
14. How can factor analysis be used for item analysis?
15. What is a second-order factor? How can it be useful?
16. How can factor analysis aid in test construction and in the interpretation of test scores?
17. Explain how floor and ceiling effects affect the observed-score distribution.
18. What situations can produce bimodal, leptokurtic, platykurtic, or U-shaped score distributions?
19. What is cross validation? Why is it necessary?
20. Explain the item-analysis problems introduced when some examinees do not attempt to answer some items.
21. What methods can be used to create a test with high internal consistency?
22. What methods can be used to create a test that will be used to select the best 5% of the applicants?
23. What methods can be used to create a test with good discrimination over a wide range of scores?
24. What methods can be used to create a test with high criterion-related validity?
25. What indices reflect the relationship between an item and the total test score?
26. How does the size of the sample affect the choice of item-analysis technique?
27. What questions should be considered in choosing a published test?
28. What publications are available to aid the test user in choosing a published test?
29. What properties should a test manual (or supplementary materials) have?

## 6.14 Computational Problems

1. For each of the items in the following tables, calculate $p_i$ and $d_i$. (Assume that equal numbers of examinees are in the $U$, $M$, and $L$ groups.) Discuss the value of each item for a general-purpose test. (An asterisk marks the correct answer.)

| Item 1 | L | M | U |
|---|---|---|---|
| a. | .30 | .25 | .20 |
| *b. | .10 | .30 | .50 |
| c. | .30 | .20 | .15 |
| d. | .30 | .25 | .15 |

| Item 2 | L | M | U |
|---|---|---|---|
| a. | .00 | .00 | .00 |
| b. | .05 | .05 | .05 |
| c. | .60 | .75 | .80 |
| *d. | .35 | .20 | .15 |

| Item 3 | L | M | U |
|---|---|---|---|
| *a. | .10 | .40 | .90 |
| b. | .45 | .30 | .03 |
| c. | .40 | .28 | .04 |
| d. | .05 | .02 | .03 |

| Item 4 | L | M | U |
|---|---|---|---|
| a. | .20 | .20 | .20 |
| b. | .20 | .20 | .20 |
| *c. | .40 | .40 | .40 |
| d. | .20 | .20 | .20 |

2. a. Using the following data, calculate the item difficulties, $p_i$, and the item/total-test-score point-biserial correlations, $r_{ix}$, for all five items.

b. Which four items would make the best general-purpose test? (Each table entry indicates whether the examinee passed (1) or failed (0) the item.)

|  |  | Examinee |  |  |  |  |  |  |  |  |  |
|---|---|---|---|---|---|---|---|---|---|---|---|
|  |  | 1 | 2 | 3 | 4 | 5 | 6 | 7 | 8 | 9 | 10 |
|  | 1 | 1 | 0 | 0 | 0 | 0 | 0 | 0 | 0 | 0 | 0 |
|  | 2 | 1 | 1 | 1 | 0 | 1 | 0 | 0 | 0 | 0 | 0 |
| Item | 3 | 1 | 1 | 1 | 1 | 0 | 0 | 1 | 0 | 0 | 0 |
|  | 4 | 1 | 1 | 1 | 1 | 1 | 1 | 0 | 0 | 0 | 1 |
|  | 5 | 0 | 1 | 1 | 0 | 1 | 1 | 1 | 1 | 1 | 1 |

3. a. Calculate the reliability and validity indices for the following items.
   b. Form the best two-item test for internal-consistency reliability. Calculate the estimated mean, standard deviation, reliability, and validity for this best test.
   c. Form the best two-item test for criterion-related validity. Calculate the estimated mean, standard deviation, reliability, and validity for this best test.

| Item | $p_i$ | $r_{ix}*$ | $r_{iY}$ |
|---|---|---|---|
| 1 | .5 | .72 | .58 |
| 2 | .6 | .74 | .62 |
| 3 | .2 | .95 | .12 |
| 4 | .8 | .93 | .24 |
| 5 | .2 | .09 | .04 |

4. Draw an ICC that would be best for:
   a. a general-purpose test.
   b. a test to be used to select the lowest 10% of the population.
   c. a test to be used to select the highest 15% of the population.
5. Using the following data, calculate and plot the estimated item-characteristic curves for Items 2 and 5.

|  |  | Item |  |  |  |  |  |  |
|---|---|---|---|---|---|---|---|---|
|  |  | 1 | 2 | 3 | 4 | 5 | 6 | 7 |
|  | 1 | 1 | 1 | 1 | 0 | 0 | 0 | 0 |
|  | 2 | 1 | 0 | 1 | 1 | 0 | 0 | 0 |
|  | 3 | 1 | 1 | 1 | 0 | 0 | 0 | 0 |
|  | 4 | 0 | 1 | 1 | 1 | 0 | 0 | 0 |
|  | 5 | 1 | 1 | 1 | 0 | 1 | 0 | 0 |
| Examinee | 6 | 1 | 1 | 1 | 1 | 0 | 0 | 0 |
|  | 7 | 1 | 1 | 1 | 0 | 0 | 1 | 0 |
|  | 8 | 1 | 1 | 1 | 1 | 1 | 0 | 0 |
|  | 9 | 1 | 1 | 1 | 1 | 1 | 0 | 1 |
|  | 10 | 1 | 1 | 1 | 1 | 1 | 1 | 0 |
|  | 11 | 0 | 1 | 1 | 1 | 1 | 1 | 0 |
|  | 12 | 1 | 0 | 1 | 1 | 1 | 1 | 0 |

6. Do an "eyeball" factor analysis for the following item-correlation matrix. What scores might be reported for this test?

|   | 1 | 2 | 3 | 4 | 5 | 6 |
|---|---|---|---|---|---|---|
| 1 | 1.0 | .8 | .1 | .9 | .1 | .2 |
| 2 | .8 | 1.0 | .2 | .8 | .1 | .1 |
| 3 | .1 | .2 | 1.0 | .1 | .1 | .2 |
| 4 | .9 | .8 | .1 | 1.0 | .1 | .2 |
| 5 | .1 | .1 | .1 | .1 | 1.0 | .9 |
| 6 | .2 | .1 | .2 | .2 | .9 | 1.0 |

# Transforming and Equating Test Scores

## 7.1  Introduction

David took a test and received a score of 32. How well did he do? The *raw score*—that is, the observed score—does not carry enough information to answer this question. However, if we knew something about the distribution of raw scores, we could get a better idea of what David's score means. For example, if we knew that David's score fell at the 90th percentile (meaning that he scored as well as or better than 90% of the examinees who took the test), we would have a much better idea about how well he did. By dealing with a percentile rather than a raw score, we have made a raw-score transformation. In this chapter we will discuss several different types of raw-score transformations that aid in the interpretation of test scores. Chapter 8 discusses the levels of measurement (nominal, ordinal, interval, and ratio) of the scores produced.by these transformations.

Because there are a number of disadvantages in retaining the raw scores on any test, most scores are transformed before being reported. A major problem with raw scores was just mentioned: a raw score by itself is difficult to interpret. Even if raw scores are accompanied by information about the number of items on the test, an

148

isolated raw score does not give any information about how one examinee's performance is related to the performance of the other examinees. If a raw-score distribution is irregular (for example, if it is skewed or bimodal), common statistical techniques that require normality cannot be applied reasonably. Another problem with the use of raw scores is that raw scores may not be comparable across tests. For example, if Gene has a raw score of 60 on Test 1 and a raw score of 20 on Test 2, we cannot easily assess his relative performance on the two tests, particularly if the distributions of scores for the two tests have quite different shapes. All of these problems have led to the development and use of common transformations that result in more easily interpretable reported scores. Common forms of expressing *transformed scores* are: (1) percentiles, (2) age and grade scores, (3) expectancy tables, (4) standard and standardized scores, (5) normalized scores, (6) formula scores, and (7) equal-interval scales.

Transformations of scores are of two basic types: linear and nonlinear. A *linear transformation* can be defined by a linear equation of the form $Y = aX + b$, where $a$ and $b$ are constants, $X$ is the raw score, and $Y$ is the transformed score. In making this transformation, every examinee's $X$ is transformed to a $Y$ using the linear rule. If the transformation equation is known, the transformed score corresponding to any raw score can be calculated easily. For example, if $Y = 3X - 2$, the transformed score corresponding to a raw score of 12 is $3(12) - 2 = 34$. When raw scores are linearly transformed, the shape of the distribution of the transformed scores is the same as the shape of the distribution of the raw scores. For example, if the raw-score distribution is skewed to the right, the linearly-transformed-score distribution also will be skewed to the right. Furthermore, linear transformations do not alter the size of correlations (see Section 2.8). The construction of standard and standardized scores and some formula scores involves a linear transformation of raw scores.

A *nonlinear transformation* cannot be expressed in the form of a linear equation. For example, $Y = X^2$ is a nonlinear transformation of $X$. In general, nonlinear transformations will change correlations and the shape of the score distribution, so that the transformed-score distribution can be very different from the raw-score distribution. All of the seven transformations listed previously, except for standard and standardized scores and some formula scores, involve nonlinear transformations.

The raw-score transformations (except for some formula scores) that are discussed in this chapter are all *monotonic* transformations of the raw scores. This means that, if one examinee's raw score is greater than another examinee's raw score, the first examinee will have a greater transformed score than the second examinee. In other words, monotonic transformations will not alter an examinee's rank order in the sample. If the scores are to be used in a ranking or sorting situation, there is nothing to be gained by using these transformations. If, however, we want to communicate the meaning of a score more effectively or to perform special statistical manipulations with the scores, one or another of the transformations can be useful.

The raw-score transformations discussed in this chapter transform scores in order to make them more meaningful. In most cases, this meaning is derived by comparing an examinee's performance to the performance of other examinees; that is, the scores derive meaning through reference to a norm group. This technique is called a *norm-referenced* approach. An alternative approach, criterion-referencing, is discussed in Section 10.5. In *criterion-referenced* testing, an attempt is made to determine whether the examinee has reached a certain specific criterion performance or mastered a specific task (for example, can the examinee subtract single-digit numbers?). In criterion-referenced testing, a raw score (number-right score) can be meaningful and does not require transformation.

## 7.2  Percentiles

Percentiles are defined with respect to a *norm*, or *reference, group*. A norm group is a specified sample of examinees—for example, a certain sample of sixth-grade students randomly chosen from schools across the United States. If it were possible to determine the actual trait values for a continuous trait (for example, intelligence or hyperactivity) for each person in a norm group, then we could determine the percentage of people with trait values less than or equal to any specified value. The *percentile rank* (or *percentile* or *percentile score*) of a trait value is defined as the percentage of people in a norm group who have trait values less than or equal to that particular trait value. For example, if 75 out of 100 people in the norm group have spelling abilities less than or equal to 17.3, then 17.3 is assigned a percentile of 75. In practice, we cannot obtain trait values, but we can obtain observed test scores. We can assume that each test score represents a range of trait values. For example, an observed test score of 17 represents a range of trait values from 16.5 to 17.5. We can further assume that every trait value in the range represented by an observed test score is equally likely to occur. For example, for an observed test score of 17, all trait values between 16.5 and 17.5 are equally likely to occur. Thus, if six examinees receive an observed test score of 17, three examinees are assumed to have trait values less than 17, and three are assumed to have trait values greater than 17.

Using these assumptions, we can use frequency distributions of observed test scores to estimate the percentiles associated with various trait values. Consider the score distribution in Table 7.1. For each score, the frequency (number) of

Table 7.1. A Score Frequency Distribution

| Score | Frequency | Cumulative Frequency |
|-------|-----------|----------------------|
| 118 | 4 | 20 |
| 117 | 6 | 16 |
| 116 | 8 | 10 |
| 115 | 2 | 2 |

examinees obtaining the score appears in the middle column. The next column on the right contains the cumulative frequency of each score, which is the number of examinees who have scores less than or equal to that score. For example, the cumulative frequency of a score of 116 is the frequency of a score of 116 (8) plus the frequency of a score of 115 (2), which equals 10. Using this observed-test-score distribution, let's estimate the percentile rank for a trait value of 117. Remembering our assumptions, we recognize that the observed test score of 117 represents a range of trait values from 116.5 to 117.5 and that the six examinees who got a test score of 117 are evenly distributed from 116.5 to 117.5. Therefore, we conclude that 13 examinees had trait values at or below 117—the ten examinees below 116.5 plus the three examinees between 116.5 and 117. (Since we assume the trait distribution is continuous, no one falls at exactly 117. Whether 13 examinees fell at and below or just below 117 is philosophically, but not practically, significant.) Since there are 20 examinees in all, 13/20 is the desired proportion. Since 13/20 = .65, the percentile rank for a trait value of 117 is estimated to be 65.

Using similar logic to calculate the percentile rank for a trait value of 116, we see that there are six examinees at or below a trait value of 116 (two below 115.5 and four between 115.5 and 116). The proportion at or below 116 is 6/20 = .30, so the percentile rank for a trait value of 116 is estimated to be 30. We also see that 18 examinees fall at or below a trait value of 118 (16 below 117.5 plus two between 117.5 and 118), so the percentile rank for a trait value of 118 is estimated to be (100)(16 + 4/2)/20 = 90. Similarly, the percentile rank for a trait value of 115 is estimated to be (100)(0 + 2/2)/20 = 5.

Calculations to find trait values corresponding to given percentiles are slightly more tedious but conceptually similar. To estimate the trait value falling at the 75th percentile rank, we need to find the trait value that 75% of the examinees fall at or below. For the data in Table 7.1, there are 20 examinees in all, so the trait value at the 75th percentile must have .75(20) = 15 examinees at or below it. Looking at the cumulative frequencies of the scores and remembering the assumptions, we see that 16 examinees have trait values at or below 117.5 and that ten examinees have trait values at or below 116.5; therefore, the trait value we want must be somewhere between 116.5 and 117.5. To make the calculations easier, we can construct a table like Table 7.2. We see that a trait value of 117.5 corresponds to a cumulative frequency of 16 and that a trait value of 116.5 corresponds to a cumulative frequency

Table 7.2. Information Table for
Calculation of a Trait Value
Corresponding to a Percentile

| Trait Value | Cumulative Frequency |
|---|---|
| 117.5 | 16 |
| ? | 15 |
| 116.5 | 10 |

of 10; we want to know the trait value corresponding to a cumulative frequency of 15. We find this trait value using linear interpolation: 15 is 5/6 of the way between 10 and 16, so the trait value we need must be 5/6 of the way between 116.5 and 117.5. The desired trait value is approximately $116.5 + .83 = 117.33$. This calculation and its logic are illustrated in Figure 7.1. On the right side of Figure 7.1, we see that we must go up 5/6 of the distance between 10 and 16. We must go up proportionately the same amount on the left side (between 116.5 and 117.5) or 5/6 times 1, which is about .83. This produces the answer of 117.33.

Occasionally frequency distributions are grouped in terms of score intervals. For example, we may know that 27 examinees earned scores from 1 to 5 without knowing how many examinees earned a score of 1, how many earned a score of 2, and so on. In such a case, we assume that the score interval from 1 to 5 covers trait values from .5 to 5.5 and that every trait value within this interval is equally likely to occur. If this last assumption is false, the percentile calculated from grouped data may differ markedly from the percentile calculated from ungrouped data. For example, when the percentile rank for a trait value of 6 is calculated for the ungrouped data in Table 7.3, it is approximately 28.6. However, for the grouped distribution the calculated percentile rank is approximately 44.6.

When dealing with grouped frequency distributions, the logic of calculating percentiles is the same as it is with ungrouped frequency distributions. For the distribution in Table 7.4, we will calculate the percentile rank for a trait value of 37 and the trait value that falls at the 70th percentile. These calculations are illustrated in Figures 7.2 and 7.3, respectively. As shown in Figure 7.2, there are 15 examinees at or below a trait value of 29.5 and 32 examinees at or below a trait value of 39.5. For a trait value of 37, we go up 7.5 units of a distance of 10 units on the left side of Figure 7.2, so on the right side we must go up 7.5/10 of a distance of 17. We conclude that there are 27.75 examinees at or below a trait value of 37. Since there are 50

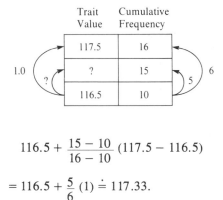

$$116.5 + \frac{15 - 10}{16 - 10}(117.5 - 116.5)$$

$$= 116.5 + \frac{5}{6}(1) \doteq 117.33.$$

Figure 7.1. Illustration of the calculation of a trait value corresponding to a percentile

Table 7.3. Ungrouped and Grouped Frequency Distributions

| Ungrouped | | | Grouped | |
| --- | --- | --- | --- | --- |
| Score | Frequency | | Score | Frequency |
| 8 | 12 | | 5–8 | 31 |
| 7 | 8 | | 1–4 | 4 |
| 6 | 10 | | | |
| 5 | 1 | | | |
| 4 | 2 | | | |
| 3 | 1 | | | |
| 2 | 1 | | | |
| 1 | 0 | | | |

Table 7.4. A Grouped Frequency Distribution

| Score | Frequency | Cumulative Frequency |
| --- | --- | --- |
| 50–59 | 6 | 50 |
| 40–49 | 12 | 44 |
| 30–39 | 17 | 32 |
| 20–29 | 10 | 15 |
| 10–19 | 2 | 5 |
| 0–9 | 3 | 3 |

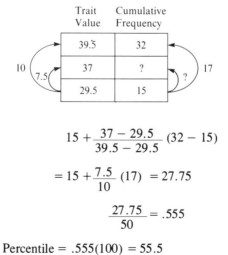

$$15 + \frac{37 - 29.5}{39.5 - 29.5} (32 - 15)$$

$$= 15 + \frac{7.5}{10} (17) = 27.75$$

$$\frac{27.75}{50} = .555$$

Percentile $= .555(100) = 55.5$

Figure 7.2. Calculation of the percentile rank for a trait value of 37

examinees in all, 27.75/50 = .555 of the examinees fall at or below a trait value of 37, which corresponds to a percentile rank of 55.5.

In Figure 7.3 we need to find the trait value that 70% of 50 examinees fall at or below—that is, the trait value with a cumulative frequency of 35. There are 44 examinees with trait values at or below 49.5, and there are 32 examinees with trait values at or below 39.5. Therefore, our answer is somewhere between 39.5 and 49.5. On the right side we go up 3/12 of the way, so on the left side we must go up 3/12 of the distance to a score of 42. Figures 7.4 and 7.5 illustrate similar calcula-

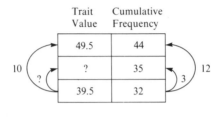

$$.70(50) = 35$$

$$39.5 + \frac{35 - 32}{44 - 32}(49.5 - 39.5)$$

$$= 39.5 + \frac{3}{12}(10) = 42$$

Figure 7.3. Calculation of the trait value at the 70th percentile

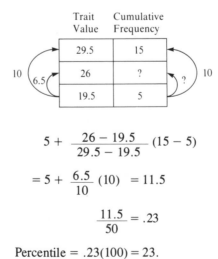

$$5 + \frac{26 - 19.5}{29.5 - 19.5}(15 - 5)$$

$$= 5 + \frac{6.5}{10}(10) = 11.5$$

$$\frac{11.5}{50} = .23$$

Percentile = .23(100) = 23.

Figure 7.4. Calculation of the percentile rank for a trait value of 26

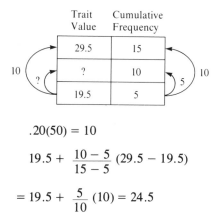

$$.20(50) = 10$$

$$19.5 + \frac{10 - 5}{15 - 5} (29.5 - 19.5)$$

$$= 19.5 + \frac{5}{10} (10) = 24.5$$

Figure 7.5. Calculation of the trait value at the 20th percentile

tions; we find that the percentile rank for a trait value of 26 is 23 and that the trait value at the 20th percentile is 24.5.

Percentiles, like any transformed scores, have some advantages and some disadvantages. The primary advantages of percentiles are that they are straightforward to calculate, regardless of the shape of the distribution of observed scores, and that they are easy to interpret. For communicating with people who have little background in statistics, percentiles are probably the most popular and meaningful transformed scores.

There are a number of limitations of percentile scores. Percentiles can be assumed to form ordinal scales (see Sections 2.2 and 8.2); thus, arithmetical manipulations of percentiles (for example, the calculation of means and variances of percentiles) can produce misleading results. Suppose that five seniors from two high schools have taken a college entrance exam. The scores for this exam are constructed on an equal-interval scale with a national mean of 420 and a standard deviation of 40. The scores and national percentiles for the two groups appear in Table 7.5. It is clear that the equal-interval scores from the two schools have the same variances. However, the variance of percentiles from School B is much smaller than the variance of percentiles from School A. Use of the variances of the percentiles could lead to inaccurate conclusions about the relative variance in performance for the two schools.

Keep in mind, also, that the distribution of percentiles within the norm group is *rectangular*, not normal, since by definition 1% of the examinees are at each percentile. Unlike the bell-shaped normal curve, a rectangular distribution curve looks like a horizontal line. Therefore, researchers who desire to use common statistical techniques that assume normal distributions should avoid the use of percentiles.

A third problem with percentile scores is that they may lead to exaggerated interpretations of small differences, especially when the test is short. Consider a test

Table 7.5. Scores and Percentiles for Students from Two Schools

|  | School A | | School B | |
| --- | --- | --- | --- | --- |
|  | Score | Percentile | Score | Percentile |
|  | 400 | 31 | 450 | 77 |
|  | 410 | 40 | 460 | 84 |
|  | 420 | 50 | 470 | 89 |
|  | 430 | 60 | 480 | 93 |
|  | 440 | 69 | 490 | 96 |
| Mean | 420 | 50 | 470 | 88 |
| Variance | 200 | 184 | 200 | 45 |

with an approximately normal score distribution. What happens to percentiles for examinees scoring near the center of the curve? As illustrated in Figure 7.6, small score differences near the center of the distribution may lead to large percentile differences. Suppose four examinees ($P_1$, $P_2$, $P_3$, and $P_4$) receive scores of 10, 12, 17, and 19, respectively, on a test. Only two score points separate $P_1$ from $P_2$ and $P_3$ from $P_4$, but, as illustrated in Figure 7.6, there will be a much larger difference in the percentiles for $P_1$ and $P_2$ than for $P_3$ and $P_4$. For example, the four percentiles for the examinees might be 25, 50, 97, and 99. Someone examining these percentiles would probably conclude that $P_1$ is subnormal, $P_2$ is average, and $P_3$ and $P_4$ are both extremely high on the trait, without realizing that only two items marked incorrectly separate $P_1$ from $P_2$ and $P_3$ from $P_4$. This problem is not restricted to normal distributions; it will occur whenever a large proportion of examinees get the same or similar observed scores, causing a one- or two-point score difference to result in a large percentile difference. Since this problem is more likely to occur on short tests, on which only a limited number of scores are possible, the test user should exercise great caution when dealing with percentiles based on short tests.

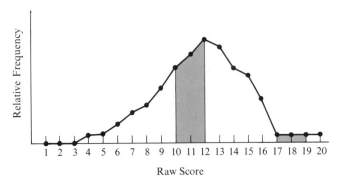

Figure 7.6. An equivalent raw-score difference generating very different percentile differences

## 7.3    Age and Grade Scores

Often test scores are reported in terms of *age* or *grade scores,* sometimes called *age* or *grade equivalents.* For example, a third-grader may be said to read at the fifth-grade level or have the mental ability of a 10-year-old. To calculate an age or grade score, the median raw score for examinees of a particular age (or grade) is determined, and this median raw score is transformed to be that age (or grade) score. For example, if the median raw score on a reading test for fourth-graders is 17.2, the raw score of 17.2 is transformed to a grade score of ''grade 4.'' Sometimes mean raw scores for a group are used instead of median scores to determine age or grade scores. In either case, interpolation is used to fill in the gaps between scores. For example, if the median grade-3 raw score is 13.3 and the median grade-4 raw score is 17.2, a raw score of 16 is transformed to a grade 3.7, or about ¾ of the way between grades 3 and 4. This calculation is illustrated in Figures 7.7 and 7.8.

Despite their popularity, age and grade scores have a number of serious limitations. Because they are assumed to form ordinal scores (Section 8.2), arithmetical manipulations of these scores can lead to misleading results. Also, the interpretation of these scores is not as straightforward as it appears. For example, one might infer that two children with the same *mental age* or age score think similarly, which is generally not true. There are enormous cognitive differences between a 5-year-old with a mental age of 8 and an 8-year-old with a mental age of 8. There will be large differences between the children in background knowledge and experiences, matu-

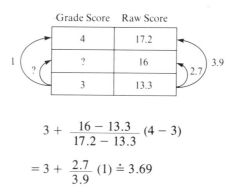

$$3 + \frac{16 - 13.3}{17.2 - 13.3} (4 - 3)$$

$$= 3 + \frac{2.7}{3.9} (1) \doteq 3.69$$

Figure 7.7. Interpolation of grade scores

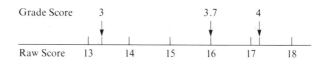

Figure 7.8. Representation of grade scores

rity of value systems, interests, cognitive styles, and reasoning ability. Similarly, a 5-year-old who is average and a 10-year-old with a mental age of 5 are very different, despite their similar mental ages. This limitation is also true for grade scores. A third-grader who is at the fifth-grade level on a science-achievement exam probably knows very different items of information and has a very different perception of the physical world than the average fifth-grader. Children with the same age or grade scores, especially when widely disparate in age, probably got different answers correct, used different test-taking strategies or styles, and are prepared for different types of subsequent training. These facts suggest that the use of age or grade scores could mislead most interpreters to perceive equalities that are not real.

A third problem with age and grade scores is that score distributions for adjacent grades typically tend to have increasing overlap as grade level increases (see Figure 7.9). Consider reading-level grade norms. A first-grader who is reading one grade level ahead may be in the 85th percentile among first-graders, but a fifth-grader who is one year ahead may only be at the 65th percentile among fifth-graders. Even though both students are one grade level ahead, the interpretation of their reading levels is quite different. The situation with age scores is the same. A 5-year-old who is two years ahead would be truly exceptional; for an 11-year-old, being two years ahead in mental age would not be as extraordinary. This problem also makes it difficult to compare examinees' performances at different age or grade levels. If two third-graders score at grade 3 and grade 4 on a mathematics exam, the one who scores higher might be very superior to the other. But, if two seventh-graders score at grade 7 and grade 8, they might be very similar to each other in mathematical competence. A new teaching method that improves performance by one grade level in only a few months' time would be marvelous if it worked for third-graders but less impressive if it worked for seventh-graders. Similar problems occur in age scores. A change of one year in cognitive or social development is an enormous leap for an infant; it is a much less dramatic change for a 16-year-old.

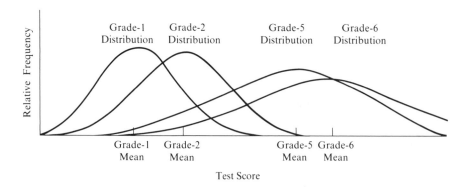

Figure 7.9. Example of increasing overlap of within-grade-score distributions as grade increases

Another fact that is often forgotten is that, when we consider all those children with the same chronological age (or the same grade), about half of them will be above average, and the other half will be below average. For example, about half of the third-graders read below the grade-3 norm. Therefore, probably very few children will fall where one might expect them to on the basis of their age or grade level.

Another problem, especially for grade scores, is that schools may differ in their curricula and may introduce topics at different rates. Thus, a whole school may be below average in arithmetic and above average in history. In a case such as this, the grade scores might suggest that the individual students are retarded or gifted in these areas, when actually it is differential exposure that accounts for their score patterns.

Obviously, the use of age or grade scores is only reasonable when the trait being measured increases (or decreases) monotonically with age or grade. The test scores illustrated in Figure 7.10 should not be transformed to age scores, because the test does not discriminate between 2-year-olds and 4- or 5-year-olds. Only when the relationship between mean or median score and age or grade is monotonically increasing or decreasing, as illustrated in Figure 7.11, should age or grade scores be considered.

A final problem with age and grade scores is that interpolation between tests may be inaccurate. School achievement exams are usually age graded. For example, there might be different mathematics-achievement tests for grades 3 to 6 and for grades 7 to 12. Unless these different tests can be equated (see Section 7.9), a fourth-grader who scores at the eighth-grade level on the lower level of the test probably will not score at the eighth-grade level on the higher level of the test. In summary, age and grade scores, despite their seeming appropriateness for use with children, have a large number of serious drawbacks that make meaningful interpretation extremely difficult.

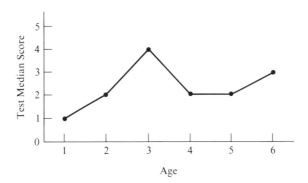

Figure 7.10. A relationship between test scores and age that is not appropriate for the development of age scores

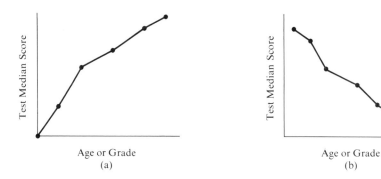

Figure 7.11. Relationships between test scores and age that are appropriate for the development of age or grade scores

## 7.4  Expectancy Tables

Expectancy tables are probably the best transformations available for tests that can be tied to a reasonable criterion. An *expectancy table* gives the conditional distribution (see Section 2.13) of criterion scores for different test scores. Table 7.6 gives a hypothetical expectancy table relating pre-course test scores to performance in a statistics class. Of the people in the norm group who scored between 25 and 30 on the pre-course test, 50% earned "A's," 30% earned "B's," and so on. For the people scoring between 5 and 9, none earned "A's," 2% earned "B's," and so on. A counselor would advise a student with a high pre-course test score to take the course, perhaps with a warning that a few students from this test-score level still did poorly in the course. When advising a person with a low test score, the counselor might suggest remedial work for the student before he or she enrolled in the class. The expectancy table illustrates the probabilistic nature of psychological prediction. Although most high scorers did well in the class, some did not—making it clear that a student with a high pre-course test score is not guaranteed an "A."

The main advantages of expectancy tables are especially apparent in counseling applications. The expectancy table makes clear the relationship between the test score and the criterion and the probabilistic nature of this relationship. Expec-

Table 7.6. Expectancy Table Relating Pre-Course Test Scores to Course Grades

| Test Score | Grade | | | | |
| | A (4) | B (3) | C (2) | D (1) | F (0) |
|---|---|---|---|---|---|
| 25–30 | .50 | .30 | .15 | .04 | .01 |
| 20–24 | .35 | .34 | .20 | .10 | .01 |
| 15–19 | .10 | .15 | .58 | .15 | .02 |
| 10–14 | .05 | .06 | .59 | .25 | .05 |
| 5–9 | 0 | .02 | .48 | .40 | .10 |
| 0–4 | 0 | .01 | .27 | .42 | .30 |

tancy tables built on local norms for schools, mental-health clinics, factories, and so on are conceptually easy to develop and use.

There are, however, some disadvantages to expectancy tables. These tables often cannot be developed, either because of time or monetary considerations or because a clear-cut criterion is not available. The norm group used to develop expectancy tables should be large enough to ensure that the probabilities in the table are reasonably stable. For a test with wide applications, a large number of expectancy tables may be necessary to relate the test scores to an array of criteria. Local norms, rather than norms based on a national sample, may be necessary for specific school programs, therapy situations, or careers. These problems with expectancy tables are practical rather than theoretical. When specific criteria and reasonable sample sizes for the norm groups are available, norms displayed in expectancy-table form are one of the most useful transformations possible.

An alternative to the expectancy table that can be used in similar situations involves the regression of the criterion on the test (see Sections 2.9 and 2.14). A predicted criterion score is provided for each test score or range of test scores. In the preceding example, the predicted (expected) course grade for every score on the test could be provided. The advantages and disadvantages of the transformation using regression techniques are very similar to those for expectancy tables.

## 7.5  Standard and Standardized Scores

Section 2.7 demonstrated how to calculate *standard scores,* often called $Z$ scores, where $Z = (X - \mu_X)/\sigma_X$. To get a standard score corresponding to any raw score, the mean of the raw scores is subtracted from the raw score, and the resulting number is divided by the standard deviation of the raw scores. A standard score indicates how many standard deviations from the mean a score lies. For example, if $Z = +1$, the raw score lies one standard deviation above the mean; if $Z = -2$, the raw score is two standard deviations below the mean. Since the standard-score transformation equation is linear, the shape of the standard-score distribution will be the same as the shape of the raw-score distribution, and correlations will not be affected. Contrary to popular belief, not all standard scores have a normal distribution. If the raw scores are skewed or bimodal, the standard-score distribution will have these same properties.

Standard scores always have a mean of 0 and a standard deviation of 1. One major disadvantage of standard scores is that about half the scores are negative. Most people prefer not to deal with negative numbers, because transcription and mathematical errors are more common (negative signs are easily lost) and because examinees dislike having negative scores. For these reasons, standard scores generally are not used in reporting scores.

*Standardized scores* are linear transformations of raw scores (or their standard-score equivalents) that eliminate the problems involved with negative numbers. Any set of standard scores can be transformed to have an arbitrary mean, $\mu^*$, and standard deviation, $\sigma^*$, by applying the formula $Y = \sigma^*Z + \mu^*$, where $Z$ is the standard score and $Y$ is the standardized score. For example, if you want to have $\mu^* = 100$ and $\sigma^* = 16$, the transformation from $Z$ to $Y$ would be: $Y = 16Z + 100$. An examinee with a standard score of 2 would have a standardized score of 132. This formula can also be easily applied to the raw scores. Since $Z = (X - \mu_X)/\sigma_X$,

$$Y = \sigma^* \left( \frac{X - \mu_X}{\sigma_X} \right) + \mu^*. \tag{7.1}$$

For example, if the raw-score mean and standard deviation are $\mu_X = 36$ and $\sigma_X = 3$, and you want to transform to standardized scores with $\mu^* = 50$ and $\sigma^* = 5$, the equation would be

$$Y = 5 \left( \frac{X - 36}{3} \right) + 50.$$

For a raw score, $X$, of 30, the transformed standardized score, $Y$, would be $Y = 5(30 - 36)/3 + 50 = 40$.

There are several standardized scale transformations in common use. The Army General Classification Test (AGCT) scores, developed in World War II, are standardized scores with $\mu^* = 100$, $\sigma^* = 20$. The College Entrance Exam Board (CEEB) test scores have $\mu^* = 500$, $\sigma^* = 100$. The subtest scores on the Wechsler tests (WISC and WAIS) are standardized to have $\mu^* = 10$, $\sigma^* = 3$. The Stanford-Binet IQ test score is standardized to have $\mu^* = 100$, $\sigma^* = 16$. Some personality-test scores, such as the California Psychological Inventory (CPI) and Minnesota Multiphasic Personality Inventory (MMPI) scales, have $\mu^* = 50$, $\sigma^* = 10$.

For people with a basic statistics background, standard and standardized scores are relatively simple to understand. Since they are linear transformations of the raw scores, these transformed scores will have a distribution with the same shape as the raw-score distribution. If the raw-score distribution is approximately normal, it is fairly easy to transform the standard or standardized scores to approximate percentiles, such as those given in Table 7.7. (This table was created using the standard normal table in the Appendix.) For example, if an examinee's standard score is 1.9, you can guess that the examinee is at about the 95th percentile (actually, from the table in the Appendix, it is the 97th percentile). If the standardized scores

Table 7.7. $Z$ Scores and Their
Approximate Percentiles in a Normal
Distribution

| $Z$ | Approximate Percentile |
|-----|------------------------|
| $-2$ | 2 |
| $-1$ | 16 |
| 0 | 50 |
| $+1$ | 84 |
| $+2$ | 98 |

have a mean of 100 and a standard deviation of 10, a score of 90 is one standard deviation below the mean, or at about the 16th percentile.

One disadvantage of standard or standardized scores is that they may be difficult for those unfamiliar with statistics to understand fully. Another disadvantage is that, since these transformations are linear, the distribution of transformed scores will contain any irregularities found in the raw-score distribution. Irregular "bumps" in this distribution, usually due to sampling irregularities, will be preserved by the transformation. A third problem with standard or standardized scores is more subtle. Suppose Juan had two standard scores, .19 on Test A and .14 on Test B, that lead us to the conclusion that he di' about equally well on the two tests. However, if the shapes of the two score distributions are quite different, our conclusion would be wrong. Figure 7.12 illustrates one possible pair of standard-score distributions. The distribution for Test A is skewed to the right, and the distribution for Test B is skewed to the left. The standard score of .19 is at the 64th percentile for Test A, and the standard score of .14 is at the 50th percentile for Test B. Similar standard or standardized scores can lead to different interpretations of relative merit. Thus, unless the test interpreter knows that two frequency distributions have the same shape, it is difficult to compare scores on two standardized scales, and it is particularly risky to interpret small differences in standard scores.

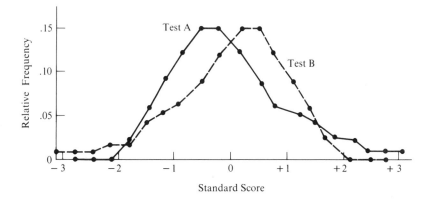

Figure 7.12. Similar standard scores fall at different percentile ranks for frequency distributions with different shapes

## 7.6  Normalized Scores

The transformation to *normalized scores* involves forcing the distribution of transformed scores to be as close as possible to a normal distribution by smoothing out, stretching, or condensing irregularities and departures from normality in the raw-score distribution. This transformation can be reasonably applied if the test developer believes that the underlying trait has a normal distribution and that the nonnormality of the raw-score distribution represents error due to sampling or test-construction problems.

The normalization process involves several steps:

1. Transform the raw scores to percentiles.
2. Find the standard score in the normal distribution corresponding to each percentile.
3. (Optional) Transform these standard scores to standardized scores with a desired mean and standard deviation.

To illustrate this process, we will normalize the raw scores given in Table 7.8 to have a transformed-score mean of 100 and standard deviation of 10. The column labeled $Z$ gives the score in the standard normal distribution corresponding to each percentile, obtained by referring to the Appendix; $Z$ is a normalized score with a mean of 0 and a standard deviation of 1. The last column is obtained by the formula $Y = 10Z + 100$, which gives the desired normalized and standardized scores. In the first row, a raw score of 118 has been transformed to a normalized and standardized score of 114.1.

Two normalized scores are in common use: $T$ scores and stanines. *T scores* are normalized scores with $\mu = 50$ and $\sigma = 10$. Nonnormalized, standardized scores with $\mu = 50$ and $\sigma = 10$ are called $T$ scores by some test publishers, so the test user should read the manual carefully to determine whether the ''$T$ scores'' are normalized. If the raw-score distribution is approximately normal, then the normalized and nonnormalized standardized ''$T$ scores'' will be approximately equal.

*Stanines* are one-digit normalized scores. They have a mean of 5 and a standard deviation of approximately 2; consequently, the difference between adjacent stanine scores is approximately one half of a standard deviation. The main advantages to the use of stanines are that their distributions are approximately normal and that each stanine involves only one number. Stanine scores are useful for rough screening of examinees, but because there are only nine different stanine scores, fine

Table 7.8. Calculation of Normalized Scores

| X Raw Score | Frequency | Cumulative Frequency | Percentile for Trait | Z Normalized Standard Score | Y Normalized and Standardized Score |
|---|---|---|---|---|---|
| 118 | 4 | 24 | 92 | 1.41 | 114.1 |
| 117 | 10 | 20 | 62 | .31 | 103.1 |
| 116 | 8 | 10 | 25 | −.67 | 93.3 |
| 115 | 2 | 2 | 4 | −1.75 | 82.5 |

discriminations among examinees can't be made with them. The percentile ranks and the percentile ranges for each stanine are given in Table 7.9. Transformations to stanines can be done by calculating the percentile rank for any raw score and then referring to Table 7.9. For example, a score at the 83rd percentile would be transformed to a stanine of 7, and a score at the 12th percentile would be transformed to a stanine of 3.

The advantage of transforming to normalized scores is that the transformed distribution has a well-known form that is easily interpretable and is amenable to common statistical manipulations. Scores on different tests, if normalized and converted to the same mean and standard deviation, become directly comparable, thus avoiding the complications involved when frequency distributions have different shapes. It is also easy to convert any normalized score to its equivalent percentile.

The use of normalized scores may not be reasonable if the underlying trait has a very nonnormal distribution. For example, if a score distribution is bimodal due to the presence of two disparate types of examinees (see Figures 6.12 and 6.13), it would not make sense to normalize the distribution. Also remember that normalized scores do not have a truly normal distribution. The normal distribution is continuous from negative infinity to positive infinity. However, normalized scores, because they are based on raw scores, are discrete and generally will fall within three standard deviations of the mean. Usually the problem of discreteness is not serious, especially if there are a large number of scores and the normalized distribution is fairly well approximated by the continuous normal curve. However, if the raw-score distribution is highly skewed, small raw-score differences between extreme scores may be exaggerated or compressed by the normalization. A last problem is that the transformed scores, with their approximately normal distribution, may lead the test user to believe that the test yields ''perfect, normal'' scores. Normalized scores based on a poor test (for example, a test with an inappropriate difficulty level or with poor discrimination among examinees) will not be very useful, despite their apparently pleasing, approximately normal distribution.

Table 7.9. Percentile Ranks and Ranges Corresponding to Stanines

| Stanine | Percentile Rank | Percentile Range |
|---------|-----------------|------------------|
| 9 | 98 | 96–100 |
| 8 | 94.5 | 89–96 |
| 7 | 83 | 77–89 |
| 6 | 68.5 | 60–77 |
| 5 | 50 | 40–60 |
| 4 | 31.5 | 23–40 |
| 3 | 17 | 11–23 |
| 2 | 5.5 | 4–11 |
| 1 | 2 | 0–4 |

## 7.7  Corrections for Guessing and Omissions

Transformations of scores can also be made to adjust for the effects of guessing and the effects of omitting items. These transformations can aid in the interpretation of an examinee's performance and in the comparison of the performances of different examinees. Transformations that take into account guessing or omissions traditionally have been called *formula scores*.

On multiple-choice tests, examinees can get an item correct, without knowing the right answer, simply by guessing. Guessing is not a problem on personality or attitude tests, where there are no right answers, but it can cause concern on aptitude, performance, or achievement tests. If there are three possible answers for each question on a test, an examinee who simply guesses at random has a probability of 1/3 of getting each item correct. On a 30-item test, an examinee who answered randomly would be expected, on the average, to obtain a score of $(30)(1/3) = 10$.

It is possible to estimate the effects that guessing has on a test score and correct or adjust the observed score accordingly. This procedure involves estimating the number of items that the individual would have gotten correct if he or she had not guessed. Suppose there are $A$ options (answer choices) for each item on an $N$-item multiple-choice test, and assume that the probability of guessing correctly is $1/A$. If an examinee guesses on $G$ of the items, the expected number of items guessed correctly is $G/A$, and the expected number of items guessed incorrectly is $G - G/A$. If we assume that an examinee gets an item wrong only through incorrect guessing, then the number of wrong responses, $W$, equals $G - G/A$, so $G = AW/(A - 1)$. The number of items that are guessed correctly is $G/A = W/(A - 1)$. If an examinee got $X$ items correct on a test, we can estimate that he or she got $F_1$ items correct without guessing, where

$$F_1 = X - G/A$$

$$= X - W/(A - 1). \tag{7.2}$$

$F_1$ is the first formula score discussed in this section, and $W/(A - 1)$ is the *correction for guessing*. If the examinee answers all items, $F_1$ is linearly related to the number of right responses, $X$, by the formula

$$F_1 = X - (N - X)/(A - 1)$$

$$= \left(\frac{A}{A - 1}\right) X - \frac{N}{A - 1}. \tag{7.3}$$

When there are no omitted items, $F_1$ is a linear function of $X$, is perfectly correlated with $X$, and has the same reliability and validity as $X$. In other words, the correction for guessing has no important effect when all the items are answered. However, when there are omitted items, $F_1$ and $X$ are not perfectly correlated.

Suppose that an examinee gets 16 items correct and 24 items wrong on a 40-item, five-option multiple-choice test. We can estimate that this examinee got

$W/(A - 1) = 24/4 = 6$ items correct by guessing and $16 - 6 = 10$ items correct without guessing. Notice that this is just an estimate of the number of items correctly answered without guessing. Some examinees may be "lucky" or "unlucky" and may guess correctly more or less than $1/A$ of the time. Given limited information and a simple model, the formula score $F_1$ uses the best estimate available for assessing the effects of guessing.

Because examinees sometimes don't answer all the items on a test, we need a formula score that takes item omissions into account. Otherwise, examinees who randomly guess on some items can obtain higher scores than those examinees who omit those items. Let $N$ be the total number of items in a test and $B$ be the number of items that are blank or not answered. $X$, $W$, and $A$ are defined as before. Then,

$$N = X + W + B; \qquad (7.4)$$

the total number of items in the test equals the number of items that are right plus the number of items that are wrong plus the number of items that are blank or omitted. The number-right scores, $X$, for examinees who answer all items are comparable to $F_2$ scores for examinees who omit items, where

$$F_2 = X + B/A. \qquad (7.5)$$

The second formula score, $F_2$, is the estimated number of items that would be correct if every blank item were replaced by a random guess. For example, if an examinee had 10 right answers and 2 blanks on a test with four options per item, that examinee's formula score would be $10 + 2/4 = 10.5$.

The scoring formula $F_2$ is a linear function of the scoring formula $F_1$ (Equation 7.2), since

$$F_2 = X + (N - X - W)/A$$

$$= \frac{(A - 1)X}{A} - \frac{W}{A} + \frac{N}{A}$$

$$= \left(\frac{A - 1}{A}\right) F_1 + \frac{N}{A} .$$

Scores based on scoring formula $F_2$ are perfectly correlated with and have the same reliability and validity as scores based on $F_1$. $F_2$, like $F_1$, is perfectly correlated with the number-right score, $X$, only if all of the examinees answer all of the items. That is, if $B = 0$, then $F_1$, $F_2$, and $X$ are perfectly correlated. When there are omissions, $F_1$ and $F_2$ are not perfectly correlated with $X$.

There has been a long controversy about the propriety and usefulness of formula scores. In most cases, examinees don't guess randomly on items they don't know. Usually some of the possible answers can be eliminated as clearly impossible or untrue; therefore, the probability of guessing correctly among the remaining alternatives is greater than $1/A$. Also examinees may differ in their tendencies to guess on or omit items. If the test directions clearly state that examinees are to omit items only when they feel that they would have to guess randomly, and if the examinees follow these directions, then a formula score is appropriate (Lord, 1975). However, a formula score is not appropriate theoretically when the test directions either give no instructions about omissions or state that an examinee's score is the number of questions answered correctly. If the theoretical results about the effects of formula scores on a test's reliability and validity are based on the assumption of random guessing, then these results are suspect unless it can be verified that examinees do omit those items on which they would have to guess randomly.

Empirical examinations of the reliability and validity of formula scores do not present a clear case either for or against formula scoring. Sabers and Feldt (1968) altered test-taking directions with respect to guessing by giving an admonition against guessing versus giving no instructions about guessing. They found that the directions and formula scoring did not alter the reliability of selected mathematics tests. Traub, Hambleton, and Singh (1969) found that changes in test directions and formula scoring had small effects on test reliability. Diamond and Evans (1973) reviewed a number of studies on formula scoring and concluded that, if it has any consistent effect, formula scoring tends to slightly increase test validity. In short, evidence about the usefulness of formula scoring is not clear cut. Formula scores may help, hinder, or not affect test reliability and validity.

The value of formula scoring depends on many factors: the difficulty of the test, the probability of correctly guessing answers, the variability of examinees' tendencies to omit items, and the reliability and validity of the tendency to omit items. Appropriate evaluation of a formula score requires that the test directions be compatible with the scoring formula and that the examinees understand the implications of the test directions and act accordingly. For example, if the test directions say that the examinees should not guess but these directions aren't followed, then the meaning of omissions and formula scores becomes unclear. Similarly, if the examinees are directed not to omit items but they omit them anyway, then the meaning of the number-right scores becomes unclear. The test user must make a careful evaluation of the meaning of omissions for the test at hand and score it accordingly. In most cases, the effect of formula scoring on the reliability and validity of a test must be evaluated empirically.

## 7.8  Equal-Interval Scales

In Section 2.2, the concept of equal intervals was introduced. A set of scores has equal intervals if any given difference between scores always represents the same amount of difference in the trait being measured. For example, if a one-point difference in spelling-test scores between the scores of 100 and 101, 101 and 102, and so on always represents the same amount of increase in spelling ability, the test has equal intervals. A test whose scores form equal intervals is particularly useful for measuring growth or change in a trait or behavior. Typically, a test's raw scores do not display equal intervals, but sometimes the raw scores can be transformed into a set of scores (a scale) that does have equal intervals.

In order to form an *equal-interval scale* (usually called an *interval scale*) from a test's raw scores, the test must measure a trait that has equal intervals. The scale developer first makes predictions about how the trait is related to test performance and then examines the accuracy of these predictions. If the predictions are accurate, the scale developer can transform the raw scores into an interval scale. This section examines one commonly used method for constructing an interval scale—*Thurstone's absolute scaling method*. Chapters 8 and 11 describe a number of other methods for forming interval (and ratio) scales.

Thurstone's absolute scaling method (which is described by Gulliksen, 1950) hypothesizes that the continuous trait being measured by a test has a normal distribution in some specified population. It also hypothesizes that raw scores on the test are monotonically related to trait values. (A *monotonic relationship* is one in which every increase in the raw score reflects an increase in the trait value.) If these hypotheses are true and the raw scores are normalized, then the normalized scores have equal intervals. In order to examine the accuracy of these hypotheses, the test is administered to two samples of examinees, each of which is assumed to have a normal distribution of trait values. For example, a spelling test might be administered to a national sample of seventh-grade students and a national sample of eighth-grade students. The resulting raw-score distributions are normalized within each sample. Each raw score is thereby transformed into one normalized score in one sample and another normalized score in the other sample. If these two sets of normalized scores are linearly related, then the normalized test scores obtained from either sample form an equal-interval scale.

Thurstone's absolute scaling method can be illustrated with a simple example. Table 7.10 contains raw-score frequency distributions, percentiles, and normalized scores (Z scores) for a hypothetical spelling test administered to seventh- and eighth-grade students. Figure 7.13 displays a plot of the Z scores obtained from

Table 7.10. Testing Results for a Hypothetical Spelling Test

| Raw Score | Seventh Grade | | | Eighth Grade | | |
|---|---|---|---|---|---|---|
| | Frequency | Percentile | Z Score | Frequency | Percentile | Z Score |
| 0 | 4 | 1 | − 2.3 | 4 | 1 | − 2.3 |
| 1 | 10 | 5 | − 1.7 | 6 | 4 | − 1.8 |
| 2 | 18 | 12 | − 1.2 | 8 | 7 | − 1.5 |
| 3 | 30 | 24 | − .7 | 14 | 13 | − 1.1 |
| 4 | 38 | 41 | − .2 | 18 | 21 | − .8 |
| 5 | 38 | 60 | + .2 | 24 | 31 | − .5 |
| 6 | 30 | 77 | + .7 | 26 | 44 | − .2 |
| 7 | 18 | 89 | + 1.2 | 26 | 57 | + .2 |
| 8 | 10 | 96 | + 1.7 | 24 | 69 | + .5 |
| 9 | 2 | 99 | + 2.3 | 18 | 80 | + .8 |
| 10 | 2 | 99.5 | + 2.6 | 14 | 88 | + 1.2 |
| 11 | 0 | 100 | + ∞ | 8 | 93 | + 1.5 |
| 12 | 0 | 100 | + ∞ | 10 | 98 | + 2.0 |
| 13 | 0 | 100 | + ∞ | 0 | 100 | + ∞ |

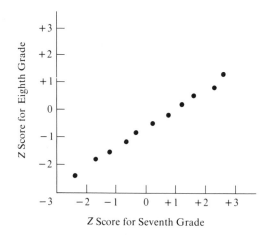

Figure 7.13. Relationship between Z scores from Table 7.10.

the two samples. (The plot does not include points containing $+\infty$.) Since the Z scores for the two grades are linearly related, the Z scores for either grade can be used as an equal-interval scale. Of course, the Z scores also could be standardized to have any desired mean and standard deviation.

Equal-interval scales can be used in arithmetical manipulations, such as the calculation of means, standard deviations, and so on. The major disadvantage of equal-interval scales is that the process involved in deriving them is so complex that some test users may be unable to understand the scores or to communicate their understanding.

Figure 7.14 displays how an equal-interval scale obtained from Thurstone's absolute scaling method might be related to other scores.

## 7.9    Equating Test Scores

When alternate forms of a test are constructed, it is often desired to transform the test scores to make them equivalent, if possible. This procedure is called *test equating*. Lord (1977b) defines test forms as being equated when it would be a matter of indifference to each examinee which test form he or she takes. Thus, for tests to be equated they must measure the same trait, and every level of the trait must be measured with equal accuracy by the two tests. Unequally reliable tests cannot be equated. When test forms are successfully equated, the examinees' scores will not be affected by the particular forms administered to them; consequently, the forms can be used interchangeably. Similarly, it is often desired to equate different levels of a test so that an examinee will get the same score regardless of whether an easier or harder level of the test is administered. This is sometimes called *articulation of test levels* or *vertical equating*, in contrast to the *horizontal equating* of test

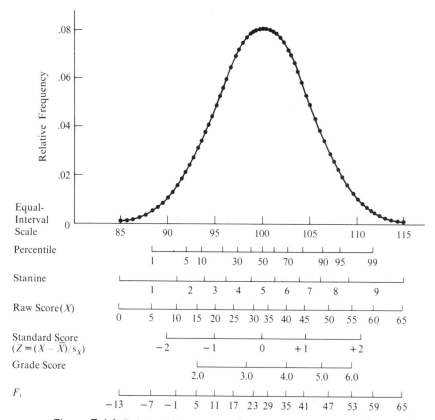

Figure 7.14. Relationships among various scores

forms within a specified difficulty level. Several procedures for equating tests will be very briefly described. These procedures determine which scores on two tests can be said to be equivalent; the problems of unequal reliabilities of the tests will not be discussed here. More detailed information about test equating methods is available from Angoff (1971) and Lord (1977b).

The two test forms to be equated can be administered to the same sample of examinees. The major disadvantage of this equating method is that the scores on the test that is administered second can be affected by practice or fatigue. Such effects can be examined by reversing the order of administration of the tests for a random half of the sample. If the raw scores from the two tests are linearly related (which can be determined by examining scatterplots of the scores), the score distributions for the two tests will have very similar shapes, and standard scores for the two tests will be equivalent. This results in a linear equating of the two tests. If the scores for the two tests are nonlinearly related, which is typically the case, standard scores for the tests will not be equivalent. In such a case, a table or graph would be used to show how a score on one of the tests would be transformed to a score on the other test.

Two tests can also be equated by administering them to different, but equivalent, samples. Equivalent samples can be obtained by very carefully controlled sampling procedures. Since the samples are equivalent, scores that are at the same percentile in the two samples are said to be equivalent. For example, suppose that a score of 10 on Test A is at the 25th percentile for Sample 1, a score of 12 on Test B is at the 22nd percentile for Sample 2, and a score of 13 on test B is at the 28th percentile for Sample 2. Using linear interpolation, a score of 10 on Test A is said to be equivalent to a score of 12.5 on Test B. This is called the *equipercentile method* of equating. If the two distributions of scores differ only in terms of their means and standard deviations, the equipercentile method will produce a linear equating of the scores. If the two distributions differ in more than their means and standard deviations, a nonlinear equating will result.

The advantage of the equipercentile method of equating is that each examinee only needs to take one test instead of two. The main disadvantage of the equipercentile method is the need to obtain equivalent samples. Also, the equipercentile method does not determine whether the two tests *should* be equated; it simply equates them. Using this method, it is possible to appear to equate tests that measure very different traits (for example, vocabulary and mathematical computation).

Thurstone's method of absolute scaling (Section 7.8) can also be used to equate tests. To use this method, one must assume that the trait being measured by the two tests is normally distributed within each of two equivalent samples. Thurstone's method has the advantage of involving the administration of only one test to each examinee, and it allows an examination of the degree to which the two tests are equatable. The major disadvantage of this method is the necessity of obtaining samples in which the trait is normally distributed; this method typically involves expensive sampling procedures.

In another method of equating, the two tests are administered to different and not necessarily equivalent samples. In addition both groups take a test called an *anchor test* that measures the same trait as the tests being equated. Scores on the anchor test are used to control for differences in the two groups that could affect the equating. The latent-trait models described in Chapter 11 are particularly useful for this type of equating. The advantage of this method is not having to obtain equivalent samples; the disadvantages are the need to administer the anchor test and the need to deal with the statistical complexities of controlling for differences between the equating groups.

Vertical equating of tests can be more difficult than horizontal equating, because different levels of a test typically involve different types of items. For example, Level 1 of a mathematics-achievement test may involve addition of single-digit numbers, but Level 2 may involve addition of two-digit numbers as well. It may be difficult to equate these tests, and, even if the test scores appear to equate statistically, there are conceptual problems in interpreting "equivalent" scores from the two tests. Also, in vertical equating it is common to link many levels together to form one scale. Level 1 is equated to Level 2, Level 2 is equated to Level 3, and so forth. Scores on Level 1 are equated to scores on Level 3 only indirectly, through

Level 2. It may be impossible to equate Levels 1 and 3 directly, because it may be that few examinees who perform reasonably well on Level 1 can answer any of the questions on Level 3, whereas most of the examinees who do reasonably well on Level 3 get perfect or nearly perfect scores on Level 1. Thus, it may be impossible to double-check the equating of scores from Levels 1 and 3. When vertical equating is accomplished by the successive equating of adjacent test levels, the use of scores from a wide variety of test levels in one data analysis may be inappropriate or may produce results that are difficult to interpret.

## 7.10  Summary

Most raw scores are transformed to other numbers so that they can be more easily interpreted. There are two main types of transformations of raw scores: linear and nonlinear. Linear transformations do not alter the basic shapes of distributions or the size of correlations. Nonlinear transformations can alter both of these properties of scores.

A popular nonlinear transformation is the percentile rank. The percentile rank of any trait value is the percentage of examinees in a norm group who obtain scores at or below the trait value in question. Percentiles are a popular transformation and are relatively easy to calculate and interpret. However, it can be misleading to deal with means or standard deviations for percentiles. Moreover, since the distribution of percentile ranks is rectangular in shape, common statistical techniques that assume normality should not be used with them. If the test is short, or if a large number of examinees obtain the same raw score, the transformation to percentile ranks may lead to exaggerated interpretations of small differences in raw scores.

Other types of nonlinear transformations result in age and grade scores. Age and grade scores are common transformations with serious limitations. They are ordinal scales, and arithmetical operations with them (for example, calculations of means) can be misleading. It often is forgotten that half of the norm group scores above its nominal age or grade level, and half scores below. Age and grade scores can reflect curriculum or environmental differences, and comparisons using age and grade scores based on different tests may cause misunderstandings. Age and grade scores can lead users to perceive equalities that aren't real.

Another nonlinear transformation is the expectancy table. Expectancy tables give the conditional distribution of criterion scores for various levels of test performance. If an explicit criterion and reasonable sample sizes are available, expectancy tables are easy to construct and especially useful for counseling applications. As an alternative, regression techniques offer similar advantages.

Standard and standardized scores are frequently used linear transformations of raw scores. If the distributions of two raw scores are different in shape, comparisons of their corresponding standard or standardized scores can be misleading.

Normalized scores are nonlinear transformations created by smoothing the raw-score distribution into an approximately normal shape. $T$ scores and stanines are common normalized scores. Normalization transforms scores to a known, easily interpretable distribution that is required by many common statistical tests. This transformation is not reasonable if the underlying trait distribution is not normal, and it is not a cure for a poorly designed test.

Formula scores ($F_1$ and $F_2$) are designed to improve the information provided by raw scores about the performance of examinees who guess on or omit items. $F_1$ estimates the number-right score if correct answers due to guessing are eliminated. $F_2$ estimates what the number-right scores would have been if examinees had randomly guessed on all omitted items. Experimental evidence for the value of calculating such scores is contradictory; consequently, the test developer must evaluate each of these transformations empirically for use with specific tests for specific purposes.

Equal-interval scales reflect the trait being measured on an interval level of measurement. If the required assumptions are reasonable, equal-interval scales are particularly useful in the assessment of growth or change. Thurstone's absolute scaling method is a common method of obtaining an equal-interval scale.

Tests are equated so that their scores can be used interchangeably. Two tests can be equated by administering both of them to one sample of examinees and determining their relationship. If they are linearly related, standard scores based on the tests are equivalent. If they are nonlinearly related, a table or graph can be used to show which scores are equivalent. Tests can also be equated by administering different tests to each of two equivalent samples and equating scores with the same percentiles in the two groups (the equipercentile method). Finally, tests can be equated using Thurstone's absolute scaling method or by the use of an anchor test.

## 7.11  Vocabulary

age equivalent
age scores
anchor test
articulation of test levels
correction for guessing
criterion-referenced testing
equal-interval scale
equipercentile equating
expectancy table
$F_1$
$F_2$
formula score
grade equivalent
grade scores
horizontal equating
interval scale
linear transformation
mental age
monotonic relationship

monotonic transformation
nonlinear transformation
normalized scores
norm group
norm-referenced testing
percentile
percentile rank
percentile score
raw score
rectangular distribution
reference group
standardized score
standard score
stanine
test equating
Thurstone's absolute scaling
transformed score
$T$ scores
vertical equating

## 7.12   Study Questions

1. Why are raw scores transformed?
2. What are the differences between linear and nonlinear transformations?
3. Explain how to calculate the percentile for a given trait value and the trait value corresponding to any given percentile. What are the advantages and disadvantages of the percentile transformation?
4. How are age and grade scores calculated? What are the advantages and disadvantages of age and grade scores?
5. How are expectancy tables constructed? What are the advantages and disadvantages of expectancy tables?
6. How can a regression equation be used to provide information similar to that provided by an expectancy table?
7. Explain how to calculate standard and standardized scores. What are the advantages and disadvantages of standard and standardized scores?
8. Explain how to normalize a set of scores. What are the advantages and disadvantages of normalized scores?
9. Assuming that the raw-score distribution in the following table is approximately normal with $\mu_X = 48$ and $\sigma_X = 2$, verify the column entries.

| Raw Score | Z | Percentile | T | Stanine |
|---|---|---|---|---|
| 54 | 3.0 | 99+ | 80 | 9 |
| 53 | 2.5 | 99 | 75 | 9 |
| 52 | 2.0 | 98 | 70 | 9 |
| 51 | 1.5 | 93 | 65 | 8 |
| 50 | 1.0 | 84 | 60 | 7 |
| 49 | .5 | 69 | 55 | 6 |
| 48 | 0 | 50 | 50 | 5 |
| 47 | − .5 | 31 | 45 | 4 |
| 46 | − 1.0 | 16 | 40 | 3 |
| 45 | − 1.5 | 7 | 35 | 2 |
| 44 | − 2.0 | 2 | 30 | 1 |
| 43 | − 2.5 | 1 | 25 | 1 |
| 42 | − 3.0 | 1− | 20 | 1 |

10. Describe the two formula scores developed as corrections for guessing and omissions.
11. What problems are involved in the use of formula scores? How useful are formula scores?
12. What is an equal-interval scale? How can equal-interval scales be constructed?
13. Describe four procedures for equating test scores. What are the advantages and disadvantages of each procedure?

## 7.13   Computational Problems

1. Using the data in the following table:
   a. Calculate the percentile ranks for trait values of 86, 92, and 107.
   b. Calculate the trait values at the 3rd, 22nd, and 75th percentiles.

| Score | Frequency |
|---------|-----------|
| 110–119 | 10 |
| 100–109 | 5 |
| 90–99 | 8 |
| 80–89 | 12 |
| 70–79 | 18 |

2. On a cognitive-maturity test, the median score for six-year-olds is 23 points and the median score for seven-year-olds is 32 points. Estimate the mental age (age score) of a child earning 28 points on this test.

3. Two potential students for a statistics class take a pre-course exam. Micah gets 21 points, and Becky gets 13 points. Using the expectancy table (Table 7.6), what advice would you give each student?

4. (Optional) Using the definition of regression contained in Section 2.14, obtain the expected course grade for each of the six pre-course test-score ranges in Table 7.6.

5. The raw scores for a test have a mean of 83 and a standard deviation of 12.
   a. What is the standard score corresponding to a raw score of 89?
   b. What is the standardized score for a raw score of 80 if the scores are standardized to be comparable to CEEB scores?

6. Transform the following scores to $T$ scores and then to stanines.

| Raw Score | Frequency |
|-----------|-----------|
| 37 | 6 |
| 36 | 124 |
| 35 | 58 |
| 34 | 10 |
| 33 | 2 |

7. Carey obtains 20 correct answers on a 39-item four-option multiple-choice test.
   a. Estimate the number of items Carey got correct by guessing.
   b. Estimate the number of items Carey got correct without guessing.
   c. What assumptions were used in making these estimates?

8. Two examinees take a true/false test with 50 items. Examinee A gets 40 items correct and omits four items. Examinee B gets 35 items correct and omits 12. Estimate the number of items each examinee would have gotten correct if their omissions were replaced with random guesses. Evaluate the relative performance of the two examinees.

9. a. Using the test-score frequency distributions in the following table, create an equal-interval scale using Thurstone's absolute scaling method.
   b. Do the data appear to form a good equal-interval scale?

|        | Frequency |       |
|--------|-----------|-------|
| Score  | Women     | Men   |
| 0      | 1         | 1     |
| 1      | 2         | 5     |
| 2      | 4         | 7     |
| 3      | 5         | 5     |
| 4      | 4         | 1     |
| 5      | 3         | 1     |
| 6      | 1         | 0     |

10. Assume the data in the following table are the result of administering two different tests to two different, but equivalent, samples.
   a. Equate the test scores (giving the Test B score equivalent to each Test A score) using the equipercentile method.
   b. Equate the test scores using Thurstone's absolute scaling method.
   c. Compare the results from a. and b.

| Test A |           | Test B |           |
|--------|-----------|--------|-----------|
| Score  | Frequency | Score  | Frequency |
| 10     | 5         | 105    | 10        |
| 11     | 10        | 115    | 15        |
| 12     | 20        | 125    | 15        |
| 13     | 20        | 135    | 30        |
| 14     | 25        | 145    | 20        |
| 15     | 10        | 155    | 5         |
| 16     | 10        | 165    | 5         |

# Scaling

## 8.1 Introduction

In Chapter 1, measurement was defined as the assignment of numbers to individuals in a systematic manner as a means of representing properties of the individuals. The discussions in Chapters 2 through 6 centered on observed test scores as measurements. In Chapter 7, some limitations of observed scores were discussed, and several transformations of observed scores were presented. These transformations resulted in new numbers being assigned to the individuals.

When we want to measure some property, we may wonder what numbers to use. Clearly, we should choose numbers that give the best measurement. There are several different ways to evaluate the quality of measurement. One approach we can use is to evaluate measurements in terms of their reliability and validity, as discussed in Chapters 4 and 5; the measurements that should be used are the ones that are the most reliable or the most valid.

There is another framework we can use for evaluating measurements—a framework that involves several characteristics we would like our measurements to have. These characteristics, which were introduced in Section 2.2, relate to how well the measurements represent the property or trait being measured. The first characteristic is distinctiveness; if examinee A and examinee B have different reading-comprehension levels, then the numbers assigned to them should be distinct. The second characteristic is ordering in magnitude; if examinee A has a higher reading-comprehension level than examinee B, we want the number assigned to examinee A to be larger than the number assigned to examinee B. The third characteristic is that of equal intervals; if the difference in reading-comprehension levels between examinees A and B is the same as the difference in reading-comprehension levels between examinees C and D, then the difference between the numbers assigned to A and B should equal the difference between the numbers assigned to C and D. The fourth characteristic is that of an absolute zero; if examinee D cannot read, he or she would be assigned a 0.

These four characteristics are used in determining the level of measurement —nominal, ordinal, interval, or ratio—and are contained within a theoretical framework called *scaling theory*. Scaling theory is a branch of measurement theory that focuses on rationales and mathematical techniques for determining what numbers should be used to represent different amounts of a property being measured. The main objective of scaling theory is to produce good scales. A *scale* is an organized set of measurements, all of which measure one property or trait. The number assigned to a particular object or examinee is called a *scale value*. For example, a set of observed test scores assigned to examinees on the basis of their vocabulary-test performances can be called an observed-score, or raw-score scale; a set of percentiles based on mathematical-computation performance can form a percentile scale. Scaling theory presents rationales and techniques for choosing particular scales, and it also describes the properties of the scales in terms of their levels of measurement.

Section 8.2 describes how a scale's level of measurement is determined, and Section 8.3 discusses the levels of measurement reached by the scales presented in Chapters 3, 7, and 11. Historically, most developments in scaling have dealt with the scaling of stimuli, such as attitudes or psychophysical stimuli. Unlike most of test theory, scaling methods are not based on observed test scores, and they involve different ways of observing and analyzing behavior, several of which are described in Section 8.4. More examples of the uses of scaling appear in Dawes (1972), and Torgerson (1958) covers scaling methods in detail.

## 8.2  Determining the Level of Measurement

Scales yield numbers that represent properties of the objects they measure. The scales cannot be changed or transformed in ways that will disrupt this representation. The types of transformations of a scale that are *admissible* (that is, the types of transformations that maintain the correct representation) define the type of scale that has been produced. For example, scales that reach a nominal level of measurement (*nominal scales*) have unique numbers assigned to distinct objects or types of objects. These numbers can be changed in any way as long as the numbers assigned to the distinct objects remain different.

Scales that reach an ordinal level of measurement (*ordinal scales*) have larger numbers assigned to objects with more of the property being measured than to objects with less of that property. If object A is greater (faster, more liberal, more blue, or more difficult) than object B, A has a larger scale value than B. Any numbers can be assigned as the scale values for A and B, as long as the number assigned to A is greater than the one assigned to B. Once a scale has been assigned, it can be transformed in any fashion as long as the correct ordering of the scale values is preserved. For example, if the scale values of 1, 2, and 3 are assigned to a set of objects, the values of 5, 10, and 11 or of 1, 22.5, and 1003 would produce the same order and would be admissible. Admissible transformations for ordinal scales are called *monotonic transformations*. A monotonic transformation is any transformation that does not affect the relative order of the scale values—for example, adding a constant or multiplying by a positive number.

Scales that reach an interval level of measurement (*interval scales*) have numbers that allow us to calculate and interpret the ratios of intervals (distances) between pairs of objects. For example, if the distance between objects A and B is twice the distance between objects C and D, then the difference between the numbers assigned to A and B is twice the difference between the numbers assigned to C and D. Any linear transformation of an interval scale is admissible. As defined in Section 7.1, a linear transformation is of the form $Y = aX + b$, where $a$ and $b$ are constants, $Y$ is the new scale value, and $X$ is the original scale value. In order to preserve the original ordering of the objects, the constant $a$ must be greater than 0. A linear transformation of an interval scale doesn't alter the ratio of the distances between scale values. For example, suppose three objects, L, M, and N, are measured on an interval scale and are given scale values of 1, 2, and 4. The distance between the scale values for M and L is $2 - 1 = 1$, and the distance between N and M is $4 - 2 = 2$. The ratio of the distance from M to L to the distance from N to M is 1/2. If a new scale, $Y$, is created from the original scale, $X$, by the linear transformation $Y = 2X + 10$, then the new scale values for the three objects are 12, 14, and 18, respectively. The ratio of the distance from $M$ to $L$ to the distance from N to M is $(14 - 12)/(18 - 14) = 1/2$; the linear transformation didn't alter the ratio of the distances between the scale values.

Scales that reach a ratio level of measurement (*ratio scales*) have numbers that allow us to calculate and interpret the ratios of the scale values. For example, if A is twice as great (fast, liberal, blue, or difficult) as B, A is assigned a scale value twice as large as the scale value assigned to B. The only transformation admissible with a ratio scale is multiplication by a constant. This transformation takes the form $Y = aX$, where the constant $a$ must be greater than 0 to preserve the original ordering of the objects. For instance, if two objects are measured on a ratio scale and are given values of 3 and 9, the ratio of the scale values of the two objects is $3/9 = 1/3$. If a new scale is formed by the transformation $Y = 5X$, the new scale values are 15 and 45. Their ratio remains 1/3; the second object still has a scale value three times as large as the first object. Note that, for a ratio scale, a linear transformation involving an additive constant is not admissible. For example, the transformation $Y = 5X + 5$ produces values of 20 and 50, which do not have the ratio 1/3.

A scale's level of measurement is determined by the type of transformation that will maintain the scale's representation of the property being measured. The scale developer identifies this transformation by using a *scaling model,* which is a symbolic representation of the relationship between the property being scaled and a set of observations, such as scores. For a scaling model to be useful, it must make testable predictions about a set of observations. In other words, the model should present a hypothesis whose statistical significance for a set of observations can be examined. If a model makes accurate predictions, it is said to *fit* the observations. When a model fits a set of observations, the model will determine which scale value should be assigned to each observation. The type of transformation of scale values that will preserve the accuracy of the model predictions defines the level of measurement obtained by the scale. Most scaling models have been developed for obtaining interval and ratio scales.

This procedure for proposing and using a scaling model can be illustrated with Thurstone's absolute-scaling model, presented in Section 7.8. This model hypothesizes that the trait being scaled has a normal distribution in certain populations of examinees and that the observed test scores are monotonically related to the trait. Thurstone's model predicts that, if the observed test scores are normalized within each of two samples of examinees from appropriate populations, the resulting normalized scales will be linearly related across populations. This prediction is tested by obtaining appropriate samples of examinees, testing them, normalizing the resulting scores within each sample (see Table 7.10), and determining whether the normalized scores have a linear plot (see Figure 7.13). If the model fits the data, the normalized scale will assign a scale value ($Z$ score) to each observed score. Any linear transformation of this scale will produce the same model predictions. That is, the $Z$ scores (standard scores) could be transformed to standardized scores by a linear equation like Equation 7.1. The standardized scores will have a normal distribution within each sample of examinees (just like the $Z$ scores), and the standardized scores will produce a linear plot that looks like the plot based on $Z$ scores. A nonlinear monotonic transformation of the $Z$ scores would not be admissible, because it would alter the normal distribution of observed scores. Since a linear transformation is admissible and a nonlinear monotonic transformation is not, Thurstone's absolute-scaling model, when it fits a set of data, produces an interval scale. If the model does not fit the data (that is, if the normalized scores do not form a linear plot), an interval scale is not produced.

In some cases a scaling model is not tested with a set of observations. Instead, scale values are assigned to observations by definition or by fiat. For example, observed test scores assign scale values by definition. Thus, the observed test scores are not necessarily linearly related to trait values, particularly if there is a floor or ceiling effect on the test. The relationship between observed test scores and trait values can appear as depicted in Figure 8.1 if there is a ceiling effect. When

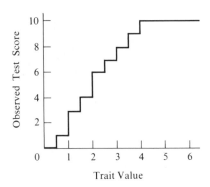

Figure 8.1. A possible relationship between observed test scores on a ten-item test and trait values when there is a ceiling effect for the test

scale values are assigned by definition or fiat, they may appear reasonable, but their reasonableness has not been empirically verified and their level of measurement is undetermined. However, it is usually assumed that scaling by fiat produces ordinal scales. The main difficulty in using scales that are assigned by fiat is the possibility of drawing inappropriate conclusions about the trait being measured.

Keep in mind that, even though they may not be linearly related to the trait or property being measured, scales obtained by fiat can be very useful. For example, observed test scores that are reliable and valid are valuable in many practical applications. In particular, observed test scores that have high predictive or concurrent validity clearly are useful.

## 8.3   Levels of Measurement Produced by Selected Scales

The levels of measurement produced by observed test scores and the scales presented in Chapters 7 and 11 can be described. As discussed previously, an observed test score is obtained by definition and does not involve testing the fit of any model. Observed test scores are assumed to form ordinal scales. Similarly, the percentile scale, described in Section 7.2, is a scale produced by definition. It does not involve testing the fit of any scaling model, and it is assumed to be an ordinal scale.

By definition, age and grade scales have equal scale intervals representing differences between the mean or median scores of the norm group for examinees a year apart in age or grade; that is, the score interval from the median grade-5 score to the median grade-6 score is defined to be the same as the score interval from the median grade-7 score to the median grade-8 score. Periods of time during the year that fall between norming dates are assigned scores by linear interpolation. This interpolation is based on the assumption that growth in the score proceeds at the same rate throughout the year. However, this assumption may not be valid. For example, we would expect more mathematics-achievement gain during a month when school is in session than during a month of summer vacation, and we might expect more achievement to occur during a school month with few vacation days than during a month with many vacation days. Age and grade scales are defined to be equal-interval scales in terms of time, but they are not necessarily of equal intervals in terms of the trait being measured. Age and grade scales do not involve testing the fit of any model, and they are assumed to be ordinal scales.

Normalized scales (described in Section 7.6) that don't involve testing the fit of a scaling model are ordinal scales. As discussed earlier in this chapter, Thurstone's absolute-scaling method involves testing a model; when the model fits, it produces an interval scale. The latent-trait models described in Chapter 11 allow estimation of an interval trait (ability) scale and an interval item-difficulty scale; these two scales can be superimposed, as shown in Figure 8.2.

We interpret Figure 8.2 in the following way. Examinee B has more ability than examinee C, who has more ability than examinee A. The difference in abilities between examinees A and C is about half the size of the difference in abilities between examinees C and B. Item 5 is more difficult than item 3, which is more difficult than item 4, which is more difficult than item 2. The difference in difficulty between items 3 and 5 is about half the difference in difficulty between items 2 and 4. Since examinee B's ability is greater than the difficulties of items 2, 4, and 3, examinee B probably will get these three items correct; it is less likely that examinee B will get item 5 correct. An examinee's placement on the scale, when augmented with additional information about the latent-trait model, can be used to obtain an exact prediction of the probability that the examinee will pass any given item. The fit of the scaling model can be tested by examining the accuracy of the model predictions of the probabilities that examinees with certain (estimated) trait values will pass items with certain (estimated) difficulties.

Rasch's Poisson model, a strong true-score-theory model described in Chapter 11, produces ratio scales whose fit to a battery of tests is examined. When a set of tests and examinees satisfy this model, we can make statements such as "Jack is twice as able as Jim" and "test A is twice as difficult as test B." The first statement is interpreted under the model to mean that Jack is half as likely as Jim to

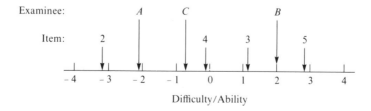

Figure 8.2. Placement of items and examinees on a difficulty/ability scale

make an error on any of the tests in the battery. The second statement means that everyone is twice as likely to make an error on test A as on test B. The binomial-error model, another strong true-score model described in Chapter 11, also produces a ratio scale of (estimated) true scores when it fits a set of data.

## 8.4  Additional Methods for Obtaining Scales

In addition to the methods already described for obtaining scales, several other methods are presented in this section. These methods are grouped according to the type of scale they produce.

### Nominal Scales

A nominal scale of objects can be obtained in a straightforward manner. People can be asked to categorize or sort the objects into mutually exclusive and exhaustive sets. Sets are mutually exclusive if each object can be sorted into only one set. (For example, "male" and "female" are mutually exclusive categories; "U.S. citizen" and "California citizen" are not.) Sets are exhaustive if every object can be classified in a set. (For instance, if we are classifying cars and the category "Ford" is left out, the sets would not be exhaustive for the categorization of cars in an American community.) After the sorting is completed, each distinct set can be assigned a distinct number.

### Ordinal Scales

Ordinal scales of objects can be obtained by having people rank-order the objects in terms of some property. Those objects that are ranked higher are assigned higher scale values. Similarly, people can be rank-ordered by their total score on some task; the total score, or any monotonic transformation of it, can be used as a scale value.

Ordinal scales can be produced by *sorting techniques*. People are given a set of stimuli (such as occupational titles, pictures, or politicians' names) and are asked to sort them into piles representing different levels along some specified dimension (such as prestige, attractiveness, or political conservatism). People may be directed to create as many piles and to place as many stimuli in a pile as they wish, or they may be constrained to use a certain number of piles with a specified number of stimuli in each pile. An example of the latter type of instruction is the *Q-sort,* a technique that constrains people to produce a specified distribution of stimuli, usually a normal distribution across piles. Scale values are assigned to the piles, and a stimulus's scale value is determined by which pile it is sorted into. The scale value of a stimulus may be determined by averaging the different values (pile scores) given to it by many different people.

In sorting studies it is important to ensure that stimuli are sampled appropriately from the population about which inferences will be made. Changes in the overall composition of a sample may change the apparent similarity of two stimuli.

For example, in a study of food preference, *apple pie* and *chocolate cake* may be sorted into the same pile when a wide variety of food types are sampled but may be sorted into different piles if only desserts are sampled. Furthermore, to produce a scaling along one dimension, the stimuli must be compatible or scalable along the same dimension. It would be inappropriate to include, in a sorting on the basis of similarity, items that differ along two or more dimensions—such as color and shape. It is also important to consider how characteristics of the raters may influence sorting behavior. For example, their degree of familiarity with a topic could have an important impact on sorting.

Paired comparisons also can be used to produce ordinal scales. The *method of paired comparisons* involves asking people to choose which object in each of a series of pairs of objects has more of a particular characteristic. If object A is selected over object B more than 50% of the time, object *A* is given a higher scale value, indicating that it is higher with respect to the characteristic. The fit of the model can be checked by determining that, if object A is judged to be greater than object B and object B is judged to be greater than object C, then object A is judged to be greater than object C.

*Rating scales* frequently are used to produce ordinal scales. Rating scales typically involve having people indicate their opinions, beliefs, feelings, or attitudes in some manner. Some examples of rating scales are:

1. I am frequently impatient with people.              yes      no
                                                     (Circle one.)

2. MY MOTHER    active___:___ :___:___:___ :___:___passive

3. How well does your present job fit in with your long-range goals?
   a. extremely well
   b. very well
   c. fairly well
   d. hardly at all
   e. not at all

4. How effective do you feel the President is as a moral leader?

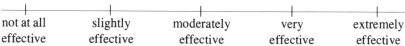

   not at all      slightly       moderately        very        extremely
   effective       effective       effective       effective      effective

5. "A woman's place is in the home."

   strongly                                                       strongly
   agree           agree         uncertain       disagree         disagree

The scale developer or user controls how rating-scale responses are transformed into numbers or scale values. For example, the values 1, 2, 3, 4, and 5 could be assigned to the answers (a) to (e) of item 3, or the values 1, 3, 9, 27, and 81 could be used. If we wanted to use responses to that item to predict whether a person will change jobs in the next three months, whichever set of scale values was most accurate in making the prediction (that is, most valid) would be the appropriate set of scale values to use. If there are great differences in the validity of different scales, the user may wish to investigate further the reasons for such differences.

In constructing rating scales, it is important for the items to be written carefully. They must not be ambiguous or "double barreled." For example, a person who doesn't have any long-range goals could have trouble answering item 3. It is also important for the scale to be unidimensional. For instance, a politician might be given one approval rating if the respondent considers the politician's stand on the issue of taxes and another rating if the politician's stand on Social Security is considered. With items such as 1 and 5, it is important that a person's tendency to agree or say yes (called an *acquiescent response set*) is not confounded with the attitude being measured. For example, items for which agreement indicates disapproval of a woman working outside the home should be balanced with items for which agreement indicates approval of a woman working outside the home.

In some cases we want to simultaneously scale examinees and items or stimuli. Guttman *scalogram analysis* (Guttman, 1944) is a method that produces an ordinal scale of items and examinees. It assumes that, if an examinee passes an item with a given difficulty, then that examinee will pass all easier items, and that, if an examinee fails an item, then that examinee will fail all items that are more difficult. Similarly, it is assumed that, if an item is passed by an examinee with a given ability, then that item will be passed by all examinees who are more able, and that, if an item is failed by an examinee, then that item will be failed by all less able examinees.

This method can be described with a simple example. Table 8.1 contains a set of dichotomous (pass = 1, fail = 0) item scores for a group of examinees. Examinee A got items 1, 2, 3, and 4 correct and item 5 wrong. We can rearrange the rows and columns of Table 8.1 to obtain Table 8.2, which forms triangular patterns of 1s and 0s. The items are ordered in terms of difficulty—2, 4, 3, 1, 5—with item 2 the easiest and item 5 the most difficult. In this case there is a perfect ordering of items by difficulty, because, for example, no one passes item 4 without passing item 2 as well. Similarly, there is a perfect ordering of examinees—A, B, D, C—from most able to least able. The items and examinees form perfect Guttman scales.

| | | Table 8.1. Responses to a Set of Items | | | | | | | Table 8.2. Rearrangement of the Rows and Columns of Table 8.1 | | | |
|---|---|---|---|---|---|---|---|---|---|---|---|---|---|

Table 8.1. Responses to a Set of Items

| | | Examinee | | | |
|---|---|---|---|---|---|
| | | *A* | *B* | *C* | *D* |
| | *1* | 1 | 0 | 0 | 0 |
| | *2* | 1 | 1 | 1 | 1 |
| *Item* | *3* | 1 | 1 | 0 | 0 |
| | *4* | 1 | 1 | 0 | 1 |
| | *5* | 0 | 0 | 0 | 0 |

Table 8.2. Rearrangement of the Rows and Columns of Table 8.1

| | | Examinee | | | |
|---|---|---|---|---|---|
| | | *A* | *B* | *D* | *C* |
| | *2* | 1 | 1 | 1 | 1 |
| | *4* | 1 | 1 | 1 | 0 |
| *Item* | *3* | 1 | 1 | 0 | 0 |
| | *1* | 1 | 0 | 0 | 0 |
| | *5* | 0 | 0 | 0 | 0 |

The set of responses in Table 8.1 produces perfect Guttman scales, but the set in Table 8.3 does not. For this set of data, it is not clear whether a true ordering exists but is obscured by random errors of measurement (fallibility of the data) or whether the items and examinees cannot be ordered. Guttman has proposed a coefficient of reproducibility that measures the quality of the scale produced. The *coefficient of reproducibility* is 1 minus the proportion of responses that would have to be changed in order to obtain a perfect Guttman scale. In Table 8.3, one observation out of the 20 (the response of examinee D to item 5) must be changed to produce a perfect Guttman scale; thus, the coefficient of reproducibility is .95. However, if only a small number of responses are being analyzed, a scale may appear to have a high coefficient of reproducibility even though responses are random. Because the scalogram technique doesn't test whether a prespecified ordering exists but finds the best possible ordering for a set of data, it tends to capitalize on chance. The ordering found for one group of examinees or items may not hold up when other groups are tested. Care must be taken when developing Guttman scales from data that can contain errors of measurement, especially for small numbers of responses. Nunnally (1970) discusses a number of other drawbacks of scalogram analysis.

Another technique for simultaneously scaling people and items is Coombs' *unfolding* technique (Coombs, 1950). The observations being analyzed are peoples' rank orderings of their preferences for or proximities to a set of stimuli along one dimension. For example, people may be asked to rank order a set of religions in terms of proximity or similarity to their own. If the scaling is successful across people, an analysis of the responses of all the people will produce a consistent scaling of stimuli and people.

For example, suppose there is a true scale of religions with two persons located on the scale as in Figure 8.3. Person A's rank ordering of his or her proximity to each religion would be Episcopalian, Catholic, Presbyterian, and Baptist. Person B's ordering would be Presbyterian, Baptist, Episcopalian, and Catholic. Figure 8.4 shows us one way to visualize how these orderings can be obtained from the persons' locations on the scales. Imagine that a stick is placed perpendicularly to the scale and touches the scale at person A's location. If each side of the scale is folded up until it touches the stick, and if note is made of the location of the stimulus scale points, the

Table 8.3. Item Responses That Do Not Form a Perfect Guttman Scale

|      |   | Examinee | | | |
|------|---|---|---|---|---|
|      |   | A | B | C | D |
|      | 1 | 1 | 1 | 1 | 1 |
|      | 2 | 1 | 1 | 1 | 0 |
| Item | 3 | 1 | 1 | 0 | 0 |
|      | 4 | 1 | 0 | 0 | 0 |
|      | 5 | 0 | 0 | 0 | 1 |

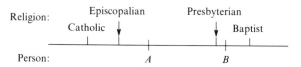

Figure 8.3. A scaling of religions and individuals

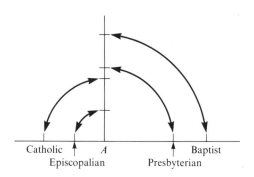

Figure 8.4. Folding and unfolding a scale

person's rank ordering of the stimuli becomes apparent by reading up from the bottom of the stick. When analyzing data, an experimenter simultaneously unfolds the set of ratings made by many people to see if these ratings are consistent with one scale (that is, to see if the model fits). When the scaling is successful, ordinal scales of people and stimuli can be created. In some cases, rank orders of the distances between stimuli or people can be obtained.

### Interval Scales

There are many methods for obtaining interval scales. One of these is through *direct estimation,* in which people are asked to assign numbers to stimuli or differences between stimuli according to some specified property of the stimuli. For example, people may be given pairs of names of breakfast cereals and be asked to judge how many more calories cereal A has than cereal B. Scale values for the stimuli usually are taken to be the mean or median of the values obtained when many people are tested.

Direct-estimation methods assume that people are skilled enough to make interval judgments. Other scaling methods make less-exacting demands on the people. In the *method of bisection,* people are given two stimuli and are asked to choose or adjust a third one to bisect or evenly divide the distance between the first two stimuli. This method could be used with lights on a dimension of intensity or statements about the United Nations on an attitude dimension.

Thurstone's *method of comparative judgments* (Thurstone, 1927) is a popular scaling technique that involves having people make order judgments about pairs of stimuli along a dimension specified by the experimenter. The scaling model transforms the ordinal judgments into an interval scale by analyzing what proportion of the time each stimulus is judged greater than another. In a simple form of this model it is assumed that the magnitude of a stimulus, $X_A$, is not always perceived to be the same but that such perception follows a normal distribution with mean, $\mu_A$, and standard deviation, $\sigma_A$. The mean is defined to be the magnitude or scale value of the stimulus. The standard deviation of the normal distribution is assumed to be the same for all the stimuli in the set being examined (that is, $\sigma_A = \sigma$ for all $A$). Since the magnitude of any single stimulus is not always perceived to be the same, perceived differences between stimuli are not always found to be the same. It is assumed that the perception of the magnitudes of any two stimuli are independent. If $X_A$ is the perceived magnitude of stimulus A, $X_B$ is the perceived magnitude of stimulus B, and $X_A$ and $X_B$ are independently, normally distributed, then the perception of the difference between the two stimuli, $X_A - X_B$, follows a normal distribution with mean $\mu_A - \mu_B$ and standard deviation $\sqrt{2\sigma^2}$. No estimate of $\sqrt{2\sigma^2}$ is made; instead, $\sqrt{2\sigma^2}$ is called the unit of measurement. The differences (for example, $\mu_A - \mu_B$) are estimated by the scaling technique in terms of this unit of measurement; for example, $\mu_A$ is two units greater than $\mu_B$, or $\mu_A - \mu_B = 2$ units. The number of units difference between the scale values of the stimuli can be estimated using the proportion of time that one stimulus is judged greater than another and the normal-distribution assumption. If two stimuli have the same magnitude ($\mu_A = \mu_B$ or $\mu_A - \mu_B = 0$), then one would be judged greater than the other 50% of the time. If stimulus A is judged to be greater than stimulus B more than 50% of the time, the magnitude of A must be greater than the magnitude of B; in other words, $\mu_A - \mu_B > 0$. If A is judged to be greater than B 84% of the time, then $\mu_A - \mu_B$ must be one unit above 0, as shown in Figure 8.5; $\mu_A - \mu_B$ is estimated to be 1 unit. If C is judged to be greater than A only 10% of the time, then $\mu_C$ must be less than $\mu_A$, and $\mu_C - \mu_A < 0$ by 1.28 units, as seen in Figure 8.6; $\mu_C - \mu_A$ is estimated to be $-1.28$ units. These values are doublechecked by having B and C compared. If the model fits, $X_C$ will be judged greater than $X_B$ 39% of the time and $\mu_C - \mu_B = -.28$ units.

Once we determine how many units separate the magnitudes of the stimuli, we can assign scale values to these magnitudes. To do this we choose one stimulus as an anchor and arbitrarily set its value equal to a constant. For example, $\mu_A = 100$. Next we assign a number to be the value of the unit of measurement. For example, we can set the unit value to be 10. Given $\mu_A = 100$ and the unit equal to 10, we can determine that $\mu_B = 100 - 10 = 90$ and $\mu_C = 87.2$. Any linear transformation of these scale values will preserve the accuracy of the predictions of the model.

## Ratio Scales

Ratio scales can be obtained using the method of direct estimation. People are asked to assign numbers to stimuli or to ratios of stimuli. The fit of a ratio-scaling model can be examined in a manner similar to that described for the construction of

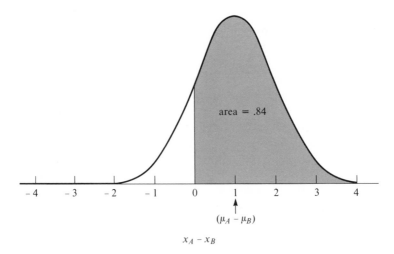

Figure 8.5. Distribution of differences in perceived magnitude for stimuli A and B when A is judged greater than B 84% of the time

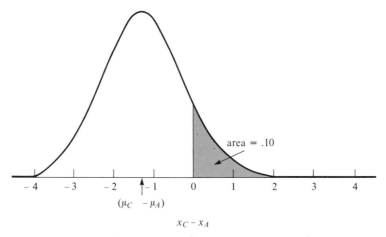

Figure 8.6. Distribution of differences in perceived magnitude for stimuli C and A when C is judged greater than A 10% of the time

ordinal scales using direct estimation. For example, if people agree that C is twice as liberal as A and that B is half as liberal as A, then the scale value for C should be four times the scale value for B.

## 8.5  Summary

Scaling theory is a branch of measurement theory that focuses on determining the numbers that should be used in a scale. A scale is an organized set of measurements for one property or trait. Scaling theory is concerned particularly with establishing the fit of a scaling model to a set of observations and with determining a scale's level of measurement—nominal, ordinal, interval, or ratio.

The type of scale that has been produced is defined by the type of transformation that can be made to the scale without disrupting its representation of the observations being examined. The numbers in a nominal scale can be changed in any way as long as the numbers assigned to distinct objects remain different. Ordinal scales permit monotonic transformations—that is, transformations that don't alter the relative order of the scale values. Interval scales permit linear transformation of the form $Y = aX + b$, where the constant $a$ is greater than 0. Ratio scales permit multiplication by a constant greater than 0.

The type of transformation that is admissible for a scale is one that does not alter the accuracy of the predictions made from the scale values (that is, it doesn't alter the fit of the scaling model). For example, for a ratio scale, if object A is judged to be twice as large as object B and object B is judged to be three times as large as object C, then object A should be judged to be six times as large as object C. If A, B, and C are assigned scale values of 6, 3, and 1, respectively, the only admissible transformation of these scale values is multiplication by a constant greater than 0.

Observed test scores, percentiles, age and grade scales, and normalized scales are all scales that are constructed by definition or fiat. These scales do not involve testing the fit of any model, and they are assumed to form ordinal scales. Thurstone's absolute-scaling model and latent-trait models involve fitting models and produce interval scales. Rasch's Poisson model and the binomial-error model also involve model fitting and produce ratio scales.

Some additional methods of obtaining scales are described. Nominal scales can be obtained through categorizing objects. Ordinal scales can be obtained by producing rank orderings of objects, by sorting, by using paired comparisons, and by using rating scales. Guttman's scalogram analysis and Coombs' unfolding technique produce ordinal scales for both people and items simultaneously. Interval scales can be obtained through direct estimation, bisection, and Thurstone's method of comparative judgments. Ratio scales can be obtained through direct estimation.

## 8.6  Vocabulary

acquiescent response set
admissible transformation
coefficient of reproducibility
direct estimation
interval scale
method of bisection
method of comparative
    judgments
method of paired comparisons
model fit
monotonic transformation
nominal scale

ordinal scale
Q-sort
rating scales
ratio scale
scale
scale value
scaling model
scaling theory
scalogram analysis
sorting techniques
unfolding

## 8.7  Study Questions

1. How are levels of measurement established?
2. What are *nominal, ordinal, interval,* and *ratio* scales?
3. What type of scale transformation is permitted with each type of scale?
4. What type of scale is produced by observed test scores?
5. What types of scales are produced by the raw-score transformations described in Chapter 7?
6. What types of scales are produced by the strong true-score-theory models and the latent-trait models described in Chapter 11?
7. How can a nominal scale be obtained and its consistency established?
8. Describe several methods of obtaining ordinal scales.
9. How are scale values assigned to stimuli when sorting techniques are used?
10. What precautions should be taken in developing scales using sorting techniques?
11. How are scale values assigned to rating scales?
12. What precautions should be taken in developing rating scales?
13. Describe *scalogram analysis*.
14. What is the *coefficient of reproducibility*?
15. What precautions should be taken in using scalogram analysis?
16. Describe the methods of direct estimation and bisection.
17. What assumptions are made and how are scale values obtained in the method of comparative judgments?
18. Describe the unfolding technique.

## 8.8  Computational Problem

1. Oranges ($X_A$) are judged to be more sour than apples ($X_B$) 75% of the time. Estimate $\mu_A - \mu_B$ using the method of paired comparisons.

# Special Considerations in the Use of Measurements

## 9.1 Introduction

In Chapter 9, various topics related to the use of test scores and other measurements are presented. First we will consider how reliability and validity are affected by systematic changes in the sample of examinees. Then we will discuss several topics related to the use of multiple scores in prediction. These topics include combining scores to maximize predictive accuracy and predicting the behavior of people in different groups in an unbiased manner. The pitfalls involved in measuring changes or differences are explained, and appropriate methods are presented for analyzing profiles based on several scores. Finally, some of the implications of test theory for the design and interpretation of research studies are described. After you've read this chapter, you should understand some of the ways to effectively and appropriately use test scores.

## 9.2 Group Heterogeneity

The level and variability of scores can differ from one group of people to another. For example, the IQ scores of residents of an institution for the mentally retarded will have a lower mean and less variance than will the scores from a random sample of an uninstitutionalized population. These two groups differ in their amounts of *group heterogeneity,* because they have different variances in their observed scores. The reliability and validity of a test can be affected in predictable ways by changes in group heterogeneity or by systematic selection of scores. Since selection occurs frequently in school admissions, job hiring, and subject selection for research studies, it is important to be aware of the effects that such selection and changes in group heterogeneity can have on test scores.

Often we have information about a test for one group of examinees and wish to have information about the properties of the test for another group but don't want to do further testing. For example, we might want to use the test's parallel-forms reliability that was determined within a selected group to estimate the reliability of the test within a larger, unselected group and, thus, avoid having to administer a parallel form of the test to the entire unselected group. Similarly, we might want to estimate a test's validity for one group when we know something about the test's validity in another group. The procedures outlined in this section will assist you in dealing with the effects of group heterogeneity on test properties. The following examples illustrate two situations in which these procedures are useful.

*Case A.* A test of self-actualization is given to a group of psychology undergraduates and to clients in an experimental clinical program. Parallel-forms reliability of the test is obtained for the undergraduates. What is the reliability of the test expected to be for the clinical group?

*Case B.* An engineering school is using an ability test to select students for admission. The first semester's grade-point averages (GPAs) for those applicants who were admitted are correlated with their test scores from the entrance exam. The correlation is found to be fairly low. Does this mean that the test should not be used in the selection process?

In these two cases, we want to compare the reliability or validity of a test in two groups that have differing degrees of heterogeneity of test scores. Each of these cases can be evaluated under the assumptions of classical true-score theory (presented in Chapter 3) if a few additional assumptions are met. Derivations of these results appear in Gulliksen (1950).

### Reliability

When we have scores for one test for two groups of examinees, the scores for one group can be designated by $X^*$ and the scores for the other group by $X$. Under the classical true-score-theory model, it is assumed that

$$\sigma_{X^*}^2 = \sigma_{T_{X^*}}^2 + \sigma_{E_{X^*}}^2, \tag{9.1}$$

and

$$\sigma_X^2 = \sigma_{T_X}^2 + \sigma_{E_X}^2. \tag{9.2}$$

The observed-score variance, true-score variance, and error variance are $\sigma_{X^*}^2$, $\sigma_{T_{X^*}}^2$, and $\sigma_{E_{X^*}}^2$ for one group and $\sigma_X^2$, $\sigma_{T_X}^2$, and $\sigma_{E_X}^2$ for the other group. The two groups could have been formed by selection of examinees from a larger group, so that the $X^*$ scores represent a subset of the $X$ scores, or the two groups could be any two separate groups of interest. In order to compare the reliabilities and variances of the test scores in the two groups, the assumption is made that the error variances are the same for the two groups:

$$\sigma_{E_{X^*}}^2 = \sigma_{E_X}^2. \tag{9.3}$$

This assumption is equivalent to the assumption that the standard errors of measurement are the same in the two groups (that is, that the factors contributing to errors of measurement, such as misunderstanding of test instructions or distractions, vary similarly in the two groups). This assumption cannot be met if it can be shown that standard errors of measurement vary as a function of true-score level and that the composition of the two groups varies with respect to the distribution of true scores (and therefore standard errors of measurement). For example, if there are substantial accumulations of scores at the floor or ceiling of a test in one group but not in the other, the assumption would not be appropriate. Using Conclusion 13 in Chapter 3, we can restate the assumption in Equation 9.3 as

$$\sigma_{X^*}^2(1 - \rho_{X^*X^*\prime}) = \sigma_X^2(1 - \rho_{XX\prime}), \tag{9.4}$$

where $\rho_{X^*X^*\prime}$ and $\rho_{XX\prime}$ are the reliabilities of the test in the two groups. Equation 9.4 contains four statistics: $\sigma_{X^*}^2$, $\sigma_X^2$, $\rho_{X^*X^*\prime}$, and $\rho_{XX\prime}$. If any three of these statistics can be obtained from a set of data, the fourth statistic can be estimated by solution of the equation. For example,

$$\sigma_{X^*}^2 = \frac{\sigma_X^2(1 - \rho_{XX\prime})}{(1 - \rho_{X^*X^*\prime})}, \tag{9.5}$$

and
$$\rho_{XX\prime} = 1 - \frac{\sigma_{X^*}^2}{\sigma_X^2}(1 - \rho_{X^*X^*\prime}). \tag{9.6}$$

Recall Case A, in which the parallel-forms reliability of a test is available for a group of undergraduates and an estimate of the test's reliability is desired for a clinical group. Let $X$ stand for the test scores in the clinical group and $X^*$ for the test scores in the group of undergraduates. Assume that the reliability of the test among the undergraduates is .8, that the test variance for the undergraduates is 10, and that the variance for the clinical group is 7. The estimated reliability of the test for the clinical group is $\hat{\rho}_{XX\prime} = 1 - (10/7)(1 - .8) \doteq .71$, which is lower than the reliability among the undergraduates. This result is reasonable when we consider one interpretation of reliability discussed in Chapter 4: reliability is the proportion of observed-score variance that is true-score variance, or

$$\rho_{XX\prime} = \frac{\sigma_T^2}{\sigma_X^2} = 1 - \frac{\sigma_E^2}{\sigma_X^2}. \tag{9.7}$$

If $\sigma_E^2$ is the same in both groups but $\sigma_X^2$ is smaller in one of the groups, then the reliability must be smaller in the group having less observed variance since $\sigma_E^2/\sigma_X^2$ must be larger. Whenever there is restriction of range (reduced observed-score variance) and constant-error variance, reliability will be lower. Remember that the above reliability for the clinical group (.71) is an estimate. This estimate will not be accurate if there are unequal error variances in the clinical and undergraduate groups. It would be preferable to actually calculate the reliability for the clinical group by administering a parallel form of the test.

## Validity

Sometimes we want to examine the validity of a test after selection has been made on the basis of test scores. When the scores on a test are used as the basis of selection, the test is said to have been subject to *explicit selection*. For example, scores on a college entrance examination are used for college admissions; the entrance examination is said to have been subject to explicit selection. When selection is based on one test (a college exam), any correlated test (for example, a test of achievement motivation) is said to have been subject to *incidental selection*. Although it was not part of the stated selection procedure, the test of achievement motivation will be affected by the explicit selection procedure because of the correlation of its scores with scores on the test that is subject to explicit selection. Another example of selection would be using only males in an experiment in which field dependence (for example, performance on a rod-and-frame apparatus) is examined. (Females are significantly more field dependent than males on this test.) Selection on the basis of gender is explicit selection. Because of the relationship between gender and field dependence, selection on the basis of gender will affect the distribution of field-dependence scores, and field-dependence scores will be subject to incidental selection.

This section examines the effects of group heterogeneity on the validity of a variable that is subject to explicit selection. Let $X$ be a variable that is subject to explicit selection and $Y$ be a validating criterion for $X$ that is subject to incidental selection. We will let $X$ and $Y$ represent the variables in a group before selection and $X^*$ and $Y^*$ represent the variables after selection has occurred. (Since all the equations in the assumptions used in this section are symmetric, it is equally acceptable to let $X^*$ and $Y^*$ stand for the variables in the group before selection and $X$ and $Y$ stand for the variables in the group after selection.) We are using $X$ to predict $Y$ and $X^*$ to predict $Y^*$ by linear regression (Sections 2.9 and 2.14). Thus,

$$\hat{Y} = \rho_{YX} \frac{\sigma_Y}{\sigma_X} (X - \mu_X) + \mu_Y \tag{9.8}$$

$$= \beta_{Y \cdot X}(X - \mu_X) + \mu_Y, \tag{9.9}$$

and

$$\hat{Y}^* = \rho_{Y^*X^*} \frac{\sigma_{Y^*}}{\sigma_{X^*}} (X^* - \mu_{X^*}) + \mu_{Y^*} \tag{9.10}$$

$$= \beta_{Y^* \cdot X^*} (X^* - \mu_{X^*}) + \mu_{Y^*}. \tag{9.11}$$

In order to examine the effect of selection on the scores, we must make two assumptions.

Assumption 1.    $\beta_{Y^* \cdot X^*} = \beta_{Y \cdot X}$ \tag{9.12}

This first assumption states that the regression coefficient for predicting the validating criterion from the variable that is subject to explicit selection is the same in the two groups. Referring to Equations 9.8 to 9.11, we can see that Assumption 1 is equivalent to the assumption that

$$\rho_{Y^*X^*} \frac{\sigma_{Y^*}}{\sigma_{X^*}} = \rho_{YX} \frac{\sigma_Y}{\sigma_X} . \tag{9.13}$$

Assumption 1 means that the regression lines for predicting the criterion from the predictor in the selected and unselected groups are parallel, or have the same slope.

The second assumption is that the population variance about the regression line for predicting the criterion from the variable subject to explicit selection is the same in the selected and unselected groups:

$$\text{Assumption 2.} \quad \sigma^2_{Y^* \cdot X^*} = \sigma^2_{Y \cdot X}. \tag{9.14}$$

If we generalize the result in Equation 2.29 from sample statistics to population statistics, we can see that Assumption 2 is equivalent to the assumption that

$$\sigma^2_{Y^*}(1 - \rho^2_{Y^*X^*}) = \sigma^2_Y(1 - \rho^2_{YX}). \tag{9.15}$$

Equation 9.15 is an assumption of homogeneity about the regression lines and states that errors of prediction have the same variance in the two groups.

Basically, the two assumptions are that the regression lines for the unselected and selected groups have the same slopes and that the variability about these regression lines is identical in the two groups.

In Figure 9.1, the regression is homogeneous in the two groups (satisfying Assumption 2), but the two regression lines are not parallel (violating Assumption 1). In Figure 9.2, the regression lines are parallel in the two groups (satisfying Assumption 1), but regression is not homogeneous (violating Assumption 2). Both assumptions are violated in Figure 9.3, and both assumptions are satisfied in Figure 9.4.

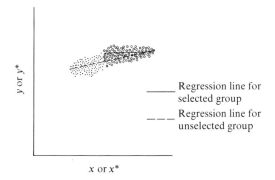

Figure 9.1. Plot of scores showing nonparallel regression lines and homogeneous regression in selected and unselected (total) groups

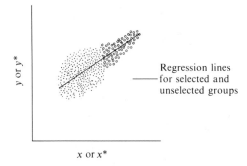

Figure 9.2. Plot of scores showing parallel regression lines and nonhomogeneous regression in selected and unselected (total) groups

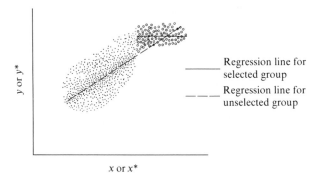

Figure 9.3. Plot of scores showing nonparallel regression lines and nonhomogeneous regression in selected and unselected (total) groups

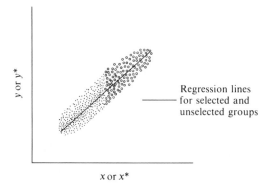

Figure 9.4. Plot of scores showing parallel regression lines and homogeneous regression in selected and unselected (total) groups

If the test user has the data necessary to verify whether the two assumptions are met, there is no need to make the assumptions. The assumptions are made when the user has incomplete data about one of the groups. An accumulation of scores at the floor or ceiling of a test in one group can cause the assumptions to be violated. If there is extreme selection (for example, if the selected group comprises the top or bottom 30% of the examinees in the unselected group), the formulas presented in this section can be very inaccurate and should not be used. If the test user suspects that there are any other special circumstances that would violate the assumptions, the results in this section should not be used.

Equations 9.13 and 9.15 can be combined to form the following equation:

$$\frac{\sigma_Y^2 - \sigma_{Y*}^2}{\sigma_{Y*}^2} = \rho_{Y*X*}^2 \left[ \frac{\sigma_X^2 - \sigma_{X*}^2}{\sigma_{X*}^2} \right]. \tag{9.16}$$

The term on the left of Equation 9.16 is the proportion of change, caused by selection, in the variance of the incidentally selected variable. Since $\rho_{Y*X*}^2 \leq 1$, the proportion of change in the variance of the incidentally selected variable must be less than or equal to the proportion change in the variance of the explicitly selected variable. The proportion of change in the variances will be equal for the two variables only when the incidentally and explicitly selected variables are perfectly correlated. There will be no change in the variance of the incidentally selected variable when the incidentally and explicitly selected variables are uncorrelated.

When the two assumptions are met, they can be used to solve for unknown statistics in terms of known statistics. For example, if we know (1) the variance of the explicitly selected variable for both groups ($\sigma_X^2$ and $\sigma_{X*}^2$), (2) the correlation between the explicitly and incidentally selected variables only in the selected group ($\rho_{Y*X*}$), and (3) the variance of the incidentally selected variable only in the selected group ($\sigma_{Y*}^2$), then the following formulas can be derived using Equations 9.13 and 9.15:

$$\rho_{YX} = \frac{\rho_{Y*X*}}{\sqrt{\rho_{Y*X*}^2 + \frac{\sigma_{X*}^2}{\sigma_X^2}(1 - \rho_{Y*X*}^2)}} \tag{9.17}$$

and

$$\sigma_Y^2 = \sigma_{Y*}^2 \left[ 1 - \rho_{Y*X*}^2 + \rho_{Y*X*}^2 (\sigma_X^2 / \sigma_{X*}^2) \right]. \tag{9.18}$$

If $\sigma_{X*}^2 / \sigma_X^2 = 1$ (that is, if selection does not affect the variance of the explicitly selected variable), the variance of the incidentally selected variable and the correlation between the two variables are estimated to be unaffected by selection.

Let us refer back to Case B, in which the engineering school is using an ability test for admissions. Scores on the ability test are designated by $X$ or $X*$, and GPA is designated by $Y$ or $Y*$. Assume that the variance of the ability-test scores among the selected engineering students is 3 ($\sigma_{X*}^2 = 3$) and that the variance among the unselected students is 10 ($\sigma_X^2 = 10$). The variance in GPA among selected students is 1 ($\sigma_{Y*}^2 = 1$), and the correlation between GPA and the ability-test performance is .4 among selected students ($\rho_{Y*X*} = .4$). Using Equation 9.18, the variance in GPA in the unselected group is estimated as $\hat{\sigma}_Y^2$

$= 1[1 - .16 + (.16)(10)/3] \doteq 1.37$. Using Equation 9.17, the estimate of the correlation between GPA and test performance in the unselected group is $\hat{\rho}_{YX} = .4/\sqrt{.16 + 3(1 - .16)/10} \doteq .62$. The correlation between GPA and the ability test scores is estimated to be more than 50% larger in the unselected group ($\rho_{YX} = .62$) than in the selected group ($\rho_{Y^*X^*} = .40$); it is the estimated correlation in the unselected group that should be used in making any decisions about whether the test is useful for selection.

The statistics available to a test user may be different from those involved in this last example. When this situation occurs, Equations 9.13 and 9.15 should be examined to see if enough is known to solve for any unknown statistics. It should be kept in mind that the equations presented in this section are designed to estimate the effects of selection on the validity of a variable used in selection. In the ideal situation, complete information would be available about the selected and unselected groups, and the effects of group heterogeneity on validity could be evaluated directly.

### Multiple Variables

In many instances there may be more than one variable that is explicitly or incidentally selected. If college admissions are influenced by high school grades as well as by test scores, there are two explicitly selected variables. If job hiring is based on an interview, a number of personality and ability variables are incidentally selected. Generalizations of the results discussed in this section to such cases are dealt with by Gulliksen (1950).

## 9.3    Combining Scores; Multiple Regression

Occasionally, scores for two or more tests are used in a select/not select, pass/fail, or admit/reject situation analogous to that described in Section 5.6. It is possible to use these scores in a variety of ways. Figure 9.5 displays the use of three

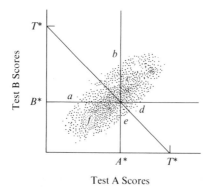

Test A Scores

Figure 9.5. Use of two scores in making a dichotomous decision

different decision rules: (1) an examinee must have a score greater than $A^*$ for test A *and* a score greater than $B^*$ for test B in order to be selected; (2) an examinee must get a score greater than $A^*$ on test A *or* a score greater than $B^*$ on test B in order to be selected; or (3) an examinee must obtain a total combined score on test A plus test B greater than $T^*$ to be selected. Examinees whose scores fall into area $c$ will be selected under rule 1. Examinees with scores in areas $a$, $b$, $c$, $d$, and $e$ will be selected under rule 2. Under rule 3, examinees with scores in areas $b$, $c$, and $d$ will be selected. This example illustrates three ways that two predictor scores can be combined to yield a dichotomous decision.

Two basic models underlie the choice of a decision rule: a compensatory model and a noncompensatory model. If high scores on one of the predictors can compensate for low scores on the other, a *compensatory model* applies and rules 2 or 3 are appropriate. If, however, minimal performance on both predictors is essential, a *noncompensatory* situation holds and rule 1 is best. For example, a typist can be effective by being very quick or very accurate or moderately quick and accurate. In selecting a typist, rules 2 or 3 would be appropriate. A prospective dentist may have to be proficient on both finger-dexterity and intelligence tests, so an admissions test for dental school might use a noncompensatory decision model such as rule 1.

A linear combination of test scores of the type displayed in rule 3 is the most frequently used method to make prediction and admission decisions or to make exact or confidence-interval predictions about criterion scores. A set of predictors related to performance on a criterion is identified—for example, quantitative and verbal scholastic-aptitude scores (predictors) are related to college grade-point average (criterion). Suppose a college admissions office wants to differentially weight and combine the predictor scores to produce one composite predictor score that maximizes the accuracy of predicting college grades. Using this one composite predictor score, the admissions office sets a cutting score for admitting students. (This cutting score is $T^*$ in Figure 9.5.) For example, the best composite predictor score might be obtained by adding three times a person's quantitative score to five times his or her verbal score. The 3 and 5 in this example are weights and are analogous to the regression coefficient, $B_{Y \cdot X}$, introduced in Section 2.9. When a person's composite predictor score is greater than 600, the person is admitted to the college.

*Multiple regression* is a statistical technique that offers a method for determining the weights that should be used to obtain the most accurate linear prediction of a criterion from several predictors. Recall from Section 2.9 that in univariate regression (predicting one criterion, $Y$, from one predictor, $X$) the following linear-prediction rule is used for a sample:

$$\hat{Y}_i = B_{Y \cdot X}(X_i - \bar{X}) + \bar{Y}, \tag{9.19}$$

where $\hat{Y}_i$ is the predicted criterion score for the $i$th examinee, $B_{Y \cdot X}$ is the regression coefficient for predicting $Y$ from $X$, $X_i$ is the predictor score for the $i$th examinee, $\bar{X}$ is the mean predictor score, $\bar{Y}$ is the mean criterion score, and

$$B_{Y \cdot X} = s_{YX}/s_X^2 = r_{YX} \frac{s_Y}{s_X} . \tag{9.20}$$

Using this prediction equation, the sum of squared errors of prediction, $\sum_{i=1}^{n} (Y_i - \hat{Y}_i)^2$, is minimized. A similar equation is used and similar results are obtained with multiple regression. The multiple-regression equation is

$$\hat{Y}_i = \sum_{j=1}^{J} B_j(X_{ji} - \bar{X}_j) + \bar{Y}, \tag{9.21}$$

where $\hat{Y}_i$ is the predicted criterion score for the $i$th examinee, $X_{ji}$ is the $j$th predictor score for the $i$th examinee, $\bar{X}_j$ is the mean of the $j$th predictor score, $B_j$ is the regression coefficient (or weight) for predicting $Y$ from $X_j$, and $\bar{Y}$ is the mean criterion score. In multiple regression, the equation for $B_j$ is more complicated than Equation 9.20. For example, when $Y$ is being predicted from two scores, $X_1$ and $X_2$,

$$B_1 = \left[ \frac{r_{YX_1} - r_{X_1X_2} r_{YX_2}}{1 - r_{X_1X_2}^2} \right] \frac{s_Y}{s_{X_1}} \tag{9.22}$$

and

$$B_2 = \left[ \frac{r_{YX_2} - r_{X_1X_2} r_{YX_1}}{1 - r_{X_1X_2}^2} \right] \frac{s_Y}{s_{X_2}}. \tag{9.23}$$

When $r_{X_1X_2} = 0$ (that is, when the predictors are uncorrelated), a predictor's weight in the multiple-regression equation is the same as its weight in a univariate regression. That is, when $r_{X_1X_2} = 0$, $B_1 = r_{YX_1} s_Y/s_{X_1}$ and $B_2 = r_{YX_2} s_Y/s_{X_2}$.

For example, an employer is predicting ratings of secretarial effectiveness using typing scores and clerical speed and accuracy scores. The means of the three scores are 35, 53, and 24, respectively, and their standard deviations are 10, 15, and 17. The correlation between the effectiveness score and the typing score ($r_{YX_1}$) is .65, and the correlation between the effectiveness score and the clerical speed and accuracy score ($r_{YX_2}$) is .50. Typing and clerical speed and accuracy have a correlation ($r_{X_1X_2}$) of .45. The regression weight for predicting secretarial effectiveness from typing scores is

$$B_1 = \left[ \frac{.65 - (.45)(.50)}{(1 - (.45)^2)} \right] \left[ \frac{10}{15} \right] \doteq .36,$$

and the weight for clerical speed and accuracy is

$$B_2 = \left[ \frac{.50 - (.45)(.65)}{(1 - (.45)^2)} \right] \left[ \frac{10}{17} \right] \doteq .15.$$

The multiple regression equation is

$$\hat{Y}_i \doteq .36(X_{1i} - 53) + .15(X_{2i} - 24) + 35$$

$$\doteq .36X_{1i} + .15X_{2i} + 12.32.$$

If a secretarial job applicant has a typing score of 51 and a clerical speed and accuracy score of 32, that applicant's predicted effectiveness score is $.36(51) + .15(32) + 12.32 \doteq 35.5$.

The multiple-regression equation is the linear combination of $X$ scores that has the greatest possible correlation with $Y$. In multiple regression, the correlation between $Y$ and $\hat{Y}$ is written $R_{Y \cdot X_1, \ldots, X_J}$ and is called the multiple correlation between $Y$ and the set of predictors. $R^2_{Y \cdot X_1, \ldots, X_J}$ is the squared multiple correlation and equals the proportion of variance in $Y$ that can be predicted from or that is shared with the linear composite of $X$ variables. The multiple-regression equation minimizes $\sum_{i=1}^{n} (Y_i - \hat{Y}_i)^2$, and confidence intervals can be constructed using multiple regression, just as is done with univariate regression.

Highly correlated predictors will each have validity coefficients, $r_{YX_j}$, almost as high as the multiple-correlation validity coefficient, $R_{Y \cdot X_1, X_2, \ldots, X_J}$, since they provide redundant or overlapping information to the prediction. When we want to add items to a test or add tests to a battery in order to improve validity, predictors that are uncorrelated with the original predictors should be added. Equation 9.24 gives the formula for the squared multiple correlation for predicting a criterion, $Y$, from two scores, $X_1$ and $X_2$:

$$R^2_{Y \cdot X_1 X_2} = \frac{r^2_{YX_1} + r^2_{YX_2} - 2r_{YX_1} r_{YX_2} r_{X_1 X_2}}{1 - r^2_{X_1 X_2}}. \tag{9.24}$$

Imagine that in the secretarial example, $Y$ is predicted from $X_1$ alone or from $X_2$ alone, producing a squared correlation of .42 or .25. If $X_1$ and $X_2$ are uncorrelated, the multiple $R^2$ using both variables would be .42 + .25 = .67. If $r_{X_1 X_2} = .45$, then $R^2_{Y \cdot X_1 X_2} \doteq .47$. If $r_{X_1 X_2} = .90$, then $R^2_{Y \cdot X_1 X_2} \doteq .45$. The squared multiple correlation decreases as the correlation between the two predictors increases, since the correlated predictors provide redundant information. Therefore, when multiple predictors are used, prediction will be most efficient when predictors tend to be uncorrelated with one another but highly correlated with the criterion.

Whenever we use a multiple-regression equation, we should cross-validate it. *Cross-validation* involves using a previously determined regression equation in a new sample of examinees and obtaining a new multiple correlation with the criterion. A set of regression weights developed in one sample probably will not produce as high a multiple correlation in another sample; this effect is called *shrinkage*. If the sample on which the weights are computed is large and is similar in composition to the cross-validating sample, less shrinkage would be expected. If, however, the sample in which the weights are computed is small and is very different from the cross-validating sample and if a large number of predictors are used in the multiple-regression equation, then there can be a great deal of shrinkage. Many statistics books give formulas for estimating the amount of shrinkage to expect under various conditions (see, for example, Lord & Novick, 1968).

When combining scores, we can use weights other than multiple-regression weights if we wish to maximize or minimize a criterion other than the sum of squared errors. For example, scores can be weighted to maximize the reliability of the resulting composite score (Gulliksen, 1950). When scores are combined, it is not possible to avoid weighting them in some manner. For example, when scores are simply summed with no explicit weights (other than $B_j = +1$ for every score), implicit weighting still occurs. This implicit weighting is produced by differences in the variances of the predictor scores and is influenced by the correlations among the predictors. We can understand this effect most easily by considering the extreme case. If one of the predictors, $X_j$, has no variance ($s_{x_j}^2 = 0$), then $X_j$ will simply add a constant to each person's score and will not have any important influence on the prediction. Variables with larger variances tend to have larger influences on decisions. When predictor scores are uncorrelated, a simple unweighted sum of observed scores gives to each score a weight proportionate to its standard deviation. For example, suppose that the standard deviation of one score, $X_1$, is twice the standard deviation of another score, $X_2$, and that the scores are uncorrelated, $r_{x_1 x_2} = 0$. The score with the larger standard deviation, $X_1$, will be given twice the weight of $X_2$ when the two scores are added together to produce a composite score. If uncorrelated predictor scores are standardized (see Section 7.5) so that all predictor scores have the same standard deviation, then the standardized scores will be given equal weight when they are added together. Giving the variables the same weight is a user-chosen weighting system. There is no such thing as a "natural" weighting system that allows us to avoid making decisions about weights. In fact, by excluding scores from the regression equation, we implicitly use a large number of zero weights.

If many predictors are used in a prediction equation and if the predictors are highly correlated, different weighting systems will not make too much difference in the predictions that are made. If few predictors are used and they are uncorrelated, weighting can have an important impact on predictions.

## 9.4    Suppressor Variables, Moderator Variables, and Bias in Selection

It is possible for a variable to be useful in predicting a criterion even though the variable isn't correlated with the criterion. Such a variable is called a *suppressor variable*. A suppressor variable is uncorrelated with a criterion, but, because of its correlation with other predictor variables, it improves prediction of the criterion. A suppressor variable acts to suppress parts of the other predictor variables that interfere with effective prediction. Horst (1966) presents an example of a suppressor variable in a study predicting success in pilot training in World War II. Scores on three tests (mechanical ability, numerical ability, and spatial ability) were positively correlated with the criterion, while scores on a fourth test (verbal ability) had a very low correlation with the criterion. The four predictor variables were fairly highly intercorrelated. When the verbal score was included in the prediction, the verbal score had a negative regression weight, and its inclusion improved the multiple correlation with the criterion. Apparently, verbal ability was a factor affecting the other predictor scores but not affecting pilot success. The inclusion of the verbal score, with a negative weight, in the regression equation controlled for (regressed out) the effects of verbal ability on performance on the other predictors and, in effect, reduced the scores of those who did well on the tests because of verbal ability alone.

Suppressor variables, although intriguing, are usually difficult to find in practice (Dicken, 1963), and it is prudent to use cross-validating samples to verify their existence. Conger and Jackson (1972) point out that there is a mathematical limitation on the increment in validity that can be expected by the addition of a suppressor variable to a regression equation. They conclude that it usually is more fruitful to search for an additional predictor variable to predict that part of the criterion that is not yet predicted than it is to search for a suppressor variable that accounts for parts of the predictor variables that are not relevant to the criterion. An additional problem with suppressor variables is that the negative weighting penalizes examinees who do well on the suppressor variable. Although predictive accuracy may be improved, it may be hard to justify this penalty to examinees who, because they did well on a test, are not selected.

Although suppressor variables may be difficult to identify, moderator variables may be more common. *Moderator variables,* like suppressor variables, are used to increase the accuracy of prediction. Zedeck (1971) distinguishes three uses of moderator variables. (1) Moderator variables can identify subgroups of examinees with different validity coefficients. This type of validity is called *differential validity*. For example, high school grades may be more highly correlated with college grade-point averages among freshmen than among sophomores. In this case, year in school is a moderator variable. (2) The criterion scores of some examinees may be more accurately predicted than the criterion scores of others. This result is called *differential predictability*. It is possible to search for a moderator variable that predicts an examinee's predictability. For example, predictability of auto-repair skills from a paper-and-pencil test score may be more accurate for those who have been employed a short time than for those who have had a long period of on-the-job experience. In this example, the number of years of job experience would be a moderator variable that identifies subgroups that differ in predictability. (3) Sometimes moderator variables are added to a regression equation that is estimated for a total group, and no subgroups are formed. This procedure is called a *moderated regression technique*. If a basic regression equation is $\hat{Y} = bX_1$, $X_2$ may be added to the equation as a moderator variable in a form such as this: $\hat{Y} = bX_1 + cX_2 + dX_1X_2$. This technique is useful if the moderated regression is more accurate than the basic regression equation. For all three uses of moderator variables, it is prudent to cross-validate the use of the moderator variable.

When regression equations are used in selection procedures and regression lines differ across groups, questions of fairness can arise. For example, suppose that, in predicting a criterion such as college grades for two groups of examinees, the regression lines are found to be parallel but generally higher for one group than the other. Such a situation is illustrated in Figure 9.6. The values $y_1$, $y_2$, and $y_c$ indicate criterion scores that would be predicted for a given $x$ (predictor) score, depending on whether the regression equation is estimated in group 1, group 2, or the combined group. The regression equation that was produced in the combined group, when compared with within-group regression equations, consistently overpredicts criterion scores for group 2 and underpredicts criterion scores for group 1. In effect, the

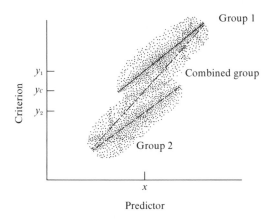

Figure 9.6. Regression lines for groups with varying levels of criterion scores

combined regression equation favors the low-scoring group rather than the high-scoring group. This effect suggests that, if there are group differences in the level of criterion scores in the regression problem, using a combined-group or the higher group's regression equation can help the "disadvantaged" group.

If there are group differences in the level of predictor scores, a combined-group regression equation can underpredict the lower group's criterion scores, as depicted in Figure 9.7. The combined-group regression line, when compared with within-group predictions, overpredicts criterion scores for most members of group 1 and underpredicts criterion scores for most members of group 2. Using the combined-group regression line in this situation would hurt the disadvantaged group (that is, the group with lower predictor scores).

When regression equations differ across groups, we cannot state (without

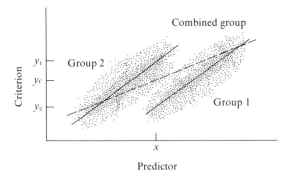

Figure 9.7. Regression lines for groups with varying levels of predictor scores

causing an argument) which procedure is more fair—the use of different regression lines for the two groups or the use of the regression line based on the combined group. If different equations are used, examinees in one group can complain that, to be attributed with the same criterion score, they need a higher predictor score than those in the other group. In other words, two examinees with the same high school grades could have different predicted college grades solely because they belong to different groups. If the regression equation based on the combined groups is used, some examinees can complain that group membership is a valid part of the prediction and their criterion scores are being underpredicted.

When regression lines are not parallel in two groups, the implications of using different regression equations will vary, depending on the range of predictor scores being dealt with. If regression equations differ in accuracy (that is, differ in the standard error of estimate, $s_{Y \cdot X}$) for two groups, decisions about the best equation to use are further complicated.

A large number of criteria have been suggested for establishing fair or unbiased selection procedures when subgroups differ in their distributions of predictor and criterion scores. Cleary (1968) has proposed the following guidelines:

> A test is biased for members of a subgroup of the population if, in the prediction of a criterion for which the test was designed, consistent nonzero errors of prediction are made for members of the subgroup. In other words, the test is biased if the criterion score predicted from the common regression line is consistently too high or too low for members of the subgroup [p. 115].

Thorndike (1971) offers a different conception of fair test use in selection:

> the qualifying scores on a test should be set at levels that will qualify applicants in the two groups in proportion to the fraction of the two groups reaching a specified level of criterion performance [p. 63].

Cole (1973) suggests that:

> for both minority and majority groups whose members can achieve a satisfactory criterion score ($Y > Y_p$) there should be the same probability of selection regardless of group membership [p. 240].

Guion (1966) proposes that:

> unfair [test] discrimination exists when persons with equal probabilities of success on the job have unequal probabilities of being hired for the job [p. 26].

At first glance, all of these concepts appear to have merit, although closer scrutiny reveals that they have different implications and that some (for example, Thorndike's and Cole's) can lead to self-contradictions (Peterson & Novick, 1976). Peterson and Novick propose the use of expected utility in developing and evaluating fair selection procedures. In the expected-utility method, each outcome (for example, selection of a successful person or rejection of a potentially successful person) is assigned a value on the basis of its judged *utility*, $x_i$. For each selection procedure, the probability of each possible outcome, $p_i$, is evaluated. The *expected utility* of a selection procedure is the sum of the products of the probabilities of the possible outcomes and their utilities; that is, $\sum_{i=1}^{I} p_i x_i$ (see the discussion of expected value in Section 2.14). The procedure with the highest expected utility is the "best" procedure.

For example, imagine that a spatial-ability test is used to choose people for an astronaut-training program. There are four possible outcomes in this selection: choosing a person who would be successful, choosing a person who would not be successful, rejecting a person who would be successful, and rejecting a person who would not be successful. Those people in charge of the astronaut-training program may assign utilities of $+20$, $-50$, $-15$, and $+5$ to these outcomes. If there are two possible selection procedures, $A$ and $B$, their expected utilities can be compared to determine the better procedure to use. Suppose that, if selection procedure $A$ is used, the probabilities of the four outcomes are .07, .03, .30, and .60, and that, if selection procedure $B$ is used, the probabilities are .14, .06, .15, and .65. The expected utility of procedure A is $.07(+20) + .03(-50) + .30(-15) + .60(+5) = -1.6$. The expected utility of procedure $B$ is $.14(+20) + .06(-50) + .15(-15) + .65(+5) = .8$. Since procedure $B$ has the higher expected utility, it is the better selection procedure to use. When different groups of applicants are being considered (for example, a group of men and a group of women are prospective astronauts), utilities and probabilities of outcomes can be figured for each group, and a total expected utility can be found in a similar fashion.

Often the most difficult part of comparing different selection procedures is assigning the utilities associated with the possible outcomes. It is clear that judgment of the utility of any outcome is not primarily a statistical consideration. Those people who are influenced by test use—schools or companies, applicants, and society in general—should be involved in deciding the utility of outcomes. The person applying the selection procedure—the educational administrator, psychologist, or statistician—cannot make this decision alone.

## 9.5  Measuring Change

Often test users are interested in measuring change. For example, a therapist may be interested in demonstrating a reduction in anxiety after treatment, or a teacher may be interested in demonstrating improved performance on an achievement test after an instructional unit. The classical true-score-theory model described in Chapter 3 is particularly useful when we have to decide on the proper way of estimating and using *change* or *difference scores*. Change scores typically are estimated using observed pretest scores, $X$, and posttest scores, $Y$; the change or difference score is $Y - X$. We assume that the scores $X$ and $Y$ measure traits on interval or ratio scales, so that taking a difference between them makes sense.

We also assume that $X$ and $Y$ both contain some measurement error; that is

$$X = T_X + E_X \tag{9.25}$$

and
$$Y = T_Y + E_Y, \tag{9.26}$$

where $T_X$ and $E_X$ are the true and error scores associated with $X$, and $T_Y$ and $E_Y$ are the true and error scores associated with $Y$. It is the error of measurement in $X$ and $Y$ that causes complications in the interpretation of difference or change scores based on $X$ and $Y$. The difference (or change) score, $D$, is

$$D = Y - X \tag{9.27}$$

$$= T_Y - T_X + E_Y - E_X \tag{9.28}$$

$$= T_D + E_D, \tag{9.29}$$

where $T_D = T_Y - T_X$ and $E_D = E_Y - E_X$.

Difference scores tend to be more unreliable than the scores entering into the difference; that is, $D$ is more unreliable than $Y$ or $X$. The explanation for this tendency can be seen in the formulas for the error variance and the reliability of a difference score. Since errors of measurement are uncorrelated under the classical model, it can be shown* that

$$\sigma_{E_D}^2 = \sigma_{E_X}^2 + \sigma_{E_Y}^2. \tag{9.30}$$

The error variance of a difference score will be as large or larger than the error variance of either of the scores entering into the difference.

Recall that the reliability of a score is the ratio of its true-score variance to its total-observed-score variance (Interpretation 3, Section 4.1). The numerator of the reliability of a difference score is

$$\sigma_{T_D}^2 = \sigma_{T_Y - T_X}^2 \tag{9.31}$$

$$= \sigma_{T_Y}^2 + \sigma_{T_X}^2 - 2\sigma_{T_Y T_X} \tag{9.32}$$

$$= \sigma_Y^2 \rho_{YY'} + \sigma_X^2 \rho_{XX'} - 2\sigma_Y \sigma_X \rho_{YX}, \tag{9.33}$$

where $\rho_{YY'}$ and $\rho_{XX'}$ are the reliabilities of $Y$ and $X$.

The denominator of the reliability of a difference score is

$$\sigma_D^2 = \sigma_{Y - X}^2 \tag{9.34}$$

$$= \sigma_Y^2 + \sigma_X^2 - 2\sigma_Y \sigma_X \rho_{YX}. \tag{9.35}$$

---

*Two facts that will be useful for following the developments in this section are that $\sigma_{W+Z}^2 = \sigma_W^2 + \sigma_Z^2 + 2\sigma_{WZ}$ and that $\sigma_{W-Z}^2 = \sigma_W^2 + \sigma_Z^2 - 2\sigma_{WZ}$, where $\sigma_{WZ}$, the covariance between $W$ and $Z$, equals $\sigma_W \sigma_Z \rho_{WZ}$. (See Section 2.14.)

The reliability of a difference score, then, is

$$\rho_{DD'} = \frac{\sigma_{T_D}^2}{\sigma_D^2}$$

$$= \frac{\sigma_Y^2 \rho_{YY'} + \sigma_X^2 \rho_{XX'} - 2\sigma_Y \sigma_X \rho_{YX}}{\sigma_Y^2 + \sigma_X^2 - 2\sigma_Y \sigma_X \rho_{YX}}. \tag{9.36}$$

If $\sigma_X = \sigma_Y$,

$$\rho_{DD'} = \frac{\rho_{YY'} + \rho_{XX'} - 2\rho_{YX}}{2(1 - \rho_{YX})} \tag{9.37}$$

$$= \frac{\frac{1}{2}(\rho_{YY'} + \rho_{XX'}) - \rho_{YX}}{1 - \rho_{YX}}. \tag{9.38}$$

If $\sigma_X = \sigma_Y$, the reliability of a difference score is the average reliability of the scores entering into the difference minus their correlation, all divided by 1 minus their correlation. The reliability of the difference will be positive only when the mean reliability is greater than the correlation of the two scores. As the correlation between the two measures decreases, the reliability of their difference increases. For example, if the average reliability of two measures is .8, if the measures have the same standard deviations, and if their correlation is .6, then the reliability of their difference score is $(.8 - .6)/(1 - .6) = .5$. If their correlation is .3, the reliability of their difference score is higher (it is .71). The implications for the assessment of change are obvious and important, particularly if the two testings are highly correlated and have low reliability.

It can be seen from Equation 9.28 that $D$ shares error terms with both $Y$ and $X$. Correlations between $D$ and $Y$ or $X$ are called *spurious correlations,* because part of their correlation is due to shared errors of measurement. In effect, the correlation will tend to be spuriously high or low, since part of it reflects a correlation of errors in $Y$ or $X$ with themselves. The correlation between $T_D$ and $T_X$, which is not spurious, can be estimated from the following (Lord, 1963):

$$\rho_{T_D T_X} = \frac{\rho_{DX} + \frac{\sigma_X}{\sigma_D}(1 - \rho_{XX'})}{\sqrt{\rho_{DD'} \rho_{XX'}}}. \tag{9.39}$$

The problem of spurious correlations occurs only when we correlate $D$ with $X$ or $Y$. When $D$ is correlated with any score other than $X$ or $Y$, there will be no problem of spurious correlation due to shared errors of measurement. However, the size of the correlation will be affected by the degree of unreliability of $D$. Any correlation between $D$ and another score can be corrected for attenuation (see Section 5.4) if it is desired to estimate the correlation of $T_D$ with the score.

When comparing change for different groups, it is important to consider differences between the groups on pretest scores. If there is a ceiling effect in one group, it will be more difficult to change scores in that group than in a lower-scoring group. If there are group differences in pretest scores, it is not clear how these differences should be taken into account when comparing posttest scores or change scores for the groups (Lord, 1967; 1969b). The best way to attempt to eliminate pretest differences is by random assignment of examinees to groups. When pretest scores are equal for the two groups, the groups' posttest means can be compared without the necessity for the researcher to become involved with change scores. When pretest scores are not equal for the two groups, the researcher will have a difficult time comparing the groups.

Harris (1963) has edited a book, *Problems in Measuring Change,* that contains extended discussions of the topics covered in this section. Linn and Slinde (1977) present a review of methods of determining the significance of change scores.

## 9.6 Profile Analysis

A test user may wish to interpret simultaneously an examinee's scores on several tests or other measurements. The analysis of several scores for one examinee is called *profile analysis.* Figure 9.8 contains a profile for Sally on a set of personality scales. On the face of it, Sally appears to be high on Inferiority and Excitability and low on Sociability and Masculinity. However, we have not been told the means and standard deviations of the scales, and without such information we cannot interpret the scores correctly. In Figure 9.9 each scale has been standardized to have a mean of zero and a standard deviation of 1. Now a somewhat different picture emerges from the scales. Sally appears to be relatively high on Inferiority and Masculinity and low on Sociability.

We still don't have enough information to adequately evaluate Sally's profile. The reliabilities of the scales have not been taken into account. In Figure 9.10 vertical bars have been added to each point, indicating Sally's score plus or minus one standard error of measurement ($\pm \sigma_X \sqrt{1 - \rho_{XX'}}$, Section 4.8). Now it

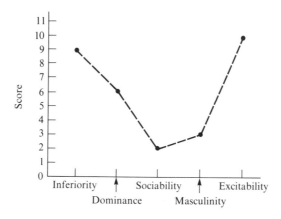

Figure 9.8. Sally's profile on the *Acme Personality Inventory*

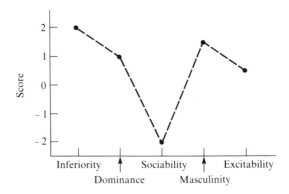

Figure 9.9. Sally's profile on the *Acme Personality Inventory* standardized scales

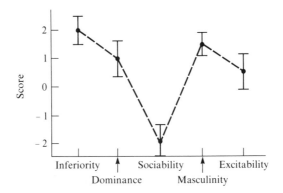

Figure 9.10. Sally's profile on the *Acme Personality Inventory* standardized scales, with standard errors of measurement indicated

appears that Sally's Masculinity score is not substantially higher than her Excitability and Dominance scores; her most extreme scores appear to be on Inferiority and Sociability. Sally appears to be more extreme on Sociability than on Dominance. We might hypothesize that this difference between Dominance and Sociability would produce a high degree of anxiety and ambivalence when Sally is asked to direct the activities of a social club.

Can the profile analyst be satisfied that the profile has now been completely evaluated? No. In profile analysis, differences are implicitly taken between a person's standing on different scales. Recall from Section 9.5 that the reliability of a difference score is influenced by the correlation between the scores entering into the difference. For example, suppose that the reliability of the Dominance and Sociability scores are .7 and .6 and that their correlation is .45. Using Equation 9.38, we find that the reliability of a difference between standard scores on the two scales is $\hat{\rho}_{DD'}$ = $\left[ (.7 + .6)/2 - .45 \right]/(1 - .45) \doteq .36$. A difference between these two scores is not very reliable. In other words, there are no apparent important individual differences in the contrast between these measures of Dominance and Sociability, and it probably would not be worthwhile to construct theories explaining the meaning of differences between these two scales. It also wouldn't be fruitful to attempt to relate a difference between these two scales to some other personality or behavioral characteristic, since the low reliability of .36 indicates that observed differences are likely to reflect chance fluctuation.

Conger and Lipshitz (1973) present different measures of the reliability of a profile. They demonstrate that a profile's reliability must be less than or equal to the average reliability of the scores entering into the profile; the higher the correlation among the scores, the lower the profile's reliability.

## 9.7 Implications of Measurement Theory for the Design and Interpretation of Research Studies

In analyzing measurements and in interpreting others' analyses, it is important to keep in mind the implications of measurement theory. For example, imagine that a paired-associates-learning test and a verbal-fluency test are administered to two groups of children. One group has been given training in imagery production aimed at improving paired-associates learning. The other group has received no such training. It is hypothesized that verbal fluency will be correlated more strongly with the learning task in the untrained group than in the trained group. The observed correlation between paired-associates learning and verbal fluency for the untrained group is .40 and for the trained group is .25. The observed correlations are ordered in the hypothesized direction, and a statistical test finds them to be significantly different. However, without further information about the reliabilities of the tests in the two groups, it is not possible to state whether the hypothesis is being supported. For example, suppose that the reliabilities of the paired-associates test scores and the verbal-fluency test scores are .7 and .8 in the untrained group but only .40 and .45 in the trained group. The correlations between the two measures corrected for attenuation (see Section 5.4) are $.4/\sqrt{(.7)(.8)} \doteq .53$ in the untrained group and $.25/\sqrt{(.4)(.45)} \doteq .59$ in the trained group. These corrected correlations do not support the hypothesis.

Any investigation of differences between correlations should consider the reliabilities of the measures involved. If a researcher is concerned only about correlations between observed measures, then reliability is not important. But if a researcher is, in fact, concerned about relationships among traits or true scores that the tests are intended to measure, then reliabilities are crucial. Furthermore, if a test is unreliable, it is unlikely that it will display significant mean differences between groups of interest; large amounts of error variance will mask any true-score differences that may exist between the groups. Anyone examining changes in scores must be particularly careful to examine reliabilities and preexisting differences between the groups being compared. Any conclusion of "no relationship" (that is, that a correlation or mean difference is 0) is suspect, until it is verified that the measures being examined are reliable.

Some experimental designs call for *repeated measurements* on a group of examinees. For example, a learning experiment might obtain measurements under two or more different situations (treatments). The interpretation of significant mean differences in repeated measurements should consider reliability. For example, say that each student in a class is taught two sets of facts—one under a structured practice condition and the other under an independent learning condition. An examination of the mean amount learned under the two conditions indicates that, on the average, children learn significantly better under the structured practice condition than under the independent learning condition. The researcher then might conclude that all children learn better under the structured condition. However, the reliability of the difference between the amounts learned under the two conditions should be examined. If this difference is reliable, it means that there are important individual differences in the benefits of the two conditions and that some children may learn better under independent learning than under the structured practice condition. Furthermore, with a reliable difference, it may be fruitful to attempt to relate the difference to other variables. For example, it may be that students who do significantly better under independent learning than under structured practice conditions show particularly high scores on a test of self-motivation.

It was noted in Section 9.2 that changes in the heterogeneity of a group can affect reliabilities and correlations among variables. Another condition that will affect means, variances, reliabilities, and validities is the accumulation of scores at the floor or ceiling of a test. Suppose a test is given to an average group and to an above-average group. If many people in the above-average group attain the maximum score, then the mean difference between the two groups will not reflect accurately the true differences in trait level for the two groups. If a better test were used, in which a ceiling effect was not apparent, differences in means for the two groups would be larger. Table 9.1 gives an example of means and standard deviations for two groups on a test that appears to exhibit a ceiling effect in group B. The ceiling effect is suggested by the fact that the mean for group B is close to the maximum possible score, and the standard deviation for group B is much smaller than the standard deviation for group A. If better tests were used, it is likely that mean differences between groups A and B would be larger and that the reduction in

Table 9.1. Means and Standard Deviations for Two
Groups on a Ten-Item Test

| Group A | | Group B | |
|---|---|---|---|
| $\bar{X}$ | $s_X$ | $\bar{X}$ | $s_X$ |
| 5.2 | 1.3 | 8.7 | .7 |

the standard deviation in group B would not occur. If correlations among variables were being compared for these two groups, it would be reasonable to be suspicious of these comparisons. For example, Figure 9.11 displays plots that might occur for the two groups. The correlation between $X$ and $Y$ would be smaller in group B than in group A, but this situation is most likely caused by the ceiling effect for $X$ scores in group B rather than by differences in the correlations of the traits being measured by $X$ and $Y$.

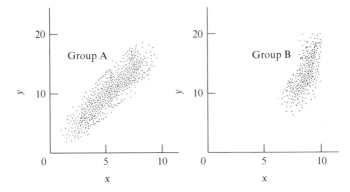

Figure 9.11. Hypothetical score plots for groups A and B

When designing and interpreting experiments, it is important to check that the measures involved are reliable and valid and that restriction of range or floor or ceiling effects are not distorting the results.

## 9.8  Summary

A change in group heterogeneity, which frequently is caused by selection of examinees, can change the reliability and validity of tests in predictable ways. The effects of a change in observed-score variance on reliability can be estimated, if it is assumed that error variance remains constant after selection. The effects of changes in group heterogeneity on the validity of an explicitly selected test (the test whose scores are the basis for selection) can be estimated by assuming that (1) the slope of the regression line for predicting the criterion (an incidentally selected test) from the explicitly selected test is not altered by selection and (2) the variance about this regression line is not altered by the selection.

Multiple test scores can be used in prediction and selection according to various models. If a certain minimum performance on each test must be obtained for a person to be selected, a noncompensatory model is being followed. If high performance on one test can compensate for low performance on another test, a compensatory model is being followed. Linear combinations of test scores follow compensatory models. Multiple linear regression is a popular method of linear combination of scores. A multiple regression assigns weights for predictors; these weights are used when adding together scores on the predictors to predict a criterion. The multiple-regression equation minimizes the sum (over examinees) of squared errors of prediction and maximizes the multiple correlation between the predictors and the criterion. When using a multiple-regression equation, it is important to cross-validate the equation on a new sample.

Multiple regressions sometimes involve suppressor and moderator variables. A suppressor variable is a variable that is uncorrelated with the criterion but, because of its correlations with the predictors, improves predictive accuracy. Suppressor variables may be difficult to find. A moderator variable, which may be easier to find, identifies subgroups with different validity coefficients or degrees of predictability; a moderator variable also can be incorporated into a regression equation.

When different groups have different regression equations that involve the same predictors and criterion, it is not always clear whether it is more fair to use different equations for people in different groups or to use one equation found by pooling the groups. Many methods proposed for fair selection procedures have hidden, undesirable implications, and comparisons of these methods can become complex. Often the most difficult part of comparing different selection procedures is in defining the desirability (utility) of different possible outcomes of the selection process.

Difference or change scores (for example, differences between pre- and posttest performance) are difficult to deal with because of their unreliability. The more highly correlated the pre- and posttest scores are, the more unreliable their difference score will tend to be. Correlations of change scores with pre- or posttest scores tend to be spuriously low or high, because of shared errors of measurement. Such correlations can be corrected to eliminate this spuriousness. When comparing change for different groups, it is important to consider group differences on pretest scores; if such differences exist, they make it very difficult to interpret group differences in change scores.

To conduct proper profile analysis, it is important to consider the means, standard deviations, reliabilities, and correlations of the scores entering into the profile. Lack of consideration of these factors can lead to misinterpretation of the profile.

Measurement theory has many implications for the design and interpretation of research studies. Reliabilities should be taken into account when comparing means or correlations across groups. When comparing the effects of different treatments within one group of examinees, it is important to consider the reliability of the differences between treatments; it may be that conclusions based on mean differences do not apply to all examinees. Floor and ceiling effects can influence means, variances, and correlations, and they can also influence comparisons between groups.

## 9.9  Vocabulary

change score
compensatory model
cross-validation

difference score
differential predictability
differential validity

expected utility
explicit selection
group heterogeneity
incidental selection
moderated regression technique
moderator variable
multiple regression

noncompensatory model
profile analysis
repeated measurements
shrinkage
spurious correlation
suppressor variable
utility

## 9.10 Study Questions

1. What assumption is made in order to predict a change in reliability as a result of a change in group heterogeneity? When is this assumption violated? When this assumption is met, what does a decrease in test variance imply about a test's reliability?

2. What is an explicitly selected variable? An incidentally selected variable? Give an example of each.

3. Which is affected more by selection—the variance of an incidentally selected variable or the variance of an explicitly selected variable? Why?

4. Which is affected more by selection—the validity of an incidentally selected variable or the validity of an explicitly selected variable? Why?

5. What assumptions are made in order to estimate the effects of explicit selection on a test's validity? Describe these assumptions with words, formulas, and graphs. When are these assumptions violated?

6. What are Equations 9.17 and 9.18 used for? Describe the effects that decreasing $\sigma_X^2*/\sigma_X^2$ has on these equations.

7. What alternative models can be used to combine two variables for a single decision? When is each model preferable?

8. What are compensatory and noncompensatory models? When might each be used?

9. Give the formula for a multiple-regression equation, and explain the terms involved.

10. How is a multiple-regression equation similar to a univariate-regression equation? How does it differ?

11. What does a multiple-regression equation maximize? What does it minimize?

12. If predictors were to be added to a multiple-regression equation, what types of predictors should be sought? Why?

13. Why is cross-validation of regression equations important?

14. In creating one composite score, describe some alternative methods of weighting the variables.

15. When we combine variables into one score, why can't we avoid weighting decisions?

16. When do changes in weights make the most difference in predictions? The least difference?

17. What is a suppressor variable? A moderator variable? Give an example of each, and explain why they can be useful.
18. Explain the implications of using different regression lines for different groups in order to predict the same criterion.
19. When two groups are at different levels on a predictor and a criterion but have parallel regression lines, what is ''unfair'' about using a combined regression line for both groups? What is ''unfair'' about using separate regression lines?
20. Discuss the different definitions of fair test use in a prediction situation. Which definition seems most ''fair'' to you? Why?
21. What do you believe is the most difficult step in making ''fair'' selection decisions?
22. What is expected utility? How can it be applied in creating ''fair'' selection procedures?
23. Why is a change or difference score usually not as reliable as the scores entering into the difference?
24. What are the formulas for (1) the standard error of measurement and (2) the reliability of a difference score, in terms of the reliabilities and variances of the scores entering into the difference?
25. When two scores have the same variance, what is the formula for the reliability of their difference? How is this formula affected by an increase in the correlation of the two scores?
26. What is a spurious correlation? How can the problem of spurious correlations be avoided?
27. Why is it important to control for pretest differences when comparing change scores for two groups?
28. What information is needed about test scores in order to interpret a profile properly?
29. Profile analysis appears simple but is very complex. Why?
30. Is it easier to interpret a profile composed of uncorrelated scores or correlated scores? Why?
31. When can the concept of test reliability help in the interpretation of experimental results?
32. Why is it difficult to interpret differences in correlations among fallible (possibly unreliable) measures?
33. How are floor and ceiling effects detected?
34. How are floor and ceiling effects related to test reliabilities, validities, and mean differences between groups?
35. Why is it important to examine the reliability of difference scores when interpreting significant mean differences in treatment effects?

## 9.11  Computational Problems

1. A standardized achievement test is administered in a school district, and the resulting standard deviation of the total score is 75. The standard deviation and

standard error of measurement of that test in a national norming sample are 100 and 30, respectively. Estimate the reliability of the test within the school district, and compare this estimate to the national reliability.

2. Only subjects who report consuming at least 100 ml of "hard" liquor daily are included in a study on alcohol consumption and dreaming. It is known that the national variance in hard-liquor consumption among drinking adults is 1600 ml. Among those people included in the study, the variance in hard-liquor consumption is 900 ml. The number of minutes of rapid-eye-movement (REM) sleep in which the subjects engage each night is measured. The standard deviation of minutes of REM sleep is found to be 20, and the correlation between amount of hard liquor consumed and amount of REM sleep is found to be $-.32$.

   a. Estimate the correlation between hard-liquor consumption and amount of REM sleep in the national population.

   b. Estimate the variance in REM sleep in the national population.

3. Verbal and quantitative aptitude-test scores are used to predict college grade-point average (GPA). Numerical information about these scores is as follows:

|  | GPA | Verbal Score | Quantitative Score |
|---|---|---|---|
| Mean | 2.0 | 502 | 483 |
| Standard deviation | 1.1 | 100 | 124 |
| Correlation with GPA | — | .62 | .48 |
| Correlation of aptitude scores |  | .40 |  |

   a. Calculate the multiple-regression equation for predicting GPA from the verbal ($X_1$) and quantitative ($X_2$) scores.

   b. What is the squared multiple correlation between GPA and the aptitude measures?

   c. What is the predicted GPA of a student with a verbal score of 525 and a quantitative score of 472?

4. Students are chosen for admission to special programs for the mentally retarded either on the basis of their intelligence-test scores or on the basis of teacher evaluations. If test scores are used for selection, the probabilities of the various outcomes are:

|  |  | Student Benefits | | |
|---|---|---|---|---|
|  |  | Yes | No | Total |
| Student | Yes | .15 | .05 | .20 |
| Admitted | No | .05 | .75 | .80 |
|  | Total | .20 | .80 | 1.00 |

If teacher evaluations are used, the probabilities of the various outcomes are:

|  |  | Student Benefits | | |
|  |  | Yes | No | Total |
| --- | --- | --- | --- | --- |
| Student | Yes | .10 | .10 | .20 |
| Admitted | No | .10 | .70 | .80 |
|  | Total | .20 | .80 | 1.00 |

If the utilities are + 50 (correct assignment to the special program), − 50 (incorrect assignment to the special program), − 20 (incorrect exclusion from the special program), and + 50 (correct exclusion from the special program), determine the expected utility of each of the selection procedures.

5. A study is made of a film's effects on the degree of prejudice toward a certain minority group. A test of prejudicial attitudes is administered to subjects both before and after they view the film. Use the data from the table below to answer the following questions. (Note: attitude change is measured by subtracting the prefilm score from the postfilm score, and a higher attitude score reflects less prejudice.)
   a. What is the variance of the change score?
   b. What is the reliability of the change score?
   c. How strongly correlated are the true amount of change in attitude and the true level of prejudice exhibited before the film was shown?
   d. How strongly correlated are the true amount of change in attitude and the number of years of formal education previously obtained by the subjects?

|  | Mean | Standard Deviation | Reliability |
| --- | --- | --- | --- |
| Prefilm attitude | 17.1 | 3.4 | .75 |
| Postfilm attitude | 22.0 | 5.1 | .70 |
| Education (in years) | 14.2 | 3.3 | (assumed = 1.0) |

The correlation of pre- and postfilm attitudes = .47.
The correlation of prefilm attitude and change in attitude = − .36.
The correlation of education and attitude change = .17.

6. Change the following profile of a high school senior's occupational interests into a form suitable for interpretation. The statistics under the profile are based on a national sample of high school seniors.

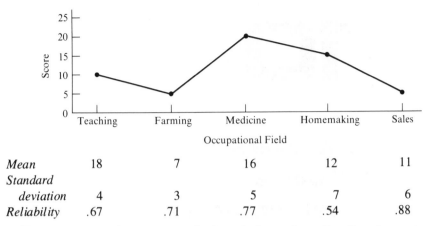

| | Teaching | Farming | Medicine | Homemaking | Sales |
|---|---|---|---|---|---|
| *Mean* | 18 | 7 | 16 | 12 | 11 |
| *Standard deviation* | 4 | 3 | 5 | 7 | 6 |
| *Reliability* | .67 | .71 | .77 | .54 | .88 |

7. A 20-item questionnaire measures attitude on the issue of equality of employment opportunities for men and women. The questionnaire is scored so that high scores indicate a favorable attitude toward equality. (Scores range in value from 0 to 20.) A 25-item questionnaire measuring job satisfaction also is used, and both questionnaires are administered to a group of men and a group of women. Discuss the meaning of the following results.

| | Women ($n = 50$) | | | Men ($n = 50$) | | |
|---|---|---|---|---|---|---|
| | $\bar{X}$ | $s_X$ | $r_{XX'}$ | $\bar{X}$ | $s_X$ | $r_{XX'}$ |
| *Attitude on equality* | 18.2 | 1.3 | .40 | 14.2 | 3.4 | .71 |
| *Job satisfaction* | 10.3 | 5.6 | .72 | 18.8 | 4.7 | .69 |
| *Correlation of measures* | −.16 | | | .35 | | |

# Controversies and Current Developments in Measurement

## 10.1  Introduction

Many controversies have arisen in the fields of testing and measurement. One of these controversies debates the relative benefits of clinical versus statistical prediction. Another deals with the advantages and disadvantages of homogeneous and nonhomogeneous tests. A third controversy deals with criticisms of tests—that they can be biased and invalid and may be invasions of privacy. Chapter 10 describes these controversies, as well as some relatively recent developments that are intended to make tests more useful. These recent developments include criterion-referenced tests, strong true-score theories and latent-trait models, generalizability theory, Bayesian methods, tailored testing, and computer interpretations of test results.

## 10.2  Clinical and Statistical Prediction

There has been a long controversy over the relative effectiveness of clinical versus statistical predictions of behavioral outcomes. One contributor to the length of this controversy has been the lack of consensus about the meaning of the terms *clinical* and *statistical prediction*. For the most part, early studies discriminated among prediction types on the basis of the method used to compile or combine the existing data. If data were compiled "in a person's head," without reference to statistical-prediction equations, the prediction was called *clinical*, regardless of the source or quality of the input data or the extent of clinical training or competence of the person making the prediction. If data from any source, including clinical observations, were compiled by use of a statistical equation, the prediction was called *statistical*.

When linear-regression equations (see Section 2.9) are used to create a score, $\hat{Y}_i$, to predict a score, $Y_i$, for examinee *i*, the accuracy of the prediction is best in one sense: the sum over examinees of the squared deviations of $Y_i$ from $\hat{Y}_i$ is minimized (the least-squared-error criterion). That is, a linear-regression equation minimizes the sum of squared errors, $\sum_{i=1}^{n} (Y_i - \hat{Y}_i)^2$. Using the criterion of minimizing the sum of squared errors, no procedure—statistical or clinical—that uses the same predictors and one linear-prediction rule for all examinees can do better than the linear-regression equation. But, if a clinician can successfully develop prediction rules that vary with the person tested or that use predictors beyond those used in the regression equation, then it is possible for a clinical judgment to be superior to a linear-regression equation in terms of the least squared error.

After reviewing a number of studies related to this issue, Meehl (1954, 1965) concluded that statistical methods of prediction were usually as good as or better than clinical methods. Focusing on one area of prediction (managerial performance), Korman (1968) concluded that clinical prediction was generally superior to statistical prediction. Sawyer (1966) classified 45 studies on the basis of their method of data collection: clinical, *mechanical* (for example, using a test or check list), or some combination of clinical and mechanical methods. Sawyer also classified the studies by their method of data compilation—clinical or mechanical (statistical). The reviewed studies varied widely in sample size, method used for prediction, type of behavior being predicted, and quality of research. Sawyer concluded that there was a general superiority of mechanical modes of data collection and compilation. Clinical methods appeared to make a greater contribution in the realm of data collection than in the realm of data compilation. Holt (1970) has described six different steps at which clinical judgment can enter into a prediction study: specification of the criterion to be predicted, identification of the variables to be used in predicting the criterion, choice of measuring instruments, tryouts of the prediction scheme, collection of cross-validating data (see Section 9.3), and compilation of cross-validation data to make the prediction. The possible superiority of statistical prediction at one step does not preclude the importance of clinical judgment at other steps.

Generalizations about the superiority of one method of prediction over another are hazardous, because there is a paucity of high quality, relevant research on which definitive conclusions can be based. Any conclusions that are made must be carefully limited to situations similar to those studied. Clinicians and statisticians frequently disagree about what data should be collected and what types of predictions should be made. The design and execution of good comparisons of clinical and statistical predictions should involve collaboration of statisticians and clinicians to assure that the goals and methods of both sides are represented fairly.

## 10.3  Homogeneous and Nonhomogeneous Tests

Tests can differ substantially in the variety of items they contain. A *homogeneous test* contains items that measure only one trait, and a *nonhomogeneous* (or heterogeneous) *test* contains items that measure a variety of traits. Examples of homogeneous tests are tests that contain only mathematical computation problems or contain only items measuring hypochondria. Examples of nonhomogeneous tests are tests of academic aptitude or intelligence, which typically contain a wide variety of item types, such as vocabulary, analogies, sequences, spatial relations, arithmetic reasoning, information, digit span, mazes, and so on. These different types of items can be scored as separate, homogeneous scales. Scores on these homogeneous scales usually are combined to create more heterogeneous subscales, such as verbal and nonverbal IQ. These subscales may also be combined to produce very heterogeneous scales, such as total IQ.

As more items are combined, scales usually have higher test/retest or parallel-forms reliability. The greater the variety of items that are included in a score, the greater the variety of criteria to which the test score will be related; thus, the test is more useful for a variety of predictions. However, interpretation of composite scales can become complicated, if not impossible. For example, it is fairly clear what a high score on a vocabulary test or a high score on an analogies test means. But, when the vocabulary and analogy scores are summed, it is difficult to say what the total score means in terms of a single trait or facility; it is difficult to think of an appropriate name for the total test score that is not extremely abstract or vague. Total scores also are difficult to interpret. For example, an examinee could get a moderately high score by scoring high on vocabulary and low on analogies, by scoring low on vocabulary and high on analogies, or by scoring moderately well on both tests. The total score doesn't tell us how well the individual did on the component tests (except in extreme cases).

Homogeneous tests are more easily interpreted than heterogeneous tests, and, in order to apply the strong true-score and latent-trait models described in Chapter 11, it is necessary for a test to be homogeneous. However, scores on a homogeneous test will not correlate as highly with as great a variety of criteria as will scores on a heterogeneous test. If we want to measure or predict one trait or type of behavior, we would prefer to use a homogeneous test containing items intended to measure that trait. If we want to predict performance on a variety of tasks— for example, success in a variety of occupations—we would be wise to use a heterogeneous test or a battery of homogeneous tests. If a battery of homogeneous tests is used, scores on these tests can be combined with different weights to predict different criteria; these weights can be determined using multiple regression (Section 9.3).

## 10.4   Criticisms of Standardized Testing

Standardized tests are a pervasive part of American life. Their use in education ranges from preschool-readiness tests to exams for admission to graduate and professional schools. Ability and intelligence tests are used for class placement and for the diagnosis of learning disorders. Achievement tests are widely used in elementary and secondary schools to measure student progress and to evaluate the effectiveness of school programs. Occupational testing is widespread, and employers such as corporations, the armed forces, and the federal government frequently use tests as a part of job-applicant screening and placement procedures. Tests are available for professional use in career counseling, personality description, and diagnosis of psychological abnormalities.

The field of testing has not been immune from attack. In 1965 congressional hearings were held on the use of tests by government agencies. (An extensive report of these hearings is contained in the November, 1965, issue of the *American Psychologist.*) Senators and representatives were particularly concerned with the use of personality tests for screening job applicants. Concerns were expressed about the validity and reliability of the tests and about the possibility that some test questions—particularly those dealing with sexual, religious, and political attitudes—were invasions of privacy. These investigations led to a restatement of the Civil Service Commission's policy on the use of personality tests; they are to be used only by qualified psychologists and psychiatrists in connection with medical determinations of the continued fitness of employees and in the evaluation of applicants for exceptionally demanding positions. The Civil Service Commission emphasized its policy that personality tests are not to be used routinely.

Two issues of *The National Elementary Principal* (March/April, 1975, and July/August, 1975) have been devoted to airing criticisms of intelligence and achievement testing. Intelligence testing has been attacked as being ethnically biased, because such testing may not accurately measure the intelligence of members of minority groups. Since such tests are frequently used for placement of students in classes for the mentally retarded, ethnic bias could result in disproportionate numbers of minority children being placed in classes for the mentally retarded. In response to just such concerns, a 1975 California law banned the use of group-administered aptitude tests in public schools, except for research purposes, placement of students in programs for the mentally gifted, and determination of postsecondary-school scholarships. The issue of ethnic bias is just one aspect of the general concern about the validity of intelligence tests. It was long accepted that such tests did indeed measure "intelligence," but the issue of ethnic bias has brought to public attention questions about the nature of intelligence and the suitability of the items on intelligence tests for measuring the trait. It has been argued that intelligence is a multidimensional concept and that the use of a single total IQ score grossly oversimplifies a complex set of psychological faculties.

Like intelligence tests, achievement tests have been attacked as being biased and invalid and as not measuring the important learning that goes on in the classroom. Probably many people who criticize the content of achievement tests would not agree on what should be covered by these tests, and this would leave the development of local tests and norms up to the individual users. However, in many cases, the expertise and investment required to develop good tests could be prohibitive. Also, when local tests are used, they preclude comparisons of achievement levels across schools or states and make evaluation of large-scale publicly funded programs very difficult. Standardized achievement tests do offer a common basis on which to compare school programs, which is valuable when it can be agreed that the tests measure behaviors of interest.

General criticism of standardized tests frequently centers around the multiple-choice format and the timing of the tests. The multiple-choice format is criticized on the grounds that it does not measure complex psychological processes, that it is vague, that it penalizes the creative examinee, and that it places too much emphasis on speed and rote memory. It has been argued that untimed essay exams or individual exams are preferable to group-administered multiple-choice exams. But timed multiple-choice exams have the advantage of being much easier to standardize and score than other test formats. Furthermore, the scores on such tests are usually found to be highly correlated with scores on reliably scored open-ended exams dealing with the same topics.

There has also been concern about the confidentiality and secrecy of test results. The Buckley amendment, an amendment to the 1974 elementary- and secondary-education bill, gives parents and college students the right to review the official school records, including test scores. They are also given the right to challenge inaccurate, misleading, or otherwise inappropriate data in the records.

The Civil Rights Act of 1964 has also put legal limitations on test use. Title VII of that act forbids employment discrimination on the basis of sex, race, color, religion, or national origin. The Tower amendment to Title VII allows the use of professionally devised ability tests in employment selection, as long as they are not used to discriminate on the basis of the above characteristics. Court cases centered on employment testing have led to government guidelines for test use. If an employer's selection procedures disqualify a disproportionate number of people from a target group, then the burden of proof lies with the employer to demonstrate that the selection procedure is not illegally discriminatory. Employers in such a situation must provide validating evidence for the relevance of the testing procedure to job performance. If a selection procedure has an adverse impact on a target group and test validation in different groups produces different prediction equations, then compensation must be made in the selection procedure—for example, the use of different cutting scores for members of different groups. Thus, the government has become involved in defining and enforcing the fair use of tests—a very complex problem, as was noted in Section 9.4.

Due to the increased use of tests and the possibility for their misuse, education about appropriate methods of test construction and use is very important. Test publishers must provide as much information as possible about the validity of their tests, and, if the test publishers become aware of common misuses of their tests, they have the responsibility to warn against such use. Scores should be reported in a manner that reflects their fallibility. It may not be sufficient to report a reliability coefficient in a technical manual and ignore it in a score report (for example, by reporting a three-digit score when the standard error of measurement indicates that differences in the third digit are meaningless). Reported scores can be surrounded by confidence intervals, either numerically or graphically, to indicate the degree of accuracy with which the measurement was made. It is the test developer's responsibility to attempt to reduce bias in test construction. Other responsibilities of the test publisher and user are covered in the *Standards for Educational and Psychological Tests* (American Psychological Association, 1974). If tests are to continue to be used in the fields of education, industry, and mental health, publishers must develop psychometrically sound tests with proven usefulness. The conscientious test publisher and user can help society in the struggle with the problems of group heterogeneity, limited budgets, the desire to give every child as good an education as possible, and the need to give all people fair treatment in job hiring and promotion. The following sections present several developments in testing that have been made in an attempt to make tests more useful.

## 10.5   Criterion-Referenced Tests

One development intended to increase the usefulness of achievement tests is *criterion-referenced* testing. Most achievement tests are *norm-referenced*; that is, a student's score is reported with reference to a norm, usually a distribution of test scores for a specific grade. Norm-referenced tests usually produce scores that are fairly global in nature, with names such as "math computation" or "language mechanics." Criterion-referenced tests, on the other hand, report how the student stands with respect to some fixed criterion. The criterion is some specific educational objective, such as being able to add single-digit numbers or to identify the number of syllables in printed words. The student is given a score either of mastery or of nonmastery for each objective. A total, global score is not of interest in a criterion-referenced test.

For criterion-referenced testing, it is desirable to have objectives that are ordered hierarchically—that is, to have the mastery of some objectives be prerequisite to the mastery of others. For example, it is unlikely that a student will master two-digit addition with carrying before mastering single-digit addition or will understand the concept of cause and effect before mastering the idea of verb tense. These hierarchies give teachers information about desirable sequences of teaching objectives. With the knowledge of which objectives a particular student has mastered, the teacher has information that is directly applicable to the organization of classroom teaching. In this sense the test is used as a diagnostic instrument, and teaching is individually tailored for the student. This is very different from using the test to label the student—that is, to label the student as *gifted* or *retarded*.

There are special psychometric problems involved in the construction of criterion-referenced tests. The first area of concern is the careful specification of the objectives to be measured and the construction of the items intended to measure these objectives. Because of the great number of specific objectives that might be covered in a criterion-referenced test, each objective needs to be measured as efficiently as possible. Desirable items are those that discriminate between examinees who have mastered the objective and those who have not. If a group of examinees includes those who have and those who have not mastered an objective, the distribution of scores on the objective should appear as a U-shaped curve, as in Figure 10.1.

For educational planning, it is desirable to select items that have proven responsiveness to instruction. In order to select those items that are the most sensitive to instruction, item tryouts for criterion-referenced tests typically include studies in which pre- and posttest scores of students who receive instruction toward an objective are compared with pre- and posttest scores of students who have not received instruction toward that objective.

A second special problem involved in criterion-referenced testing is the specification of cutting scores for mastery of an objective. For items with U-shaped distributions, the *antimode* (least-frequent score) can be taken as the cutting score. For the objective in Figure 10.1, a score greater than or equal to 3 could indicate mastery. However, if the score distribution for an objective has only one mode (for example, if it is a normal distribution), selection of a cutting score is much more difficult. Typically in these cases, the cutting score is set arbitrarily; for example, the student must get four out of five items correct to demonstrate mastery.

A third special problem with criterion-referenced tests concerns creating confidence intervals for a student's true probability of having mastered an objective. Because there usually are only a few items measuring each objective, this confidence interval can be very wide, particularly if there is a fairly high probability of correctly

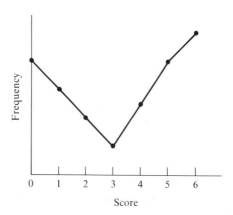

Figure 10.1. Expected distribution of scores when the sample includes examinees who have and who have not mastered the objective

guessing the answers. Bayesian methods, discussed in Section 10.8, might be used to help reduce the width of this confidence interval.

Another major problem involved in developing criterion-referenced tests is in the specification of the hierarchy of the items. The problem is largely one of separating correlation from causation. For example, the probability of mastering objective 2, given that objective 1 is not mastered, may be low. This does not necessarily mean that objective 1 must be mastered before objective 2 can be. It may be that objective 2 is rarely taught before objective 1 has been taught but that it is not necessary to teach the objectives in this order. For example, long division may be taught in the fifth grade and the Pythagorean theorem in the seventh grade. Although long division does not have to be mastered before the Pythagorean theorem can be learned, a correlational study would suggest this hierarchy. Cause/effect relationships cannot be established from correlational data, and we must be cautious in interpreting such data in establishing hierarchies.

Some criterion-referenced tests also offer some norm-referenced information (see, for example, the *Prescriptive Reading Inventory,* 1976). Studies correlating performance on criterion-referenced tests with performance on norm-referenced tests in the same subject areas have shown that norm-referenced performance can be accurately predicted from criterion-referenced performance. However, it is much less accurate to predict performance on criterion-referenced objectives from norm-referenced scores. For example, knowing how well a student has mastered a set of mathematical objectives may provide good information about the student's probable total score on a norm-referenced mathematics exam. However, the single score on the mathematics exam does not provide sufficient information to predict which specific skills have and have not been mastered (except in extreme cases when a very low or very high total score indicates that very few or very many of the criterion-referenced objectives have been mastered). By offering predictions of norm-referenced performance, criterion-referenced tests offer information of value to the administrator evaluating school programs as well as diagnostic information of value to the classroom teacher.

Hambleton, Swaminathan, Algina, and Coulson (1978) review a number of technical issues that arise with criterion-referenced tests.

## 10.6 Strong True-Score Theories and Latent-Trait Models

*Strong true-score theories* and *latent-trait models* are used to analyze homogeneous test scores when an examinee's performance is assumed to be a function of a single true score or latent (unobservable) trait. These models predict the probability of an examinee with a certain true-score or latent-trait value getting a particular item correct or obtaining a certain number-right score. The models allow estimation of an examinee's true-score or latent-trait value, and most models permit estimation of test or item difficulty. Estimates of additional item characteristics (for example, item-discriminating power) can be obtained from some of the models.

These models can be useful in many ways. Latent-trait and true-score estimates help reduce misunderstandings that can arise from using number-right scores. Some models can produce interval- or ratio-level trait or true-score scales. All of these models produce standard errors of latent traits or true scores that can vary as the level of the trait or true-score varies. In other words, some examinees' trait or true-score values are estimated more accurately than those of other examinees, and the degree of this accuracy can be estimated. Some of the models offer ways of weighting item responses in order to produce the most accurate estimates of latent traits. The models can facilitate the development and equating of alternate test forms, and they also offer a means of examining a test or an item for bias against any given group.

These models are described in more detail in Chapter 11. A thorough understanding of them involves more complicated mathematical considerations than those involved in the other chapters of this book. The nonmathematically inclined reader can obtain more information about these models by skimming the mathematical considerations and concentrating on the verbal descriptions that accompany them.

## 10.7  Generalizability Theory

Cronbach and his colleagues (Cronbach, Gleser, Nanda, & Rajaratnam, 1972) have developed the concept of *generalizability* as an attempt to increase the accuracy of test interpretation. Generalizability theory explicitly considers different systematic sources of variance in measurements and describes ways of estimating the amounts of variance contributed by these sources. Generalizability theory sees classical or weak true-score theory (Chapter 3) as being oversimplified and ambiguous, and many aspects of classical true-score theory are seen to be special cases of the more general test-theory formulation provided by generalizability theory.

In generalizability theory, observations (for example, examinees' scores on tests) are seen as samples from a universe of *admissible observations*. The *universe* describes the conditions, under which examinees can be observed or tested, that produce results that are equivalent to some specified degree. An examinee's *universe score* is defined to be the expected value of his or her observed scores over all admissible observations; the universe score is directly analogous to the true score used in classical true-score theory. Generalizability theory emphasizes that different universes exist and makes it the test publisher's responsibility to define carefully his or her universe. This definition is done in terms of *facets* or dimensions. For example, facets could be the size of the testing group, the types of training received by the examiners, the test form, the occasion for testing, and so on. Levels of these facets are specified, and their effects are examined. For example, the size of the testing group could distinguish between groups of 1 to 15 students, 15 to 30 students, or greater than 30 students. Examiners could be classroom teachers or specialists who have received extensive training in test administration. The test publisher might specify that the test results for test forms A and B are equivalent to a certain specified degree if the group size is 30 or fewer examinees, if the examiners have a certain minimum level of training, and so on.

The use of generalizability theory involves conducting two types of research studies: a *generalizability (G) study* and a *decision (D) study*. A G study is done as part of the development of the measurement instrument. The main goal of the G study is to specify the degree to which test results are equivalent when obtained under different testing conditions. In simplified terms, a G study involves collecting data for examinees tested under specified conditions (that is, at various levels of specified facets), estimating variance components due to these facets and their interactions using analysis of variance (see Hays, 1973), and producing coefficients of generalizability. A *coefficient of generalizability* is the ratio of universe-score variance to observed-score variance and is the counterpart of the reliability coefficient used in classical true-score theory. A test does not have one generalizability coefficient, but many, depending on the facets examined in the G study. The G study also provides information about how to estimate an examinee's universe score most accurately.

In a D study, the measurement instrument produces data to be used in making decisions or reaching conclusions, such as admitting people to programs or identifying children who display certain reading skills. The information from the G study is used in interpreting the results of the D study and in reaching sound conclusions.

Many test publishers present data on equivalence (that is, correlations) of alternate test forms, but frequently the conditions under which these data have been collected are not fully specified and possible systematic influences on this equivalence are not examined. The result can be ambiguities or decisions that are made without enough information. For example, using the Spearman-Brown formula, a researcher can predict that doubling the number of observations can produce a certain desired level of reliability. Suppose that the observations are made by several different observers, who rate the behavior of children on successive days. Without doing a G study, the researcher wouldn't know whether it is appropriate to double the number of observers and keep the same number of days of observation, to keep the same number of observers and double the number of days of observation, or to make some intermediate adjustment. Generalizability theory explicitly considers such problems and makes it clear that the accuracy of measurement should be considered separately for each application of the measurement device; the coefficient of generalizability (that is, the reliability) of a test is not an invariant property of the test but is influenced by the situation in which the test is administered.

A G study provides useful, detailed information about test characteristics under different testing conditions, but analysis of the data in such a study does involve developing a statistical sophistication greater than that involved in classical true-score theory.

## 10.8    Bayesian Methods

Another line of investigation intended to increase the usefulness of test scores involves applications of Bayesian statistics. *Bayesian methods* increase the accuracy of estimation of an examinee's true score by augmenting the information provided by the examinee's test score with collateral information about the examinee's group membership or about the examinee's performance on other measures. For example, an examinee's test score, $X$, can be augmented by the mean score, $\bar{X}$, for the group of which the person is a member. That is, the score $Y$ is used instead of $X$ in making decisions, where

$$Y = wX + (1 - w)\bar{X}. \tag{10.1}$$

The weight to be given the test score is $w$. This weight could be the reliability of $X$; that is, $w = r_{XX'}$. As the reliability of the score decreases, the group mean is given more weight.

If only one group is being considered, $Y$ and $X$ will produce the same conclusions about differences among examinees, because $Y$ is a linear function of $X$. If different groups are considered together, the use of $Y$ will most likely produce different conclusions than will the use of $X$. If two people come from groups having different means, they can have the same $X$ scores on the test but different $Y$ scores based on Bayesian estimation methods. In some cases it may not appear fair to use the group information. Suppose scores on an achievement test, $X$, are being used as the criterion for admission to graduate school. If both student A and student B have the same score on the achievement test, but student A comes from an undergraduate school with a lower mean achievement score than does student B, then student A will have a lower $Y$ score than student B. Student A, from the school with the lower mean, could be seen as having had to show initiative and learn more on his or her own than student B, coming from the school with the higher mean. In that case student A, with the lower $Y$ score, could be seen as the better student. On the other hand, supporters of Bayesian procedures would argue that when a higher-scoring student comes from a lower-scoring group, it is more likely that his or her test score exhibits a positive error of measurement that is corrected by the Bayesian estimation procedure. Thus, there can be complications involved in the interpretation of the use of Bayesian estimators (Novick & Jackson, 1974).

Meredith and Kearns have used Bayesian methods in connection with strong true-score and latent-trait models (Kearns & Meredith, 1975; Meredith & Kearns, 1973). Novick and his colleagues (Novick & Jackson, 1970, 1974; Novick, Jackson, & Thayer, 1971) have investigated a wide variety of uses of Bayesian methods for measurement applications.

## 10.9    Tailored Testing

The most efficient way of measuring a trait or true score is to match the item difficulty to the examinee's trait or true-score level—that is, to give more difficult items to examinees with high true scores or trait levels and to give easier items to examinees with low true scores or trait levels. If the items on a test are much too difficult or much too easy for an examinee, all that will be gained from testing is some knowledge of the upper or lower limits of the examinee's trait level. When an examinee incorrectly answers moderately difficult items, it is inefficient to administer very difficult items. As described in Section 6.3, when there is no guessing possible, the most efficient items are those that the examinee has about a 50% chance of answering correctly. When a group of examinees with a variety of trait values are tested with the same test, it is impossible for the test to be maximally efficient for all examinees simultaneously. It would be ideal to administer to an examinee only those items that are likely to give substantial amounts of information about his or her trait level. This involves administering different items to different examinees—that is, *individualized* (*tailored* or *adaptive*) testing. The psychometric problems involved in individualized testing center around two major areas: (1) choosing items for each examinee and (2) having used different items for different examinees, obtaining trait estimates that are on the same scale for the different examinees.

Tailored testing presently is done with some individually administered intelligence tests, such as the Stanford-Binet or Wechsler tests. The examiner uses his or her own judgment to choose a difficulty level at which to start testing. If the initial items are too difficult for the examinee, easier items are substituted. An examinee is given items that are more and more difficult, until he or she begins to miss a certain proportion of the items, at which point testing on that set of items is terminated. In scoring the test, it is assumed that the examinee would have correctly answered items that were easier than the items he or she did get correct and would have missed items that were more difficult than the items he or she answered incorrectly.

Wright and Douglas (1975) have proposed a method of tailored testing that uses items scaled for difficulty by Rasch's logistic model (Section 11.6). They propose letting the examinees determine for themselves which items to take. The examinee is given a test with items ordered in terms of increasing difficulty and is told to begin with moderately difficult items and to work in both directions—taking more difficult and easier items until, in the examinee's opinion, the items are too difficult or too easy. The examinee's score is the number of items that were correctly answered plus the number of items that were judged to be too easy to offer any challenge. The practicality of this procedure remains to be evaluated.

Another type of tailored testing involves *two-stage testing*. The examinee's score on one test, usually a short *locator* or *routing test,* determines which level of a *second-stage test* should be taken. In some cases the examinee's score on the locator test is used only for assignment to the second-stage test and is not used as part of the estimate of the examinee's true score or trait value. Lord (1969c) proposes a method of combining a trait estimate based on the routing test with a trait estimate based on the second-stage test. By using simulation studies, Lord has examined the information functions or efficiencies (see Section 11.7) of various combinations of routing and second-stage test designs. The two-stage testing procedure can be superior to traditional single-stage testing in estimating extreme traits, but it is not particularly helpful for medium trait levels.

A more complicated method of tailored testing involves having a computer choose the items while the examinee is taking the test (*computer-assisted testing*). When an examinee gets an item right, he or she is given a more difficult item, chosen according to some formula; a wrong answer is followed by an easier item. The choice of the difficulty level of successive items is based on a *step function*: the difficulty of item $i + 1$ is taken to be the difficulty of item $i$ plus or minus some specified value called the *step size*. Some procedures, called *shrinking-step-size procedures*, start out with large step sizes and decrease the step size as the test items approach the difficulty level that matches the examinee's trait level. Other tests use a *fixed-step-size procedure* throughout. The shrinking-step-size procedure gives a very good estimate of the trait for the administration of a given number of items; however, it requires an extremely large item pool from which items are chosen. If the examinee is to answer $N$ items, about $2^N$ items are required for the pool. For $N = 5$, the item pool must have about 32 items; for $N = 10$, the item pool must have about 1024 items. Such large item pools are rarely available. If a fixed-step-size procedure is used, the trait estimate is somewhat less accurate than that obtained with a shrinking-step-size procedure using the same $N$. However, for the fixed-step-size procedure, only $N(N + 1)/2$ items are needed in the item pool. For $N = 5$, 15 items are needed; for $N = 10$, the item pool must have 55 items. Thus, the fixed-step-size procedure, although somewhat less efficient, is a much more practical procedure than the shrinking-step-size procedure. When a fixed-step-size procedure is used, the examinee's trait score is estimated to be the average of the difficulties of the items chosen, including the difficulty of the last, $(N + 1)$th, item chosen by the computer but not answered by the examinee (Stocking, 1969). These item difficulties are estimated using a latent-trait model (see Chapter 11).

Tailored testing allows the examiner to quickly assess the examinee's level, without subjecting the examinee to a boring series of very easy problems or to an unpleasant, embarrassing series of extremely difficult problems. Thus, such methods are desirable for both the examiner and examinee. More information about tailored testing is available from Lord (1977a), Weiss (1976), and Wood (1973).

## 10.10   Computer-Interpreted Testing

Another use of computers in testing is for *computer-interpreted testing* or diagnosis. The most widespread use of computers in this area has been with the *Minnesota Multiphasic Personality Inventory* (MMPI), a personality test that involves yes/no answers to hundreds of statements about personal behavior and beliefs. Several publishers offer narrative reports interpreting the pattern of the examinee's responses in terms of personality characteristics and psychiatric diagnoses. The publishers have developed computer programs that take an examinee's pattern of responses and select computer-stored statements to be presented as descriptions or interpretations of this pattern. In his review, Eichman (1972) discusses the strengths and weaknesses of computer-assisted interpretation of the

MMPI. Among the strengths are clerical scoring convenience, reliable and systematic interpretations of the score patterns, and the firm foundation of the interpretations on the latest research findings. The main disadvantage of computer-assisted diagnosis is a lack of information about how the computer program comes up with its narrative interpretation. Details of the computer programs usually are not published; the user must rely on the reputation of the persons developing the programs, the face validity of the reports, or testimonials from other clinicians about the accuracy and usefulness of the reports. These computer programs could benefit from extensive empirical validation studies. Eichman suggests that in their present form the programs are best used by trained, experienced clinicians.

Used with proper precautions, such computer-based test-interpretation and scoring systems could be used to accumulate an enormous and valuable data base for the further refinement and development of the systems. Some people, however, object to such plans, because of the possibility of unethical use of the data base.

## 10.11  Summary

Linear regression is the most accurate means of predicting one type of behavior from another by using one linear prediction rule to make all predictions. Clinical prediction can be more accurate than statistical prediction, if the clinician can develop successful prediction rules that vary with the person involved or if the clinician can use data that are not included in the statistical prediction. Different reviews of the literature have reached different conclusions about the relative benefits of clinical and statistical predictions, and studies comparing the methods should involve collaboration between statisticians and clinicians to assure that the goals and methods of both sides are represented fairly.

All the items on a homogeneous test measure the same type of behavior, while nonhomogeneous tests contain items that measure a variety of behaviors. Scores on homogeneous tests are easier to interpret than nonhomogeneous test scores, and homogeneity is required for using the strong true-score and latent-trait models discussed in Chapter 11. Sets of scores on different homogeneous tests can be combined to predict complex criteria. Heterogeneous tests can be more useful than homogeneous tests when we want to predict a wide variety of behaviors from one score.

Standardized tests have been criticized as being invasions of privacy and as being unreliable or invalid. These concerns have been raised in particular with respect to the use of intelligence tests with minority-group members. Federal and state governments have begun regulating test use by employers and schools.

Criterion-referenced tests were developed in an effort to increase the usefulness of achievement tests. A criterion-referenced test is designed to measure whether an examinee has mastered a particular well-defined task; criterion-referenced tests, unlike norm-referenced tests, do not emphasize how well an examinee performs in comparison with other examinees. The processes involved in the development of criterion-referenced tests differ from those involved in the development of norm-referenced tests.

Strong true-score theories and latent-trait models hypothesize ways in which an examinee's performance on a particular item or test is influenced by an unobserved true score or trait. The models can be useful in test construction and scaling and in examining and increasing the accuracy of latent-trait or true-score estimates. Detailed information about these models appears in Chapter 11.

Generalizability theory specifies the conditions under which measurements can be considered to be equivalent. This specification is done by identifying the sources of variance that systematically influence the measurements and by estimating the amounts of variance contributed by these sources. A universe of admissible observations is delineated in terms of facets and levels of these facets; an examinee's universe score, which is analogous to a true score, is defined as the expected value of observed scores taken over the universe of admissible observations. A generalizability $(G)$ study estimates the score variance produced by changing levels of the facets and estimates coefficients of generalizability, which are analogous to reliabilities. A coefficient of generalizability is the ratio of variance in universe scores to variance in observed scores. In a decision $(D)$ study, data are gathered and interpreted in order to make decisions about examinees.

The basic purpose for the use of Bayesian techniques in testing is to increase the accuracy of estimation of an examinee's true score. This result is achieved by augmenting the information from the examinee's test score with collateral information about the examinee's group membership or his or her performance on other tasks. Although the use of Bayesian estimators increases accuracy, their interpretation generally is more complicated than that of traditional estimators.

Tailored testing involves giving an examinee tests or items that provide the most information about the examinee's capabilities. In two-stage testing, an examinee is given a short locator or routing test that indicates which level of a longer second-stage test should be given. When a computer is available for computer-assisted testing, successive items to be administered to an examinee can be chosen on the basis of fixed-step-size or shrinking-step-size procedures. The shrinking-step-size procedure produces more accurate estimates of examinee characteristics but requires an extremely large item pool.

Computer-interpreted testing services have been developed largely for the *Minnesota Multiphasic Personality Inventory*. The interpretations offered by the computer programs are convenient and reliable and are based on a large variety of research findings. However, the procedures that have been followed in developing the interpretive programs usually are not published, and more empirical validations of the programs should be provided. These computer services should be used only by trained, experienced clinicians.

## 10.12  Vocabulary

adaptive testing

admissible observations

antimode

Bayesian methods

clinical prediction

coefficient of generalizability

computer-assisted testing
computer-interpreted testing
criterion-referenced test
decision ($D$) study
facets
fixed-step-size procedures
generalizability ($G$) study
generalizability theory
homogeneous test
individualized testing
latent-trait models
locator test
mechanical data collection
mechanical data compilation

nonhomogeneous test
norm-referenced test
routing test
second-stage test
shrinking-step-size procedures
statistical prediction
step function
step size
strong true-score theory
tailored testing
two-stage testing
universe
universe score

## 10.13  Study Questions

1. Discuss possible variations in the definitions of *clinical* and *statistical* prediction.
2. Describe a study that involves both clinical and mechanical methods of data collection and statistical methods of data compilation.
3. Describe a study that involves a mechanical method of data collection and a clinical method of data compilation.
4. Why is a linear-regression equation as good as or better than a clinical prediction based on the same data?
5. Give an example of a case in which a clinical prediction of behavior probably would be more accurate than a statistical prediction.
6. What are the advantages and disadvantages of homogeneous and nonhomogeneous tests?
7. Give examples of situations in which each type of test (homogeneous and nonhomogeneous) would be preferred.
8. List some common criticisms of standardized testing. What additional criticisms can you think of?
9. What changes in test construction or test usage could adequately respond to the criticisms of standardized testing?
10. How has the government become involved in the regulation of test use?
11. Contrast the intent and construction of criterion-referenced and norm-referenced tests.
12. In what situations are criterion-referenced tests more useful than norm-referenced tests?
13. In what situations are norm-referenced tests more useful than criterion-referenced tests?
14. What special problems are involved in the construction of criterion-referenced tests?

15. In what situations are strong true-score theories and latent-trait models useful?
16. What distinguishes generalizability theory from classical true-score theory? How are the two theories similar?
17. What is a universe of admissible observations? How is it specified?
18. What is a universe score? A coefficient of generalizability? What are their counterparts in classical true-score theory?
19. What are the purposes of $G$ and $D$ studies?
20. Why are Bayesian methods employed? What distinguishes them from traditional methods of test scoring?
21. When different groups are considered and Bayesian methods are used, what ethical issues emerge?
22. Why is tailored testing desirable?
23. Describe several ways in which a test could be tailored or individualized.
24. What is a locator test? When is it useful?
25. Describe fixed-step-size and shrinking-step-size tailored-testing procedures. What are the advantages and disadvantages of each?
26. What are the advantages and disadvantages of computer-assisted test interpretation or diagnosis?

# Strong
# True-Score Theories
# and
# Latent-Trait Models

## 11.1 Introduction

Many of the preceding chapters examined the properties of test scores after making the assumptions of classical or weak true-score theory; these assumptions are concerned with the means and correlations of true and error scores. The classical model assumes nothing about the frequency distribution of scores, and formal statistical tests of the suitability of the classical model for a set of data are not available.

The classical model produces many practical results. This chapter examines more-detailed models or theories for test scores that also can be very useful. These models include strong true-score and latent-trait models. The models discussed in this chapter assume that there is one important characteristic (a true score or latent trait) that influences performance on all items in a test. *Strong true-score theory* is similar to weak true-score theory in that the expected value of an observed score is the true score (or a constant times the true score), but strong true-score theory involves additional assumptions about the probability that an examinee with a certain true score will have a particular observed score. Using these assumptions, the appropriateness of strong true-score theories for a given set of data can be examined. The strong true-score theories described in this chapter produce ratio-level true-score scales, and these theories imply that standard errors of measurement are different for different true scores. Binomial-error models and Poisson models are discussed as examples of strong true-score theories.

In *latent-trait theories,* it is assumed that the most important aspects of test performance can be described by an examinee's standing on one *latent trait*—a hypothetical and unobserved characteristic or trait (for example, verbal ability, knowledge of history, or extroversion). Latent-trait theories propose models that describe how the latent trait influences performance on each test item. Unlike test scores or true scores, latent traits theoretically can take on values from $-\infty$ to $+\infty$. Although in latent-trait theory the expected value of the observed score is the true score, the true score generally is not a linear function of the latent trait, so the expected value of the observed score is not equal to the latent-trait value. Computer programs are used to obtain estimates of latent-trait values. Latent-trait theories, like strong true-score theories, can be tested for their appropriateness for a set of data, and, when they fit a set of data, latent-trait models produce interval scales. Normal-ogive and logistic models are presented as examples of latent-trait theories.

Because the models considered in this chapter make powerful assumptions about the processes underlying observed scores, these models can lead to a great variety of predictions about the observed scores. When such predictions are verified, the test theorist can feel that he or she has a good model for the statistical (and sometimes the psychological) processes influencing test performance. The test user should keep in mind that these test models must be examined for their appropriateness for the data at hand.

Strong true-score and latent-trait theories go beyond a conception of one standard error of measurement being used for all examinees; instead, these models produce standard errors that vary with latent-trait or true-score level. These standard errors, unlike those obtained in classical true-score theory using sample variances and reliabilities, are not influenced by the distribution of scores in the sample being tested. With these models, standard errors also are available for estimates of item parameters (for example, item difficulty and discrimination indices).

Strong true-score and latent-trait theories can be very helpful. A researcher can hypothesize ways in which a true-score or latent-trait distribution has been transformed into an observed-score distribution. From this hypothesis, assorted predictions about the properties of the observed scores can be made. If these predictions are upheld, the researcher can obtain estimates of the true scores or latent traits and, thus, can help eliminate possible misinterpretations caused by the use of raw scores. The models can also be used to help determine whether one latent trait alone appears to be influencing test performance. Some theories can assist in determining whether the same latent trait is affecting test scores for different groups of people, which is helpful in examining test bias. Interval- and ratio-level scales with desirable properties can be created using these test models. The precision of estimation of a trait can be increased by using item selection and weighting techniques involving test models, and the development and equating of alternate test forms can be facilitated.

Working with strong true-score and latent-trait models involves knowledge of several distribution functions. Distributions that are central to the understanding of a model are described in this chapter. If you are not comfortable with the mathematics in this chapter, you can become familiar with the assumptions and implications of the models by concentrating on the verbal descriptions. If you're interested in obtaining more detailed information about the models, see Lord and Novick (1968).

## 11.2  Local Independence

In strong true-score and latent-trait theories, it is assumed that the true-score or latent-trait value gives all the information that is available for predicting an examinee's performance on any item (or test); additional information about how the examinee performed on other items or how other examinees performed will not improve the prediction. This assumption implies that there is local independence of items and examinees. *Local independence of items* means that, for a given true-score or latent-trait value, item scores are independent of one another. When two items are locally independent, the probability that an examinee with a given true-score or latent-trait value passes both items is the product of the probabilities that the examinee passes each item. For example, if an examinee with a certain true score has a probability of .8 of passing item 1 and a probability of .9 of passing item 2 and if the items are locally independent, then the examinee has a probability of $(.8)(.9) = .72$ of passing both items. Another way to express local independence of items is to say that the probability that examinee A passes item 2, given that examinee A passes item 1, is just the probability that examinee A passes item 2. Similarly, *local independence of examinees* implies that the scores of different examinees are independent, given their true scores or latent-trait values. For example, if examinee A has a probability of .2 of passing a certain item and examinee B has a probability of .9 of passing that same item and if the examinees' responses are locally independent, then the probability that both will pass the item is $(.2)(.9) = .18$.

If the act of answering one item or the knowledge of one item's answer influences the answering of other items, then the items are not locally independent. For example, an attitude survey in which the context created by answers to some questions influences subsequent answers would not be suitable for latent-trait or strong true-score models. If changing the order of administration of a set of items influences test performance, the items are not locally independent. Chained items (that is, items for which answers are dependent on the answers to preceding items) are not locally independent. If one examinee's scores influence another examinee's scores through discussion or collaboration on answers, then the scores are not locally independent and strong true-score and latent-trait models would not be appropriate.

Local independence of items does not mean that the items will necessarily be independent when the scores of examinees with a variety of true scores or latent traits are pooled together. Suppose two examinees, Ben and Jane, are tested with two ability items, 1 and 2. Ben passes item 1, and Jane fails item 1. If we had to guess whether Ben or Jane is more likely to pass item 2, it would make sense to bet on Ben, because their scores on item 1 give us some information about their true-score or latent-trait values. It is likely that, since Ben passed item 1 and Jane failed it, Ben has a higher latent-trait or true-score value and, therefore, has a higher probability of passing item 2. When examinees with different true-score or latent-trait values are considered together, locally independent items can be related.

Another way to look at local independence is by examining scores on two variables obtained for two groups of people, labeled A and B. Everyone in group A has the same high true-score or latent-trait value; everyone in group B has the same low true-score or latent-trait value. Within each group, the observed scores for variables 1 and 2 are independent. Plots of the observed scores for each group appear in Figure 11.1. Figure 11.2 displays the plot obtained when the two groups are pooled. Because group B has lower scores than group A on both variables, the variables are positively related when the groups are pooled. Between-group differences in scores represent real trait or true-score differences; within-group differences in scores are not meaningful or predictable and are due to random variation (measurement error). The two variables, although correlated in the combined sample, are locally independent within the groups that are formed on the basis of trait level.

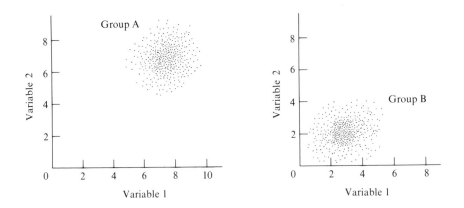

Figure 11.1. Plots for locally independent variables within two groups

## 11.3  Binomial-Error Models

The *binomial-error model* (Lord, 1965) allows us to determine how similar a true score and an observed score are likely to be. In simplified terms, the binomial-error model assumes that the observed score is a number-right score for a test whose locally independent items are all of equal difficulty. The model produces

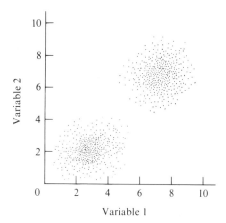

Figure 11.2. Plot obtained when groups A and B are pooled

standard errors of measurement that vary with true-score level; that is, the model implies that some true scores have smaller standard errors of measurement than others and allows the user to determine these standard errors.

The following list presents the formal assumptions of the binomial-error model.

1. The observed test score for examinee $j$, $X_j$, is the sum of scores for $N$ locally independent, *binary items*—that is, items producing scores of 1 (correct) or 0 (incorrect). Therefore, the binomial-error model is suitable for number-right scores. If the score for any item could take on more than one of two values, the binomial-error model would not be suitable.
2. The probability that an item is correct (that is, takes on the value 1) is $\zeta_j$ (Greek letter *zeta*) for each and every item for examinee $j$. $\zeta_j$ is the $j$th examinee's true score. If the items vary in difficulty or if an examinee does not finish the test, this assumption would be violated.
3. $X_j = N\zeta_j + E_j$, where $E_j$ is the error of measurement for examinee $j$. This assumption is analogous to the additivity assumption for true and error scores in classical true-score theory (Assumption 1, Section 3.1).
4. The expected observed score for an examinee with true score $\zeta_j$ is $N\zeta_j$: $\mathcal{E}(X_j|N\zeta_j) = N\zeta_j$. (The vertical bar "$|$" in this expectation is read "given." See Section 2.14.) This assumption implies that $\mathcal{E}(E_j|N\zeta_j) = 0$. A similar assumption is made in classical true-score theory (Assumption 2, Section 3.1).

When the four assumptions are met, the binomial-error model holds and $X_j$ has a *binomial distribution*. Let's examine the binomial distribution with the simple example illustrated in Table 11.1. For this discussion, the $j$ subscript will be dropped from $X$ and $\zeta$ for simplicity, and you should bear in mind that observed scores and true scores refer to observed scores and true scores for a specific examinee. Suppose that a three-item test is being used and that an examinee's true probability of obtaining a score of 1 on any one item on the test is .75; the probability of a score of 0 on any one item is $1 - .75 = .25$. There is only one pattern of item scores that will produce a total number-right score of 0, and that pattern is (0, 0, 0). (The first number in the pattern is the score for item 1, the second is the score for item 2, and the third is the score for item 3.) Because the items are locally independent, the probability of the (0, 0, 0) pattern is $(1 - .75)^3$. The overall probability of observing a total score of 0 is the number of item-score patterns that will produce a total score of 0 times the probability of one such pattern: $(1)(1 - .75)^3 \doteq .02$. There are three patterns of item scores that will produce a total number-right score of 1: (1, 0, 0), (0, 1, 0), and (0, 0, 1). The probability of any one of these patterns occurring is $.75^1(1 - .75)^2$. The overall probability of observing a total score of 1 is $(3)(.75)(1 - .75)^2 \doteq .14$. The probabilities of other scores can be figured similarly, by multiplying the number of item-score patterns that will produce a given total score by the probability of observing one such pattern.

Table 11.1. Calculating Binomial Probabilities for an $N$-Item Test[a]

| Total Score | Patterns of Item Scores Producing Total Score | Number of Patterns Producing Total Score | Probability of One Pattern Producing Total Score | Probability of Total Score |
|---|---|---|---|---|
| $x$ | Any pattern with $x$ out of $N$ responses equal to 1 | $\binom{N}{x} = \dfrac{N!}{x!(N-x)!}$ | $\zeta^x(1-\zeta)^{N-x}$ | $\binom{N}{x}\zeta^x(1-\zeta)^{N-x}$ |
| 0 | (0, 0, 0) | $\dfrac{3!}{0!3!} = 1$ | $.75^0(1-.75)^{3-0}$ | $(1-.75)^3 \doteq .02$ |
| 1 | (1, 0, 0), (0, 1, 0), (0, 0, 1) | $\dfrac{3!}{1!2!} = 3$ | $.75^1(1-.75)^{3-1}$ | $3(.75)(1-.75)^2 \doteq .14$ |
| 2 | (0, 1, 1), (1, 0, 1), (1, 1, 0) | $\dfrac{3!}{2!1!} = 3$ | $.75^2(1-.75)^{3-2}$ | $3(.75)^2(1-.75) \doteq .42$ |
| 3 | (1, 1, 1) | $\dfrac{3!}{3!0!} = 1$ | $.75^3(1-.75)^{3-3}$ | $(.75)^3 \doteq .42$ |

[a]Example is for $N = 3$, $\zeta = .75$.

In general, under the binomial-error model, the probability that an examinee with true score $\zeta$ gets $x$ items correct on an $N$-item test is

$$p(X = x \mid \zeta) = \binom{N}{x}\zeta^x(1-\zeta)^{N-x} \qquad \text{for } x = 0, 1, \ldots, N, \qquad (11.1)$$

where $\qquad \dbinom{N}{x} = \dfrac{N!}{x!(N-x)!} ,$ $\qquad\qquad$ (11.2)

and $\qquad\qquad N! = N(N-1)(N-2) \; \cdots \; (2)(1).$ $\qquad\qquad$ (11.3)

$\dbinom{N}{x}$ (read "$N$ choose $x$," or the number of combinations of $N$ things taken $x$ at a time) reflects the number of patterns of item scores that will produce a total score of $x$, and $\zeta^x(1-\zeta)^{N-x}$ reflects the probability of observing one of those patterns. ($N!$ is read "$N$ factorial"; $0! = 1$.) Equation 11.1 states that the test score, $X$, follows a binomial distribution for a fixed true score. Figure 11.3 contains several binomial distributions produced by various true scores for a 15-item test. Each of these distributions can be thought of as being produced by repeated independent administrations of a test to the same examinee or by a single testing of a group of examinees, all with the same true score. (These curves are analogous to those in Figure 4.1.) For example, if 100 examinees, all with a true score of .05, take a 15-item test, we would expect about 46 of these examinees to obtain a score of 0, 37 to obtain a score of 1, 13 to obtain a score of 2, and so on. Remember that the binomial distribution (Equation 11.1 and Figure 11.3) is the distribution of observed scores for a fixed true score, $p(X = x \mid \zeta)$. The distribution of observed scores, $p(X = x)$, for a group of examinees with a variety of true scores depends on the distribution of the true scores, $f(\zeta)$, in that group.

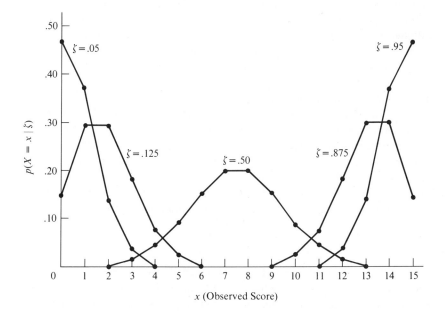

Figure 11.3. Five binomial distributions for a 15-item test

By Assumption 4, $\mathcal{E}(X|N\zeta) = N\zeta$. The variance of the observed score for a fixed value of $N\zeta$ is $\sigma^2_{X \cdot N\zeta}$. Since any deviation of $X$ from $N\zeta$ is error of measurement, $\sigma^2_{X \cdot N\zeta}$ is the error variance for a given value of $N\zeta$:

$$\sigma^2_{E \cdot N\zeta} = \sigma^2_{X \cdot N\zeta} \tag{11.4}$$

$$= N\zeta(1 - \zeta). \tag{11.5}$$

Under the binomial-error model, error variance depends on true score. Error variance is greatest for $\zeta = 1/2$ and decreases as $\zeta$ approaches 0 or 1. Error variance is zero for $\zeta = 0$ or 1, and, since $\mathcal{E}(E|N\zeta)$ is zero (Assumption 4), all errors of measurement are assumed to be zero for $\zeta = 0$ or 1. In other words, under the binomial-error model, examinees with true scores of 0 or 1 are assumed to be measured without error. Remember that, although true scores of 0 or 1 imply observed scores of 0 or $N$, observed scores of 0 or $N$ do not necessarily imply true scores of 0 or 1; for example, an examinee with a true score less than 1 may have a positive error of measurement that produces an observed score of $N$.

The regression of errors of measurement on $N$ times true scores, $\mathcal{E}(E|N\zeta)$, is contained in Figure 11.4. (See Section 2.14 for discussion of expectation and regression.) $\mathcal{E}(E|N\zeta)$ is a horizontal line, indicating that the correlation over examinees of true scores and errors of measurement is zero under the binomial-error model. Thus, the binomial-error model is consistent with one of the basic assumptions of classical true-score theory (Assumption 3, Section 3.1). Also contained in Figure 11.4 is an indication of the range of values of $E$ for each $N\zeta$. Most errors of measurement will be close to 0, but when a true score is fairly extreme (but not equal to 0 or 1) it is possible, but unlikely, to have extreme values of $E$. When $N\zeta$ is extreme, $E$ will have a skewed distribution, as shown in Figure 11.3. Under the binomial-error model, the sizes of errors of measurement are not independent of true scores, but they are uncorrelated with true scores. (The teams *independence* and *lack of correlation* are not necessarily synonymous except when applied to variables that have a bivariate normal distribution. See Section 2.13 and Hays, 1973.)

The binomial-error model is consistent with much of classical true-score theory. Assumptions 3 and 4 of the binomial model are analogous to Assumptions 1 and 2 of the classical model (Section 3.1). Under the binomial model $\rho_{E\zeta} = 0$, which satisfies Assumption 3 of the classical model. The binomial-error model also can be consistent with Assumptions 4 and 5 of the classical model; therefore, all the conclusions in Chapter 3 based on these assumptions can be valid under the binomial-error model. For example, under the binomial-error model,

$$KR21 = \frac{N^2 \sigma^2_\zeta}{\sigma^2_X} , \tag{11.6}$$

where KR21 is the coefficient of item homogeneity used to assess internal consistency reliability described in Section 4.5. Equation 11.6 is similar to the conclusion in classical true-score theory that $\rho_{XX'} = \sigma^2_T/\sigma^2_X$. Also, under the binomial-error model

$$\rho^2_{X\zeta} = KR21; \tag{11.7}$$

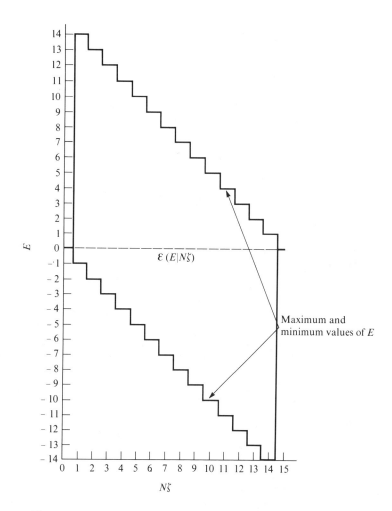

Figure 11.4. Regression of errors of measurement, $E$, on $N$ times true scores, $N\zeta$, for a binomial-error model for a 15-item test

the squared correlation between observed scores and true scores equals the coefficient of item homogeneity. This fact is analogous to the classical-theory statement that $\rho_{XT}^2 = \rho_{XX'} = $ KR21 when items have equal difficulties.

There are differences, however, between the binomial-error model and classical true-score theory. Under the classical model, the standard error of measurement ($\sigma_E = \sigma_X \sqrt{1 - \rho_{XX'}}$) depends on characteristics of the sample being tested; changing the sample can easily change the standard deviation and reliability of the test scores as well as the standard error of measurement. Under the binomial-error model, the standard error for a fixed true score ($\sigma_{E \cdot N\zeta}$) depends only on the model and does not depend on the distribution of scores in the sample being tested. The binomial-error model specifies how the standard error of measurement varies with true-score level, but classical true-score theory makes no such specification. In Section 4.8, a method is described for constructing confidence intervals for true scores using the untested assumptions of a normal distribution of errors of measurement and a constant standard error of measurement for all true scores. Section 4.8 notes that these assumptions may not be reasonable, particularly when there are floor or ceiling effects. In such instances, the binomial-error model is more reasonable, and with the binomial-error model it is possible to examine the reasonableness of the assumption of a binomial distribution of errors of measurement. When the binomial-error model fits a set of data, it produces true-score estimates, $\hat{\zeta}$, that form a ratio scale.

The binomial-error model assumes that item difficulties are equal. If item difficulties are not equal, a generalization of the binomial-error model—called the *compound binomial-error model*—can be used. The compound binomial-error model, like the binomial-error model, produces standard errors that vary with true-score level and that are not influenced by the distribution of scores in the sample being tested.

A major goal of strong true-score theories is to obtain a good true-score estimate, $\hat{\zeta}$, for an examinee with a given observed score, $x$. This result can be achieved by obtaining the regression of true score on observed score—that is, by obtaining the true score expected for a given observed score, $\varepsilon(\zeta | x)$ (Section 2.14). This regression equation can be very complicated, and a computer program usually is used to obtain true-score estimates (see Wingersky, Lees, Lennon, & Lord, 1969). In some cases, however, a simple linear rule for predicting true scores from observed scores is available (Lord & Novick, 1968, p. 515*ff*). Lord (1969a) notes that estimation of the true-score distribution, $f(\zeta)$, has the following uses.

1. To estimate the frequency distribution of observed scores that will result when a given test is lengthened.
2. To equate true scores on two tests by the equipercentile method [see Section 7.9].
3. To estimate the frequencies in the scatterplot between two parallel (nonparallel) tests of the same psychological trait, using only the information in a (the) marginal distribution(s).
4. To estimate the frequency distribution of a test for a group that has taken only a short form of the test (this is useful for obtaining norms).
5. To estimate the effects of selecting individuals on a fallible measure [observed score].
6. To effect matching of groups with respect to true score when only a fallible measure is available.
7. To investigate whether two tests really measure the same psychological function when they have a nonlinear relationship.
8. To describe and evaluate the properties of a specific test considered as a measuring instrument.

An additional use, of some interest, is

9. To estimate the item-true score regression [which is analogous to the item

characteristic curve, see Section 6.5] for particular items, without strong prior assumption as to its mathematical form.*

When using the binomial-error model, it is necessary to test the fit of the model to the data at hand. This is done by estimating true scores for a group of examinees and then by determining if their distribution of observed scores is consistent with this estimated distribution of true scores and the predictions of the binomial model (Equation 11.1). Wingersky, Lees, Lennon, and Lord (1969) provide a computer program for this purpose. Lord (1965) has successfully applied a compound binomial model to several 25- to 60-item vocabulary tests and a 30-item nonverbal reasoning test; these applications involved test scores for about 1000 to 6000 college seniors. Although the binomial-error models have fit some data sets and can be of practical value, to date their use has not been widespread.

## 11.4  Poisson Models

*Poisson models* are appropriate for test scores based on a large number of items. The Poisson model can be applied to the number of right or wrong answers on these tests. If the number of right answers is examined, the probability of a right answer must be small; if the number of wrong answers is examined, the probability of a wrong answer must be small for the model to fit. The *Poisson distribution* is a limiting distribution for the binomial distribution; as the number of items becomes very large and the probability of a right (or wrong) answer remains small, the binomial distribution approaches a Poisson distribution. In this sense the Poisson distribution can be considered to be a special case of the binomial distribution.

There are many different types of Poisson models. This section examines in detail one model that has been proposed by Rasch (1960). This model produces ratio scales (Sections 2.2 and 8.2) for examinee ability and test difficulty. These ratio scales permit statements such as "Jack is twice as able as Jim and is half as likely as Jim to make an error," "Test A is twice as difficult as test B, and the probability of making an error on test A is twice that of making one on test B," and "Jack will do as well on test A as Jim will do on test B." Statements such as these cannot be made with most traditional scales; for example, it is incorrect to state that an examinee with an IQ of 150 is twice as intelligent or is half as likely to make an error as an examinee with an IQ of 75.

We will describe *Rasch's Poisson model* as being applied to the number of incorrect answers made by a group of examinees on a set of tests; however, keep in mind the fact that the model could be applied to the number of correct answers when the probability of a correct answer is small. Rasch's Poisson model can be described with the following assumptions.

*From "Estimating true-score distributions in psychological testing (An empirical Bayes estimation problem)" by F. M. Lord, *Psychometrika*, 1969, *34*, 259–299. Copyright 1969 by the Psychometric Society. Reprinted by permission.

1. Every test in the set being examined has a large number of locally independent binary items. There is no strict cutoff for the number of items in each test, but 75 or more items appears to be a suitable number.
2. The average probability of an incorrect answer is small on each test being examined. There is no strict definition of "small," but probabilities of incorrect answers should be less than about .10.
3. The average probability of examinee $j$ making an incorrect answer to an item in test $i$, $p_{ij}$, is the ratio of two parameters—the test's difficulty, $\delta_i$ (Greek letter *delta*), and the examinee's ability, $\zeta_j$:

$$p_{ij} = \delta_i / \zeta_j. \tag{11.8}$$

The values of $\delta_i$ and $\zeta_j$ are such that $p_{ij}$ has a value between 0 and 1. The probability of an incorrect answer increases as the difficulty of the test increases and as the ability of the examinee decreases. Therefore, the probability of an incorrect answer is highest for a difficult test and an unable examinee. $p_{ij}$ is analogous to the true score in the binomial-error model.
4. Let $X_{ij}$ be the variable standing for the number of incorrect answers made by examinee $j$ on test $i$ ($x_{ij}$ is a specific observed value of $X_{ij}$ for a given $i$ and $j$).

$$X_{ij} = N_i p_{ij} + E_{ij}, \tag{11.9}$$

where there are $N_i$ items on test $i$ and $E_{ij}$ is the error of measurement for test $i$ and examinee $j$. This assumption is similar to the additivity assumption for true and error scores that is made in classical true-score theory.
5. $\mathcal{E}(X_{ij} | N_i p_{ij}) = N_i p_{ij}$; the expected number of incorrect answers for the $j$th examinee on the $i$th test is $N_i p_{ij}$ or $N_i \delta_i / \zeta_j$. (A similar type of assumption is made in classical true-score theory.) For example, if a test with $\delta_i = .3$ is taken by an examinee with $\zeta_j = 10$, the examinee would have an average probability of $(.3/10) = .03$ of making an incorrect answer on an item. If there are 100 items in the test, we would expect the examinee to make $(100)(.03)$ or 3 incorrect answers and 97 correct answers. If we let $\lambda_{ij}$ (Greek letter *lambda*) stand for the expected number of incorrect answers made by examinee $j$ on test $i$, then

$$\lambda_{ij} = N_i \frac{\delta_i}{\zeta_j}. \tag{11.10}$$

Given Assumptions 1–5, Rasch's Poisson model predicts that

$$p(X_{ij} = x_{ij} | \lambda_{ij}) = \frac{e^{-\lambda_{ij}} \lambda_{ij}^{x_{ij}}}{x_{ij}!}, \qquad x_{ij} = 0, 1, 2, \ldots, N_i, \tag{11.11}$$

which is the Poisson distribution with parameter $\lambda_{ij}$. In this distribution function, $e$ is a constant approximately equal to 2.718. If $\lambda_{ij} = 1$, the probability of no errors is $e^{-1} (1^0)/0! \doteq .37$, the probability of one incorrect answer is $e^{-1} (1^1)/1! \doteq .37$, the probability of two incorrect answers is $e^{-1} (1^2)/2! \doteq .18$, and so on. Figure 11.5 contains several Poisson distributions. Each distribution can be seen to be the result of repeated independent testings involving various examinees and tests, all of which

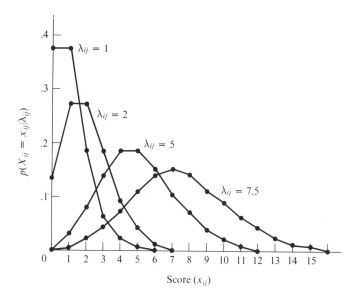

Figure 11.5. Four Poisson distributions

are based on the same value of $\lambda_{ij} = N_i \delta_i / \zeta_j$. (These distributions are analogous to those in Figures 4.1 and 11.3.) For example, if 100 testings take place with $N_i \delta_i / \zeta_j = 2$, about 14 of these testings are expected to produce no incorrect answers, 27 of these testings are expected to produce one incorrect answer, 27 are expected to produce two incorrect answers, and so on.

We can see from Equation 11.8 that $p_{ij}$ will remain unchanged if both the ability and difficulty scales are multiplied by the same constant. For example, $\delta_i = .3$ and $\zeta_j = 10$ will produce $p_{ij} = .03$. If $\delta_i = 3$ and $\zeta_j = 100$, $p_{ij}$ will still equal .03. In order to estimate difficulty and ability scale values, it is necessary to *anchor* either the ability or difficulty scale (that is, pick a zero point). Rasch anchors the difficulty scale by fixing the difficulty of the most difficult test in the set, $\delta_*$, at one; that is, $\delta_* = 1$. Then

$$\hat{\delta}_i = \frac{x_{i+}/N_i}{x_{*+}/N_*} \, , \tag{11.12}$$

where $x_{i+} = \sum_{j=1}^{n} x_{ij}$. That is, $x_{i+}$ is the total number of errors made on test $i$. Abilities are estimated from

$$\hat{\zeta}_j = \frac{\sum_{i=1}^{I} N_i \hat{\delta}_i}{x_{+j}} \, , \tag{11.13}$$

where $x_{+j}$ is the total number of incorrect answers made by examinee $j$.

Table 11.2 contains a numerical example of incorrect answers made by

Table 11.2. Numbers of Incorrect Answers Made by Two Examinees on Two Tests[a]

|  |  | Examinee | | |
|---|---|---|---|---|
|  |  | 1 | 2 | Total $(x_{i+})$ |
| Test | 1 | 4 | 8 | 12 |
|  | 2 | 12 | 4 | 16 |
|  | Total $(x_{+j})$ | 16 | 12 | 28 |

[a]Test 1 has 100 items; test 2 has 150 items.

two examinees on two tests. In this example test 1 is the most difficult test in the set, and the difficulty of test 1 is set equal to 1. The difficulty of test 2 is estimated by Equation 11.12 as $\hat{\delta}_2 = (16/150)/(12/100) \doteq .89$. Using Equation 11.13 the ability of examinee 1 is estimated as $\hat{\zeta}_1 = [(100)(1) + (150)(.89)]/16 \doteq 14.59$; the ability of examinee 2 is estimated as $\hat{\zeta}_2 = [(100)(1) + (150)(.89)]/12 \doteq 19.46$.

Rasch anchors the ability and difficulty scales to the most difficult test. However, it isn't necessary to use the most difficult test for this anchoring; we could use the least difficult test, the average difficulty of the set of tests, or any other measure that facilitates interpretation of the ability and difficulty scale values. As an alternative, the scales could be anchored to the scores of the most or least able examinee in the group or to the average ability of the group. Changing the anchor results in multiplying both the ability and difficulty scales by the same constant; this will change the expectations and variances of the scales but will not affect correlations of the ability or difficulty scales with other variables.

Under the model, the estimated expected number of incorrect answers made on test $i$ by examinee $j$ is $N_i \hat{p}_{ij} = N_i \hat{\delta}_i / \hat{\zeta}_j$ (in the previous example, $N_1 \hat{p}_{11} = (100)(1)/14.59 \doteq 6.85$). All the expected numbers of incorrect answers for the previous example appear in Table 11.3. Examining the expected numbers of incorrect answers under Rasch's model in this table, we see that examinee 1 is expected to have 1.33 times as many incorrect answers as examinee 2, regardless of the test used. When a set of tests satisfies the Rasch model, any one of the tests is expected to produce the same ability estimate, except for measurement error. Similarly, any set

Table 11.3. Expected Frequency of Incorrect Answers under the Rasch Model

|  |  | Examinee | | |
|---|---|---|---|---|
|  |  | 1 | 2 | Total $(x_{i+})$ |
| Test | 1 | 6.85 | 5.14 | 11.99 |
|  | 2 | 9.15 | 6.86 | 16.01 |
|  | Total $(x_{+j})$ | 16.00 | 12.00 | 28.00 |

of examinees is expected to produce the same estimate of test difficulty, except for measurement error; this conclusion implies that if Rasch's model holds, representative (normative) samples are not necessary to estimate test difficulties. The test developer must still continue to consider the amount of measurement error that is allowable and structure samples of examinees and tests accordingly.

It is always important to test the fit of the model to a set of data; for example, a goodness-of-fit test (Hays, 1973) would reject the model for the data in Table 11.2. The model implies that tests will have the same relative difficulty regardless of the examinee tested. In the example (Table 11.2), test 1 was less difficult than test 2 for examinee 1, but test 1 was more difficult than test 2 for examinee 2. The model implies that examinees will have the same relative ability regardless of the test used. In this example, examinee 1 was more able than examinee 2 according to test 1, but examinee 1 was less able than examinee 2 according to test 2. It makes sense that a goodness-of-fit test would reject Rasch's model for this example. Of course, when the model is rejected, it is unreasonable to use ability or difficulty scale-value estimates based on the model.

Rasch (1960) describes how estimates of the standard errors of ability and difficulty estimates can be obtained. These standard errors allow estimation of the accuracy of ability and difficulty estimates for each examinee and each test. In classical true-score theory, standard errors of measurement are calculated to estimate the accuracy of true score estimation, but in classical theory the same standard error of measurement usually is used for all true scores. In Rasch's model, standard errors are estimated separately for different ability and test difficulty levels.

Rasch (1960) has been successful in fitting this model to a set of oral-reading tests. Meredith (1971) has developed a Poisson model for tests of pure speed. On speed tests the probability of an incorrect answer (or correct answer) is small and the number of items is large. This model has been applied successfully to a test of perceptual speed ("Finding A's") from the *Kit of Reference Tests for Cognitive Factors* (French, Ekstrom, & Price, 1963). Meredith's model conceivably could be suitable for tests of fluency of ideas, simple addition or subtraction, or other speed tests.

Rasch's Poisson model is suitable for sets of tests that have very small (or very large) probabilities of incorrect answers and large numbers of items. Rasch has proposed another model (a logistic model) that does not require extreme probabilities of errors and large numbers of items and has more general applicability than the Poisson model. Rasch's logistic model is described in Section 11.6.

## 11.5  Normal-Ogive and Logistic Models

Most latent-trait models have been used with tests on which performance is a function of one unobserved (latent) characteristic or trait, such as vocabulary level or mathematical-reasoning ability (see Lord & Novick, 1968). It is the goal of such models to estimate an examinee's standing on the continuous latent trait, which ranges from $-\infty$ to $+\infty$. These models also estimate two important parameters for each item—the item's difficulty and its discriminating power. These item parameters can assist greatly in item selection aimed at producing tests that give the most accurate possible estimates of the latent trait.

We will describe the assumptions of two latent-trait models—the normal-ogive and logistic models.

1. Performance on the test being examined can be described by one *latent trait*, $\theta$ (Greek letter *theta*), and the items in the test are homogeneous in measuring the trait. For example, a mathematical-reasoning test that includes some items that rely heavily on reading comprehension would not be appropriate for these models. Any test whose items can be factor analyzed into more than one significant factor (Sections 5.11 and 6.6) usually would not be suitable for the normal-ogive and logistic models.
2. The test is composed of locally independent binary items.
3. The probability that an examinee with latent-trait value $\theta$ passes item $i$ is a cumulative normal or logistic function. In the *normal-ogive model*, the probability that an examinee with latent trait $\theta$ passes item $i$ is

$$p_i(\theta) = \int_{-\infty}^{a_i(\theta - b_i)} \frac{1}{\sqrt{2\pi}} e^{-z^2/2} \, dz, \tag{11.14}$$

where $b_i$ is the *item difficulty*, $a_i$ is the *item-discriminating power*, and $z$ is the standard normal variable defined in Section 2.7. The integral on the right side of Equation 11.14 is the cumulative normal distribution, sometimes called the *normal ogive*. Evaluating Equation 11.14 is the same as finding the probability of obtaining a value less than or equal to $a_i(\theta - b_i)$ from a standard normal distribution. In the *logistic model*

$$p_i(\theta) = \frac{1}{1 + e^{-Da_i(\theta - b_i)}}, \tag{11.15}$$

where $D$ is an arbitrary constant. Equation 11.15 is the cumulative logistic function.

In each model, $p_i(\theta)$ is the *item-characteristic function* that gives the probability of passing item $i$ for any value of $\theta$. These models are called *two-parameter latent-trait models*, because they are a function of two item parameters —$a_i$, the item-discriminating power, and $b_i$, the item difficulty. $D$ is an arbitrary constant. When $D = 1.7$, the normal-ogive and logistic item-characteristic functions (Equations 11.14 and 11.15) produce very similar results. Since the logistic and normal-ogive models are almost interchangeable when $D = 1.7$, the logistic often is preferred because it is easier to work with mathematically than the normal ogive.

Figure 11.6 contains three item-characteristic curves that are consistent with the normal-ogive and logistic models. The normal-ogive and logistic models imply that the item-characteristic curves must be smooth, must increase as $\theta$ increases, and must have horizontal asymptotes for extreme values of $\theta$. An item that is more likely to be answered correctly by examinees with moderate trait values than by those with high trait values would not be suitable for the normal-ogive or logistic models. For example, a violation of this assumption would occur with a multiple-choice item having a distractor (wrong answer) that is particularly attractive to very able examinees. If an item-characteristic curve is monotonically nondecreasing (that is, $p_i(\theta)$ never decreases as $\theta$ increases), it is always possible to adjust the scale of $\theta$ so that the item produces a normal-ogive or logistic item-characteristic curve. It may be, however, that different $\theta$ scales would be produced for different items in the same test. For the model to be reasonable, it is necessary to find one $\theta$ scale that transforms all the item-characteristic curves for the items in the test to normal-ogive or logistic curves. Thus, whenever these models are used, their goodness-of-fit to the data at hand must be considered.

Referring to Figure 11.6, we can see that the item difficulty, $b_i$, is a measure of the item's location on the horizontal (latent-trait) scale. The item difficulty is defined such that an examinee has a 50% chance of passing item $i$ when $\theta = b_i$ (that is, when the examinee's trait level matches the item difficulty). If an examinee's latent-trait value is greater than an item's difficulty, then the examinee has a greater than 50% chance of passing that item. When an examinee's trait level is much higher than an item's difficulty, the examinee is very likely to pass the item. Similarly, when an examinee's latent-trait value is lower than an item's difficulty, the examinee has less than a 50% chance of passing the item.

The latent-trait level at which an item discriminates most effectively among examinees is $b_i$, and the item-characteristic curve is steepest at $b_i$. The slope of the item-characteristic curve at $b_i$ is a constant times $a_i$. It can be seen in Figure 11.6 that, as $a_i$ increases, the slope of the item-characteristic curve at $b_i$ increases and item

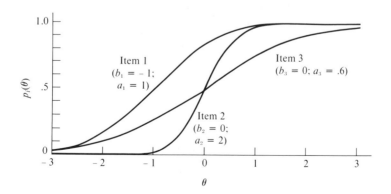

Figure 11.6. Three normal-ogive or logistic item-characteristic curves

discrimination at that one latent-trait level increases. For example, item 1 discriminates best at $\theta = -1$ (that is, the item-characteristic curve for item 1 is most steep at $\theta = b_1 = -1$) and also gives some information about $\theta$ anywhere between $-2$ and $0$. Item 2 discriminates very well near $0$; a small change in $\theta$ near $0$ makes a big difference in $p_2(\theta)$. In other words, examinees who answer item 2 correctly are likely to have $\theta > 0$, and examinees who do not answer item 2 correctly are likely to have $\theta < 0$. Item 2 gives little information about other trait levels, since its item-characteristic curve is fairly flat for $\theta$ less than $-.5$ or greater than $.5$. Item 3 also reflects $\theta$ best near $0$, but, unlike item 2, item 3 gives some information about $\theta$ for values of $\theta$ from $-2$ to $+2$. Item 3 is less discriminating than item 2 at $\theta = 0$; examinees who answer item 3 correctly may or may not be above $\theta = 0$.

To use the normal-ogive or logistic models, it is necessary to obtain estimates of the item parameters and latent-trait values. Obtaining these estimates is a fairly complicated process, and computer programs have been developed to obtain them using the pass/fail scores for all the examinees for every item (Kolakowski & Bock, 1973a, 1973b; Wood, Wingersky, & Lord, 1976). In general, large sample sizes and fairly lengthy tests are recommended for the estimation processes to work well. Standard errors of the latent-trait estimates and item parameters are provided by the programs or can be calculated from the program output. A goodness-of-fit test for the model, available from some programs, determines whether the estimated item-characteristic curve for each item (based on finding the proportions of examinees with various $\hat{\theta}$s who pass that item) conforms to the predictions of Equations 11.14 or 11.15 using $\hat{a}_i$, $\hat{b}_i$, and $\hat{\theta}$ in place of $a_i$, $b_i$, and $\theta$.

The item difficulty, $b_i$, and latent trait, $\theta$, are represented on the same interval scale. This scale can be transformed linearly without changing the predictions of the model, as long as the item-discriminating power, $a_i$, is also transformed appropriately. For example, suppose we are working with one scale for $\theta$, $b_i$, and $a_i$ and we create a new scale for them: $\theta^* = 8\theta + 5$, $b_i^* = 8b_i + 5$, and $a_i^* = a_i/8$. The only term in the item-characteristic function (Equations 11.14 and 11.15) that depends on these values is $a_i(\theta - b_i)$. It is clear that

$$a_i^*(\theta^* - b_i^*) = \frac{a_i}{8}\left[8\theta + 5 - (8b_i + 5)\right] \tag{11.16}$$

$$= a_i(\theta - b_i); \tag{11.17}$$

the new scale would produce the same predictions and would be just as effective as the old scale. Therefore, the zero point and the scale unit are chosen arbitrarily, usually by setting the mean latent-trait value equal to 0 and the standard deviation of the latent-trait values equal to 1 for some specified group of examinees. Another way of selecting a scale is to set the mean item difficulty equal to 0 and the average item-discrimination index equal to $1/D$ for some specified group of items.

Imagine that a scale for the items and latent trait is determined using one group of examinees. Scaling with any other group of examinees probably would produce a somewhat different set of scale values for the item parameters. If the model fits both sets of data, the item parameters obtained from one group of examinees would be linearly related to the item parameters obtained from the other group, just as $a_i^*$ and $b_i^*$ are linearly related to $a_i$ and $b_i$. Similarly, if latent-trait values are estimated for one group of examinees using two different sets of items and if both sets of data fit the latent-trait model, the latent-trait values determined from one set of items ($\theta^*$) would be linearly related to the latent-trait values determined from the other set of items ($\theta$). This linear-transformation property will hold as long as the changes in the examinees or items are not so extreme as to make the items of totally inappropriate difficulty for the examinees.

One problem with the traditional methods of item analysis discussed in Section 6.3 is that changes in item-tryout samples can alter in unpredictable ways the proportion of examinees passing an item, $p_i$, the item-discrimination index, $d_i$, and the item/test point biserial, $r_{iX}$. If the test developer is satisfied that the item-tryout sample is representative of the groups for which the test will be used, then $p_i$ and $d_i$ or $r_{iX}$ can be used for choosing the best items, as discussed in Section 6.3. If the sample is not representative, $p_i$ and $d_i$ or $r_{iX}$ should not be used.

If a latent-trait model is appropriate, nonextreme changes in the item-tryout sample will do no more than make a linear transformation of the $a_i$ and $b_i$ scale. However, estimating $a_i$ and $b_i$ is a more complicated computational procedure than estimating $d_i$ or $r_{iX}$ and $p_i$. Also, in order to use $\hat{a}_i$ and $\hat{b}_i$, the latent-trait model must fit the data at hand. The parameter estimates $\hat{a}_i$ and $\hat{b}_i$ do not indicate how useful a set of items will be with a particular group of examinees (that is, how well the item difficulties will match the examinees' abilities), unless latent-trait estimates, $\hat{\theta}$, are available for that group. When $\hat{a}_i$, $\hat{b}_i$, and $\hat{\theta}$ are available, they can be used in selecting items that provide the most efficient estimation of the latent-trait values, as described in Sections 11.7 and 11.8.

Some aspects of the latent-trait models can be related to classical true-score theory (Chapter 3). When a latent-trait model fits a set of data, it is possible to express an examinee's true score on a test in terms of $p_i(\theta)$, where $\theta$ is the examinee's latent-trait value. Recall that a true score is defined as an expected observed score (Section 3.1). For each item there are only two possible scores, 0 and 1, and an examinee's true score for an item is, by the definition of expectation in Section 2.14, $(1)p_i(\theta) + (0)[1 - p_i(\theta)] = p_i(\theta)$. If a test score, $X$, is the sum of $N$ item scores, the expected test score or true score is $\varepsilon(X \mid \theta) = T(\theta) = \sum_{i=1}^{N} p_i(\theta)$; $T(\theta)$ is known or fixed when $\theta$ is known. Any variance of $X$ for a fixed $T(\theta)$ is error variance in the classical sense. Thus, $\sigma_{X \cdot \theta}^2 = \sigma_{X \cdot T(\theta)}^2 = \sigma_{E \cdot T(\theta)}^2$, which is the squared standard error of measurement for one value of $\theta$. Notice that $\sigma_{E \cdot T(\theta)}^2$ can vary as a function of $\theta$ or $T(\theta)$. The total squared standard error of measurement in Chapter 3, $\sigma_E^2$, depends on the particular sample of examinees that is tested; $\sigma_E^2$ is the mean of $\sigma_{E \cdot T(\theta)}^2$ taken over all obtained values of $\theta$.

The latent-trait models have many practical uses. For example, it is possible to estimate an examinee's latent-trait value from any subset of items that fits the models, thereby reducing testing time. It is also possible to estimate item parameters from any group of examinees that covers an appropriate range of latent-trait values, thus making representative item-tryout samples unnecessary. Subsets of items and examinees are equivalent in terms of producing latent-trait and item-parameter estimates that are the same except for measurement error. However, keep in mind that the standard errors of the latent-trait and item-parameter estimates are dependent on and can vary as a function of the items and examinees used. The better the item difficulties match the examinees' latent-trait values and the greater the number of items and examinees, the lower these standard errors will be (see Sections 11.7 and 11.8).

The latent-trait models can make item tryouts more economical and informative. Suppose we are constructing a new spelling test. In the item-tryout stage we want to obtain an estimate of the proportion of children in a nationally representative sample who would pass each item. However, obtaining a nationally representative sample of several thousand students is too expensive at the item-tryout stage. Luckily, we have an old, nationally standardized spelling test that fits a latent-trait model. We administer the old test and the new items to a relatively small, not necessarily representative sample at the appropriate grade levels. Parameters for the new and old items are obtained as if all the items comprised one test. From norms for the old test we estimate a national distribution of latent-trait values. Using this latent-trait distribution and the parameters of the new items, we can obtain a good estimate of the proportion of students in a nationally representative sample who would pass each new item. Items that are too easy or too difficult can be discarded. We can, if desired, identify and retain items that show substantial growth (that is, change in difficulty level) from grade to grade. After the final version of the new test is constructed, we would obtain a nationally representative sample to provide current norms for the new test. Given the information from the item tryout, we should not run into any bad surprises (such as floor or ceiling effects), in the norming.

Latent-trait models can be helpful in examining test items for ethnic or sex bias. To do this, item parameters are estimated separately for each group of interest—for example, Blacks and Whites. If the items are measuring the same latent trait in the two groups, the item parameters will be linearly related across groups. Any items whose parameters are not linearly related across groups can be modified or deleted from the test.

Normal-ogive and logistic models can be used to develop successive pools of items that produce the same $\theta$ scale. Suppose we have developed a test with items that are consistent with a normal-ogive or logistic model. Sometime later, we want to develop an alternate form of the test that produces the same $\theta$ scale. The new test and the old test are administered to a new group of examinees. The $\theta$ scale for the new sample is transformed linearly, so that the items in the old test produce the same $a_i$'s and $b_i$'s in the new sample as in the old sample. Once the $\theta$ scale for the new sample is established, the $a_i$'s and $b_i$'s for the new test for the new sample can be estimated. If the items in the new test fit the logistic or normal-ogive model, the new and old forms of the test will produce the same latent-trait values, except for errors of measurement. Standard errors of measurement for the latent-trait estimates for the new and old forms of the test may vary, depending on differences in the items used in the two forms. If it is desired to have the test forms produce the same standard errors for every value of $\theta$, items must be matched across forms. That is, if one form has an item with $a = 1$ and $b = 0$, the other form must have an item with the same parameters. This method can be used to equate forms of a test without causing concern about whether differences in the distribution of the latent trait have affected the equating—as might happen with equipercentile equating (Lord & Novick, 1968).

Two important uses of the normal-ogive and logistic models are item selection and weighting aimed at producing test scores that measure the latent trait most efficiently. This is useful in tailored testing (see Section 10.9) or in creating a test that minimizes the standard error of the latent-trait estimate for those latent-trait values in which the test developer is most interested. These uses of the latent-trait models are discussed in Sections 11.7 and 11.8.

As we stated earlier, for the normal-ogive or logistic models to be appropriate, all items must measure the same trait. Speed tests are not appropriate for these models, because, when an item is not attempted, performance is not a function of the latent trait and the characteristic curve cannot be a normal ogive or logistic. Generalizations of these models are available to deal with omitted responses that will occur on a speed test (Lord, 1974a) and other possible additional scores (Bock, 1972).

If examinees with very low trait values can correctly answer items (for example, if they can guess the answers correctly), the normal-ogive and logistic models are not appropriate in the form previously described. (See Birnbaum's description of latent-trait models in Lord and Novick, 1968.) If the probability that someone with a very low latent-trait value will get item $i$ correct is $c_i$, then the item-characteristic curve will have its lower asymptote at $c_i$ rather than at 0 (see Figure 11.7). Items 1 and 3 in Figure 11.7 have $c_1 = c_3 = .25$; item 2 has $c_2 = .2$. Using $c_i$ as a third item parameter, the models can accommodate this type of

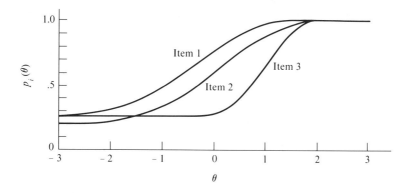

Figure 11.7. Three-parameter normal-ogive or logistic items

guessing. The item-characteristic functions of the *three-parameter normal-ogive* and *logistic models* are

$$p_i(\theta) = c_i + (1 - c_i) \left[ \int_{-\infty}^{a_i(\theta - b_i)} \frac{1}{\sqrt{2\pi}} e^{-z^2/2} \, dz \right] \qquad (11.18)$$

and

$$p_i(\theta) = c_i + (1 - c_i) \left[ \frac{1}{1 + e^{-Da_i(\theta - b_i)}} \right]. \qquad (11.19)$$

More information about the latent-trait models can be obtained from Lord and Novick (1968). Lord (in press) discusses in detail many of the technical issues that arise in the use of latent-trait models. Information also is available from increasing numbers of journal articles that explain and examine latent-trait theories. For example, an entire edition of the *Journal of Educational Measurement* (Summer, 1977) has been devoted to explaining latent-trait models and their uses.

## 11.6  Rasch's Logistic Model

There is an interesting *one-parameter logistic model* that Rasch developed independently of the logistic models described in the previous section. *Rasch's logistic model* (see Rasch, 1960, 1966a, 1966b) has the same assumptions as the two-parameter model—with one additional assumption: item-discriminating powers ($a_i$'s) are constant for all items. The item-characteristic function for Rasch's logistic model is

$$p_i(\theta) = \frac{1}{1 + e^{-Da(\theta - b_i)}}, \qquad (11.20)$$

where $a$ is the item-discriminating power common to all the items, $b_i$ is the item difficulty, which can vary over items, and $D$ is an arbitrary constant. Since $a$ is constant for all items, the slopes of the item-characteristic curves will all be the same; since item difficulties vary, the locations of the item-characteristic curves vary. Figure 11.8 shows the item-characteristic curves of three items that would be consistent with Rasch's logistic model. These items have difficulties of $-1, 0$, and $+2$; all have the same slope. Wright and Panchapakesan (1969) have developed computer programs for obtaining estimates of Rasch's item difficulties and latent-trait values.

Rasch's logistic model has the practical benefits described for the two- and three-parameter logistic models. There is an additional practical benefit gained from using the Rasch model, given that the model fits the data. Under Rasch's model there is no need to differentially weight items in order to produce a total score that gives the maximum possible amount of information about the latent trait; the number-right score is the best possible total score to use. With two- or three-parameter logistic models, the number-right score is not the best possible total score to use. (This subject is discussed more fully in Section 11.8.)

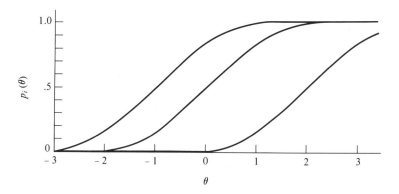

Figure 11.8. Three item-characteristic curves consistent with Rasch's logistic model

Since the Rasch logistic model makes stronger assumptions than either the two- or three-parameter latent-trait models, it generally is more difficult to fit the Rasch model to a set of data. Anderson (1973) examined a subset of the items in the *Verbal Scholastic Aptitude Test* for their fit to Rasch's model. The model was rejected, and it appeared that the items had unequal discriminating powers. Anderson, Kearney, and Everett (1968) found Rasch item- and examinee-parameter estimates to be substantially equivalent when subgroups of items and examinees were systematically examined for an intelligence test used by the Australian army and navy for screening recruits. Hambleton and Traub (1973) compared the fit of the two-parameter logistic model with the fit of Rasch's logistic model for selected items from the verbal and mathematics sections of the *Ontario Scholastic Aptitude Test* and the *Verbal Scholastic Aptitude Test*. The two-parameter model fit the data better than Rasch's model for every test; differences between the models decreased as the number of items in the test being examined increased.

Whitely and Dawis (1974) present a thought-provoking discussion of the appropriate uses and interpretations of Rasch's model. They examined Rasch's model for a 60-item multiple-choice test of verbal analogies used with college and high school students. About 30–40% of the items did not fit the model. Latent-trait estimates based on odd/even or random-half splits of the items were as equivalent as the standard errors of the estimates would lead one to expect. Two subtests, formed by grouping the easiest items and the hardest items, produced substantially different latent-trait estimates. Further discussion and clarification of this article and the Rasch model are contained in Wright (1977) and Whitely (1977).

Rasch's logistic model produces latent-trait and item-difficulty scales that have desirable properties, but, like any other model, the suitability of the model for a set of items must be established before the scales are used. The *Keymath Diagnostic Arithmetic Test* (Connolly, Nachtman, & Pritchett, 1976) and the *Woodcock*

*Reading Mastery Tests* (Woodcock, 1973) are two published tests that employ Rasch's model.

## 11.7    Test Information

One way in which latent-trait models can assist in constructing better tests is in improving the amount of information that the test conveys about the latent trait (see Birnbaum's discussion in Lord and Novick, 1968). This section describes how test information is measured and interpreted. The following section demonstrates how logistic models are particularly well suited to measuring test information.

Figure 11.9 contains hypothetical curves relating observed scores to latent-trait scores. From these curves it is possible to examine how well the tests are measuring the traits. For example, observed scores for test 1 (Figure 11.9a) increase regularly with latent trait in the low and high ranges of the trait, and observed-score variances for a given trait value are relatively small in these ranges. Test 1 measures the trait well in the upper and lower ranges of the trait. However, in the middle ranges of the latent trait, observed scores are relatively constant, and observed-score variances are relatively large. Although test 1 measures the latent trait well at high and low trait values, it does not measure the trait well in the middle ranges. Test 2 (Figure 11.9b), on the other hand, measures medium values of the latent trait well, but does not discriminate well at the extremes.

It is possible to convey by a formula the effect that is seen graphically in Figure 11.9. We use an information function, $I(X, \theta)$, where $X$ is any score (for example, a test or item score) and $\theta$ is the latent trait. The *information function* is defined as

$$I(X, \theta) = \frac{\left[\varepsilon'(X \mid \theta)\right]^2}{\sigma_{X \cdot \theta}^2} . \tag{11.21}$$

$\varepsilon(X \mid \theta)$ is the *expectation* (or *regression*, see Section 2.14) of $X$ for a given value of $\theta$; $\varepsilon'(X \mid \theta)$ is the *slope of the expectation or regression curve* at $\theta$ (that is, the first derivative of the regression curve at $\theta$). $\sigma_{X \cdot \theta}^2$ is the variance of $X$ around the regression curve at $\theta$ or the squared standard error of measurement at $\theta$. Notice that the regression curve need not be linear. The information function for a given $\theta$ is the squared slope of the regression curve divided by the variance about the regression curve at $\theta$. Since the score, $X$, best reflects the trait when the slope is steep and the variance is small, large values of the information function are desirable. Small values for the information function will occur when the slope is small (that is, when the regression curve becomes horizontal) and the variance is large, as is found in the middle range of $\theta$ for Test 1 (Figure 11.9a). As demonstrated in Figure 11.9, the information that a score conveys about a latent trait can vary depending on the value of the latent trait being examined. The information function of a score should be large for all values of $\theta$ that are important to the user.

If $X$ is an unbiased estimator of $\theta$ (see Section 2.14), then $\varepsilon(X \mid \theta) = \theta$, and

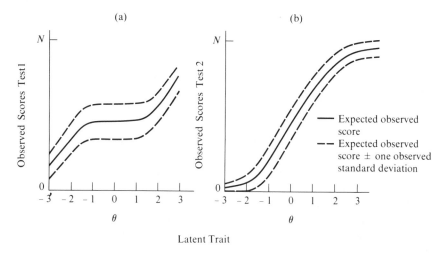

Figure 11.9. Observed test scores for a range of latent-trait values

this expectation is a straight line with a slope of 1. In this case, $I(X, \theta) = 1/\sigma^2_{X \cdot \theta}$, and increasing the information function of $X$ at $\theta$ results in decreasing the standard error of measurement of $X$ at $\theta$. If two scores are linearly related, a comparison of their information functions involves a comparison of the reciprocals of their squared standard errors of measurement. When two scores are not linearly related, a comparison of their information functions at $\theta$ will be influenced both by their squared standard errors of measurement and by the slopes of their regression curves at $\theta$.

Information theory can aid in determining how to score a test to ensure that the scores convey the most possible information about the latent trait. For example, a test score, $X$, can be a number-right score, such as

$$X = \sum_{i=1}^{N} u_i, \tag{11.22}$$

where $u_i$ is the score (0 or 1) obtained on item $i$ of an $N$-item test. Or, a test score can be a weighted sum of item scores such as

$$X = \sum_{i=1}^{N} w_i u_i, \tag{11.23}$$

where $w_i$ is the weight given to the score on the $i$th item. Information theory offers a basis for choosing item weights, $w_i$, that produce a total test score that conveys the maximum amount of information about $\theta$ (see Section 11.8). The amount of information that a test conveys about $\theta$ when the best item weights are used can be denoted $I(X^*, \theta)$. The amount of information that is conveyed by any scoring of a test, $I(X, \theta)$, must be less than or equal to $I(X^*, \theta)$. It can be shown that $I(X^*, \theta)$ equals the sum of the information functions of the items, $\sum_{i=1}^{N} I(u_i, \theta)$, so that

$$I(X, \theta) \leqslant I(X^*, \theta) \tag{11.24}$$

$$= \sum_{i=1}^{N} I(u_i, \theta); \tag{11.25}$$

the information function of a test score must be less than or equal to the sum of the item-information functions. It is apparent from Equation 11.25 that increasing the number of items in a test will increase the amount of information the test can convey. If each of a set of items contributes the same amount of information, a $k$ percent increase in test length will produce a $k$ percent increase in maximum test information.

The computer programs that estimate latent-trait values produce latent-trait estimates that are "best" according to some criterion (for example, maximum likelihood). (Maximum-likelihood estimation leads to latent-trait and item-parameter estimates that maximize the probability of having obtained the set of pass/fail item scores that were used in the estimation.) These best estimates of the latent traits have a one-to-one relationship with the test scores based on using the best item weights, although this relationship does not have to be linear. The maximum-likelihood estimate of $\theta$, $\hat{\theta}$, is unbiased and has asymptotically (as the number of items becomes large) a normal distribution with expectation

$$\varepsilon(\hat{\theta} \mid \theta) = \theta \tag{11.26}$$

and standard deviation

$$\sigma_{\hat{\theta} \cdot \theta} = 1/\sqrt{I(X^*, \theta)} \tag{11.27}$$

$$= 1/\sqrt{\sum_{i=1}^{N} I(u_i, \theta)}; \tag{11.28}$$

the standard error of a maximum-likelihood estimate of $\theta$ equals the reciprocal of the square root of the sum of the item-information functions. As the sum of the item-information functions increases, the standard error of the latent-trait estimate decreases. (The item-information function, $I(u_i, \theta)$, depends on the true values of $\theta$ and the item parameters. These true values are rarely known, but a good approximation to $I(u_i, \theta)$ can be obtained by using maximum likelihood estimates of the item parameters and latent traits in evaluating $I(u_i, \theta)$.) Thus, it is possible to construct confidence intervals for latent-trait values by using information functions (see Section 4.8), and an information function can be interpreted as a measure of the precision of estimation of the latent trait. Notice that, when the best weights are used, the amount of information contributed by an item is not influenced by the characteristics of the other items in the test. This is in contrast to classical true-score theory, wherein the contribution of one item to a test's standard error of measurement is not easily identified. Also notice that the standard errors based on information functions are influenced by the model and item parameters and are not influenced by the distribution of the latent trait in the sample being examined. This is in contrast to the standard error for a true-score estimate produced under classical true-score theory (that is, $\sigma_E = \sigma_X \sqrt{1 - \rho_{XX'}}$), which is influenced by the characteristics of the sample being examined.

Figure 11.10 contains the item-characteristic curves of two hypothetical items. Figure 11.11 displays the information functions of the items, $I(u_i, \theta)$, the information function of the sum of the item scores, $I(X, \theta)$, and the information function of the optimally weighted sum of the items, $I(X^*, \theta)$. The item-information curves are greatest at the $\theta$'s corresponding to the greatest slopes of the item-characteristic curves. Item 2 has a steeper maximum slope than item 1, and the information function of item 2 is correspondingly higher at its maximum than the information function of item 1; the range of values of $\theta$ for which item 2 conveys substantial information is narrower than the range for item 1. $I(X^*, \theta)$, the sum of the information functions of the two items, would be the information function of a test composed of items 1 and 2 if the items were optimally weighted. $I(X, \theta)$ would be the

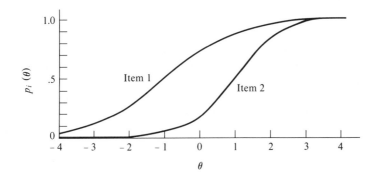

Figure 11.10. Item-characteristic curves for two items

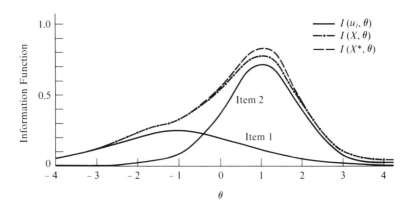

Figure 11.11. Information functions of the items in Figure 11.10

information function of a test if the item scores were simply summed; $I(X, \theta)$ is slightly less than $I(X^*, \theta)$ everywhere. In this example, differential item weighting would not improve test information very much, and $I(X, \theta)$ and $I(X^*, \theta)$ are very similar.

In Section 6.5 we noted that tests can be created to have maximum discrimination at a certain proportion-correct score by choosing items whose characteristic curves have maximum slopes at that score. The same goal of maximizing test discrimination at important latent-trait values can be achieved by using information functions in item selection. For example, if we were most interested in accurately measuring latent-trait values greater than 0 and we had to choose between items 1 and 2, we would choose item 2, based on the information curves in Figure 11.11.

It is often desirable to compare the amounts of information offered by different test models, scoring procedures, or tests. This comparison is made by computing the ratio of the two information functions of interest. This ratio is called the *relative-precision* function, $RP(X_1, X_2, \theta)$;

$$RP(X_1, X_2, \theta) = I(X_1, \theta)/I(X_2, \theta), \tag{11.29}$$

where $X_1$ is one test score and $X_2$ is a second test score. In the special case where two scoring or estimation procedures are being compared for one test model, the relative-precision function is called the *relative efficiency*, $RE(X_1, X_2, \theta)$. Although information functions can be greatly affected by any nonlinear changes in the scale of the latent trait, relative-efficiency functions are not affected by changes in the latent-trait scale (Lord, 1974d). If a researcher has an important reason for using one particular latent-trait scale, it is reasonable to evaluate a test in terms of its information function; in most cases, relative efficiency functions are preferred.

Figure 11.12 contains a comparison of the efficiencies of two published vocabulary sections of reading-achievement tests for sixth grade (Lord, 1974c); the *Comprehensive Tests of Basic Skills* (CTBS) is compared to the *Metropolitan Achievement Tests* (MAT). The horizontal line labeled $N_{CTBS}/N_{MAT}$ is the ratio of the number of items in the two tests and would be the relative efficiency expected if the item-information functions were the same for the two tests and if the tests differed only in length. The curving line is the relative-efficiency function. For percentile ranks less than 45, CTBS provides about 50% of the information that MAT provides. For percentile ranks between about 45 and 55, the relative efficiency of the CTBS is greater than $N_{CTBS}/N_{MAT}$ but is still less than 1. For percentile ranks between 55 and 80, the two tests have roughly equivalent efficiency. For percentile ranks greater than 80, CTBS provides about 50% more information than MAT. If a test user were more concerned with lower ranges of the latent trait for this grade, then MAT would be the more efficient test to use; if the test user were more concerned with the high range of $\theta$, then CTBS would be preferred. Remember that test publishers generally publish several levels of a test, and test users should be comparing tests at the levels and grades of interest.

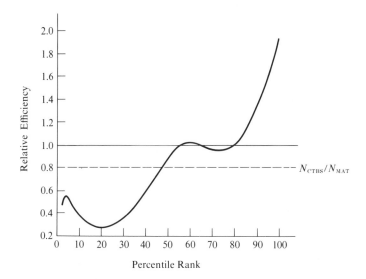

Figure 11.12. Relative efficiency of CTBS vocabulary to MAT vocabulary at grade 6. Adapted from "Quick estimates of the relative efficiency of two tests as a function of ability level" by F. M. Lord, *Journal of Educational Measurement*, 1974, *11*, 247–254. Copyright 1974 by the National Council on Measurement in Education. Reprinted by permission.

## 11.8 Information Functions and the Logistic Models

The logistic models are particularly well suited for the estimation of the information functions of items and tests. If such models apply, choosing and weighting items to maximize test information becomes simplified.

The information function for a two-parameter logistic item is

$$I(u_i, \ \theta) = D^2 a_i^2 \ \frac{e^{-Da_i(\theta - b_i)}}{\left[1 + e^{-Da_i(\theta - b_i)}\right]^2} \tag{11.30}$$

$$= D^2 a_i^2 p_i(\theta)\left[1 - p_i(\theta)\right], \tag{11.31}$$

where $p_i(\theta)$ is defined as in Equation 11.15. A two-parameter logistic item contributes the most information when $p_i(\theta)\left[1 - p_i(\theta)\right]$ is maximized (that is, when $p_i(\theta) = .5$); this happens when $\theta = b_i$. In other words, an item contributes the most information for latent-trait values that are near the item difficulty. Another way to say this is that, when an item's difficulty is well matched to an examinee's latent-trait level, the item will give the most information about the latent trait.

The information curves for three logistic items appear in Figure 11.13. Items 1 and 2 have $b = 0$; item 1 has $a_1 = .59$, while item 2 has $a_2 = .80$. Item 3 has $b_3 = -2$ and $a_3 = .80$. If we need to find an item that measures the latent trait well for $\theta$ greater than $-1$ and if only one item can be used, then item 2 would be chosen; item 3 would give the most information about the trait value for $\theta$ less than $-1$. Thus, when the logistic model fits a set of items, it is fairly straightforward to choose items that maximize information at a particular trait level. This is useful when a test constructor desires to make a test that is particularly effective at one trait value—for example, when a cutting score is being used (see Section 6.5).

Notice that an item-information function is solely a function of $\theta$ and the item parameters. If two test forms contain items with matching item parameters, the tests will produce equated latent-trait estimates with the same information functions. Tests such as these would be more rigorously equated than tests equated by, say, the equipercentile method (see Section 7.9).

Items can be selected for inclusion in a test on the basis of the total amount of information, $A_i$, that they offer. $A_i$ is the sum (integral) of the information offered at all $\theta$'s; this sum is the same as the total area under the information curve. For the two-parameter logistic,

$$A_i = Da_i. \tag{11.32}$$

Since $D$ is an arbitrary constant, we see that items with large $a_i$'s (discrimination indices) give the most total information. Choosing logistic items on the basis of

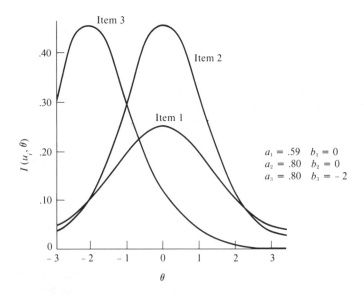

Figure 11.13. Information functions for three two-parameter logistic items

maximizing total information simply involves choosing items with maximum discriminating power.

As we noted in Section 11.7, it is possible for a test score to be a weighted sum of item responses. For the two-parameter logistic, the item weight that maximizes the test-information function is

$$w_i = Da_i; \qquad (11.33)$$

for the two-parameter logistic, the best weight for an item is $D$ times its discriminating power. If a weighted test score were to be based on the items in Figure 11.13, the optimal weight for item 1 would be $(1.7)(.59) = 1$. The optimal weights for items 2 and 3 would be about 1.4. When Rasch's one-parameter logistic model fits a set of items, there is no need for differential item weighting since all items would have the same discrimination indices and would contribute equally to total test information.

When examinees with low latent-trait values can correctly guess on items (that is, when a three-parameter logistic model is appropriate), an item's information function and best weight are more complicated to describe. Essentially, guessing tends to decrease the amount of information that an item provides at lower trait levels and to decrease the item's weight at the lower trait levels.

Extended discussions of the effects of item selection and weighting on total test information for the *Verbal Scholastic Aptitude Test* have been made by Lord (1968, 1974b). Information functions can be used for item selection and weighting with the normal-ogive model, but the formulas involved become much more complicated than with the logistic model.

## 11.9  Summary

The strong true-score and latent-trait theories examined in this chapter assume that there is one important characteristic influencing an examinee's performance on all the items in a test; differences in this characteristic explain differences in examinees' test performance. This assumption implies that there is local independence of items and examinees.

Binomial-error models are examples of strong true-score theories. The basic binomial-error model is suitable for number-right scores on tests where all items have equal difficulties; the compound binomial model is suitable when items have unequal difficulties. For these models it is assumed that the observed score is a linear combination of true score and error of measurement. A test consistent with the binomial-error model is consistent with much of classical true-score theory. The binomial-error model implies that standard errors of measurement vary with true-score level and that these standard errors are not influenced by the distribution of scores in the sample being tested. This model produces ratio scales for the true scores.

Rasch's Poisson model is a strong true-score model suitable for tests with a large number of items with very low (or very high) probabilities of being correctly answered. Rasch's model assumes that an examinee's true probability of producing an incorrect answer to an item in a test is the ratio of the test's difficulty to the examinee's ability. This model produces ratio scales for the test difficulties and examinee abilities.

Normal-ogive and logistic models are examples of latent-trait theories. In these models the latent trait is assumed to vary between $-\infty$ and $+\infty$. These models are suitable for homogeneous tests that have monotonically increasing item-characteristic curves. The normal-ogive and logistic models are virtually inter-changeable, although the logistic model is easier to work with. In these models item difficulties and item-discrimination indices are estimated, and changes in the sample used for this estimation will do no more than linearly transform the item parameters. An examinee's latent-trait value can be estimated from any items that fit the model. Rasch's logistic model is a special version of the logistic model that assumes that all item-discrimination indices are equal. Of the many practical uses of these models, two of the most important are their uses in test equating and in the selection and weighting of items to maximize the information that the test score conveys about the latent trait (that is, to minimize the standard error of the latent-trait estimate). These models produce latent traits and item difficulties on interval scales.

## 11.10   Vocabulary

anchoring scales
binary items
binomial distribution
binomial-error model
compound binomial-error model
item-characteristic function $(p_i(\theta))$
item difficulty $(b_i)$
item-discriminating power $(a_i)$
item-information function
    $(I(u_i, \theta))$
latent trait $(\theta)$
latent-trait theory
local independence of examinees
local independence of items
logistic model

normal ogive
normal-ogive model
one-parameter latent-trait model
Poisson distribution
Poisson model
Rasch's logistic model
Rasch's Poisson model
regression curve
relative efficiency
relative precision
slope of the regression curve
strong true-score theory
test-information function $(I(X, \theta))$
three-parameter latent-trait model
two-parameter latent-trait model

## 11.11   Study Questions

1. Discuss the differences between strong true-score theory and classical or weak true-score theory.
2. What are the similarities and differences between strong true-score theory and latent-trait theory?

3. How are strong true-score and latent-trait theories useful?

4. What do the terms *local independence of items* and *local independence of examinees* mean?

5. Give a few examples of tests that would not produce locally independent scores.

6. What are the assumptions of the binomial-error model?

7. For what type of test is the binomial-error model suitable?

8. How are observed scores related to true scores under the binomial-error model?

9. How is the compound binomial model related to the basic binomial-error model?

10. How is the binomial-error model related to classical true-score theory?

11. Describe some of the practical uses of the binomial-error model.

12. What are the assumptions of Rasch's Poisson model?

13. Describe some tests for which Rasch's Poisson model might be suitable.

14. How can ability and difficulty scale values be obtained in Rasch's Poisson model?

15. Name the advantages obtained when Rasch's Poisson model fits a set of test scores.

16. What are the assumptions shared by the normal-ogive and logistic models? How are the two models different?

17. What type of test is suitable for the normal-ogive and logistic models?

18. How do the latent-trait models deal with tests on which there is the possibility of correct guessing among examinees with low latent-trait values?

19. Compare and contrast the item parameters obtained with the latent-trait models with the item parameters obtained in Section 6.3.

20. What are some of the practical uses of the latent-trait models?

21. How is Rasch's logistic model related to the logistic models described in Section 11.5?

22. What advantages and disadvantages does Rasch's logistic model have relative to the other logistic models?

23. What does the term *test information* mean? Explain the term pictorially, in words, and in a formula.

24. How is test information related to item information?

25. What is the maximum information that a test based on a given set of items can have? How is this maximum obtained?

26. How is test information related to the standard error of a latent-trait estimate?

27. How are relative precision and relative efficiency related to test information?

28. How can item and test information be used to evaluate the usefulness of different items and tests?

29. Why is the logistic model particularly useful for examining item and test information?

30. What is $A_i$? How is it used in comparing items?

31. What item-weighting scheme maximizes test information for the two-parameter logistic model? For Rasch's logistic model?

## 11.12  Computational Problems

1. Two items on a test are locally independent. An examinee has probabilities of .5 of passing the first item and .3 of passing the second.
   a. What is the probability that the examinee will pass both items?
   b. What is the probability that the examinee will pass the second item, given that he or she passes the first item?
2. A test satisfies the requirements of local independence of examinees. Two examinees have the same true score and have a probability of .1 of passing a certain item.
   a. What is the probability that both examinees will pass the item?
   b. If the first examinee passes the item, what is the probability that the second examinee will pass that item?
3. A four-item test fits the binomial-error model.
   a. What is the probability that an examinee with a true score of .6 will have an observed score of 1?
   b. What is the probability that he or she will have an observed score of 4?
4. What are the probabilities of observing each of the scores of 0, 1, 2, 3, 4, and 5 in a binomial distribution with $N = 5, p = .4$?
5. An examinee has a true score ($\zeta$) of .9 and takes a ten-item test.
   a. What is $N\zeta$ for that examinee?
   b. What is the possible range of error of measurement ($E$) for that examinee when the binomial-error model is used?
   c. What is this range for a true score ($\zeta$) of .5?
6. What is the probability of observing a score of 4 in a Poisson distribution with $\lambda = 3$? ($e^{-3} \doteq .05$.)
7. The following table contains the numbers of errors made by two examinees on two addition tests.
   a. Estimate the difficulties of the tests and the abilities of the examinees.
   b. Calculate expected numbers of errors for each examinee on each test.
   c. Does the model appear to fit the observed data?

Numbers of Errors Made by Two
Examinees on Two Addition Tests*

|  |  | Examinee | | |
|---|---|---|---|---|
|  |  | 1 | 2 | Total |
| Test | A | 5 | 8 | 13 |
|  | B | 15 | 17 | 32 |
|  | Total | 20 | 25 | 45 |

*Test A has 75 items; test B has 150 items.

8. Item 1 has a logistic item-characteristic curve with parameters $a_1 = .7$, $b_1 = -.3$, and $c_1 = 0$. Assume $D = 1.7$.

   a. Calculate the probabilities of passing the item for $\theta$ equal to $-2$, $-1$, $-.3$, $.5$, $1$, $2$, and $3$.

   b. For the same $\theta$'s, calculate the probabilities of passing item 2 with $a_2 = 1.2$, $b_2 = 1$, $c_2 = .2$.

   c. Plot the item-characteristic curves for these two items on the same graph.

9. Three items, with difficulties of $-1.5$, $.4$, and $2.1$, fit Rasch's logistic model with $Da = 1$.

   a. What are the probabilities of passing the items for $\theta$ values of $-2$, $0$, $1.5$, and $3$?

   b. Plot the item-characteristic curves of these items on the same graph.

10. Two logistic items have the following parameters: $a_1 = 1$, $b_1 = .5$, $c_1 = 0$, and $a_2 = .5$, $b_2 = 0$, $c_2 = 0$. Assume $D = 1.7$.

   a. Plot the information functions of the items on the same graph.

   b. What are the total areas under the information curves for each item?

   c. At what value of $\theta$ is the information function maximized for each item?

   d. What are the maximum values that the information functions reach?

   e. What item weights would maximize the amount of information given by the two-item test?

   f. Using the best weights, how much information is given by the two-item test at $\theta = -1$ and $\theta = +1$?

   g. Estimate the standard error of estimate of $\hat{\theta}$ at $\hat{\theta} = -1$ and $\hat{\theta} = +1$ when the best item weights are used.

# Appendix:
# Areas under the
# Standard Normal Curve

| z | | | z | | | z | | |
|---|---|---|---|---|---|---|---|---|
| 0.00 | .0000 | .5000 | 0.55 | .2088 | .2912 | 1.10 | .3643 | .1357 |
| 0.01 | .0040 | .4960 | 0.56 | .2123 | .2877 | 1.11 | .3665 | .1335 |
| 0.02 | .0080 | .4920 | 0.57 | .2157 | .2843 | 1.12 | .3686 | .1314 |
| 0.03 | .0120 | .4880 | 0.58 | .2190 | .2810 | 1.13 | .3708 | .1292 |
| 0.04 | .0160 | .4840 | 0.59 | .2224 | .2776 | 1.14 | .3729 | .1271 |
| 0.05 | .0199 | .4801 | 0.60 | .2257 | .2743 | 1.15 | .3749 | .1251 |
| 0.06 | .0239 | .4761 | 0.61 | .2291 | .2709 | 1.16 | .3770 | .1230 |
| 0.07 | .0279 | .4721 | 0.62 | .2324 | .2676 | 1.17 | .3790 | .1210 |
| 0.08 | .0319 | .4681 | 0.63 | .2357 | .2643 | 1.18 | .3810 | .1190 |
| 0.09 | .0359 | .4641 | 0.64 | .2389 | .2611 | 1.19 | .3830 | .1170 |
| 0.10 | .0398 | .4602 | 0.65 | .2422 | .2578 | 1.20 | .3849 | .1151 |
| 0.11 | .0438 | .4562 | 0.66 | .2454 | .2546 | 1.21 | .3869 | .1131 |
| 0.12 | .0478 | .4522 | 0.67 | .2486 | .2514 | 1.22 | .3888 | .1112 |
| 0.13 | .0517 | .4483 | 0.68 | .2517 | .2483 | 1.23 | .3907 | .1093 |
| 0.14 | .0557 | .4443 | 0.69 | .2549 | .2451 | 1.24 | .3925 | .1075 |
| 0.15 | .0596 | .4404 | 0.70 | .2580 | .2420 | 1.25 | .3944 | .1056 |
| 0.16 | .0636 | .4364 | 0.71 | .2611 | .2389 | 1.26 | .3962 | .1038 |
| 0.17 | .0675 | .4325 | 0.72 | .2642 | .2358 | 1.27 | .3980 | .1020 |
| 0.18 | .0714 | .4286 | 0.73 | .2673 | .2327 | 1.28 | .3997 | .1003 |
| 0.19 | .0753 | .4247 | 0.74 | .2704 | .2296 | 1.29 | .4015 | .0985 |
| 0.20 | .0793 | .4207 | 0.75 | .2734 | .2266 | 1.30 | .4032 | .0968 |
| 0.21 | .0832 | .4168 | 0.76 | .2764 | .2236 | 1.31 | .4049 | .0951 |
| 0.22 | .0871 | .4129 | 0.77 | .2794 | .2206 | 1.32 | .4066 | .0934 |
| 0.23 | .0910 | .4090 | 0.78 | .2823 | .2177 | 1.33 | .4082 | .0918 |
| 0.24 | .0948 | .4052 | 0.79 | .2852 | .2148 | 1.34 | .4099 | .0901 |
| 0.25 | .0987 | .4013 | 0.80 | .2881 | .2119 | 1.35 | .4115 | .0885 |
| 0.26 | .1026 | .3974 | 0.81 | .2910 | .2090 | 1.36 | .4131 | .0869 |
| 0.27 | .1064 | .3936 | 0.82 | .2939 | .2061 | 1.37 | .4147 | .0853 |
| 0.28 | .1103 | .3897 | 0.83 | .2967 | .2033 | 1.38 | .4162 | .0838 |
| 0.29 | .1141 | .3859 | 0.84 | .2995 | .2005 | 1.39 | .4177 | .0823 |
| 0.30 | .1179 | .3821 | 0.85 | .3023 | .1977 | 1.40 | .4192 | .0808 |
| 0.31 | .1217 | .3783 | 0.86 | .3051 | .1949 | 1.41 | .4207 | .0793 |
| 0.32 | .1255 | .3745 | 0.87 | .3078 | .1922 | 1.42 | .4222 | .0778 |
| 0.33 | .1293 | .3707 | 0.88 | .3106 | .1894 | 1.43 | .4236 | .0764 |
| 0.34 | .1331 | .3669 | 0.89 | .3133 | .1867 | 1.44 | .4251 | .0749 |
| 0.35 | .1368 | .3632 | 0.90 | .3159 | .1841 | 1.45 | .4265 | .0735 |
| 0.36 | .1406 | .3594 | 0.91 | .3186 | .1814 | 1.46 | .4279 | .0721 |
| 0.37 | .1443 | .3557 | 0.92 | .3212 | .1788 | 1.47 | .4292 | .0708 |
| 0.38 | .1480 | .3520 | 0.93 | .3238 | .1762 | 1.48 | .4306 | .0694 |
| 0.39 | .1517 | .3483 | 0.94 | .3264 | .1736 | 1.49 | .4319 | .0681 |
| 0.40 | .1554 | .3446 | 0.95 | .3289 | .1711 | 1.50 | .4332 | .0668 |
| 0.41 | .1591 | .3409 | 0.96 | .3315 | .1685 | 1.51 | .4345 | .0655 |
| 0.42 | .1628 | .3372 | 0.97 | .3340 | .1660 | 1.52 | .4357 | .0643 |
| 0.43 | .1664 | .3336 | 0.98 | .3365 | .1635 | 1.53 | .4370 | .0630 |
| 0.44 | .1700 | .3300 | 0.99 | .3389 | .1611 | 1.54 | .4382 | .0618 |
| 0.45 | .1736 | .3264 | 1.00 | .3413 | .1587 | 1.55 | .4394 | .0606 |
| 0.46 | .1772 | .3228 | 1.01 | .3438 | .1562 | 1.56 | .4406 | .0594 |
| 0.47 | .1808 | .3192 | 1.02 | .3461 | .1539 | 1.57 | .4418 | .0582 |
| 0.48 | .1844 | .3156 | 1.03 | .3485 | .1515 | 1.58 | .4429 | .0571 |
| 0.49 | .1879 | .3121 | 1.04 | .3508 | .1492 | 1.59 | .4441 | .0559 |
| 0.50 | .1915 | .3085 | 1.05 | .3531 | .1469 | 1.60 | .4452 | .0548 |
| 0.51 | .1950 | .3050 | 1.06 | .3554 | .1446 | 1.61 | .4463 | .0537 |
| 0.52 | .1985 | .3015 | 1.07 | .3577 | .1423 | 1.62 | .4474 | .0526 |
| 0.53 | .2019 | .2981 | 1.08 | .3599 | .1401 | 1.63 | .4484 | .0516 |
| 0.54 | .2054 | .2946 | 1.09 | .3621 | .1379 | 1.64 | .4495 | .0505 |

From Runyon/Haber, *Fundamentals of Behavioral Statistics*, 2nd ed., © 1971, Addison-Wesley, Reading, Massachusetts. Pp. 290–291. Reprinted with permission.

| z | | | z | | | z | | |
|------|-------|-------|------|-------|-------|------|--------|--------|
| 1.65 | .4505 | .0495 | 2.22 | .4868 | .0132 | 2.79 | .4974 | .0026 |
| 1.66 | .4515 | .0485 | 2.23 | .4871 | .0129 | 2.80 | .4974 | .0026 |
| 1.67 | .4525 | .0475 | 2.24 | .4875 | .0125 | 2.81 | .4975 | .0025 |
| 1.68 | .4535 | .0465 | 2.25 | .4878 | .0122 | 2.82 | .4976 | .0024 |
| 1.69 | .4545 | .0455 | 2.26 | .4881 | .0119 | 2.83 | .4977 | .0023 |
| 1.70 | .4554 | .0446 | 2.27 | .4884 | .0116 | 2.84 | .4977 | .0023 |
| 1.71 | .4564 | .0436 | 2.28 | .4887 | .0113 | 2.85 | .4978 | .0022 |
| 1.72 | .4573 | .0427 | 2.29 | .4890 | .0110 | 2.86 | .4979 | .0021 |
| 1.73 | .4582 | .0418 | 2.30 | .4893 | .0107 | 2.87 | .4979 | .0021 |
| 1.74 | .4591 | .0409 | 2.31 | .4896 | .0104 | 2.88 | .4980 | .0020 |
| 1.75 | .4599 | .0401 | 2.32 | .4898 | .0102 | 2.89 | .4981 | .0019 |
| 1.76 | .4608 | .0392 | 2.33 | .4901 | .0099 | 2.90 | .4981 | .0019 |
| 1.77 | .4616 | .0384 | 2.34 | .4904 | .0096 | 2.91 | .4982 | .0018 |
| 1.78 | .4625 | .0375 | 2.35 | .4906 | .0094 | 2.92 | .4982 | .0018 |
| 1.79 | .4633 | .0367 | 2.36 | .4909 | .0091 | 2.93 | .4983 | .0017 |
| 1.80 | .4641 | .0359 | 2.37 | .4911 | .0089 | 2.94 | .4984 | .0016 |
| 1.81 | .4649 | .0351 | 2.38 | .4913 | .0087 | 2.95 | .4984 | .0016 |
| 1.82 | .4656 | .0344 | 2.39 | .4916 | .0084 | 2.96 | .4985 | .0015 |
| 1.83 | .4664 | .0336 | 2.40 | .4918 | .0082 | 2.97 | .4985 | .0015 |
| 1.84 | .4671 | .0329 | 2.41 | .4920 | .0080 | 2.98 | .4986 | .0014 |
| 1.85 | .4678 | .0322 | 2.42 | .4922 | .0078 | 2.99 | .4986 | .0014 |
| 1.86 | .4686 | .0314 | 2.43 | .4925 | .0075 | 3.00 | .4987 | .0013 |
| 1.87 | .4693 | .0307 | 2.44 | .4927 | .0073 | 3.01 | .4987 | .0013 |
| 1.88 | .4699 | .0301 | 2.45 | .4929 | .0071 | 3.02 | .4987 | .0013 |
| 1.89 | .4706 | .0294 | 2.46 | .4931 | .0069 | 3.03 | .4988 | .0012 |
| 1.90 | .4713 | .0287 | 2.47 | .4932 | .0068 | 3.04 | .4988 | .0012 |
| 1.91 | .4719 | .0281 | 2.48 | .4934 | .0066 | 3.05 | .4989 | .0011 |
| 1.92 | .4726 | .0274 | 2.49 | .4936 | .0064 | 3.06 | .4989 | .0011 |
| 1.93 | .4732 | .0268 | 2.50 | .4938 | .0062 | 3.07 | .4989 | .0011 |
| 1.94 | .4738 | .0262 | 2.51 | .4940 | .0060 | 3.08 | .4990 | .0010 |
| 1.95 | .4744 | .0256 | 2.52 | .4941 | .0059 | 3.09 | .4990 | .0010 |
| 1.96 | .4750 | .0250 | 2.53 | .4943 | .0057 | 3.10 | .4990 | .0010 |
| 1.97 | .4756 | .0244 | 2.54 | .4945 | .0055 | 3.11 | .4991 | .0009 |
| 1.98 | .4761 | .0239 | 2.55 | .4946 | .0054 | 3.12 | .4991 | .0009 |
| 1.99 | .4767 | .0233 | 2.56 | .4948 | .0052 | 3.13 | .4991 | .0009 |
| 2.00 | .4772 | .0228 | 2.57 | .4949 | .0051 | 3.14 | .4992 | .0008 |
| 2.01 | .4778 | .0222 | 2.58 | .4951 | .0049 | 3.15 | .4992 | .0008 |
| 2.02 | .4783 | .0217 | 2.59 | .4952 | .0048 | 3.16 | .4992 | .0008 |
| 2.03 | .4788 | .0212 | 2.60 | .4953 | .0047 | 3.17 | .4992 | .0008 |
| 2.04 | .4793 | .0207 | 2.61 | .4955 | .0045 | 3.18 | .4993 | .0007 |
| 2.05 | .4798 | .0202 | 2.62 | .4956 | .0044 | 3.19 | .4993 | .0007 |
| 2.06 | .4803 | .0197 | 2.63 | .4957 | .0043 | 3.20 | .4993 | .0007 |
| 2.07 | .4808 | .0192 | 2.64 | .4959 | .0041 | 3.21 | .4993 | .0007 |
| 2.08 | .4812 | .0188 | 2.65 | .4960 | .0040 | 3.22 | .4994 | .0006 |
| 2.09 | .4817 | .0183 | 2.66 | .4961 | .0039 | 3.23 | .4994 | .0006 |
| 2.10 | .4821 | .0179 | 2.67 | .4962 | .0038 | 3.24 | .4994 | .0006 |
| 2.11 | .4826 | .0174 | 2.68 | .4963 | .0037 | 3.25 | .4994 | .0006 |
| 2.12 | .4830 | .0170 | 2.69 | .4964 | .0036 | 3.30 | .4995 | .0005 |
| 2.13 | .4834 | .0166 | 2.70 | .4965 | .0035 | 3.35 | .4996 | .0004 |
| 2.14 | .4838 | .0162 | 2.71 | .4966 | .0034 | 3.40 | .4997 | .0003 |
| 2.15 | .4842 | .0158 | 2.72 | .4967 | .0033 | 3.45 | .4997 | .0003 |
| 2.16 | .4846 | .0154 | 2.73 | .4968 | .0032 | 3.50 | .4998 | .0002 |
| 2.17 | .4850 | .0150 | 2.74 | .4969 | .0031 | 3.60 | .4998 | .0002 |
| 2.18 | .4854 | .0146 | 2.75 | .4970 | .0030 | 3.70 | .4999 | .0001 |
| 2.19 | .4857 | .0143 | 2.76 | .4971 | .0029 | 3.80 | .4999 | .0001 |
| 2.20 | .4861 | .0139 | 2.77 | .4972 | .0028 | 3.90 | .49995 | .00005 |
| 2.21 | .4864 | .0136 | 2.78 | .4973 | .0027 | 4.00 | .49997 | .00003 |

# Glossary of Symbols

The numbers in parentheses following the definitions of the symbols indicate the sections in which the symbols are introduced.

| | |
|---|---|
| $a_i$ | item-discriminating power for item $i$ for latent-trait models (11.5) |
| $A_i$ | total amount of information provided by item $i$ (11.8) |
| $\alpha$ | lower-case Greek letter *alpha*; coefficient alpha (4.4) |
| $\alpha(20)$ | coefficient alpha reliability for a test with unequal item difficulties (4.5) |
| $\alpha(21)$ | coefficient alpha reliability for a test with equal item difficulties (4.5) |
| $\lvert a \rvert$ | absolute value of $a$ |
| $\doteq$ | approximately equals |
| $b_i$ | difficulty of item $i$ for latent-trait models (11.5) |

| | |
|---|---|
| $B_{Y \cdot X}$ | regression coefficient for predicting $Y$ from $X$ in a sample (2.9) |
| $\beta$ | lower-case Greek letter *beta* |
| $\beta_j$ | population regression weight for predicting $Y$ from $X_j$ in a multiple-regression equation (9.3) |
| $\beta_{Y \cdot X}$ | regression coefficient for predicting $Y$ from $X$ in a population (2.14) |
| $c_i$ | lower asymptote of the item-characteristic curve for item $i$ for three-parameter latent-trait models (11.5) |
| $d_i$ | item-discrimination index (6.3) |
| $D$ | constant usually set equal to 1.7, used in latent-trait models (11.5) |
| $\delta$ | lower-case Greek letter *delta* |
| $\delta_i$ | difficulty of test $i$ for Rasch's Poisson model (11.4) |
| $e$ | constant approximately equal to 2.718 |
| $e^{-b}$ | the reciprocal of $e$ taken to the power of $b$; $1/e^b$ (2.4; 11.4) |
| $E$ | error score (3.1) |
| $E, E'$ | error scores for two parallel tests (3.1) |
| $\mathcal{E}(X)$ | expected value (population mean) of variable $X$ (2.6; 2.14) |
| $\mathcal{E}(Y \mid x)$ | conditional expectation of variable $Y$ given variable $X = x$; the regression of $Y$ on $X$ (2.14) |
| $\mathcal{E}'(X \mid \theta)$ | first derivative with respect to $\theta$ of the regression of $X$ on $\theta$; the slope of the regression of $X$ on $\theta$ at the value $\theta$ (11.7) |
| $F_1, F_2$ | formula scores that correct for guessing or omissions (7.7) |
| $f(x)$ | frequency of the value $x$ of the discrete variable $X$; density function for the continuous variable $X$ at the value $x$ (2.4) |
| $>$ | greater than; "$X > Y$" is read "$X$ is greater than $Y$." |
| $\geq$ | greater than or equal to; "$X \geq Y$" is read "$X$ is greater than or equal to $Y$." |
| $i$ | subscript indicating the $i$th value of a variable (2.3) |
| $\infty$ | infinity |
| $I(X, \theta)$ | information provided by test score $X$ at latent trait $\theta$ (11.7) |
| $I(X^*, \theta)$ | maximum amount of information that a sum of weighted item scores ($X^*$) can provide about the latent trait $\theta$ (11.7) |

| | |
|---|---|
| $I(u_i, \theta)$ | information provided by item score $u_i$ about the latent trait $\theta$ (11.7) |
| $\int_a^b f(x)dx$ | integral of the function $f(x)$ with respect to $x$ between the values $a$ and $b$; area under the curve $f(x)$ as cut off on the $X$ axis by the limits $a$ and $b$, $a < b$ (2.4) |
| KR20 | Kuder-Richardson reliability for a test with unequal item difficulties (4.5) |
| KR21 | Kuder-Richardson reliability for a test with equal item difficulties (4.5) |
| $L_i$ | the number of examinees who have total test scores in the lower range of total test scores and who have item $i$ correct (6.3) |
| $\lambda$ | lower-case Greek letter *lambda* |
| $\lambda_{ij}$ | expected number of errors for test $i$ by examinee $j$ in Rasch's Poisson model (11.4) |
| $\ln x$ | natural logarithm of $x$, $\log_e x$ |
| $<$ | less than; "$X < Y$" is read "$X$ is less than $Y$." |
| $\leq$ | less than or equal to; "$X \leq Y$" is read "$X$ is less than or equal to $Y$." |
| $\mu$ | lower-case Greek letter *mu* |
| $\mu_X$ | population mean for variable $X$ (2.6; 2.14) |
| $n, N$ | number of elements (for example, number of examinees or number of items) (2.3) |
| $N!$ | $N$ factorial; $N! = N(N-1)(N-2) \cdots (2)(1)$. (11.3) |
| $\binom{N}{x}$ | "$N$ choose $x$"; number of combinations of $N$ things taken $x$ at a time for $0 \leq x \leq N$; coefficient of the binomial distribution (11.3) |
| $p_c$ | proportion of examinees obtaining a score of 1 on two dichotomous variables (2.11) |
| $p_i$ | population item-difficulty index for item $i$ (6.3) |
| $p_i(\theta)$ | item-characteristic function for item $i$, which is a function of the latent trait $\theta$; probability of getting item $i$ correct given $\theta$ (11.5) |
| $p_X$ | proportion of examinees obtaining a score of 1 on dichotomous variable $X$ (2.11) |
| $p(x); p(X = x)$ | relative frequency of the value $x$ of the discrete variable $X$ in a |

|  | population; probability that the variable $X$ takes on the value $x$ (2.4) |
|---|---|
| $p(X = x, Y = y)$ | joint probability that the variable $X$ takes on the value $x$ and the variable $Y$ takes on the value $y$ (2.13) |
| $p(X = x \mid Y = y)$; $p(X = x \mid y)$ | conditional probability that the variable $X$ takes on the value $x$ given that the variable $Y$ takes on the value $y$ (2.13) |
| $\phi$ | lower-case Greek letter *phi* |
| $\phi_{XY}$ | phi coefficient for variables $X$ and $Y$ (2.11) |
| $\pi$ | lower-case Greek letter *pi*; constant approximately equal to 3.142 |
| $r$; $r_{XY}$ | sample correlation coefficient; sample correlation coefficient between variables $X$ and $Y$ (2.8); estimate of the validity coefficient (5.3) |
| $r_{iX}$ | point-biserial correlation between item $i$ and test score $X$ (2.11; 6.3) |
| $r_{pbis}$ | point-biserial correlation coefficient (2.11) |
| $r_S$ | Spearman correlation coefficient (2.11) |
| $r_{tet}$ | tetrachoric correlation coefficient (2.11) |
| $r_{XX'}$ | sample estimate of a reliability coefficient (4.2) |
| $R_{Y \cdot X_1 X_2, \ldots, X_J}$ | multiple correlation of variable $Y$ with variables $X_1$, $X_2$, . . . , $X_J$ (9.3) |
| $RE(X_1, X_2, \theta)$ | relative efficiency of test score $X_1$ to test score $X_2$ at the latent trait $\theta$ (11.7) |
| $RP(X_1, X_2, \theta)$ | relative precision of test score $X_1$ to test score $X_2$ at the latent trait $\theta$ (11.7) |
| $\rho$ | lower-case Greek letter *rho* |
| $\rho_{T_X T_Y}$ | validity coefficient that has been corrected for attenuation (5.4) |
| $\rho_{XY}$ | population correlation coefficient between variables $X$ and $Y$ (2.8; 2.14); validity coefficient (5.3) |
| $\rho_{XX'}$ | population correlation coefficient between parallel test scores; population reliability coefficient (4.1) |
| $s$; $s_X$ | sample standard deviation; sample standard deviation for variable $X$ (2.5) |
| $s^2$; $s_X^2$ | sample variance; sample variance for variable $X$ (2.5) |

| | |
|---|---|
| $s_E$ | estimate of the standard error of measurement (3.3; 4.8) |
| $s_i^2$ | sample variance of scores for item $i$ (6.4) |
| $s_i r_{iX*}$ | item-reliability index (6.4) |
| $s_i r_{iY}$ | item-validity index (6.4) |
| $s_{XY}$ | sample covariance of variables $X$ and $Y$ (2.8) |
| $s_{Y \cdot X}$ | sample standard error of estimate (2.8) |
| $s_{Y \cdot X}^2$ | sample variance of variable $Y$ given variable $X$; variance in $Y$ not explained by $X$ (2.8) |
| $s_{Y \cdot x}^2$ | sample variance of variable $Y$ given $X = x$ (2.8) |
| $\sigma$ | lower-case Greek letter *sigma* |
| $\sigma_E$ | population standard error of measurement (3.3; 4.8) |
| $\sigma_X$ | population standard deviation for variable $X$ (2.14) |
| $\sigma_{XY}$ | population covariance of variables $X$ and $Y$ (2.14) |
| $\sigma_{Y \cdot X}$ | population standard error of estimate; standard deviation of $Y$ given $X$ (9.2) |
| $\sigma^2; \sigma_X^2$ | population variance; population variance for variable $X$ (2.6; 2.14) |
| $\Sigma$ | capital Greek letter *sigma* |
| $\displaystyle\sum_{i=1}^{n}$ | summation sign with limits 1 and n (2.3) |
| $T$ | true score (3.1) |
| $T, T'$ | true scores for two parallel tests (3.1) |
| $\tau$ | lower-case Greek letter *tau* (2.11; 3.1) |
| $\theta$ | lower-case Greek letter *theta*; the latent trait in normal-ogive and logistic models (11.5) |
| $u_i$ | the score (0 or 1) for item $i$ (11.7) |
| $U_i$ | the number of examinees who have total test scores in the upper range of total test scores and who have item $i$ correct (6.3) |
| $w_i$ | weight to be given scores on item $i$ (11.7) |
| $x$ | a value of variable $X$ (2.3) |
| $x_{i+}$ | summation of the observed values of the variable $X_{ij}$ over the values of subscript $j$ (11.4) |

| | |
|---|---|
| $X$ | random variable $X$ (2.3); observed test score (3.1) |
| $X, X'$ | observed scores for two parallel tests (3.1) |
| $X_i$ | the $i$th $X$ variable; a subscripted variable (2.3) |
| $X_{ij}$ | a doubly subscripted variable (2.3) |
| $\bar{X}$ | sample mean of the variable $X$ (2.5) |
| $y$ | a value of variable $Y$ (2.3) |
| $y = f(x)$ | $y$ is a function of $x$ |
| $y = f(x, z)$ | $y$ is a function of $x$ and $z$ |
| $Y$ | random variable $Y$ (2.3) |
| $\bar{Y}$ | sample mean of the variable $Y$ (2.8) |
| $\hat{Y}; \hat{Y}_i$ | estimated or predicted score for variable $Y$; estimated $Y$ for examinee $i$ (2.9; 5.5) |
| $\bar{Y}_1$ | sample mean of $Y$ scores for examinees with $X = 1$ (2.11) |
| $Z$ | random variable $Z$ |
| $Z = \dfrac{X - \mu_X}{\sigma_X}$ | standard score or $Z$ score corresponding to variable $X$, where $X$ has population mean $\mu_X$ and standard deviation $\sigma_X$ (2.7) |
| $Z = \dfrac{X - \bar{X}}{s_X}$ | estimated standard score, based on sample mean and standard deviation (2.8) |
| $z_c$ | critical value from a normal table for confidence probability $c$ (2.9) |
| $\zeta$ | lower-case Greek letter *zeta*; the true score in some strong true-score-theory models (11.3; 11.4) |

# Answers
# to Computational
# Problems

## Chapter 2

**1.** a. $-11$ b. $-2$ c. $-30$   **2.** a.

| $x_i$ | $f(x_i)$ | $p(x_i)$ |
|---|---|---|
| 7 | 1 | .05 |
| 6 | 3 | .15 |
| 5 | 4 | .20 |
| 4 | 2 | .10 |
| 3 | 3 | .15 |
| 2 | 3 | .15 |
| 1 | 3 | .15 |
| 0 | 1 | .05 |

b. .45   **3.** 3.55; 3.5; 5

**4.** 7; 3.95; 1.99   **5.** a. .3085 b. .8413 c. .5328 d. .1359 e. .50 f. 49 g. 46.64

**6.** $-.76$

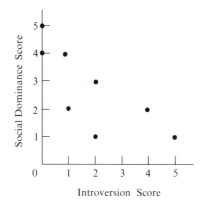

**7.** a. $\hat{Y} = -.63X + 3.92$ b. 2.66 c. .90 d. .55 to 3.51 (2.03 ± 1.48)    **8.** .64
**9.** .41; there is a tendency for more females than males to have "long" hair.
**10.** .65    **11.** .82    **12.** .82; there is a strong rank order correlation between empathy
and nurturance.    **13.** a. .20 b. .02 c. .45 d. .03
**14.** a.

| $x$ | $\varepsilon(Y\|x)$ |
| --- | --- |
| 0 | 0 |
| 1 | 1.0 |
| 2 | 2.0 |
| 3 | 1.0 |
| 4 | 0 |

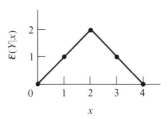

b. No.    **15.** 3.5    **16.** 73    **17.** a. Independent b. Not independent

## Chapter 3

**1.** 8    **2.** 5    **3.** .33    **4.** .75    **5.** 10; .3    **6.** a. .8; .2; .2; .8 b. 20; 5    **7.** 15; 10;
3.16    **8.** .67    **9.** a. four times larger b. two times larger c. .75

## Chapter 4

**1.** .89; .45; 20; 5    **2.** 1; 1    **3.** .89    **4.** .5    **5.** a. .66 b. .67    **6.** Pairs: (1,5), (2,4),
(3,8), (6,7). Any complementary sets of four items will do, where one item from
every pair is contained in a set. For example, the matched random subsets could
be (1, 2, 3, 6) and (5, 4, 8, 7).    **7.** a. .79 b. .71    **8.** .55    **9.** .82    **10.** .90
**11.** 150 items or three times longer.    **12.** 100.6 to 113.4 (107 ± 6.4)

## Chapter 5

**1.** .77   **2.** .68   **3.** 47.0 to 60.2 (53.6 ± 6.6)   **4.** a. .52 b. 5; .85 c. 8 to 10 d. 3 to 5   **5.** a. approximately 70 b. .60 c. 80   **6.** 214   **7.** No; for convergent validity the following correlations should be high but are low: $r_{A_1 A_2}$, $r_{B_1 B_3}$, $r_{A_2 A_3}$, $r_{B_2 B_3}$. For discriminant validity the following correlations should be low but are high: $r_{A_1 B_1}$, $r_{A_2 B_3}$.   **8.** a. Two factors: (Tests 1, 3) (Tests 2, 4) b. Two factors: (Tests 1, 2, 4) (Test 3) c. Two factors: (Tests 1, 2, 5) (Tests 3, 4)

## Chapter 6

**1.**

| Item | $p_i$ | $d_i$ |
|------|-------|-------|
| 1 | .30 | .4 |
| 2 | .23 | − .2 |
| 3 | .47 | .8 |
| 4 | .40 | 0 |

Items 1 and 3 would be good for a general-purpose test; items 2 and 4 are not good items.

**2.** a.

| Item | $p_i$ | $r_{iX}$ |
|------|-------|----------|
| 1 | .1 | .45 |
| 2 | .4 | .91 |
| 3 | .5 | .63 |
| 4 | .7 | .68 |
| 5 | .8 | − .22 |

b. 1, 2, 3, 4

**3.** a.

| Item | $s_i r_{iX*}$ | $s_i r_{iY}$ |
|------|---------------|--------------|
| 1 | .36 | .29 |
| 2 | .36 | .30 |
| 3 | .38 | .05 |
| 4 | .37 | .10 |
| 5 | .04 | .02 |

b. Items 3 and 4; 1.0; .75; .86; .20

c. Items 1 and 2; 1.1; .72; .11; .82

**4.**

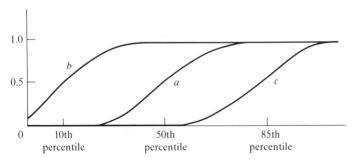

**5.**

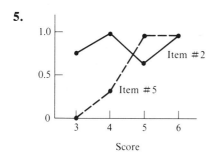

**6.** A score based on items 1, 2, and 4 and a score based on items 5 and 6 would be appropriate.

## Chapter 7

**1.** a. 49; 60; 79 b. 70.4; 76.0; 103.0   **2.** 6.56   **3.** Micah appears adequately prepared to take the course, and most students with similar test scores have obtained "A's" and "B's." Becky might need remedial help before the course or will need special effort during the course to do well, since most students with similar test scores have obtained "C's" and "D's."

**4.**

| Score (x) | $\varepsilon\,(Y\,|\,x)$ |
|-----------|--------|
| 25–30     | 3.24   |
| 20–24     | 2.92   |
| 15–19     | 2.16   |
| 10–14     | 1.81   |
| 5– 9      | 1.42   |
| 0– 4      | .99    |

**5.** a. .5 b. 475   **6.** $T$ scores: 71.7; 54.1; 41.8; 31.9; 24.3 Stanines: 9; 6; 3; 1; 1   **7.** a. 6.33 b. 13.67 c. The probability of guessing correctly is 1/4, and an answer is wrong only from incorrect guessing. **8.** Examinee A: 42; Examinee B: 41; Examinee A did better than examinee B in terms of raw score, but B omitted a lot more answers than A; when omissions are taken into account, A and B scored similarly.   **9.** a.

| Score | Scale is | Either |
|-------|---------|--------|
| 0     | − 1.96  | − 1.96 |
| 1     | − 1.28  | − .93  |
| 2     | − .67   | − .06  |
| 3     | − .06   | .76    |
| 4     | .52     | 1.44   |
| 5     | 1.15    | 1.96   |
| 6     | 1.96    | ∞      |

b. Yes   **10.**

| Score<br>Test A | Equivalent score for Test B<br>using method | |
|---|---|---|
| | a | b |
| 10 | 100 | — |
| 11 | 109 | 110 |
| 12 | 120 | 120 |
| 13 | 131 | 131 |
| 14 | 140 | 140 |
| 15 | 149 | 148 |
| 16 | 160 | 159 |

c. The two equating methods produce very similar results.

## Chapter 8

**1.** .67

## Chapter 9

**1.** School: .84; national: .91   **2.** a. − .41 b. 431.7   **3.** a. $\hat{Y} = .0056(X_1 − 502) +$ .00245($X_2$ − 483) + 2.0 b. .45 c. 2.10   **4.** Test scores: 41.5; teachers: 33   **5.** a. 21.27 b. .50 c. − .29 d. .24
**6.**

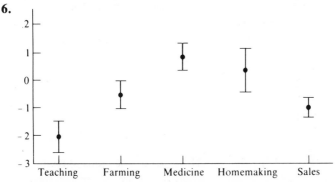

**7.** Women appear to have lower average job satisfaction than men and a more favorable attitude toward equality of job opportunities. There appears to be a ceiling effect on the equality attitude among women, making it risky to interpret the correlations.

## Chapter 11

**1.** a. .15 b. .30   **2.** a. .01 b. .10   **3.** a. .1536 b. .1296   **4.** .0778; .2592; .3456; .2304; .0768; .0102   **5.** a. 9 b. −9≤E≤+1 c. −5≤E≤+5   **6.** .17   **7.** a. .81 for

A; 1 for B; 10.54 for 1; 8.43 for 2 b. 5.76 for 1A; 14.23 for 1B; 7.21 for 2A; 17.79 for 2B c. Yes.

**8.** a. and b.

| $\theta$ | probability of passing item | |
|---|---|---|
| | 1 | 2 |
| − 2 | .12 | .20 |
| − 1 | .30 | .21 |
| − 0.3 | .50 | .25 |
| 0.5 | .72 | .41 |
| 1 | .82 | .60 |
| 2 | .94 | .91 |
| 3 | .98 | .99 |

c.

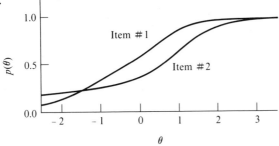

**9.** a.

| $\theta$ | probability of passing item | | |
|---|---|---|---|
| | 1 | 2 | 3 |
| − 2.0 | .38 | .08 | .02 |
| 0.0 | .82 | .40 | .11 |
| 1.5 | .95 | .75 | .35 |
| 3.0 | .99 | .93 | .71 |

b.

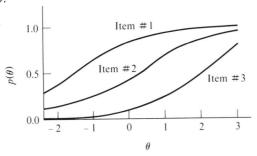

**10.** a.

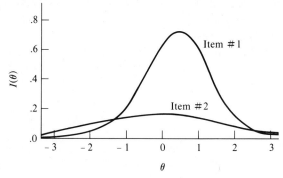

b. 1.7; .85 c. .5; 0 d. .72; .18 e. 1.7; .85 f. .34; .76 g. 1.70; 1.15

# References

American Psychological Association, American Educational Research Association, & National Council on Measurement in Education. *Standards for educational and psychological tests.* Washington, D.C.: American Psychological Association, 1974.

Anastasi, A. On the formation of psychological traits. *American Psychologist, 1970, 25,* 899–910.

Anastasi, A. *Psychological testing* (4th ed.). New York: Macmillan, 1976.

Anderson, E. B. A goodness of fit test for the Rasch model. *Psychometrika, 1973, 38,* 123–140.

Anderson, J., Kearney, G. E., & Everett, A. V. An evaluation of Rasch's structural model for test items. *The British Journal of Mathematical and Statistical Psychology, 1968, 21,* 231–238.

Angoff, W. H. Scales, norms, and equivalent scores. In R. L. Thorndike (Ed.), *Educational measurement.* Washington, D.C.: American Council on Education, 1971.

Bock, R. D. Estimating item parameters and latent ability when responses are scored in two or more nominal categories. *Psychometrika, 1972, 37,* 29–51.

Buros, O. K. (Ed.). *Personality tests and reviews.* Highland Park, N.J.: Gryphon Press, 1970.

Buros, O. K. (Ed.). *The seventh mental measurements yearbook.* Highland Park, N.J.: Gryphon Press, 1972.

Buros, O. K. (Ed.). *Tests in print II*. Highland Park, N.J.: Gryphon Press, 1974.

Campbell, D. T., & Fiske, D. W. Convergent and discriminant validation by the multitrait-multimethod matrix. *Psychological Bulletin,* 1959, *56,* 81–105.

Chun, K., Cobb, S., & French, J. R. P., Jr. *Measures for psychological assessment.* Ann Arbor, Mich.: Survey Research Center of the Institute for Social Research, The University of Michigan, 1975.

Cleary, T. A. Test bias: Prediction of grades of Negro and White students in integrated colleges. *Journal of Educational Measurement,* 1968, *5,* 115–124.

Cole, N. S. Bias in selection. *Journal of Educational Measurement,* 1973, *10,* 237–255.

Conger, A. J., & Jackson, D. N. Suppressor variables, prediction, and the interpretation of psychological relationships. *Educational and Psychological Measurement,* 1972, *32,* 579–599.

Conger, A. J., & Lipshitz, R. Measure of reliability for profiles and test batteries. *Psychometrika,* 1973, *38,* 411–427.

Connolly, A. J., Nachtman, W., & Pritchett, E. M. *Keymath diagnostic arithmetic test.* Circle Pines, Minn.: American Guidance Service, 1976.

Coombs, C. H. Psychological scaling without a unit of measurement. *Psychological Review,* 1950, *57,* 145–158.

Cronbach, L. J. Coefficient alpha and the internal structure of tests. *Psychometrika,* 1951, *16,* 297–334.

Cronbach, L. J. *Essentials of psychological testing* (3rd ed.). New York: Harper & Row, 1970.

Cronbach, L. J., Gleser, G. C., Nanda, H., & Rajaratnam, N. *The dependability of behavioral measurements: Theory of generalizability for scores and profiles.* New York: Wiley, 1972.

Cronbach, L. J., & Meehl, P. E. Construct validity in psychological tests. *Psychological Bulletin,* 1955, *52,* 281–302.

Cureton, E. E. The upper and lower twenty-seven per cent rule. *Psychometrika,* 1957, *22,* 293–296.

Dawes, R. M. *Fundamentals of attitude measurement.* New York: Wiley, 1972.

Diamond, J., & Evans, W. The correction for guessing. *Review of Educational Research,* 1973, *43,* 181–191.

Dicken, C. Good impression, social desirability, and acquiescence as suppressor variables. *Educational and Psychological Measurement,* 1963, *23,* 699–720.

DuBois, P. H. *A history of psychological testing.* Boston: Allyn & Bacon, 1970.

Ebel, R. L. *Essentials of educational measurement.* Englewood Cliffs, N.J.: Prentice-Hall, 1972.

Eichman, W. J. (MMPI) Computerized scoring and interpreting services. In O. K. Buros (Ed.), *The seventh mental measurements yearbook.* Highland Park, N.J.: Gryphon Press, 1972.

French, J. W., Ekstrom, R. B., & Price, L. A. *Manual for kit of reference tests for cognitive factors.* Princeton, N.J.: Educational Testing Service, 1963.

Ghiselli, E. E. *Theory of psychological measurement.* San Francisco: McGraw-Hill, 1964.

Gorsuch, R. L. *Factor analysis.* Philadelphia: Saunders, 1974.

Guilford, J. P. *The nature of human intelligence.* New York: McGraw-Hill, 1967.

Guion, R. Employment tests and discriminatory hiring. *Industrial Relations,* 1966, *5,* 20–37.

Gulliksen, H. *Theory of mental tests.* New York: Wiley, 1950.

Guttman, L. A basis for scaling qualitative data. *American Sociological Review,* 1944, *9,* 139–150.

Hambleton, R. K., Swaminathan, H., Algina, J., & Coulson, D. B. Criterion-referenced testing and measurement: A review of technical issues and developments. *Review of Educational Research,* 1978, *48,* 1–47.

Hambleton, R. K., & Traub, R. E. Analysis of empirical data using two logistic latent trait models. *British Journal of Mathematical and Statistical Psychology*, 1973, *26*, 195–211.

Harris, C. W. (Ed.). *Problems in measuring change*. Madison: University of Wisconsin Press, 1963.

Hays, W. L. *Statistics for the social sciences*. San Francisco: Holt, Rinehart & Winston, 1973.

Henryssen, S. Gathering, analyzing, and using data on test items. In R. L. Thorndike (Ed.), *Educational measurement* (2nd ed.). Washington, D.C.: American Council on Education, 1971.

Holt, R. R. Yet another look at clinical and statistical prediction: Or, is clinical psychology worthwhile? *American Psychologist*, 1970, *25*, 337–349.

Horst, P. *Psychological measurement and prediction*. Belmont, Calif.: Wadsworth, 1966.

Kearns, J., & Meredith, W. Methods for evaluating empirical Bayes point estimates of latent trait scores. *Psychometrika*, 1975, *40*, 373–394.

Kelley, T. L. The selection of upper and lower groups for the validation of test items. *Journal of Educational Psychology*, 1939, *30*, 17–24.

Kolakowski, D., & Bock, R. D. *LOGOG: Maximum likelihood item analysis and test scoring—logistic model for multiple item responses*. Ann Arbor, Mich.: National Educational Resources, 1973. (a)

Kolakowski, D., & Bock, R. D. *NORMOG: Maximum likelihood item analysis and test scoring—normal ogive model*. Ann Arbor, Mich.: National Educational Resources, 1973. (b)

Korman, A. K. The prediction of managerial performance: A review. *Personnel Psychology*, 1968, *21*, 295–322.

Kuder, G. F., & Richardson, M. W. The theory of the estimation of test reliability. *Psychometrika*, 1937, *2*, 151–160.

Linn, R. L., & Slinde, J. A. The determination of the significance of change between pre- and posttesting periods. *Review of Educational Research*, 1977, *47*, 121–150.

Lord, F. M. An application of confidence intervals and of maximum likelihood to the estimation of an examinee's ability. *Psychometrika*, 1953, *18*, 57–76.

Lord, F. M. Elementary models for measuring change. In C. W. Harris (Ed.), *Problems in measuring change*. Madison: University of Wisconsin Press, 1963.

Lord, F. M. A strong true-score theory, with applications. *Psychometrika*, 1965, *30*, 239–270.

Lord, F. M. A paradox in the interpretation of group comparisons. *Psychological Bulletin*, 1967, *68*, 304–305.

Lord, F. M. An analysis of the Verbal Scholastic Aptitude Test using Birnbaum's three-parameter logistic model. *Educational and Psychological Measurement*, 1968, *28*, 989–1020.

Lord, F. M. Estimating true-score distributions in psychological testing (An empirical Bayes estimation problem). *Psychometrika*, 1969, *34*, 259–299. (a)

Lord, F. M. Statistical adjustments when comparing preexisting groups. *Psychological Bulletin*, 1969, *72*, 336–337. (b)

Lord, F. M. *A theoretical study of two-stage testing*. (ETS RB-69-95). Princeton, N.J.: Educational Testing Service, 1969. (c)

Lord, F. M. Estimation of latent ability and item parameters when there are omitted responses. *Psychometrika*, 1974, *39*, 247–264. (a)

Lord, F. M. *Practical methods for redesigning a homogenous test, also for designing a multilevel test*. (ETS RB-74-30). Princeton, N.J.: Educational Testing Service, 1974. (b)

Lord, F. M. Quick estimates of the relative efficiency of two tests as a function of ability level. *Journal of Educational Measurement,* 1974, *11,* 247–254. (c)

Lord, F. M. The relative efficiency of two tests as a function of ability level. *Psychometrika,* 1974, *39,* 351–358. (d)

Lord, F. M. Formula scoring and number-right scoring. *Journal of Educational Measurement,* 1975, *12,* 7–11.

Lord, F. M. A broad-range tailored test of verbal ability. *Applied Psychological Measurement,* 1977, *1,* 95–100. (a)

Lord, F. M. Practical applications of item characteristic curve theory. *Journal of Educational Measurement,* 1977, *14,* 117–138. (b)

Lord, F. M. *Applications of item response theory to practical testing problems.* New York: Lawrence Erlbaum Associates, Inc., in press.

Lord, F. M., & Novick, M. R. *Statistical theories of mental test scores.* Menlo Park, Calif.: Addison-Wesley, 1968.

*Manual for the 16PF.* Champaign, Ill.: Institute for Personality and Ability Testing, 1972.

Meehl, P. E. *Clinical versus statistical prediction: A theoretical analysis and a review of the evidence.* Minneapolis: University of Minnesota Press, 1954.

Meehl, P. E. Seer over sign: The first good example. *Journal of Experimental Research in Personality,* 1965, *1,* 27–32.

Meredith, W. Poisson distributions of error in mental test theory. *British Journal of Mathematical and Statistical Psychology,* 1971, *24,* 49–82.

Meredith, W., & Kearns, J. Empirical Bayes point estimates of latent trait scores without knowledge of the trait distribution. *Psychometrika,* 1973, *38,* 533–554.

Mulaik, S. A. *The foundations of factor analysis.* New York: McGraw-Hill, 1972.

Novick, M. R., & Jackson, P. H. Bayesian guidance technology. *Review of Educational Research,* 1970, *40,* 459–494.

Novick, M. R., & Jackson, P. H. *Statistical methods for educational and psychological research.* New York: McGraw-Hill, 1974.

Novick, M. R., Jackson, P. H., & Thayer, D. T. Bayesian inference and the classical test theory model reliability and true scores. *Psychometrika,* 1971, *36,* 261–288.

Nunnally, J. C., Jr. *Introduction to psychological measurement.* New York: McGraw-Hill, 1970.

Peterson, N. S., & Novick, M. R. An evaluation of some models for culture-fair selection. *Journal of Educational Measurement,* 1976, *13,* 3–29.

*Prescriptive reading inventory technical report.* Monterey, Calif.: CTB/McGraw-Hill, 1976.

Rasch, G. *Probabilistic models for some intelligence and attainment tests.* Copenhagen: The Danish Institute for Educational Research, 1960.

Rasch, G. An individualistic approach to item analysis. In P. F. Lazarsfeld & N. W. Henry (Eds.), *Readings in mathematical social sciences.* Chicago: Science Research Associates, 1966. (a)

Rasch, G. An item analysis which takes individual differences into account. *British Journal of Mathematical and Statistical Psychology,* 1966, *19,* 49–57. (b)

Richardson, M. W. The relation between the difficulty and the differential validity of a test. *Psychometrika,* 1936, *1,* 33–49.

Sabers, D. L., & Feldt, L. S. An empirical study of the effect of the correction for chance success on the reliability and validity of an aptitude test. *Journal of Educational Measurement,* 1968, *5,* 251–258.

Sawyer, J. Measurement *and* prediction, clinical *and* statistical. *Psychological Bulletin,* 1966, *66,* 178–200.

Spearman, C. The proof and measurement of association between two things. *American Journal of Psychology,* 1904, *15,* 72–101.

Stanley, J. C., & Hopkins, K. D. *Educational and psychological measurement and evaluation.* Englewood Cliffs, N.J.: Prentice-Hall, 1972.

Stocking, M. *Short tailored tests*. (ETS RB-69-63). Princeton, N.J.: Educational Testing Service, 1969.

Taylor, H. C., & Russell, J. T. The relationship of validity coefficients to the practical effectiveness of tests in selection: Discussion and tables. *Journal of Applied Psychology*, 1939, *23*, 565–578.

Thorndike, E. L. *An introduction to the theory of mental and social measurements*. New York: Science Press, 1904.

Thorndike, R. L. Concepts of culture-fairness. *Journal of Educational Measurement*, 1971, *8*, 63–70.

Thorndike, R. L., & Hagen, E. P. *Measurement and evaluation in psychology and education*. New York: Wiley, 1977.

Thurstone, L. L. A law of comparative judgment. *Psychological Review*, 1927, *34*, 273–286.

Thurstone, L. L. *The reliability and validity of tests*. Ann Arbor, Mich.: Edwards Brothers, 1931.

Thurstone, L. L. Primary mental abilities. *Psychometric Monographs*, No. 1, 1938.

Torgerson, W. S. *Theory and methods of scaling*. New York: Wiley, 1958.

Traub, R. E., Hambleton, R. K., & Singh, B. Effects of promised reward and threatened penalty on performance of a multiple-choice vocabulary test. *Educational and Psychological Measurement*, 1969, *29*, 847–861.

Weiss, D. J. *Final report, computerized ability testing 1972–1975*. Psychometric Methods Program, Department of Psychology, University of Minnesota, 1976.

Wesman, A. G. Writing the test item. In R. L. Thorndike (Ed.), *Educational measurement* (2nd ed.). Washington, D.C.: American Council on Education, 1971.

Whitely, S. E. Models, meanings and misunderstandings: Some issues in applying Rasch's theory. *Journal of Educational Measurement*, 1977, *14*, 227–235.

Whitely, S. E., & Dawis, R. V. The nature of objectivity with the Rasch model. *Journal of Educational Measurement*, 1974, *11*, 163–178.

Wingersky, M. S., Lees, D. M., Lennon, V., & Lord, F. M. *A computer program for estimating true-score distributions and graduating observed-score distributions*. (ETS RM-69-4). Princeton, N.J.: Educational Testing Service, 1969.

Wood, R. Response-contingent testing. *Review of Educational Research*, 1973, *43*, 529–544.

Wood, R. L., Wingersky, M. S., & Lord, F. M. *LOGIST—A computer program for estimating examinee ability and item characteristic curve parameters*. (ETS RM-76-6). Princeton, N.J.: Educational Testing Service, 1976.

Woodcock, R. W. *Woodcock reading mastery tests manual*. Circle Pines, Minn.: American Guidance Service, 1973.

Wright, B. D. Misunderstanding the Rasch model. *Journal of Educational Measurement*, 1977, *14*, 219–225.

Wright, B. D., & Douglas, G. A. *Best test design and self-tailored testing*. Research Memorandum No. 19, Statistical Laboratory, Department of Education, University of Chicago, 1975.

Wright, B., & Panchapakesan, N. A procedure for sample-free item analysis. *Educational and Psychological Measurement*, 1969, *29*, 23–48.

Zedeck, S. Problems with the use of "moderator" variables. *Psychological Bulletin*, 1971, *76*, 295–310.

# Name Index

Algina, J., 229
Anastasi, A., 131, 141
Anderson, E. B., 261
Anderson, J., 261
Angoff, W. H., 171

Binet, A., 3
Birnbaum, A., 259, 262
Bock, R. D., 256, 259
Buros, O. K., 141

Campbell, D. T., 109
Cattell, R. B., 131
Chun, K., 141
Cleary, T., 207
Cobb, S., 141
Cole, N. S., 207
Conger, A. J., 205, 213
Connolly, A. J., 261
Coombs, C. H., 187
Coulson, D. B., 229
Cronbach, L. J., 79, 84, 108, 141, 230
Cureton, E. E., 122

Dawes, R. M., 179
Dawis, R. V., 261
Diamond, J., 168
Dicken, C., 205
Douglas, G., 233
Du Bois, P. H., 2, 3

Ebel, R. L., 120
Eichman, W. J., 234, 235
Ekstrom, R. B., 131, 253
Evans, W., 168
Everett, A. V., 261

Feldt, L. S., 168
Fiske, D. W., 109
French, J. R. P., Jr., 141
French, J. W., 131, 253

Galton, F., 3
Ghiselli, E. E., 40
Gleser, G. C., 230
Gorsuch, R. L., 111, 133
Guilford, J. P., 131

Guion, R., 207
Gulliksen, H., 81, 86, 125, 169, 194, 200, 203
Guttman, L., 186-187

Hagen, E. P., 141
Hambleton, R. K., 168, 229, 261
Harris, C. W., 211
Hays, W. L., 41, 231, 253
Henryssen, S., 121
Holt, R. R., 223
Hopkins, K. D., 120
Horst, P., 204

Jackson, D. N., 205
Jackson, P. H., 232

Kearney, G. E., 261
Kearns, J., 232
Kelley, T. L., 122
Kolakowski, D., 256
Korman, A. K., 223
Kuder, G. F., 84

Lees, D. M., 248, 249
Lennon, V., 248, 249
Linn, R. L., 211
Lipshitz, R., 213
Lord, F., 39, 121, 168, 170, 171, 203, 210, 211, 233, 234, 242, 248, 249, 253, 256, 259, 260, 266, 267, 269

Meehl, P. E., 108, 223
Meredith, W., 232, 253
Mulaik, S. A., 111, 133

Nachtman, W., 261
Nanda, H., 230
Novick, M. R., 39, 203, 207, 232, 248, 253, 259, 260
Nunnally, J. C., Jr., 187

Panchapakesan, N., 260
Pearson, K., 3
Peterson, N. S., 207
Price, L. A., 131, 253
Pritchett, E. M., 261

Rajaratnam, N., 230
Rasch, G., 249, 253, 260
Richardson, M. W., 84, 121
Russell, J. T., 105, 106

Sabers, D. L., 168
Sawyer, J., 223
Singh, B., 168
Slinde, J. A., 211
Spearman, C., 3, 98
Stanley, J. C., 120
Stern, W., 3
Stocking, M., 234
Swaminathan, H., 229

Taylor, H. C., 105, 106
Thayer, D. T., 232
Thorndike, E. L., 3
Thorndike, R. L., 141, 207
Thurstone, L. L., 131, 188
Torgerson, W. S., 179
Traub, R. E., 168, 261

Weiss, D. J., 234
Wesman, A. G., 120
Whitely, S. E., 261
Wingersky, M. S., 248, 249, 256
Wood, R., 234
Wood, R. L., 256
Woodcock, R. W., 262
Wright, B. D., 233, 260, 261

Zedeck, S., 205

# Subject Index

Absolute zero, 7, 179
Achievement tests, criticisms of, 225–226
Acquiescent response set, 186
Adaptive testing, 232–234, 236, 259
Additivity of true and error scores, 57, 60
Admissible observations, 230, 236
Admissible transformation, 179–180, 191
Age equivalent (*see* Age score)
Age score, 157–159, 173
  definition of, 157
  disadvantages of, 5, 157–159, 173
  equated tests, 159
  level of measurement of, 157, 173,
    182–183, 191
  nonlinear transformation of raw score, 149
  related to other scores, 170
Algebra:
  of expectations, 44–48, 49
  of summation signs, 11
Alpha (*see* Coefficient α)
Alternate forms, 78
Alternate forms reliability, 77–78, 91 (*see
  also* Parallel forms reliability)

Alternative measures of association, (*see
  Association, alternative measures of)*
Anchoring a scale, 189, 251, 252
Anchor test equating, 172, 174
Antimode, 228
*Army General Classification Test,* 162
Articulation of test levels, 170
Artificially dichotomized variable, 37
Association, alternative measures of, 36–41,
  49
  biserial correlation, 39–41, 49
  comparison of, 42
  Kendall's tau, 40–41, 49
  phi coefficient, 37–38, 41, 49
  point–biserial correlation, 38–41, 49
  Spearman rank–order correlation, 40–41, 49
  tetrachoric correlation, 38, 41, 49
Attenuation of correlation, 34, 49, 139 (*see
  also* Correction for attenuation)

Base rate:
  for dichotomous screening, 102, 114
  for Taylor–Russell tables, 105, 114

Bayesian methods, 229, 232, 236
Bias:
    in intelligence tests, 225
    examining with item analysis, 129, 131,
        140, 143
    examining with latent–trait models, 230,
        240, 258
    in selection, 205–208, 216
Bimodal distribution, 16, 136
Binary item, 243
Binomial distribution, 243–245
Binomial–error model, 240, 242–249, 269
    (*see also* Strong true–score theories)
    assumptions of, 242–243
    and classical true–score theory, 91, 243,
        247–248, 269
    compound binomial–error model, 184, 248,
        269
    confidence intervals for true scores, 91, 248
    equating, 248
    error variance, 246–247
    KR21, 246
    level of measurement of, 184, 191, 248,
        269
    standard errors, 91, 246, 247–248, 269
    uses of, 248–249
Bisection, method of, 188, 191
Biserial correlation, 39–41, 49
    use in item analysis, 40, 123
Bivariate normality:
    Taylor–Russell tables, 105
    tetrachoric correlation, 38
Buckley amendment, 226

*California Personality Inventory*, 162
Carry-over effect, 77, 78
Ceiling effect (*see also* Floor effect):
    confidence intervals for true scores, 91
    definition of, 58, 133
    difference score, 210
    group heterogeneity, 195
    interpreting research, 214, 216
    level of measurement, 181
    predicting a criterion, 101
    Taylor-Russell tables, 105
    test-score distribution, 133
Central tendency, 16–17, 48 (*see also* Mean;
    Median; Mode)
Chained item, 241
Chance success level, 121
Change score (*see* Difference score)
Chi-square goodness-of-fit test, 3
Civil Rights Act of 1964, 226
Classical true-score theory, 56–71
    assumptions of, 57–60
    and binomial-error model, 91, 243,
        247–248
    conclusions of, 60–65

Classical true-score theory (*continued*)
    difference score, 208–209
    and generalizability theory, 230
    and group heterogeneity, 194
    and information functions, 264–265
    and latent-trait models, 257
    proofs of conclusions, 65–70
    and Rasch's Poisson model, 253
    and strong true-score theories, 239–240
Clinical versus statistical predictions, 222–224,
    235
Coefficient $\alpha$, 79–80, 83–85, 88, 91 (*see also*
    Kuder-Richardson formulas)
Coefficient of generalizability, 231, 236
Coefficient of reproducibility, 187
Cognitive factors, 131
College Entrance Exam Board, 162
Combining groups:
    effects on correlations, 35–36, 49
    effects on distributions, 136
Comparative judgments, method of, 188–189,
    191
Compensatory model, 201, 215
Composite scores (*see* Multiple scores,
    combining)
Compound binomial-error model, 248, 269
*Comprehensive Tests of Basic Skills*, 266
Computer-assisted testing, 234, 236
Computer-interpreted testing, 234–235, 236
Concurrent validity, 97–98, 113, 182 (*see
    also* Criterion-related validity)
Conditional distribution (*see also* Conditional
    probability):
    binomial, 244
    definition of, 28
    expectancy table, 160, 173
    normal, 89
    Poisson, 250
    variance of, 28–29, 246, 257, 264
Conditional expectation, 47–48
Conditional probablilty, 43–44, 49 (*see also*
    Conditional distribution)
Confidence interval, 19, 32–34, 49
    assumptions, 32–33, 49, 89, 100, 114
    binomial-error model, 248
    for a criterion, 100–101, 114
    for a criterion-referenced test, 228–229
    interpretation of, 33, 101
    for a latent trait, 264
    multiple regression, 203
    for a true score, 89–91, 92, 248
    width of, 34, 90
Confidence probability, 34
Confidentiality of test scores, 226
Constant, 9, 48
    expected value of, 45
    summations of, 11
Construct validity, 108–109, 113, 114, 130

Construct validity (*continued*)
  (*see also* Factorial validity;
    Multitrait-multimethod validity)
Content validity, 95–96, 113, 130
  related to construct validity, 108
Continuous variable, 9–10, 48
Convergent validity, 110, 112, 114
Coombs' unfolding technique, 187–188, 191
Correction for attenuation, 63–64, 98–99,
    113–114
  definition of, 63–64, 98
  for different scores, 210
  proof of, 68
  use of, 98–99, 213
Correction for guessing, 139, 166–168, 174
  (*see also* Formula scores; Guessing)
Correlation (*see also* Association, alternative
    measures of; Attenuation of correlation;
    Biserial correlation; Kendall's tau;
    Multiple correlation; Pearson
    product-moment correlation; Phi
    coefficient; Point-biserial correlation;
    Spearman rank-order correlation;
    Tetrachoric correlation)
  choice of, 36–41, 49
Correlation matrix, 109
Covariance, 24, 46
Criterion, 97, 113 (*see also* Criterion-related
    validity; Linear regression)
Criterion-referenced test, 150, 227–229,
    235–236
  construction of, 227–228
Criterion-related validity, 95, 96, 97–98,
    113–114
  attenuation, correction for, 98–99
  choosing items to maximize, 125, 143
  concurrent, 97–98, 113
  confidence intervals, 100–101
  and construct validity, 108
  dichotomous screening, 101–104, 114,
    200–204
  effect of group heterogeneity, 196–200, 215
  effect of item-response omissions, 139
  moderator variables, 205, 216
  multiple predictors or criteria, 108,
    200–204, 215
  predictive, 97, 113
  suppressor variables, 204–205, 216
  Taylor-Russell tables, 104–107, 114
  validity coefficient, 97–98, 113, 114
Criticisms of standardized tests, 225–227, 235
Cross validation:
  clinical versus statistical prediction, 223
  item analysis, 139, 143
  moderator variables, 205
  multiple regression, 203, 216
  suppressor variables, 205
Curvilinear relationship, 27

Cutting score, 101–104
  criterion-referenced test, 228
  definition of, 101
  determining the best, 103–104
  information functions, 268
  item analysis, 121–122, 129, 143
  multiple regression, 201

Decision study, 231, 236
Density:
  definition of, 15, 48
  normal, 16, 20–21
Descriptive statistics, 16–18, 48
Deviation, 24
Dichotomous screening (*see also* Cutting
    score; Taylor-Russell tables):
  multiple predictors, 200–201, 215, 216
  single predictor, 101–104, 114
Dichotomous variable, 37, 49
  correlation between dichotomous and
    continuous, 38–40, 49
  correlation between two dichotomous,
    37–38, 49
Difference score, 208–211, 212, 214, 216
  reliability of, 210, 213, 214
Differential predictability, 205, 216
Differential validity, 205, 216
Difficulty, item (*see* Item difficulty)
Direct estimation, 188, 189, 191
Discrete variable, 9, 48
Discriminant validity, 110, 112, 114
Discrimination, item (*see* Item discrimination)
Distinctiveness, 7, 179
Distractor, 123, 140, 143
Distribution (*see* Conditional distribution;
    Density; Frequency distribution;
    Probability; Relative frequency
    distribution)
Distribution rule, 11, 45

Educational Testing Service, 131
Efficiency, relative, 266
Employment testing, 1–2, 225–226, 235
Equal intervals, 7, 168, 179
Equal-interval scale (*see* Interval scale)
Equating, 170–173, 174
  binomial-error model, 248
  information function, 268
  latent-trait models, 172, 230, 241, 258–259,
    270
  strong true-score theories, 230, 241
  of true scores, 248
Equipercentile equating, 171–172, 174
Error of measurement (*see* Error score)
Error score:
  binomial-error model, 243
  classical true-score theory, 57–59

Error score (*continued*)
  correlation with other error scores, 57, 58–59
  definition of, 57, 60
  for a difference score, 209
  expected value of, 61, 65
  and observed score, 57, 60, 63, 67, 73, 75, 76
  standard deviation of (*see* Standard error of measurement)
  systematic, 59
  and true score, 57–61, 65, 246
  unsystematic, 59
Error-score variance (*see also* Standard error of measurement):
  binomial-error model, 246
  and correlation of observed and true scores, 62, 66
  and correlation of parallel test scores, 63, 67
  for a difference score, 209
  estimating, 63
  group heterogeneity effect, 195, 215
  and observed-score and true-score variances, 61, 65
  for parallel tests, 57, 59, 60
  and reliability, 63, 67, 73, 75, 195
  for sums of parallel test scores, 64, 69
  and testing conditions, 195
  and test length, 64, 69
  varying with true score, 246
Essay item, 119, 226
Essentially τ-equivalent tests:
  definition of, 57, 60
  internal-consistency reliability, 79, 80, 83, 84, 91
Estimation, 19, 48, 99–101 (*see also* Confidence interval; Linear regression)
  unbiased, 47
Ethnic bias (*see* Bias)
Exclusive sets, 184
Exhaustive sets, 184
Expectancy table, 149, 160–161, 173
Expectation (*see also* Expected value)
  conditional, 47–48
Expected utility, 207–208
Expected value, 44–48
  conditional, 47–48
  definition of, 44
  rules for manipulating, 45
  use in population statistics, 20, 45–46
Explicit selection, 196, 215

Facet, 230, 236
Face validity, 95–96, 113
Factor, 111
Factor analysis, 111–113, 114, 130–133, 143

Factor analysis (*continued*)
  construct validity, 112–113, 114, 143
  content validity, 143
  definition of, 111
  factorial validity, 111–113, 114
  factor loading, 111, 114, 130–131
  factor score, 132
  first-order factor, 131
  influences on, 131–132
  item analysis, 130–133, 140, 143
  sampling and computing requirements, 140
  second-order factor, 130–131
Factorial validity, 111–113, 114 (*see also* Factor analysis)
Factor loading, 111, 114, 130–131
Factor score, 132
Fairness (*see* Bias)
First-order factor, 131
Fit of a model, 181, 183, 191, 240
  binomial-error model, 249
  latent-trait models, 256
  Rasch's logistic model, 261
  Rasch's Poisson model, 253
Fixed-step-size procedure, 234, 236
Floor effect (*see also* Ceiling effect):
  confidence intervals for true scores, 91
  group heterogeneity, 195
  interpreting research, 214, 216
  level of measurement, 181
  predicting a criterion, 101
  Taylor-Russell tables, 105
  test-score distribution, 133–134
Formula scores, 166–168, 174
Frequency distribution, 12–13, 48 (*see also* Probability; Relative frequency distribution)
  grouped, 152

Generalizability, coefficient of, 231, 236
Generalizability study, 231, 236
Generalizability theory, 88, 230–231, 236
Goodness-of-fit test, 3, 253, 256
Government regulation of testing, 225–226, 235
Grade equivalent (*see* Grade score)
Grade score, 157–159, 173
  definition of, 157
  disadvantages of, 5, 157–159, 173
  level of measurement of, 157, 173, 182–183, 191
  nonlinear transformation of raw score, 149
  related to other scores, 170
Group-administered test, 3
Grouped frequency distribution, 152
Group heterogeneity (*see* Heterogeneity, group)

Groups, combining (*see* Combining groups)
Guessing (*see also* Formula scores):
    correction for, 166–168, 174
    effect on item analysis, 139
    latent-trait models, 259–260, 269
Guttman's scalogram analysis, 186–187, 191

Halves, forming test, 81
Heterogeneity, group, 193–200, 215
    definition of, 194
    effects on reliability, 194–196, 215
    effects on validity, 194, 196–200, 215
Heterogeneous test, 224, 235 (*see also*
    Homogeneous test)
Heteroscedasticity, 33 (*see also*
    Homoscedasticity)
Hierarchy of objectives, 227, 229
History of testing and measurement, 2–4
Hit rate, 101–103, 114
Homogeneous regression, 197
Homogeneous test, 83, 88, 224, 235 (*see
    also* Internal-consistency reliability)
    definition of, 224
    item analysis for, 121, 130
    latent-trait models, 224, 229, 253, 254, 270
    strong true-score theories, 224
Homoscedasticity, 33, 49, 89, 100, 114
Horizontal equating, 170, 172
Hypothesis testing, 19, 48

ICC (*see* Item-characteristic curve)
Incidental selection, 196, 215
Independence, 44–46, (*see also* Local
    independence)
Individual differences, 3
Individualized testing, 232–234, 236, 259
Inferential statistics, 18–20, 48 (*see also*
    Confidence interval)
    unbiased estimate, 47
Information function, 262–269, 270
    classical true-score theory, 264
    cutting score, 268
    definition of, 262
    equating tests, 268
    guessing, 269
    item analysis, 266–269
    item-discriminating power, 267–269
    item-score weighting, 263, 265–266, 269
    logistic models, 267–269
    maximizing for a test, 263–264
    relative efficiency, 266
    relative precision, 266
    standard error of measurement, 262–263
    tailored testing, 233
    and test length effects, 264
Integrals, 15

Intelligence tests, 225
Intercorrelation (*see* Correlation)
Internal-consistency reliability, 78–85, 88, 91
    (*see also* Coefficient α; Homogeneous
    test; Kuder-Richardson formulas;
    Reliability; Spearman-Brown formula)
    advantages of, 80
    assumptions of, 79, 83
    choosing items to maximize, 125, 143
    and correction for attenuation, 99
    general case, 83–85
    interpretation of, 80, 84
    as a lower bound for reliability, 79, 83, 84
    speed test, 81–82
    split halves, 78–83
Interpolation, 152
Interval level of measurement, 7, 8, 48, 180,
    191
Interval scale, 168–170
    admissible transformation of, 180, 191
    bisection, 188, 191
    choice of correlation, 36
    comparative judgments, 188–189, 191
    definition of, 168–169, 174, 180, 191
    direct estimation, 188, 191
    latent-trait models, 183, 191, 230, 240,
        256, 270
    mathematical manipulation of, 8
    Thurstone's absolute scaling method,
        169–170, 174, 181, 191
Invasion of privacy, 225
Item analysis, 119, 120–133, 138–140,
    142–143
    bias, 129, 131, 140, 143
    comparison of methods of, 140
    content validity, 196
    criterion-referenced test, 227–228
    cross validation, 139
    distractors, examining, 123, 143
    factor analysis, 130–133, 143
    item-characteristic curves, 127–130, 143
    item difficulty and discrimination of
        point-biserials, 120–124, 142–143
    item reliability and validity indices,
        124–126, 143
    item-response omissions, 139
    latent-trait models, 255–259, 266, 268–269,
        270
    maximizing criterion-related validity, 125,
        143
    maximizing internal-consistency reliability,
        125, 143
    sample size requirements, 118–119, 140
Item-characteristic curve, 127–130, 140, 143
    item/true-score regression, 248
    latent-trait models, 255, 259–260, 265–266,
        268, 270
Item-characteristic function, 254, 260

Item difficulty, 81, 84, 120–123, 124, 139,
    140, 142–143
    effect of item-response omissions, 139
    effect on item/total-test-score point-biserial, 39
    item-characterisitc curves, 129, 254–257
    in Kuder-Richardson formulas, 84
    latent-trait models, 254–257, 260, 270
    sample considerations, 139–140
    tailored testing, 232–234
Item-discriminating power, 229, 254–257,
    260, 261, 269
Item discrimination, 122–124, 142–143
    item-characteristic curves, 127–129, 140,
    143
    and item-discriminating power, 257
    and item-response omissions, 139
    sample considerations, 139–140
Item factor analysis, 130–133, 143
Item formats, 119–120, 185
Item homogeneity (see Homogeneity, test)
Item information function, 262, 267 (see also
    Information function)
Item parameter, 254
Item-reliability index, 124–126, 140, 143
Item scores:
    correlation between, 38
    correlation with criterion, 124
    correlation with total test score, 38–39,
    122–124, 142–143
    information function, 262, 267
    mean (see Item difficulty)
    variance, 121
    weighting, 230, 240–241, 263–265, 269, 270
Item selection (see Item analysis)
Item/total-test-score point-biserial correlation,
    39, 122–123, 142–143
    related to item-discriminating power, 257
Item/true-score regression, 248 (see also
    Item-characteristic curve)
Item tryout, 119, 139 (see also Item analysis)
    for latent-trait models, 257
Item-validity index, 124–126, 140, 143
Item weighting, 230, 240, 263–265, 269, 270
Item writing, 119–120

Joint probability, 42–44, 49

Kendall's tau, 40–41, 49
Keymath Diagnostic Arithmetic Test, 261
Kit of Reference Tests for Cognitive Factors,
    131, 253
KR20, KR21 (see Kuder-Richardson formulas)
Kuder-Richardson formulas, 83–85, 88, 91
    (see also Coefficient α;
    Internal-consistency reliability)
    binomial-error model, 246–247
    choosing items to maximize, 124–125, 143

Latent trait, 240
Latent-trait models, 229–230, 236, 239–241,
    253–260, 270 (see also Information
    function; Logistic models; Normal-ogive
    model)
    ability/difficulty scale, 183, 256
    assumptions of, 254, 269, 270
    bias; 230, 240, 258
    and classical true-score theory, 56, 257
    confidence intervals for trait, 264
    in equating, 172, 230, 241, 258–259, 270
    estimation of model parameters, 256
    factor analysis, 254
    guessing, 259–260, 269
    homogeneous tests, 224, 229, 253, 254,
    270
    item analysis, 255–256, 257, 258, 259,
    266–269, 270
    item-characteristic curve, 255, 259–260,
    265–266, 268, 270
    item-characteristic function, 254
    item difficulty, 254–257, 260, 270
    item-discriminating power, 229, 254–257,
    260, 261, 269
    item parameters, 254, 256, 257, 258, 259,
    260
    level of measurement of, 183, 191, 230,
    240, 256, 270
    local independence, 254
    model fit, 256
    one-parameter model, 260–262
    Rasch's logistic model, 233, 260–262, 269,
    270
    for shortening tests, 259
    standard error of measurement, 230, 256,
    257, 258, 259, 263, 264
    and strong true-score theories, 239–240
    in tailored testing, 234
    three-parameter models, 259–260
    and traditional item-analysis procedures, 257
    true scores, 239, 240, 254, 257
    two-parameter models, 253–259, 267–269
    uses of, 230, 236, 240–241, 257–259, 270
Least-squares criterion, 31–32, 49, 223
    multiple regression, 202, 203, 215–216
Length of test (see Test length, effect of)
Leptokurtic distribution, 134–136
Level of measurement, 2, 6–8, 48, 179–182,
    182–184, 191
    absolute zero, 7, 179
    admissible transformations, 179–180, 191
    age scores, 157, 173, 182–183, 191
    binomial-error model, 184, 191, 248, 269
    ceiling effect and observed test scores, 181
    characteristics of, 7, 179
    choice of statistical technique, 8
    Coombs' unfolding technique, 187–188, 191
    determining, 179–182, 191

Level of measurement (*continued*)
  direct estimation, 188, 189, 191
  distinctiveness, 7, 179
  equal intervals, 7, 168, 179
  grade scores, 157, 173, 182–183, 191
  Guttman's scalogram analysis, 186–187, 191
  interval, 7, 8, 48, 180, 191
  latent-trait models 183, 191, 230, 240, 256, 270
  method of bisection, 188, 191
  nominal, 7–8, 48, 179–180, 184, 191
  normalized scores, 183, 191
  observed test scores, 37, 181–182, 191
  ordering in magnitude, 7, 179
  ordinal, 7, 8, 48, 180, 191
  paired comparisons, 185, 191
  percentiles, 155, 182, 191
  Rasch's Poisson model, 183–184, 191, 249, 270
  rating scales, 185–186, 191
  ratio, 7, 8, 48, 180, 191
  scaling model, 181, 191
  sorting, 184–185, 191
  strong true-score theories, 183–184, 230, 240, 248, 249, 269
  Thurstone's absolute scaling method, 169, 170, 174, 183, 191
  Thurstone's method of comparative judgments, 188–189, 191
Limits of summation, 10
Linear equating, 171–172, 174
Linear interpolation, 152, 157
Linear regression, 31–34, 49, 99–101, 114, 235 (*see also* Conditional expectation; Confidence interval; Regression)
  alternative to expectancy table, 161
  coefficient, 32, 46, 201, 202
  equation, 32, 49, 100, 201, 202
  group heterogeneity effects, 196–199, 215
  least-squares criterion, 31–32, 49, 100, 202, 203, 215–216
  multiple, 200–204, 215–216
  Pearson correlation, 30–31, 32, 49, 100, 202
  slope, 197, 215
  standard error of estimate, 29, 100
  statistical versus clinical prediction, 222–224
  use of, 32, 99–100, 201
  variance around regression line, 28, 197
  variance explained, 30–31, 49, 203
Linear relationship, 27, 32–33, 44, 48–49, 100, 114
Linear transformation, 27–28, 149, 173, 180, 191
Local independence, 241–242, 269 (*see also* Independence)
  binomial-error model, 242, 243
  latent-trait models, 254

Local independence (*continued*)
  Rasch's Poisson model, 250
Locator test, 233, 236
Logical validity, 96, 113
  and test development, 118, 139
Logistic function, cumulative, 254
Logistic models, 253–260, 270 (*see also* Latent-trait models)
  assumptions of, 254
  guessing, 260, 269
  information function, 267–269
  item-score weighting, 269
  and normal-ogive model, 254, 270
  one-parameter, 260
  Rasch's, 260–262, 270
  in tailored testing, 233
  three-parameter, 259–260
  two-parameter, 254
Lower bound on reliability, 79, 80, 83, 84, 91

Magnitude, ordering in, 7, 179
Marginal distribution, 28, 42
Marginal probability, 42
Marker test, 112–113
Mastery score, 227–229
Matched random subsets, method of, 81, 82, 83
Maximum likelihood estimation, 264
Mean, 16–17, 19, 20, 46, 47, 48 (*see also* Expected value)
Measurement, 2–4, 6 (*see also* Level of measurement)
Measurement theory, 2, 5, 6
  definition of, 2
  history of, 2–4
  implications for research, 213–215, 216
  related to scaling theory, 179, 190
*Measures for Psychological Assessment*, 141–142, 143
Measures of association, alternative (*see* Association, alternative measures of)
Median, 16–17, 48
Mental age, 157 (*see also* Age score)
*Mental Measurements Yearbook*, 141, 143
Method bias, 110, 114
Method of bisection, 188, 191
*Metropolitan Achievement Tests*, 266
*Minnesota Multiphasic Personality Inventory*, 98, 162, 234, 236
Mode, 16–17, 48
Model, test, 56
  binomial-error, 242–249, 269
  compound binomial-error, 248, 269
  Coombs' unfolding, 187–188, 191
  Guttman's scalogram, 186–187, 191
  latent-trait, 229–230, 236, 253–260, 269, 270

Model, test (*continued*)
  logistic, 254, 260, 270
  normal ogive, 254, 270
  paired comparisons, 185, 191
  Rasch's logistic, 260–262, 270
  Rasch's Poisson, 249–253, 269–270
  strong true-score theories, 229–230, 236,
    239–241, 269
  Thurstone's absolute scaling, 169–170, 191
  Thurstone's method of comparative
    judgments, 188–189, 191
Model fit (*see* Fit of a model)
Moderated regression technique, 205, 216
Moderator variable, 205, 216
Monotonic relationship, 159, 169
Monotonic transformation, 149, 159, 180,
    184, 191
Multiple-choice item, 119
  criticisms of, 226
  item difficulty, 121, 143
  latent-trait models, 255
Multiple correlation, 203, 216 (*see also*
    Correlation; Linear regression; Multiple
    scores, combining; Multiple regression;
    Pearson product-moment correlation)
Multiple regression, 200–204, 205, 215–216,
    224 (*see also* Correlation; Linear
    regression; Multiple scores, combining;
    Pearson product-moment correlation)
Multiple scores, combining, 108, 200–204,
    215–216, 224
Multi-step variable, 36, 49
  choice of correlation for, 36–41
Multitrait-multimethod validity, 109–110, 114

Nominal level of measurement, 7–8, 48,
    179–180, 184, 191
Nominal scale, 8, 179–180, 184
Nonattempted items (*see* Omissions,
    item-response)
Noncompensatory model, 201, 215
Nonhomogeneous test, 224, 235 (*see also*
    Homogeneous test)
Nonlinear equating, 171–172, 174
Nonlinear relationship, 27, 171–172, 174,
    182, 248
Nonlinear transformation, 149, 173
Normal distribution, 20–23, 48, (*see also*
    Normalized score)
  bivariate, 38
  in confidence intervals, 32–33
  density function, 16
  deviation from, 113
  discrete variables, 23
  of error scores, 89
  independence and correlation, 44
  linear relationships, 44

Normal distribution (*continued*)
  nonstandard, 23
  parameters of, 16
  standard, 21, 48
  standard score, 23, 48, 162
  table of areas under the standard normal
    curve, 275–277
Normalized score, 149, 163–165, 173–174
  disadvantages of, 165
  level of measurement of, 183, 191
  stanine, 164
  *T* score, 164
Normal-ogive model, 240, 253–260, 270 (*see
    also* Latent-trait models)
  assumptions of, 254
Norm group, 119, 150, 173
Norm-referenced test, 150, 227, 235
Norms, 119, 150
Number-right score (*see* Observed score)

Objective, 227–229
Observed score:
  binomial distribution given true score, 244
  ceiling effect, 91, 181
  in classical true-score theory, 57
  for criterion-referenced tests, 150
  for a difference score, 209
  distribution given true score, 74
  distribution over examinees, 133–138
  and error score, 57, 60, 63, 67, 73, 75,
    76
  expected value for a fixed examinee, 57
  expected value over examinees, 46
  interpretation of, 148, 173
  level of measurement of, 37, 181–182, 191
  mean, 46
  normal distribution given true score, 88–89
  for parallel tests, 57, 59, 62–64. 67–69,
    73, 91
  Poisson distribution given true score, 250
  raw score, 148
  transformation of, 148–150, 173
  and true score, 57, 60, 62, 63, 66, 68,
    73, 74, 76, 88–91
  usefulness of, 148–149, 182
Observed-score variance:
  and correlation between observed and true
    scores, 62, 66
  and correlation between parallel test scores,
    62, 63, 67
  and error and true-score variances, 61, 65,
    91
  for fixed trait, 257, 262, 264
  for fixed true score, 73–74, 246, 257
  group heterogeneity effects, 195
  for parallel tests, 62, 66
  and reliability, 62, 63, 67, 73, 75, 91
Odd/even reliability, 81, 82, 83

Omissions, item-response (*see also* Formula scores):
   correction for, 166–168, 174
   in item analysis, 139, 143
   latent-trait models, 259
One-parameter latent-trait model (*see* Rasch's logistic model)
*Ontario Scholastic Aptitude Test*, 261
Ordering in magnitude, 7, 179
Ordinal level of measurement, 7, 8, 48, 180, 191
Ordinal scale:
   admissible transformation of, 180, 191
   age score, 157, 173, 182–183, 191
   Coombs' unfolding, 187–188, 191
   correlations using, 37
   definition of, 180, 191
   grade score, 157, 173, 182–183, 191
   Guttman's scalogram analysis, 186–187, 191
   normalized score, 183, 191
   observed test score, 37, 181–182, 191
   paired comparisons, 185, 191
   percentile, 155, 182, 191
   rating scale, 185–186, 191
   sorting, 184–185, 191
   ways to obtain, 184–188, 191

Paired comparisons, method of, 185, 191
Parallel forms (*see* Parallel tests)
Parallel forms reliability, 77–78, 88, 91 (*see also* Reliability)
Parallel tests:
   correlation between observed scores, 62, 63, 67, 68, 72, 73, 77, 91
   definition of, 57, 59–60
   equality of correlations with other scores, 59, 62, 66
   equality of observed-score variances, 59, 62, 66
   and essentially $\tau$-equivalent tests, 60
   internal-consistency reliability, 79, 80
   Spearman-Brown formula, 79, 80, 85–88, 91
   sums of parallel test scores, 64, 69, 80, 85–88, 91
Parameter, item, 254
Parameter, population, 20
Pearson product-moment correlation, 23–31, 48–49, (*see also* Association, alternative measures of; Correlation)
   attenuation of, 34, 49, 139
   combining groups, effect of, 35–36, 49
   and confidence intervals, 32
   and covariance, 24
   between criterion and predictor, 97, 113
   curvilinear relationship, 27
   definition of, 27
   between dichotomous and continuous variables, 38–40, 49

Pearson product-moment correlation (*continued*)
   between dichotomous variables, 37–38, 49
   formula for, 24
   group heterogeneity effects, 199
   history of, 3
   independent variables, 44
   between item and test scores, 39, 122, 142
   between item scores, 38
   and linear regression, 30, 49
   linear relationship, 27, 44, 48
   linear transformation of variables, 27–28, 149
   nonlinear transformation of variables, 149
   between ordinal variables, 37, 40, 49
   population, 46
   and predictability, 27, 30, 31
   and proportion explained variance, 28–31, 49
   between rank orders, 40, 49
   and regression coefficient, 30–31
   and reliability, 72–73
   restriction of range, effect of, 34, 49
   sample, 24
   sign of, 25–26, 27, 48
   size of, 25–26, 27, 48
   spurious, 210, 216
   squared, 28–31, 49
   and standard error of estimate, 32
Percentile, 149, 150–156, 173
   advantages of, 155
   approximating with standard scores, 162
   calculation of, 150–155
   definition of, 150
   disadvantages of, 155–156
   distribution of, 155, 173
   level of measurement of, 155, 182, 191
   mathematical manipulation of, 155
   median as a type of, 17
   relationship with other scores, 170
Percentile rank (*see* Percentile)
Percentile score, (*see* Percentile)
Phi coefficient, 37–38, 41, 49
   use in item factor analysis, 131
Platykurtic distribution, 136
Point-biserial correlation coefficient, 38–41, 49 (*see also* Item/total-test-score point-biserial correlation)
   use in item analysis, 122–123
Point estimate, 100
Poisson distribution, 249, 250–251
Poisson models, 240, 249–253 (*see also* Rasch's Poisson model)
Pooling scores over groups (*see* Combining groups)
Population:
   definition of, 14, 18–19
   probability, 14–15, 48
   statistics, 20, 24, 46
Power test, 82

Practice effect, 77
Precision, relative, 266
Predictability, 27, 30, 31
Prediction, clinical versus statistical, 222–224, 235
Predictive validity, 97, 113, 182 (*see also* Criterion-related validity)
Predictor, 97, 202, 203
*Prescriptive Reading Inventory*, 229
Primary mental abilities, 131
Probability, 14–15, 42–44, 48–49 (*see also* Binomial distribution; Logistic function, cumulative; Normal distribution; Normal-ogive model; Poisson distribution)
Profile analysis, 211–213, 216
Proportion explained variance, 28–31, 49, 203
Proximity, 187
Psychometrics, 3 (*see also* Measurement theory)
Published test, selection of, 140–142, 143–144

Q-sort, 184

Random sample, 19
Range, 17, 48
Range, restriction of (*see* Restriction of range)
Rank-order variables, 40, 49
Rasch's logistic model, 233, 260–262, 269, 270
Rasch's Poisson model, 240, 249–253, 269–270
    estimating ability, 251, 253
    anchoring the scale, 251–252
    assumptions of, 250, 269–270
    and classical true-score theory, 253
    estimating test difficulty, 251
    level of measurement of, 183–184, 191, 249, 270
    local independence, 250
    model fit, 253
    Poisson distribution, 250
Rating scale, 185–186, 191
Ratio level of measurement, 7, 8, 48, 180, 191
Ratio scale, 180–181, 230 (*see also* Ratio level of measurement)
    admissible transformation of, 180–181, 191
    binomial-error model, 184, 191, 248, 269
    correlation with, 36
    definition of, 180
    direct estimation, 189
Rasch's Poisson model, 183–184, 191, 249, 270
    strong true-score theories, 183–184, 230, 240, 248–249, 269
    ways to obtain, 189–190, 191
Raw score (*see* Observed score)
Rectangular distribution, 155, 173
Reference group, 119, 150, 173

Regression, 47 (*see also* Conditional expectation; Linear regression; Multiple regression)
Regression coefficient, 32, 46, 201, 202 (*see also* Linear Regression)
Regression line, 31 (*see also* Linear regression)
Relative efficiency, 266
Relative frequency distribution, 13–14, 48
Relative precision, 266
Reliability, 72–92 (*see also* Alternate forms reliability; Coefficient α; Correction for attenuation; Internal-consistency reliability; Kuder-Richardson formulas; Parallel forms reliability; Spearman-Brown formula; Test/retest reliability)
    as Bayesian weight, 232
    and coefficient of generalizability, 231, 236
    and confidence interval for a criterion, 99
    and confidence intervals for true scores, 89–91, 92
    of a difference score, 210, 214
    for equal item difficulties, 84, 91
    and equating, 170–171
    essentially τ-equivalent tests, 79–80, 83–84, 91
    estimating, 76–88, 91–92
    formula scores, effect of, 166–168
    group heterogeneity, effect, 194–196, 215
    history of, 3
    of infinitely long test, 64, 70, 86
    interpretations of, 4, 72–76, 91
    item-reliability index, 124, 143
    lower bound of, 79, 80, 83, 84, 91
    of profiles, 211–213, 216
    research, interpreting, 213-215, 216
    of speed tests, 82, 83, 88
    split halves, 78–83
    and standard error of measurement, 88–91, 92
    testing conditions, effect of, 77, 78, 80–81, 88
    test length, effect of, 79, 85–88, 91–92
    for unequal item difficulties, 84, 91
    and validity, 75, 98–99, 113–114
Reliability index, item (*see* Item-reliability index)
Repeated measurements, 214, 216, (*see also* Difference score; Profile analysis)
Reproducibility, coefficient of, 187
Research, interpreting, 213–215, 216
Restriction of range (*see also* Heterogeneity, group):
    effect on correlations, 34, 49
    effect on error variance, 195
    effect on reliability, 194–196
    effect on validity, 97
    from unattempted items, 139
Routing test, 233, 236

Rules:
  for expected values, 44–48, 49
  for summation signs, 11

Sample, 18–19, 48
  statistics, 16–19, 24–31, 47
Sample characteristics, effects of:
  on correlations, 34–36, 49, 199
  on factor analysis, 131
  on item analysis, 139, 143, 257
  on item-characteristic curves, 139
  on regression, 205–207
  on reliability, 195, 215, 231
  on validity, 199, 205, 215
Sampling validity (see Logical validity)
Scale, 179–180, 190 (see also Interval scale;
    Nominal scale; Ordinal scale; Ratio scale)
Scale value, 179, 191
Scaling by fiat, 181, 191
Scaling model, 181, 191
Scaling theory, 179, 190–191
Scalogram analysis, 186–187, 191
Scatterplot, 25, 48
Score distribution, 133–138 (see also
    Frequency distribution)
Screening (see Dichotomous screening)
Second-order factor, 130–131
Second-stage test, 233, 236
Selection of a group (see Heterogeneity,
    group)
Selection of a published test, 140–142,
    143–144
Selection of predictor variables, 203
Selection ratio, 105, 114
Shrinkage, 139, 203
Shrinking-step-size procedure, 234, 236
Sixteen Personality Factor Questionnaire, 131
Skewness, 18, 133, 149
  definition of, 16
  median, use of, 17
  normal curve, 21
Slope of regression line, 197, 215, 262
Sorting techniques, 184–185, 191
Spearman-Brown formula, 64, 79–80, 85–88,
    91
  assumptions of, 79, 85, 91
  and coefficient α, 79–80
  definition of, 64, 85
  and generalizability theory, 231
  limit for infinitely long test, 64, 70
  and other reliability estimates, 88
  proof of, 69–70
  speed tests, 82
  and test length control, 88, 91
Spearman rank-order correlation, 40–41, 49
Specimen set, 142
Speed test:
  definition of, 81
  latent-trait models, 259

Speed test (continued)
  Poisson model, 253
  reliability for, 82, 83, 88
Split-half reliability, 78–83 (see also
    Internal-consistency reliability)
Spurious correlation, 210, 216
Standard deviation, 17–18, 24, 46, 48 (see
    also Variance)
Standard error of estimate:
  in confidence intervals, 32, 100
  definition of, 28–29
  homoscedasticity of, 33, 100
Standard error of measurement (see also
    Error-score variance):
  binomial-error model, 242–243, 246,
    247–248, 269
  in confidence intervals for true scores,
    88–91, 92
  definition of, 63, 88–89, 92
  for difference scores, 209
  and distribution of observed scores for fixed
    true score, 89
  estimating, 63
  homoscedasticity of, 89
  and information function, 262–263, 264–265
  for latent-trait models, 256, 257, 258, 259,
    263
  in profile analysis, 211
  for Rasch's Poisson model, 253
  varying with true score or trait level, 240,
    243, 246, 247–248, 253, 263, 269
Standardized score, 161–163, 173
Standardized tests, criticisms of, 225–226, 235
Standard normal distribution, 21, 48
Standard score, 23, 48, 161–163, 173
  advantages of, 162
  disadvantages of, 163
  effect on distribution shape, 162
  normal distribution, 23, 48
  in profile analysis, 211
  related to standarized scores, 161–162
Standards for Educational and
    Psychological Tests, 4–5, 142, 227
Stanford-Binet, 162, 233
Stanine, 164–165, 173
Statistic, definition of, 19–20
Statistical versus clinical prediction,
    222–224, 235
Step function, 234
Stepped-up reliability, 85
Step size, 234, 236
Strong true-score theories, 229–230, 239–241,
    269 (see also Binomial-error model;
    Poisson models; Rasch's Poisson model)
  and classical true-score theory, 239–240,
    243, 246–248, 250, 253
  homogeneous tests, 224, 229
  and latent-trait models, 239–240
  level of measurement of, 183–184, 230,

Strong true-score theories (*continued*)
    240, 248–249, 269
    local independence, 241–242
    standard errors, varying, 240, 243, 246,
        247–248, 253
    uses of, 229–230, 236, 240–241, 248–249
Structure of the intellect, 131
Subscripted variable, 9, 48
    two subscripts, 9, 10
Summation notation, 10–12, 48
Suppressor variable, 204–205, 216
Symmetrical distribution, 18 (*see also*
    Skewness)
Systematic errors of measurement, 59


Tailored testing, 232–234, 236, 259
Taylor-Russell tables, 104–107, 114
Test development, 118–119, 142 (*see also*
    Item analysis)
Test equating (*see* Equating)
Test information function, 262–266 (*see also*
    Information function)
Test length, effect of:
    on error-score variance, 64, 69
    on information functions, 264
    on reliability, 64, 69, 79, 85–86, 91–92
    Spearman-Brown formula, 64, 69–70,
        85–86, 91–92
    on true-score variance, 64, 69
    on validity, 98–99
Test model (*see* Model, test)
Test norming, 119, 150
Test/retest reliability, 76–77, 88, 91 (*see also*
    Reliability)
Tests:
    criticisms of standardized, 225–226, 235
    definition of, 1
    government regulation of, 225, 226, 235
    history of, 2, 3
    uses of, 1–2, 225
Test-score distribution, 133–138
*Test in Print II*, 141, 143
Test standardization, 119, 150
Test statistics, estimating for selected items,
    124–126, 143
Test theory (*see* Model, test)
Tetrachoric correlation, 38, 41, 49
    item factor analysis, 131
Three-parameter latent-trait models, 259–260
Thurstone's absolute scaling method, 169–170,
    174, 183, 191
    use in equating, 172
    level of measurement of, 169, 170, 174,
        181, 191
Thurstone's method of comparative judgments,
    188–189, 191
Tower amendment, 226
Trait, latent, 240

Transformed score, 148–150, 173–174
    age score, 157–159
    equal-interval scale, 168–170
    expectancy table, 160–161
    formula score, 166–168
    grade score, 157–159
    level of measurement of, 182–183, 191
    linearly, 149
    nonlinearly, 149
    normalized score, 163–165
    percentile, 150–156
    purpose of, 148–150
    standardized score, 161–163
    standard score, 161–163
True/false item, 121
True score:
    binomial-error model, 243–249
    in classical true-score theory, 57–58
    confidence intervals for, 89–91, 248
    correction for attenuation, 63, 68, 98–99,
        113–114
    correlation between true scores, 63, 68, 98,
        114
    definition of, 57
    of a difference score, 209
    distribution of, 244, 248
    equating, 248
    and error scores, 57, 58, 59, 60, 61, 65,
        76
    essentially τ-equivalent tests, 57, 60
    latent-trait models, 239, 240, 257
    and observed scores, 57, 60, 62, 63, 66,
        68, 73, 74, 76, 88–91, 239, 240,
        243–248, 250–251, 257
    for parallel tests, 57, 59, 60
    Rasch's Poisson model, 250–252
    strong true-score theories, 239–240
    universe score, 230
True-score variance, 61–69, 73–74, 76, 91
    binomial-error model, 246
    of a difference score, 209
*T* score, 164, 173
Two-parameter latent-trait models, 254
Two-parameter logistic model, 267–269
Two-stage testing, 233, 236


Unattempted items (*see* Omissions,
    item-response)
Unbiased estimator, 47, 262, 264
Unfolding, 187–188, 191
Unit of measurement, 189
Universe score, 230, 236
Unsystematic errors of measurement, 59
U-shaped distribution, 136–137, 228
Utility, 207–208, 216


Validity, 4, 95–114 (*see also* Content validity;
    Construct validity; Correction for

Validity (*continued*)
    attenuation; Criterion-related validity;
    Dichotomous screening; Taylor-Russell
    tables)
    choosing items to maximize, 125–126, 143
    coefficient, 97–98, 113
    comparing for tests of different length,
    98–99
    definition of, 95, 113
    effect of formula scores, 166–168
    effect of group heterogeneity, 194,
    196–200, 215
    multiple predictors or criteria, 108, 200–208
    reliability limiting, 75, 98, 113
Validity index, item (*see* Item-validity index)
Variability, measures of, 16–18, 48
Variable, 9–10, 48
    continuous, 9–10, 48
    definition of, 9, 48
    dichotomous, 37
    discrete, 9, 12, 48
    subscripted, 9, 48
    in summations, 10–12
    value of, 9, 48
Variance, 17–18, 48 (*see also* Error-score
    variance; Observed-score variance;

Variance (*continued*)
    Standard deviation; True-score variance)
    conditional, 28–29
    as a descriptive statistic, 17–18, 47, 48
    of a difference score, 209
    as an inferential statistic, 47
    of an item score, 121
    population, 20, 46
    proportion explained, 30–31, 49, 203
    sample, 17–18, 19–20
    of a sum of scores, 46
    unbiased estimator, 47
*Verbal Scholastic Aptitude Test*, 261, 269
Vertical equating, 170, 172

Weak true-score theory (*see* Classical
    true-score theory)
Wechsler tests, 162, 233
Weighting scores:
    items, 230, 240–241, 263–266, 269, 270
    predictors, 201–204
*Woodcock Reading Mastery Tests*, 261–262

Z score, 23, 24, 48, 161–162 (*see also*
    Standard score)